HISTORY OF
CHURCH OF CHRIST (HOLINESS) U.S.A.

The Late Bishop Charles Price Jones, 1865-1949
The Founder

DEDICATION

This volume is dedicated to the memory of the late Bishop Charles Price Jones, and those devout, Godly men who jeopardized their lives to blaze the way to a higher life as revealed to them, in the Holy Scripture, by the Holy Spirit.

History
of
Church of Christ (Holiness) U.S.A.
1895 - 1965

OTHO B. COBBINS, A.B., A.M., D.D.
EDITOR-IN-CHIEF

Illustrated with Photographs

NATIONAL PUBLISHING BOARD
CHURCH OF CHRIST (HOLINESS) U.S.A.
234 W. 69th Street, Chicago, Illinois 60621

PRINTED BY
VANTAGE PRESS
NEW YORK   WASHINGTON   HOLLYWOOD

FIRST EDITION

Copyright, © 1966, by Church of Christ (Holiness) U.S.A.

Printed by Vantage Press, Inc.
120 West 31st Street, New York, N.Y. 10001

Manufactured in the United States of America

Library of Congress Catalog Card Number: 66-22333

PREFACE

The history of the Church of Christ (Holiness) U.S.A. tells of a church conceived by the inspiration of the Holy Spirit and born in the adversities of oppression, suffering, deprivation and ostracism. Its survival is the result of prayer, fasting and studying God's word. Its adherents have striven to walk according to God's will and to be led by the Spirit of God.

In his annual message to the National Convention in Chicago, Illinois, in August 1936, the late Bishop Charles Price Jones advocated the publishing of the history of the church, pointing out the necessity of including in the history—

1. The events incidental to the beginning of the movement
2. The doctrine of the church
3. The inception and development of the organic structure
4. Short biographical sketches of those who labored and are laboring among us with lives rich in good works and spiritual experience.

At the National Convention in Detroit, Michigan, in 1942, it was resolved to authorize the appointment of a committee to interview the founder, Bishop C. P. Jones and those persons who were instrumental in founding the church; that a history of said church be written for information and inspiration of present laborers and their posterity.

Two years later, Mrs. Annie E. Butler, having collected much data on the general church, was appointed official historian.

In August of 1954, Sister Rosa Vance, an associate of Bishop Jones for many years, was appointed as compiler.

In August 1960, at the National Convention in Jackson, Mississippi, the Committee made its final report to the convention, recommending, on the request of Sister Rosa Vance, that Professor O. B. Cobbins be editor-in-chief, which was adopted.

The Bishops' Council later took necessary steps to "set in motion," machinery for publishing the book.

This study embraces the first 70 years of the Church, 1895-1965. It is the first such document ever made available to the general public about, and by, the Church of Christ (Holiness) U.S.A.

Pictures of historic churches, functional groups and dynamic individuals, supplement the record of Christian services and heroism. In like manner, reports of those laborers of the recent past, whose services in sustaining and projecting "The Cause," have been included.

Grateful thanks and appreciation are extended to all who have been helpful in making this publication possible, including those persons who were instrumental in gathering materials for the same, whose names were not placed in the records.

Special mention is given to Mrs. Sarah J. Land, of Cleveland, Ohio, and Mrs. Rosa C. Lee, of Lexington, Mississippi.

Mrs. Rosa Jones Vance of Magnolia, Mississippi, is known and recognized as the official compiler who worked laboriously, across the years, ultimately submitting the data to the National Convention for final editing and publication.

The names of all members of the compiling committee are:

Rev. George A. Thomas, Chairman, Jackson, Miss.

Mrs. Rosa J. Vance, Secretary and Chief Compiler, Magnolia, Miss.

Mrs. Annie E. Butler, Jackson, Miss.

Mrs. Sarah J. Land, Cleveland, Ohio

Rev. O. A. Askerneese, Washington, D.C.

Miss C. V. Johnson, Los Angeles, California

Rev. J. C. Smith, Newport News, Virginia

Rev. C. P. Jones, Jr., Washington, D.C.

CONTENTS

CHAPTER   PAGE

Preface — The Editor In-Chief   7

I   Introduction   11

II   Charles Price Jones, The Founder   17
      "The Man With A Spiritual Vision And
      A Righteous Mission"

III   "The Emerging Church Movement"   45
      The Pioneers
      Evangelism
      The Early Home Missionaries
      Foreign Mission
      Healings Through Faith And Prayers
      Testimonies
      The Manual
      The Need For Literature

IV   The Conventions   87
      The National Convention
      Diocese Conventions

V   The Local Churches   117
      The Early Churches (1895-1904)
      The Spread Of Churches (1905-1919)
      Later Church Expansion (1920-1965)

VI   The Ministry   269
      The Bishops Of The Church (1927-1965)
      The Pastors

VII   National Auxiliaries   308

VIII Church Enterprises   322

IX   Biography   352

X   The Ministry Of Songs   399

XI   Expanding Perimeter   426

XII   The Family, The Core Of The Church   441

Born in 1895 in the rural Holmes County seven miles south of Lexington, Miss., O.B. Cobbins was reared as transitory orphan who never knew mother, father nor grandmother. He was ten years old when his grandfather died in Feb. 1906. He was one of four children: Samuel T., Elizabeth, and Hallie. Both Samuel T. and Hallie have passed.

For the next five years, 1906-1911, after the passing of his grandfather, O. B. Cobbins lived seventeen miles north of Lexington on the farm in Carrell County, Miss., with his uncle Rev. Lee Porter Cobbins at Adair, Miss., who had four children of his own to care for.

During this five year period of his young life, O. B. Cobbins became besieged with a religious yearning, the impulse for an education, and economic assurance. These three motives became the guides which permeated his domestic and Christian life. He never could do enough for his Savior. He craved for more education that he might better serve his fellowman. He labored consistently that neither he nor his family would be a ward of society. At about fifteen years of age he left his uncle and went to C.M. & I. College at Jackson, Miss. He reached Jackson with only the clothes he had on and fifteen cents, with which to begin a life career on his own.

7

The very night he reached Jackson, he went to Christ Temple Church and heard Elder C. P. Jones preach. Four weeks later he joined the church and was baptized by Elder C. P. Jones.

He entered C.M. & I. College as a sixth grade boarding work student, and stayed there one school year 1911-1912. The next two years he went to school in Hattiesburg, Miss., and lived with his brother Samuel. After school closed in 1913, he worked for one week across the Leaf River, sleeping on mice-infested hay on the ground under a farm shed.

About a week later he went to a ravine near the same farm, to pick blackberries to sell. Shortly after he started picking berries a young white girl came down through the woods to pick blackberries also. But when she saw Otho, she returned to her house.

Presently her father appeared with pistol and shotgun leveled, looking for Otho. When he saw Otho, with a shotgun aimed, he cursed Otho, ordered him out and marched him up the hill to the farm house. While he held Otho at gun point, the farmer called to his grown son to bring a rope, "We got a nigger to hang." The son who could be seen plowing, stopped plowing, loosed one of the plow lines, and came running to join his father for the lynch party.

As the walk was started down through woods, Otho was asked his choice of the form of brutality: "Hanging or castration?"

"Let me pray," Otho replied. At this point the scene became dramatic. The father began asking questions of Otho. In answering the questions, Otho had chance to tell his name, to give name of white neighbor farmer, where Otho worked just a few days before; that he had come to Hattiesburg from C.M. & I. College; that he chopped cotton, picked blackberries, and did odd jobs to make money to go back to school. This seemed to have been the turning point of the dramatic scene.

The father's harsh countenance seemed to have mellowed. The melodrama here indicated a changed heart. He turned and looked toward his yard gate where the bucket of berries had been placed, and said to Otho, "Go get those berries and be out of sight within one minute; if not by that time, I will shoot you."

Running took place. Jesus had made a way of escape for the youth who trusted in His name. Thank God! Faith was increased in the blessed Saviour, Jesus.

Otho remained in the Hattiesburg Public School the next school year. The principal was his eighth grade teacher. His studies, earnest, and sincere disposition won the confidence of the principal.

The school was a two-story 10 or 12-classroom building heated with space coal heater in each classroom, with no janitor employed. Principal J. S. Love was allowed five dollars per month to be used for whatever help he could get for that sum. The principal offered that sum monthly to Otho Cobbins to do the best he could with the work. Starting fires in all the classrooms in the mornings and sweeping all the rooms and bringing in coal and kindling for all the rooms in the afternoons, was too much to be required of an under-weight eighth grade pupil. But he did his best, for the orphaned child needed that pittance to help in his personal subsistence. He considered this as another blessing from his "Jesus" whom he had learned to love.

The studiousness and faithfulness of Otho Cobbins was reported to the City Superintendent of Schools. On his visit to the school, the superintendent saw Otho, and afterward the superintendent told the principal to send Otho to the superintendent's office. When Otho appeared, he was received by the superintendent who presented Otho with an eighth grade diploma two months before the close of school, on the basis of his scholastic achievement and as a reward for his studiousness and faithfulness. Following this official act on the part of the superintendent, the teachers, led by Mrs. Hettie Simms, presented Otho with handkerchiefs, socks, and ties as "going away gifts." His brother Samuel gave Otho trainfare to Jackson to re-enter and work his way through C.M. & I. College for the next two years, 1914-1916.

In September 1916, Otho Cobbins walked the 7 miles from Jackson to Tougaloo and entered the high school department of Tougaloo College. He was only able to pay his entrance fees there. He had to depend on work-aid during the rest of the two school years, graduating from high school in May 1918 as salutatorian of his class.

Tougaloo College was operated by the American Missionary Association of New York, under the auspices of the Congregational Church.

After graduating from Tougaloo College (H.S.), his formal academic training was intermittent. He studied at the following educational institutions: Mississippi Baptist College (now defunct), Holly Spring, Miss., Alcorn A. & M. College, Alcorn, Miss.,

9

Tuskegee Institute, Tuskegee, Ala., Fisk University, Nashville, Tenn., where the M.A. Degree in Education was earned, Chicago University, Chicago, Ill., Chicago Teachers College, Chicago, Ill., University of Southern California at Los Angeles.

In August 1918, O. B. Cobbins was sent by the American Missionary Association as a teacher at Fessenden Academy, near Ocala, Florida.

In September 1919, he matriculated in Tougaloo College for the first semester.

The next major change in his career was when he was appointed as a Sunday School Missionary in thirteen counties in South East Alabama, by the American Sunday School Union of Philadelphia, Penn. In this field he worked for three years 1920-1923, until he was asked by the National Publishing Board to become editor of *Truth* and Manager of Truth Publishing Company at Jackson, in March 1923. While continuing with this as part time, he became 9th grade teacher in the Smith Robertson Public School in Jackson, for two years 1923-1925.

In September 1957, he returned to the Chicago Public Schools in the first public high school (W. H. Lanier High School) in Jackson.

In August 1927, he was elected second principal of the Lanier High School, which grew in enrollment to over 1000 pupils. Prof. A. M. Rogers was the first principal.

On November 25, 1929, he became the second supervisor. of Jackson Public Schools for Negroes, which position he retained until 1950. Prof W. H. Lanier, former president of Alcorn A. & M. College, Alcorn, Miss., was the first supervisor from 1910 to 1929.

In 1951, Prof. O. B. Cobbins joined the instructional staff of the Chicago Public Schools, under the Chicago Board of Education, Chicago, Illinois.

The school year 1954-1955, he taught in the department of education and psychology in Johnson C. Smith University, Charlotte, North Carolina.

During the two years he lived in Los Angeles, California, he spent one semester in attendance at the school of religion of the University of Southern California.

In September 1957, he returned to the Chicago Public School where he remained until he retired in 1964.

CHAPTER I

INTRODUCTION

MULTIPLE CHURCH NAMES FACED

Designating an acceptable official name for the denomination has been a problem of concern for the founders and leaders of the organization. At times the solution to the problem involved some legal aspects, as the reader may observe as he reads through the book.

At this point, it would be well to call attention to the fact that in the beginning the late Bishop C. P. Jones was a staunch Baptist himself, having pastored in Alabama, Arkansas, and in Mississippi where he labored at Mt. Helm Missionary Baptist Church. He was a member of the Jackson Missionary Baptist Association which was held at Crystal Springs, Mississippi, September 20-22, 1900, and so was Mt. Helm Baptist Church.

He had issued a call for a "holiness convocation" in 1896 about four years prior to the meeting of this Baptist Association at Crystal Springs, Mississippi. He had held his first "Holiness Convocation" at Mt. Helm Baptist Church June 6-15, 1897, three years prior to the association meeting at Crystal Springs, Miss.

The record refers to the Crystal Springs meeting as a "blot upon and a disgrace to our Lord Jesus Christ . . . . and yet, this meeting was but a repetition of the disgrace of every assembly of this association since the death of the lamented A. Reed whose wisdom and zealousness for justice to all, held the association together."

Those who opposed the then current officers and administrators of the association pointed out twelve acts of recklessness wrought by that staff.

Those who opposed were: W. J. Johnson, R. B. Brown, H. Diggs, W. S. Pleasant, A. Brown, Thomas Sanders, R. Thompson, H. Dees, E. J. Lucas (later a missionary to Africa), E. M. Bennet, S. A. Jordan, and F. S. Sheriff.

These brethren issued the following call:

"Come, Pastors and Deacons"

11

In the name of the Most High God, we beg that every pastor and deacon comprising the Jackson Baptist Association to meet at Collis Hill Baptist, Terry, Mississippi, at 10:00 A. M. Friday, October 26, 1900, for the purpose of prayerfully considering what we shall do about the unchristian way our church affairs are carried on by those who are leaders, and who will not allow us to consider it in the association. Let everyone come who believes that the 'Word of God is right'. Psa. 3:4. Let everyone come who believes that 'man shall not live by bread alone, but by every word that proceedeth out of the mouth of God.' Matt. 4:4. Let everyone come who believes in One Lord, one faith, and one baptism. Eph. 4:5.

Pursuant to the foregoing call, the Jackson Baptist Association in an extra session at Collis Hill Missionary Baptist Church, Terry, Mississippi, October 26, 1900 at 10:00 A.M. Elder Thomas Sanders was made temporary moderator and Brother S. B. Weakley was elected temporary clerk of the meeting.

An enrollment committee was appointed. The committee's report showed that 36 messengers had responded to the call.

This temporary organization proposed a new organization and a new name, and in keeping with that idea, a committee was appointed to survey the whole controversy and return with appropriate recommendations.
Committee:
W. S. Pleasant, Chairman, W. J. Johnson, R. Thompson, F. S. Sheriff, S. B. Weakley, Frank Sutton, Spencer Parker, P. M. Wiggins, T. A. Fields, S. A. Jordan, J. H. Green, Secretary.

The information given here and the data on the pages which immediately follow are based on the minutes of the "First Session and History of the Origin of Christ's Association of Mississippi, of Baptized Believers in Christ" held with China Grove Church of Christ, Myles, Mississippi, December 28-30, 1900.

The committee's report to the temporary organization:

1. The committee's recommendation to organize a new association to be named, "Christ's Association of Mississippi" of baptized believers, was adopted by the temporary organization.

2. The committee's disapproval of the anonymous injunction or peremptory or blackmailing circular purporting to have come from the SIMON PURE BAPTISTS of Jackson, Mis-

sissippi, ordering C. P. Jones to vacate the parsonage and also Mt. Helm Baptist Church and to leave Jackson at once without further trouble.

3. The committee recommended the renouncing of allegiance to the Jackson Baptist Association and to withdraw from the association, and to resolve into an association to be known as Christ's Association of Mississippi of baptized believers.

4. The committee further recommended that the churches, all baptized believers in Christ, be then called to meet and permanently organize the association, Friday, December 28, 1900 at Myles Station, Mississippi (China Grove Church, Eld. W. S. Pleasant, Pastor.)

5. All of the foregoing recommendations were adopted by the temporary organization.

The temporary organization adjourned.

Eld. Thomas Sanders, Moderator Pro tem
S. B. Weakley, Clerk Pro tem

THE MYLES MEETING

The temporary organization met to form a permanent organization at Myles, Mississippi, Friday, December 28, 1900, as appointed with Moderator Thomas Sanders in the chair. In the absence of S. B. Weakley, W. S. Keys was elected secretary pro tem.

The moderator made the necessary preliminary remarks declaring the house ready to enter into permanent organization.

A motion prevailed that the name of the association be "Christ's Association of Mississippi of Baptized Believers".

The moderator appointed the following committees: W. T. Weakley, Thomas Silas, and P. Hunt committee on enrollment.

Committee on Permanent Organization: Charles Kendrick, Hyram Wright, Frank Sutton, P. M. Wiggins, W. S. Keys, H. Diggs, W. J. Johnson, Henry Moore, and W. T. Weakley.

Committee on Finance: Henry Moore, H. P. Patrick, P. M. Wiggins.

Thomas Sanders was appointed to preach Friday night. When the hour of service arrived, C. P. Jones was present. Then Thomas Sanders yielded to C. P. Jones who preached from the text: "So the wall was finished in the twenty and fifth day of the month E-lul, in fifty and two days. And it came to pass, that when all

13

our enemies heard thereof, and all the heathen that were about us saw these things, they were much cast down in their eyes: For they perceived that this work was wrought of our God." Nehemiah 6: 15-16. The soul-stirring sermon gave strength to all the brethren. After which the moderator declared the meeting was ready to resume routine business.

The report on permanent organization was made:

W. S. Pleasant, President,
Thomas Sanders, Vice Moderator (Later became one of the
          first presidents of the CM&I College Trustee Board)
W. T. Weakley, Secretary
W. S. Keys, Corresponding Secretary
F. S. Sheriff, Treasurer

The report was adopted. Thus a permanent organization was officially established with the new names and new core of officers.

The committee on time and place recommended that the next session of the "Christ's Association of Mississippi, of Baptized Believers in Christ" convene with Damascus Church of God, Hazelhurst, Mississippi, Wednesday before the second Sunday in September 1901 at 10:00 A. M. On Saturday morning, December 29, 1900, C. H. Mason preached to the association from Isa. 21: 13. This same C. H. Mason later became Bishop C. H. Mason, the founder and head of the "Church of God In Christ". C. H. Mason preached again on Sunday, December 30, 1900 from Ezek. 46:10,11

On Saturday night E. J. Lucas preached from 2nd Tim. 2:19. E. J. Lucas later became a missionary to Africa.

The proceeding of the first annual sessions of the Christ's Sunday School Convention of Mississippi which was held with the White Oak Church of Christ, Carpenter, Mississippi, July 12-13, 1901.

When the convention opened, it was really the twenty-seventh annual session of the Jackson Missionary Baptist Sunday School and Educational Convention because the Association name was changed in December 1900 just about six months before, and the Sunday School Convention was set to change its name at the then current session.

On the first day of the convention a committee was appointed on the change of name for the convention.

14

Church	Membership	Post Office	Delegates
1. Big Creek		Jonesville	Frank Sutton
			M. Johnson
2. St. Paul		Jackson	Thomas Sanders
3. China Grove		Jackson	Thomas Sanders
4. Collis Hill		Terry	Charles Kendrick
5. Wilderness of Judea		Hazlehurst	P. M. Wiggins
			H. G. Anderson
			J. Brown, Clerk
6. China Grove	79	Myles	W. J. Johnson
			B. J. Simrall, Clerk
7. Caney Creek	25	Jackson	H. Diggs
8. Mt. Galilee		Jackson	H. Dees
			W. T. Weakley
9. Mt. Helm		Jackson	Henry Moore
			W. S. Keys
			Hiram Wright
10. Damascus	250	Jackson	W. S. Pleasant
			Idell Jefferson, Clerk
11. White Rock			Thomas Sanders
12. White Oak	235	Jackson	W. S. Pleasant
			S. A. Garner, Clerk
13. Carlton Hill	70	Hazlehurst	F. S. Sheriff
14. Hope Springs	242	Carpenter	Robt. Thompson
			Thomas Silas
			Harry Jones
			Thomas Roach, Clerk
15. Sweet Rest		Pearson	C. P. Jones
16. Holy Ghost Tabernacle	35	Silver Creek	E. J. Lucas

15

The adopted resolution provided for:

1. Change of name to Christ's Sunday School Convention of Mississippi of Baptized Believers in Christ.
2. Use of non-denominational books.
3. Redirection of educational money.
4. Open assemblage.

By this time and for more than a decade to come, an acceptable name for the church emerged into the limelight.

Before the official separation in the Jackson Association in December 1900, some of the churches were using the name *Church of God,* as in the case of Damascus at Hazlehurst and China Grove at Myles, and also seen on the corner stones on some churches. Some others were using the name *Church of Christ,* as in the case of White Oak at Carpenter, Miss., and Mt. Helm at Jackson, Miss.

The primeval insurgent was referred to as a "non-denominational religious movement" during the period 1895-1900, and persisted for nearly two decades in some areas.

In the September 7, 1911 issue of *Truth* on page two, paragraph one of the President's message is given with the heading:

President's Report

Adopted by the convocation of the churches, Aug, 22, 1911: To the brethren of the convocation of the *Churches of God in Christ,* Greetings: I, C. P. Jones, whom you under the hand of the Lord have chosen as President and Chief Overseer of the work of the Lord under our hand, beg to submit my report for the session of 1911 which is our fifth annual session as a body organized for labor. However, it would properly be the sixth session: For the winter convocation of 1906 was the summer convention 1905 deferred for a reason.

The denominational name used here was "Churches of God in Christ". Elder C. H. Mason (later Bishop C. H. Mason) who was associated with Bishop Jones from the beginning, had withdrawn by this time, but was using the same denominational name, and had the name incorporated under his leadership.

It seems to have been then that the original convocation changed to the name: Church of Christ (Holiness) U.S.A.

Recapitulation:-

1. Movement
2. Church of God
3. Church of Christ
4. Church of God in Christ
5. Church of Christ (Holiness) U.S.A.

16

CHAPTER II

C. P. JONES, THE FOUNDER

"The man with a Spiritual Vision and a Righteous Mission".
"And who knoweth whether thou art come to the kingdom for such a time as this." Esther 4:14

Bishop C. P. Jones came on the religious scene when church bigotry of his time was rampant.

Beginning of the work as reported by Brother Jones' first secretary who was in Jackson, 1892-1902, 1907-1909, 1925-1929. She was in position to know most about the history of the beginning. She wrote in her diary that when Sister Alice Brown took to Brother Jones the idea of the school, he took it to the Lord, then came with the statement the Lord sent him to *preach the Gespel* and *not* to build schools, and so sent her to the brethren. It was they who went forward at school work and *not he, as some now tell it.* Brother Jones himself left recorded names of some who were with the beginning and mentioned Brother G. A. Thomas as among later than the first, though among early ones to come in. I give this as first hand historical data. —Sister Vance

Beginning of the work as reported by Mrs. Sarah J. Thomas-Land, one of the charter members and the first secretary to the founder, reporter for the *Truth,* writer of the cards for little folks and the primary quarterly of those early days.

Brother Jones, as he preferred being called and as all our ministers were called, came from Selma, Ala., to pastor the Mt. Helm Baptist Church in Jackson, Miss., in 1895, having been elected by unanimous vote of the church.

Sister Land's Report

I had been in Jackson two years when Elder Jones came to Jackson. Another lady and I were teaching in a Congregational school on Capitol St. Our church were so few in number that our pastor was sent to North Carolina to pastor. Though we were Con-

17

gregationalists, we often attended the Mt. Helm Baptist Church and enjoyed hearing pastor preach; for he really preached the Gospel. He called us friends, and one day asked me if I could come sometimes after school and on Saturdays and help with his work. He always had so much writing to be done. I began helping him and so became his first secretary and later a member or his church. I lived with Brother and Sister Jones until I was married in the First Temple Church.

He'd held a revival meeting for the church and everybody wanted to hear him preach. Before he left Selma he'd sought and found a closer walk with God. The Holy Ghost was poured out on some who had glorified Jesus, and they had powers. He attended a convention in Vicksburg, Miss., in 1895 and some of the ministers who heard him gladly received the baptism with the Holy Ghost. In 1896 he put out his first booklet, a treatise on the 12th chapter I Cor. titled. "The Work of the Holy Spirit in the Churches." About this time God told him to publish the *Truth*. This same year he was commanded of God to call a Holiness Convention. The Spirit gave him the time, place, date, and even the duration of the meeting to be called. Many miracles were wrought in this meeting. Sins were confessed openly and privately forsaken, tears shed, sinful living given up, crutches thrown away, secret order pins thrown out the church windows and many souls were added to the church. These were days when the saints were really persecuted for Christ's sake. One time in a meeting at McComb, Miss., while Brother Jones was preaching under a brush arbor a shot was fired into the congregation. He said, "Let us pray." We all bowed in prayer and afterwards continued the services. We were taken to court after the 1898 Convention and eventually were put out of the church building. The Sunday School Convention was put out at a little church in the rural district near Jackson while we were in session in 1899. We finished our meeting in a nearby church building. One thing, Brother Jones believed in conquering Satan and driving out sin. O how we fasted and prayed! We often fasted three days at a time. Sometimes he fasted so long that he appeared unnatural. In those days of persecution many of those lovely inspiring, encouraging and heart-strengthening songs were born in the heart of our pastor. Sometimes when they were given him in the night he would have us join him through the hours and sing. For he had his own chorus. Often we remained in the church until midnight.

This movement was born in the Mt. Helm Baptist Church. Not

only were the members of that church stirred and awakened but many came from other churches. Some "searched the scriptures to see if those things were true" (Acts 17:11). Of course, when fire breaks out, if not put out, it spreads. Invitations came from near and far, and the minister went everywhere preaching the Gospel—traveled from the Atlantic to the Pacific and from the Gulf of Mexico to the Great Lakes, telling the story of the cross of Christ who came to seek and to save the lost race of man.

A Mr. Helm (white) had given the church to the colored Baptists. Sometime later these same white people tried to get Brother Jones to accept the presidency of Alcorn College, but he would not give up the leadership of his people. The night the pastor was ordered out of the Mt. Helm church those of us who believed and accepted the Gospel as it was preached and taught stood up and followed him out. We went into an empty store that belonged to a man not one of us but a friend. Brother Jones sat on the counter and we stood before him. That is when and where we held our first meeting. The brethren or trustees rented the Benevolent Hall on Farish Street and there we held services until we purchased and built on the corner of Grayson (now Lamar) and Monument Streets. I don't know how long we used the Benevolent Hall, but pretty soon all saw the need of a church house—a permanent meeting place.

The lot on the corner of Grayson and Monument Streets, covered with beautiful cedars, must have been for sale. For the pastor and leading brethren bought this place, and on a Sunday in a meeting held here the entire cost was raised in cash and subscriptions. Deacon Henry Moore, in whose home the pastor stayed during his illness of smallpox in the 1900 epidemic, paid the first $100 (as report goes). This was in 1899. Soon the Lord's ambassadors and their co-workers, by earnestly praying and fasting and working, built the First Temple Church, the mother church of the Church of Christ (Holiness) U.S.A.

This structure was a church and parsonage—a building that housed also the printing press with its workers and outfit. The Temple and school building were destroyed by fire. The Temple was rebuilt, white friends donating for the work. It seemed all those things were done by magic. The Lord God was with us and we had a mind to work; and we worked (Neh. 4:6). Not only did we work but we prayed. Prayer should precede always.

We fasted and prayed to know the will of the Lord. When people seek to know and do the Lord's will He will help them and prosper

19

what they do. Jesus came all the way to earth to do the will of the Father. "Our Father in Heaven, Thy will be done."

Our final ousting was from the parsonage on Church Street soon after we were put out of the Mt. Helm Church building. Bills signed by "The Committee of one hundred" were strung in the yard and outside, telling the pastor and his family to vacate the parsonage. Brother Jones was brave. For he loved God, feared and trusted Him and sought to obey Him.

We were already holding services in the Benevolent Hall on Sundays. That hall was then used as a public school building for Negroes; for at that time Jackson had not one public school building for my people. Now (in 1957) there are in this city about a dozen public school buildings for the education of Negroes. Jackson, Mississippi, has come a long way since 1899.

So God was with us. Certainly He had a house ready. There was in our midst a Sister Boyd who owned a five room house on Ash Street. This cottage had just been repaired. She told the pastor to move in and take over. For she was staying on the premises where she worked.

A POEM
by Bishop C. P. Jones
to Mrs. Sarah Thomas Land

How good to you and me the Lord has been!
We have lived long among the Sons of Men;
You not so long as I, I must admit,
But we were there together, *albeit.*
In 1895 I thundered loud,
You were a teacher then and in the crowd.
In age you were behind the preacher some. ....
You were a worker that to me did come.
These years you've followed in that holy way
And are still bearing fruit down to this day.
The youthful freshness gone, as go it must,
But the young heart is there among the Just,
Renewed in Faith and Truth day after day,
And so renewed in strength to keep the Way.
The Savior's Hope as new, His Word as dear,
As when we met that first eventful year.
We have seen much of good along the path;

20

And oft we have been tried; a daily *death*
The holy life demands, and we have died
To walk with God among the Sanctified.
But we have *lived* by faith; for 'tis God's plan;
And what the Lord decries is good for man.
He *prays* for us, and so our faith fails not,
Tho Satan often has us "on the spot."
The rescue bands from Heaven join in the strife,
For living faith bestows eternal life. (John 3).
Eyes lifted to the Help beyond the sky,
From the eternal hills our help draws nigh.
What if youth's beauty fail and come distress
Since we are thus renewed in holiness?
A beauty of the Heaven's that can not fade—
The strength of God Himself in all to aid.
I often think of Thee and for Thee pray —
Please do not forget me along the Way.
Eph. 6:10-19.

Autobiographical Sketch of Charles Price Jones, Founder of the Church of Christ (Holiness), U.S.A.

I was born in Texas Valley, near Rome, Georgia, December 9, 1865. I was reared at Kingston, Ga., between Rome and Atlanta; and the greatest religious influences in my life were Miss Ada Dawson, who came there from Columbus in 1874 or 75, and the Reverend Humphrey Daniels, my mother's pastor at Shiloh Baptist Church in Kingston. He signed himself U. Daniels, spelling the Humphrey without the "H". He was a man of deep, beautiful and impressive piety.

In 1882 my mother died, July 12, leaving me a boy in my seventeenth year. I had a spell of sickness nearly every year and was so afflicted as not to hope to reach my thirtieth year. My mother was the wife of Berry Latimer, a good man of the Methodist persuasion. I cannot speak too highly of this man. I love his memory. I had not sense enough when young to appreciate his worth. But the years have taught me his true value.

Mother being dead, I was bereft of the one restraining influence that now remained in my life. In after years wise children realize the value of parental restraint as they could not at first. I have heard them in deep trouble, blame their parents for not restraining them. So the poor parents must bear the blame. If they are strict they are too strict. If they are slack they are cursed for it in after years. But love beareth all things.

After the death of my mother I left Texas Valley at the age of 17, for Cedartown, and Rome, Ga., and afterwards I went to Chattanooga, Tenn., then some months later to Memphis; thence to Arkansas; and at last to Cat Island, where in 1884 I was converted and joined Locust Grove Baptist Church and was baptized by Elder J. D. Petty, a superior man and gifted minister of his day. This was in the southern part of Crittenden County, Arkansas.

After Locust Grove Church fell into the hands of Elder Geo. W. Dickey for a short while, he licensed me to preach in 1887 though I had begun preaching locally in 1885. In 1887 I left Cat Island and went to Forest City, Ark.; thence to Helena where I was under watchcare of Centennial Baptist Church under the great E. C. Morris who afterwards was president of the National Baptist Convention. From Helena I went to Little Rock, to enter the Arkansas Baptist College, then practically in its infancy. Taught school in Grant County, Arkansas, in 1888 and was elected pastor of Pope Creek Baptist Church in July, 1888. In October of 1888, I was ordained to the ministry in Mt. Zion Baptist Church, by Dr. C. L. Fisher. In November 1888 I was elected pastor of St. Paul Baptist Church on Broadway, in Little Rock, Ark. The afterward eminent Bishop J. A. Jeter was then one of my deacons. In 1891 I accepted a call to Bethlehem Baptist Church in Searcy, Ark., and become editor of the Ark. Baptist College Vanguard, published by Arkansas Baptist College. I graduated from the academic course of the college in 1891, and was married the same year to Miss Fannie Brown of Little Rock, Ark. Our only daughter, Ola Mae, was born in 1893, was severely burned and died in 1897, before she was 4 years old.

I accepted a call to the Tabernacle Baptist Church in Selma, Ala., in 1892 which was the College Church of Selma University, where I pastored for two and half years. I was very popular as a pastor and evangelist everywhere, for as Doctor J. H. Hoke of Arkansas once said, my "word was with power." I loved Jesus. Power belongs to God. *Know God.*

But it was at Selma that I found myself in need of a deeper experience of grace, a larger power. As I asked God for this grace He demanded that I let Him sanctify me; which I did. For as He demanded of me, I fasted and prayed three days and nights. He then sanctified me sweetly in His love. Rom. 5:1-5. New visions of Christ, of God, of truth, were given me. The earnestness of the Spirit was mine. I was sealed in Him unto the day of Redemption. The blessing of God rested upon me — all on the merits of Jesus. Eph. 1:14. For in myself I felt more unworthy and undone than ever. It was the nearness, the eminence, the reality of the presence of God that exalted my spirit and filled me with joy, the joy of the Holy Ghost. Yet it made me feel keenly my unworthiness and the daily need of "amazing grace."

This was in 1894 and I can only speak briefly of how my ministry was blessed in Selma; at Marion with Dr. Bacote, a wonderful man; at Tuskegee, with Reverend Archer; and with other people in other places. I glory now in the mercy of God showed me then. Its very memory elates and refreshes.

Early in 1895 I accepted a call to Mt. Helm Baptist Church in Jackson, Mississippi. I had been called there twice previously, in 1893 after a revival and in 1894. This time I went, and it was there that my largest and greatest work was done; if I might speak of my work as great. Anyway my toil and suffering were great, and in them, like Paul, I rejoice. Rom. 5:1-5; 2 Cor. 12.

If you have sought earnestly to live a good life, old age has compensations that money cannot buy — approval of conscience; wisdom of soul, comfort of fervor and spirit, future hope and assurance — all these make one, in spite of earthly poverty or of the remembrance of futilities and mistakes. Even the years the locusts have eaten become rich and fruitful under the power of the Holy Ghost. Joel 2. All things work together for good to those who love God. Rom. 8:26-39. Only keep the faith. The just live by faith. Rom. 1:14-16. Keep wisdom. Let her reprove thee, chasten thee, give thee tasks. She will surely deliver thee a crown of glory. Nor will surely wait until thou art in Heaven to let thee try on that crown.

When I first gave myself to the Lord to be sanctified, (this was in 1894 at Selma) I had no idea at all of taking up holiness as a fad, or an ism, or a creed, or the slogan of a "cult". I just wanted to be personally holy. I just wished to make my own calling and election sure to my own heart by walking with God in the Spirit. As a Baptist I had doctrinal assurance; I wanted spiritual assurance, heart peace, rest of soul, the joy of salvation in the understanding of a new heart, a new mind, a new spirit, constantly renewed and conforted by the Holy Ghost. (Titus 3:5-8; John 14:15-20) But when I reached Jackson, Miss., I became convinced by the Lord that what I needed, all His people needed; that without following peace with all men and holiness, no man could see the Lord. Heb. 12:1-14; that no man could follow Christ in his own strength; that therefore it was the privilege and duty of all to be filled with the Spirit (Eph. 5:16-18) and walk by the Spirit (Gal. 5:15-26); that Christ in us is the Hope of Glory (Col. 1:27, 28), Christ the life, as well as Christ in Heaven the Intercessor, the High Priest and Advocate. Col. 1:27-29; Heb. 4:14-16. Christ in you, in me, in all. Christ!

This conviction "ate me up." (Psa. 69:9) Maybe it was because I am like that, an extremist, likely. But it seemed that the "wee" was upon me if I withheld from the church the message of her privileges and obligations in the Spirit of Christ. (I Cor. 9:16)

One day as I staggered under the weight of this obligation, under the necessity of this ministry, I felt that I must be alone and especially talk with God about it. I went to the home of Sister Rachel Williams, a God-fearing woman, the widow of Deacon Ben Williams, and asked if I might lock myself in her parlor and remain unmolested till I had reached the Lord with this matter. Oh the relief and help possible through prayer. It is good when burdened to pray it out; some phrase it "pray through." I prayed from about 9 a.m. to about 3 p.m. This was the burden of my prayer: "Lord, give me power to convince my people and my generation of the beauty of holiness and the advantages of righteousness." (Deut. 28) My people loved beauty, but the beauty of the flesh is vain and deceiving and soon passes. They wanted to advance in the world; but worldly advantages proved only a snare; for wealth promotes robbery, engenders pride and breeds strife; which to my people was fatal. I saw that in God was our salvation temporal and eternal. I desired that they should see it. I saw how we could hasten the coming of the Lord and universal happiness and welfare. I wanted them to see it. And so I prayed. Between 3 and 4 o'clock in the afternoon I became exhausted. I lay down on the sofa on which I knelt and said, "Lord, I'm exhausted. I can pray no more." Then the Lord flooded me with blessing until laughing and crying and verily kicking like an infant for holy delight, I at last begged the Lord to desist.

24

It seemed I could stand no more, my vision was clarified, my eyes were opened. I could see apparently the golden walls and pearly gates of the "city made without hands." Surely the heavens were opened. The Spirit spoke within from the holy of holies of my redeemed spirit, and said, "You shall write the hymns for your people." This He said six or seven times till it was fixed in my mind. I got up and went to the organ in the corner of the room, wrote a song titled "Praise the Lord," ruled off a tablet, set it to music, and sang it before I left the room. This song I lost, to my regret. I sent it to a publisher, a Mr. William Roseborough, author of *Celestial Showers,* and he failed to bring it out. For it was his second book, *Celestial Showers No. II.* Before he brought the book out I was rejected by the Baptist people as a heretic. This would not occur now for they have advanced in spirituality and tolerance. All discord comes from misunderstanding. We have learned to love one another and some of the most highly and strictly spiritual men I know are Baptist. God bless them. Amen.

But those were dark days. One minister's intelligent wife, Mrs. R. J. Temple, mother of Dr. Ruth Temple of our city, said to me, "We had not so much as heard whether there be any Holy Ghost." (Acts 19) Of course that statement could not be taken in exactly the same sense as at Ephesus, but one can see what she meant. One lady writing up the minutes at a Sunday School Convention said my sermon was full of the Holy Ghost, and put the term in quotations. But thank God, many see now who did not see then. And for this we are glad. God made me see years ago that, by and by, this would be so. The earth is the Lord's and the fulness thereof. (Ps. 24) He will bring His sheep and there shall yet be "one fold and one Shepherd."

Entering A New Era

In 1894 I was pastor of the Tabernacle Baptist Church of Selma, Ala., and my ministry with that church and with the Alabama Baptist ministry at large seemed to be accepted and much loved. But as I read my Bible and observed conditions, I felt that we were not, as a brother once said to me, "toting fair with Jesus." I began then to seek Him with all my heart for that power that would make my life wholly His, so that I might realize both the blessedness and usefulness of real Bible religion. I was not satisfied with a faith that brought no fruit, or else fruit of

25

such poor a quality spiritually, and a religion that none of the signs spoken of in the Bible followed. (Mark 16:14-18; Heb. 2:1-11) I wanted to be one of wisdom's true sons and like Abraham, "a friend of God."

As we sought God, the Spirit promised us that if we would fast with light, with joy and with the Holy Ghost. Oh the splendid glory of that exalted state! Do not be satisfied with the attitude merely, that holiness is right. Get the experience. Get saved. Get a knowledge of it. Have the mind of Christ. You will really know something then that you never knew before. Try it out. (Jno. 14: 12-23)

From then on, with more or less zeal, we sought renewings of power and pushed the claims of Christ on the churches. I could not help it, for then I knew Him, and knew also that He was in the Father, and I in Him and He in me. (Jn. 14:15-18)

I beg again, get the real experience of the fullness of the Spirit. Amen. In 1895 I accepted a unanimous call to the Mt. Helm Baptist Church, Jackson, Miss. Here I began my deeper spiritual labors among the people. I worked in the Associations and at Byram, Big Creek, Mt. Olive and Carleton Hill, of which latter, Elder F. Sheriff was then pastor. From the first I found in Elder Sheriff an industrious farming minister, who bore an excellent reputation among whites and blacks (Ecc. 7) In 1895 we preached at the General Baptist Association in Vicksburg, and there Elder A. J. Bradley was much affected by the message, but he later proved unable to go all the way; yet for a time, he seemed a friend to our dear Master. Also a Brother Tate of Tougaloo, who afterwards became an Adventist, God bless them.

But in 1896 the General Association of the Baptist Church was held in Mt. Helm Church, Jackson. At that time we came to better know Elders Kelly Rucks, A. Reed, R. J. Temple, W. S. Pleasant and others who regarded our zeal with more or less apparent favor. At this association we sold our first booklet a treatise on the 12th chapter of First Corinthians, under the title, "The Work of the Holy Spirit in the Churches." We also about this time began to publish the *Truth*.

The Divine Command

Sometime after this association the Holy Spirit bade us call a Holiness Convention. Said I, "When Lord?" "The 6th of June,"

26

said He. "What day will that be, Lord?" I asked. "Sunday," said He. Later when the almanac for 1897 came out, I found it was Sunday. Then I, young as I was in the way, knew it was the Lord. In due time we made the call. We had already begun in 1896 as I said, to publish the *Truth,* so it became the special organ of the call. But special invitations, I think, were sent out to those men who seemed interested in their own souls and the souls of the people.

We began the meeting Sunday, June 6th, and continued two weeks, studying the Bible and praying night and day. For this reason, we have always opened the convention on Sunday. And later when the meeting became so large that the community could not bear it two weeks and we set its time for convenience, later in the year, and shortened the time to the Biblical period feast of eight days. We still held and yet hold to the tradition of opening it on Sunday. At this first meeting we brought out *Truth,* which was then a semi-monthly, as a daily and the Lord our God was with us and the shout of a King was among us. (Num. 23-21)

Of the men present then, there are with us now such heroes as S. F. Sheriff, J. E. Burris, T. J. Hardy, A. J. Scarborough, G. H. Funches, J. A. Jeter; W. S. Pleasant, R. H. Morris, E. W. Butler, W. T. Nickerson, C. H. Mason and a host of those who follow on, whose names we do earnestly trust are in the Book of Life.

At first, our movement was entirely inter-denominational, non-sectarian and in spirit anti-sectarian. Our motto in this matter was, "Denominationalism is slavery." We stood for the communion of the Holy Ghost. We served in the denominations if allowed, but we served Christ in the life of His people instead of a denominational "image in the plains of Dura." But alas! the sectarian spirit is hard to conquer. We are soon contending for our crown, our doctrine, our way, our sect instead of the Lord. Please read I Cor. 1, 2, and 3.

Driven Out

But we were persecuted by the churches eventually and associations and all sects combined against us. We do not blame them, because self-preservation is the first law of nature, as the saying goes. Our mission was misunderstood. What we do not understand we fear and fight. But this persecution caused us to build another sect, which was not our aim nor desire. We contend that Christ is all. But we were extreme in our fight. The times demanded it. But we from the first, only wanted to exalt Jesus and put down man-made tradition. Mark 7:1-7. In our zeal to be entirely scriptural, not anti-Baptistic, but simply scriptural, as the Baptists claimed and do now claim to be, we after the convention voted to change the name of the church. This was the second or 1898 convention. We have gone through fire and water and Satan has done us much harm, but here we are yet telling our children and the world that "God hath called His church unto holiness." II Cor. 4:1-8)

As a holiness convention we date from June, 1897, when we were interdenominational, called together by the Holy Spirit that He might take the things of Christ and show them to us. Present were delegates from many parts of our country: from Arkansas, Tennessee, Missouri, Illinois, North Carolina, Louisiana, Alabama, Georgia and all over, as the saying goes. This meeting being called a holiness convention, the study of the Bible, prayer in and for the Holy Ghost and testimonies were the dominant features thereof. To know the Lord better and to receive power and joy for His service; these were our goal. The Spirit who called us together met with us in power.

Not all were convinced that we were right, but all could see that something must be done to make the religion of Jesus a more effective and fruitful thing. Those of a doubtful mind were bewildered as to just what was happening and scarcely knew whether to fight or to surrender and seek the Lord. The sick were healed, the blind were made to see, the afflicted were blessed, and the Gospel of the New Testament was preached to the poor. And for those who labored with singleness of heart Christ was all and in all. Black and white, Jew and Gentile sought God together.

During our convocation at Mt. Helm in 1898 the fight began hard against us. The move on the part of Mt. Helm to change the name of the church to "Church of Christ" gave the enemies of the Holy Spirit a chance, and they put us in court. And though we won our liberty in the lower court, the Supreme Court put us out; not on general law, but on a technicality involved in the Mt. Helm holding. But we were out and that for the name's sake of the Lord. (John 16)

The Spirit said to me, "You Baptists are liars. Nowhere in Holy

Writ is the church called a Baptist Church. John was called Baptist because he baptized the people unto a clean life and organized no church at all. I am robbed of My glory. I said I will build My church. The church is Mine. There is salvation in no other name but Mine. Give Me My glory."

Like Paul, know nothing but Christ crucified and all men will hate you. Add not to His Word lest you be found a liar. (Pro. 30) And nowhere in the Bible is there a Church of Christ (Holiness). Holiness belongs to God. He is righteous in all His ways and holy in all His works I complained to Him: "Lord, people are dubious about this holiness and I don't blame them. So many men have professed holiness and taken other men's wives or killed some one or committed other crimes and gone to prison. How about it?" Said He to me, "You preach Me. I am holiness. I said preach the Gospel: the good news of salvation. Preach Me. I have done no sin neither was guile found in My mouth." Said Paul, "We preach Christ crucified, to the Jew a stumbling block, to the Greeks foolishness; but to those who we called, both Jews and Greeks Christ is the power of God and the wisdom of God."

Our ministers and churches who were fostering the glorious and scriptural doctrine that we are to follow peace with all men and holiness, without which no man shall see the Lord, submitted to persecutions of all kinds till after a few years when those churches and ministers who held forth the doctrine that the Holy Spirit was building a holy church as the body of a holy Christ, were put out of the churches as they then existed and of which most of us were members (the Baptist denomination), and were compelled to build our own church houses, beginning with Christ Temple on Grayson and Monument Streets in Jackson, Damascus at Hazlehurst, Miss., Church of God in Little Rock, Ark., and many others too numerous to mention here, that joined us in those glorious attempts to honor the Lord. Many of our heroes are gone; some are still here.

The Lord has crowned our labors with moderate success and in some cases with splendid success. We congratulate ourselves that the Lord of hosts is with us and the God of Jacob is our refuge. Yet there remaineth very much land to be possessed. So we must seek the unity of the Spirit in the bond of peace and press the battle to the gate. My brethren, let nothing discourage you, but be strong and fear not and work. Quit yourselves like

29

men! A mere fault finder is not a man. Men help men lay hold and help. Glory. Are we of the fibre of Joshua? Have we the faith of Abraham?

Our first entirely independent church was organized at Lexington, Miss. Our first Sunday School convention was organized at Carleton Hill Church near Jackson, in 1899 and continued under the leadership of Fathers W. S. Pleasant and Thos. Sanders till our work was reorganized in 1906. During our National Convention held with Christ Temple, Jackson, in 1921, thru influence of Elder Wm. Mitchell, the Virginia and North Carolina Convocation, with Elder John F. Morrison as President, sought our fellowship. After proper investigation by Committee on New Churches and Fellowship, this Convocation with all their ministers, churches and members were accepted into fellowship of the National Convention of the Church of Christ (Holiness) U.S.A. with headquarters at Jackson. Yet there remaineth very much land to be possessed (1935).

A Larger Ministry

An old white gentleman came from Meridian, Miss., who asked me what was my theory of holiness; was sin eradicated, according to the theory of the eradicationalists or according to the doctrine of the Keswick Movement, was it merely kept under by the presence of the Spirit? I answered him that the Bible bid us to reckon ourselves dead indeed unto sin but alive unto God; that sin was put to death by Christ and that faith claimed victory over sin in Christ and in Him is no sin. That walking in Christ the life in Him is ours. It is God's business to make the mystery effective; it is ours to believe it and be saved. He promised that he that believeth and is baptized shall be saved. The Holy Spirit declares without addition or equivocation that he that believeth on the Son hath everlasting life. He does not even have to go to Heaven to get it. We have it now. Christ in us is the hope of glory. Jesus Christ the same yesterday, today, and forever—made unto us wisdom, righteousness, sanctification and redemption.

Godliness Not Ours But His

Of course we know that in us, that is, in our flesh dwelleth no good thing. But does not the Spirit of Truth declare it? "Ye are not in the flesh, but in the Spirit, if so be that the Spirit of Christ dwell in you." Can it be that the Spirit of Truth is given just as we are dying, to guide us into all truth? Must we not know the Truth to be free? Do only the dead or the dying have the fellowship of the Holy Ghost? Does He give us the glory of the new birth, and then leave that new birth to the power of the natural man, the old man, the first Adam? Nay: there is a fight. The Spirit lusteth against the flesh and the flesh against the Spirit, but greater is He that is in you than he that is in the world.

Systems and Faith

Israel had a beautiful and adequate system; but it failed to do what God wanted it to do—produce men of faith—though it was the most nearly perfect system of the ages. It could not build a temple in five hundred years. Then comes a man of faith, who in a lifetime builds an empire and at his death bequeathes two million dollars to the building of a temple. The just live by faith. We are sanctified not by morals, but by faith. Paul had morals, unimpeachable: morals when he was the chief of sinners. The vilest Pharisee had morals to brag on. Morals are good, even indispensable; but we are justified by faith. Faith purifies the heart and gives us an inheritance among the sanctified. Morals are a part of the results if it is not self-determined and does not make us proud of ourselves. We are saved by grace, through faith, and that not of ourselves, but it is the gift of God.

Back to the Bible

The spiritual side of our work must not be made secondary. The Savior would not have us forget and forsake the precious truth of Divine healing. We have believed and therefore have we spoken. (Ps. 116) Since we are justified by faith, and sanctified by faith, and live by faith and stand by faith and overcome by faith and please God by faith, anything that tests and promotes faith is of incalculable value in the eternal welfare of the soul.

Don't throw away Divine healing. Covet anything that keeps you in touch with God. To know Him and Jesus Christ is eternal life. All He requires is faith out of a pure heart, to believe in Him and love the Lord with all our heart and love one another as He commands us. Nothing is too great for Him to do for us. He loves the prodigal and awaits his return with longing eyes and open arms. And to the faithful son He says, "All I have is thine;

31

make merry when thou pleasest." For what hath the Lord required of thee but to do justly, love mercy and walk humbly with thy God? Amen.

Dedication

To the memory and work of the late Bishop Charles Price Jones
1. He was the founder, editor, and former owner of *Truth*.
2. He was a poet, musician, and a nationally known pulpiteer.
3. He was an interpreter of the Bible, using the English, Latin, Greek and Hebrew translations.
4. He was editor of "The Gift of the Holy Ghost Among the Churches", "Christian Workers Handbook", and "What We Believe and Teach".
5. He was editor of "Jesus Only" song books numbers one and two, "His Fullness" and "Sweet Selections", and the "Jesus Only Standard Hymnal", the official hymnal of the Church.
6. His songs are used throughout the United States and in foreign countries.
7. He was the builder of Christ Temple—the mother church at Jackson, Mississippi, which he pastored for 22 years.
8. He was the founder of the church and President of the National Convention for 50 years.
9. But few men equaled him in varied intellectual and literary abilities.
10. His followers and admirers number into the tens of thousands.
11. During his lifetime he brought about a re-awakening in religion which affected not only the many thousands who knew him but teeming thousands who never saw or knew him. His contention for the Christ-Life was proclaimed throughout the nation. It now becomes the responsibility of the present leadership to promulgate that which he set aflame.

His Song

Jesus only is my motto, Jesus only is my song,
Jesus only is my heart tho't, Jesus only all day long.
Jesus only shall command me, Jesus only guide my way
Only He to choose my changes, None but Jesus ev'ry day.
None but Jesus, Saviour, Captain, None but Jesus help me sing;
Fill me ever with Thy presence, Jesus, Jesus, Lord and King.
                                                            Amen.

It was in Jackson, that his ministry greatly developed and spread like a mighty oak tree. He had a conviction of a deeper work of grace and an infilling of the Holy Spirit that pricked him to surpass the religious contentions of his peers.

The Late Bishop Charles Price Jones
His Last Visit to Jackson

Bishop Jones:

Thou hast neared the closing era of thy prolonged vigorous labors. Thou hast done thy work. Thou hast sung thy song. Sit down, and take thy much deserved rest. For there is laid up for thee a crown of righteousness which the Lord, the righteous judge, shall give thee. (2 Timothy 4:8)

Bishop Charles Price Jones died January 19, 1949, in Los Angeles, California.

His funeral was held at 1:00 P.M., January 25, 1949 at the Christ Temple Church where he pastored for 28 years.

* * *

A Tribute to the Late Bishop C. P. Jones
by
A Faithful Follower

Of special interest is the known truth that as long as our founder and pastor was able to minister to us in anointing and praying for the sick, the saints did not have to be confined to hospitals and submit to operations.

One scene will never erase from my mind and heart will stay with me as long as I live. I lived to see his prayer come true. During his last illness his one desire was to be able to sit once

33

more in the pulpit that he'd ministered from; and so he did. He would raise both of his arms over us and with tears streaming down his tired face, he would say in his feeble voice to those of us he pastored, "Little children, love one another." I'm glad I had the privilege to sit at his feet and learn.

For 29 years he was my pastor and teacher of God's Holy Word. Now God is using me to teach and help others grasp the true meaning of Holiness. Many shy away from it, but after taking time to study God's Word they find that it is not a fanatic state of emotions but a beautiful life of putting on Christ and being clothed in the beauty of holiness and living a life entirely for Christ.

Mrs. Pearl E. Jones

Sister Pearl E. Jones is the widow of the late Bishop Charles Price Jones. To this union three sons were born: Charles Price Jones, Jr., Vance R. Jones and Samuel S. Jones. Sister Pearl E. Jones was the second wife of Bishop C. P. Jones. His first wife, Mrs. Fannie Jones, died in 1916. To that union a daughter was born, who died during her early childhood.

34

A group of nine distinguished prelates on the occasion of the funeral of the founder of the church, the Late Bishop Charles Price Jones, on January 25, 1949, at 1:00 P.M. at Christ Temple Church, Los Angeles, California, his pastorate. Bishop E. W. Butler, officiating.

Reading from left to right:

Northern Diocese presiding Bishop Jacob M. Haywood of Chicago, Illinois; South Central Diocese presiding Bishop M. R. Conic of Jackson, Miss.; National Convention Treasurer, Mr. Walter Moore of Chicago, Illinois; North Central Diocese presiding Bishop Wm. Mitchell of St. Louis, Mo.; Pastor Louis Randall of Indianapolis, Ind.; Acting Pastor, C. L. Carhee of Christ Temple Church (formerly pastored by the deceased) Los Angeles, California; Pastor, Rev. A. B. Smith of Merced, California, Western Diocese Supervisor; South Western Diocese presiding Bishop E. W. Butler of Little Rock, Arkansas; Rev. B. M. Draugh of Los Angeles, California.

35

Otho B. Cobbins,
B.A., M.A., D.D.

Historical Sketch — Continued 1926-1952
By Bishop O. B. Cobbins, A.B., A.M., D.D.

The Historical Sketch by Bishop Charles Price Jones extends to 1926, the year in which it was written. The writer of this "continued sketch" attempted to carry this historical sketch from 1926 to 1952, a period of 26 years.

The writer's equipage and his acquaintance with the development and working of the church may be attested by the following:

1. His first acquaintance with the church was in 1906, 59 years ago.
2. He was a student of C. M. & I. College for three years; later he attended other institutions, earning the degree of Master of Arts in Education from Fisk University at Nashville, Tennessee.
3. He first saw Bishop Jones in 1909, 56 years ago.
4. He joined the Christ Temple Church at Jackson, Mississippi, in May 1911 under the pastorate of Bishop C. P. Jones, 54 years ago.
5. In March 1916 he was licensed to preach by Bishop C. P. Jones, 49 years ago.
6. In 1921 he was ordained to the ministry in Jackson, 44 years ago.

36

7. For four years, 1940-1944, he was President of the National Sunday School and Holiness Young Peoples Union Congress, one of the major auxiliaries of church.
8. He was manager and editor of the church publication and official organ for a part of five years.
9. For four years, 1942-1946, he was chairman of the National Education—Trustee Board of C. M. & I. College, the "one" educational institution of the church.
10. He served as assistant pastor of Christ Temple Church at Jackson, Mississippi, under Bishop E. W. Butler and Bishop J. L. I. Conic, and twice served as acting pastor of the Christ Temple Church, the mother church.
11. He was appointed adjutant bishop of the South Central Diocese in October 1943 by Bishop C. P. Jones, 22 years ago.
12. He was elected and consecrated bishop of the church in August 1945 in St. Louis, Missouri, by the National Convention and assigned presiding bishop of the South Central diocese, 20 years ago.
13. He attended the National Convention for the first time in 1911, and attended 40 annual sessions of the National Convention thereafter. Beginning with the convention of 1911, he has attended 41 or 75% of all the National Conventions held through 1964 in 9 different cities in 9 different States.

Against this background the writer claimed sufficient knowledge of the general church to attempt to continue this "historical sketch" of the church for the 39 year period, 1926-1965.

From the first convention in 1897 through the 1926 convention, Bishop Charles Price Jones—then Elder Jones, the founder of the church, was the undisputed leader and head of the new church in spite of two years when he was away from the brotherhood and the convention, working with another religious group, during which time Elder J. A. Jeter carried on as president of the convention. This period really began in 1896, and covered a period of 30 years 1896-1926.

During the 30 year period:—
1. Elder Jones exerted his greatest religious influence as an exponent of a new church which affected the religious life of many thousands of people throughout the nation.
2. The paper *Truth* (later *Truth Messenger*), which he

37

Delegates to the National Convention
Jackson, Mississippi, August 22-29, 1926

founded and published, reached its height of success.
3. The convention had the greatest number of church affiliates.
4. The greatest numerical following had been witnessed.
5. The educational work at C. M. & I. College, as a Christian training institution had reached its zenith.

During the 31 year period, 1895-1926, the organization had e-volved from a mere religious movement to a denominational status.

During this 30 year period the annual sessions of the national convention were held at the Christ Temple Church at Jackson, Mississippi, except four sessions held as follows: 1920 in Atlanta, Ga., Elder K. H. Burrus, host pastor; 1922 in Montgomery, Ala., Elder W. H. Dunn, host pastor; 1924 Chicago, Illinois, Elder Wm. Webb, host pastor, and 1923 in Little Rock, Ark., Elder Wm. Mitchell, host pastor.

After the end of this 30 year period in the opinion of the editor changes began to take place in rapid succession:

1. Organizational and administrative weakness began to be manifested.
2. The spiritual fever began to wane.
3. The constituency became more inquisitive.
4. Clannishness began to diminish.
5. Much of the evangelistic zeal began to disappear.
6. Proselyting began to give way to developing internal feud.
7. Much that had been *restrained* began to be *condoned* or ignored.

38

8. Much that had been held in high esteem began to be disregarded.

These changes took place in the transitory process in such manner that many were not conscious of what was actually taking place.

The next national convention, 1927, in Norfolk, Virginia, saw a partial change in the administration of the church with the view of strengthening that which was weakening.

A partial episcopal form of government was established, with the election of Elder C. P. Jones as senior bishop and president of the national convention, and election of four junior bishops: namely, Elders J. L. I. Conic, E. W. Butler, Wm. A. Washington, Bishop L. J. Morrison. At the same time the whole jurisdiction was reorganized into four dioceses under the supervision of the four elected junior bishops as follows: Bishop L. J. Morrison, Eastern Diocese; Bishop J. L. I. Conic, Northern Diocese; Bishop E. W. Butler, Southern Diocese; and Bishop Wm. A. Washington, Western Diocese.

It was hoped that this reorganization would revitalize, strengthen, and extend the scope of the movement. The expected results were only partially achieved. A large portion of the general church constituency was not ready to accede to this change in form of church government.

This transition period lasted 11 years, 1927-38. By this time there were those who questioned the expediency of continuing Bishop C. P. Jones as active president of the convention as he was nearing his 75th birthday. Manual required retirement at 75.

At the 1938 national convention in Los Angeles, California, changes were made in the administrative cabinet, dividing the diocese, electing additional bishops, and making certain transfers. These actions satisfied the minds of some while it embittered the feelings of others. Bishop Washington was changed from chairman of the publishing board to first vice-president of the national convention. Bishop J. L. I. Conic was changed from vice president of the convention to chairman of the publishing board. He was also made presiding bishop of the newly created Southeastern Diocese after being transferred from the Northern Diocese.

The Northern Diocese where Bishop J. L. I. Conic formerly presided was divided into Northern Diocese and North Central Diocese, and with Bishop H. L. Carver, a newly elected bishop, presiding in the new Northern Diocese, and with Bishop Wm.

39

Mitchell, a newly elected bishop, presiding in the new North Central Diocese.

The Southern Diocese where Bishop Butler formerly presided was divided into South Eastern Diocese and the newly formed South Western Diocese. Bishop Butler was placed over the South Western Diocese with headquarters in Little Rock, Ark. This change moved him from pastor of the Christ Temple Church at Jackson where he had pastored for 15 years. Bishop Conic was placed over the South Eastern Diocese with headquarters in Jackson, Miss.

Also at the 1938 convention a motion prevailed to convene the national convention biennially instead of annually. This action also provided that the auxiliaries would terminate in the diocese. At the 1940 session of the convention in Chicago the delegation voted its disapproval of that action and reinstated the annual sessions of the national convention with the auxiliaries, beginning with the 1942 session. (The Bishops' council met in 1941 in St. Louis, Mo.)

Following the death of Bishop J. L. I. Conic in May 1939, the president, Bishop C. P. Jones called the first extra session of the national convention to meet in Jackson, in August 1939. At the request of the president, the episcopal committee, which acted at the 1938 convention, was abolished at this extra session. Some of the leaders and officials of the convention held that the calling of this extra session was illegal and some did not attend, and disapproved the abolishing of the episcopal committee.

Following the death of Bishop Conic, Bishop C. P. Jones took charge as general bishop of the South Eastern Diocese. Bishop Willie A. Thurmond who was made adjutant bishop under Bishop Butler, and also served as such under Bishop Conic, continued as such under Bishop C. P. Jones. At the time of the death of Bishop Conic the writer was acting pastor of the Christ Temple Church at Jackson with Rev. Joe King usually filling the pulpit on Sundays.

After that 1939 extra session, Bishop Jones, after conferring with the writer and others, appointed Rev. L. J. Brunson pastor of the Christ Temple Church at Jackson. Rev. Brunson accepted but died in February following (1940). The deacon board of the church again asked the writer to take charge of the affairs of the church. Later in the Spring Bishop Thurmond who was acting as adjutant bishop of the diocese under Bishop Jones, took over the pastorage of the church, which he held until September 1942.

40

In 1941, in the absence of the annual session of the national convention, the bishops' council was held in St. Louis, Missouri. At this council Rev. J. M. Haywood of Atlanta, Ga., was admitted to the brotherhood and made overseer of the South Eastern Diocese. Also the state of Mississippi was taken out of the South Eastern Diocese and made a diocese called the South Central Diocese. Following this, Bishop Jones went to Mississippi, called a conference of ministers and leaders, and placed Bishop Butler in charge of the newly created South Central Diocese.

At the same 1941 bishops' council in St. Louis, the Northern part of the Eastern Diocese was taken away and made into a separate diocese called the North Eastern Diocese, and placed in charge of Bishop W. E. Holman.

Bishop Jones attended three more national conventions after the bishops council in 1941 in St. Louis; 1942 in Detroit, 1943 in Jackson, and 1944 in Chicago.

The 1942 convention was held in Detroit, where Rev. John W. Gilbert was the host pastor. Elders J. M. Haywood and Rev. J. Gordon Hay were elected bishops. Bishop Haywood was placed over the South Eastern Diocese, and Bishop Hay was made assistant to Bishop Holman in the North Eastern Diocese. These two dioceses were set up at the bishops council and approved by this session of the convention. Bishop W. H. Dunn was sick and not able to attend the convention but was left in charge of the divided Eastern Diocese. He died the early part of 1943.

Bishop Jones asked that Mississippi, the South Central Diocese be returned to him that he might go to Mississippi following the convention and make adjustments in the Christ Temple Church pastorate at Jackson. He went to Mississippi, called a meeting of ministers at Jackson, moved Bishop Thurmond from the Christ Temple Church pastorate and placed Rev. L. P. Johnson as pastor. In sending out the call for the meeting a typographical error was made in the notice according to Rev. G. J. Strong. Where the reference was made to Rev. George A. Thomas as district superintendent of the Jackson and Terry District, the notice actually read "state superintendent." When this error was brought to Bishop Jones' attention he said, "let it stand," since the notice had been issued.

The 1943 convention was held at Christ Temple Church, Jackson, Rev. L. P. Johnson, host pastor. At this convention representatives from the Pilgrim Holiness Church presented a proposal for beneficial affiliation with our church and convention largely in a financial way. The proposal was accepted by the convention. In spite of the fact that the affiliation was helpful to the convention and the general church, this affiliation largely in the missionary department was short-lived.

Church Name

At this 1943 convention two questions arose with reference to the Mississippi convention, partly as a result of the error of the title "state superintendent". During the year Mississippi had operated as a state and had held a state convention on the old basis as before the change 16 years ago in 1927. When the time came for the report from the state, the report was rejected on the ground that Mississippi had held a state convention with state superintendent or president instead of a diocese convention; and further that the separation of Mississippi from the South Eastern Diocese by the Bishops' council in 1941 had not been approved by the National Convention in 1942. Thus, Mississippi was not a member of the convention. The matter was immediately reported to Bishop Jones who was at his room at the time, and also reported to Rev. Geo. A. Thomas who was at his home at the time. Both came over to the convention. At the proper time a series of motions prevailed which admitted Mississippi to the convention as the South Central Diocese, and its report was accepted.

The convention closed however without making any provisions for a bishop for the diocese. After the convention Bishop Jones asked the writer to agree to become adjutant bishop of the diocese. After several weeks of prayerful consideration and urging on the part of leaders, the acceptance was written to Bishop Jones.

Bishop Holman was made presiding bishop of the Eastern Diocese at the 1943 convention when the North Eastern Diocese was reunited with the Eastern Diocese following the death of Bishop Dunn.

In December 1943 Bishop Jones was stricken and had to undergo a serious major operation. This ordeal was too strenuous for him at his age and feeble condition. After this attack he was never again the same. He recovered enough to attend the diocese convention at Jackson, in July 1944. He met in conference with the ministers and leaders of the diocese to settle the dispute in the diocese over the two men, one with the title "state superintendent," and the other whom he had named and appointed, with the title "adjutant bishop," both titles applying to the same jurisdiction. The members of the conference wanted to settle the controversy by a vote of those present at the conference. To this Bishop Jones agreed. The vote was overwhelmingly in favor of the title "adjutant bishop", and the writer was accordingly voted as their choice for the position.

From Jackson Bishop Jones went to the 1944 National Convention in Chicago. This was general election year. Bishop H. L. Caver had died during the early Spring of 1944. A pastor had to be placed at the church of Chicago. A bishop had to be placed over the Northern Diocese. The question of the presiding officer for the South Central Diocese was again raised. The tension was very acute at this convention. Bishop Jones delayed his annual message until Thursday, seeking to adjust affairs as best as could be done. Bishop Wm. A. Washington was again recommended by Bishop Jones for first vice president, and was elected by the convention. Bishop Willie A. Thurmond was made second vice president. Bishop Thurmond died in February following, in 1945. Bishop J. M. Haywood of Atlanta, Georgia, was made presiding bishop of the Northern Diocese and pastor of the Temple Church at Chicago. Bishop J. Gordon Hay was made presiding bishop of the South Eastern Diocese. He died the Spring of 1946 in Chicago. The South Central Diocese was left as was voted in the diocese in July 1944.

The close of this, the 1944 convention, was the last convention witnessed by the president, founder, and senior Bishop Charles Price Jones. After forty years of energetic and heroic leadership with the church, his energies began to wane as a natural consequence of old age infirmities, following fifty years of strenuous religious endeavors, 1894-1944, which had taken away that which had seemed undauntable.

The retiring veteran leader, in relinquishing his grip of authority, wrote a letter to the general brotherhood and the constituency of the general church. In this letter, he made it clear that his personal conditions made it impossible for him to continue to carry the responsibility of the convention and the general work, and recommended and asked that the responsibility for carrying on the executive authority and responsibility of the convention be placed on Bishop Wm. A. Washington of Los Angeles, California, who was then first Vice President of the National Convention.

On the first business session day of the 1945 convention held in St. Louis, Missouri, the letter was read to the convention, following the annual message by Bishop Washington.

Two motions were presented to the convention. One motion was by Professor W. H. Howard that the annual address of Bishop Washington be accepted in its entirety and become a part of the minutes.

The other motion was by Rev. H. R. McInnis, seconded by Bishop Wm. Mitchell that Bishop Jones' recommendation that Bishop Washington take over the executive responsibilities of the work as long as wisdom dictates be passed unanimously. A $200.00 monthly stipend was voted for Bishop C. P. Jones.

The National Convention of 1946 in Jackson was critical and sensitive. It was a time that necessitated consideration, tolerance, patience, study, understanding, prayer and counseling. "Where no counsel is, the people fall: but in the multitude of counselors there is safety." Proverbs 11:14.

The year 1926-27 may be referred to as a transitory period. 1945-47 may well be called another transitory period.

The 1946 Convention was the beginning of the end of a fellowship which lasted for a quarter of a century without serious interruption in relationships. Now grievances were seized upon and serenity dispelled, recovery from which disillusionment need not be expected within the next quarter of a century.

The excruciating events leading to this disillusionment were based on administrative malfunction rather than doctrine. The Doctrine of the Original Body has been maintained by dissenting groups.

There was another way of looking at these circumstances, when the general principles were continued in vogue by all segments concerned. Under the section headed "The Expanding Perimeter," this philosophy of religion is more fully depicted.

IN MEMORIAM

That grim reaper death struck heavily within about four years 1949-1953. The first was the founder and Senior Bishop Charles Price Jones who died January 19, 1949 in Los Angeles, California.

The second was that great organizer, Bishop William Alexander Washington, who died in May, 1949 in Los Angeles, California.

The third was that convert of Bishop Washington, Bishop William Mitchell, who died February 21, 1951 in St. Louis, Missouri.

The fourth was that pulpiteer, Bishop Edward W. Butler, who died in August 1953 in Jackson, Mississippi. on the eve of the 1953 session of the National Convention in Detroit, Michigan.

CHAPTER III

THE EMERGING CHURCH MOVEMENT

THE PIONEERS

The consequences of any great movement may be predicted on five fundamental principles.

1. The merits of the anticipated goals
2. The confirmed belief of the individual promoters in the ultimate objectives.
3. The psychic, physical and intellectual equipment of the adherents.
4. The devotion and the determination of the advocates.
5. The exhibition of the magnanimous spirit of altruism.

Like the disciples of old, the pioneers were courageous, God-fearing men who dedicated their lives to champion a controversial movement, not withstanding the overt impending perils.

Elder H. Blackman

Elder H. Blackman was born in 1870. He became a member of the Bethel A.M.B. Church, east of Lexington, Mississippi. When Elder C. H. Mason preached at the Bethel Church, young Blackman became a convert to the new teaching.

Young Blackman was with Elder Mason in the services conducted in the old gin-house, in Lexington.

He was ordained in 1899 by Elder Mason.

Because of his participation in the new movement, Elder H. Blackman, of Lexington, Mississippi, was severely beaten by a miniature mob when he would not promise to desist. Later, when he saw the mob returning, he asked, "Are you coming to beat me again?" The Spirit had pricked the conscience of the mobsters so that they were returning, not to beat him again, but to atone for their debauchery. During the more than forty years of his pastoral services, Elder Blackman pastored churches located at Acona, Artesia, Okolona, Canton, Tougaloo, Hazlehurst for

45

Elder H. Blackman

43 years and Brookhaven, Mississippi, for 38 years, and Bogalusa, Louisiana, for an indefinite period.

Elder Blackman died December 25, 1946, at his home in Canton, Mississippi.

The life of Elder Blackman was expressed by a friend Mr. Clint Bonner in the following lines:

"There are men who sweat and toil just to get a name.

"There are men who squander a whole life for money and fame.

"But I know a man who counted not gold.

"His only Treasure was his brother's Soul."

Rev. L. J. Brunson

Rev. Louis J. Brunson was with the pioneers at the turn of the century. He was pastoring the Tabernacle Baptist Church near Franklinton, La., where his preaching embraced the holiness tenets which caused him to be put out of the church. He was a good pastor and a forceful preacher. His chief pastorates included McComb, Terry, Norfolk, Virginia, and Christ Temple, the mother church, Jackson.

He died in early 1941 while pastoring the Christ Temple Church at Jackson.

Rev. L. J. Brunson

Rev. John Vance

Rev. Lee Porter Cobbins, 1866-1913

47

Rev. Jacob C. Cartwright

Rev. Jacob C. Cartwright, Natchez, Miss., and pastor of church at Greenville, Miss. He was gifted in getting church factions to harmonize their differences. He was one of the stablizing factors among the brethren in the rift which resulted from the doctrine imbibed by some of the leaders from the "1906 California experience."

Rev. Lee Porter Cobbins, 1866-1913

Rev. Lee Porter Cobbins was the son of Samuel and Mary Cobbins. He was born in 1866 in Holmes County, seven miles south of Lexington, Miss.

He was married to Martha Hobbs and moved to Carroll County seventeen miles north of Lexington.

He was the first in Carroll County to accept sanctification and holiness in the new church movement. He soon became the one outstanding leader throughout his community. He pastored the first church established in the county in 1896, known as Mt. Perea 16 miles north of Lexington. It was through him that the editor, O. B. Cobbins, his sister, Elizabeth Cobbins Hines and brother S. T. Cobbins came to know about sanctification and holiness in 1906 following the death of their grandfather.

Rev. L. P. Cobbins began pastoring a church at Tchula about 1900, Goodman about 1904, and Yeager about 1907. He always attended the annual convocation at Jackson, in August. He was accepted as a gifted soul-stirring preacher.

The Lord blessed him to own his 320-acre farm and he felt willing to be used of the Lord in establishing and promoting churches for the Lord's saints in the new faith.

He died in 1913 from an accident which occurred while working on his farm.

Rev. John Vance

Rev. John Vance was credited with having established more churches than any other minister of the church and pastored more different churches than any other minister of the church.

He was fearless, courageous, often endangered, but never bodily harmed.

He was a gifted evangelist and conducted many evangelistic meetings in many parts of the country. He felt duty bound to meet all appointments, even under the most adverse circumstances.

His special gift seemed to have been in the divine healing service, for many were they who called on him for prayer for healing
and who testified to bodily healing through faith.

He died May 3, 1956.

Elder John Vance's Own Reports

On one occasion Elder W. T. Nickerson called me to help him
in a meeting in Scott County, Mississippi. During the sermon we
noticed that a man would come into the audience and whisper to
someone. So the brethren abruptly ushered us two ministers through
an open window. Of course we ran. Along the road we saw groups
of men some with dogs, some with ropes and guns. Arriving at
Brother Nickerson's lodging, we ran through the house and on
through the field and were lost in a thicket. So we escaped mob
violence.

We heard later that ministers were reported as separating husbands and wives by their preaching against adultery. That seemed to
be the misunderstanding nearly everywhere. John the Baptist was
beheaded because he dared to tell the governor, "It is not lawful
for thee to have thy brother's wife." . . . . "for he had married
her." (Mark 6:18, 17)

I have been shot at and my meetings have been shot into. I have
ridden horseback and have walked for miles in the rain after night
services. Yet I've come through it all unharmed, by the grace
of God.

God Bless the Vances

God bless the noble Vances—We're glad to hear from them.
No nobler breed e'er held a plow or wore a diadem.
Year by year and day by day they keep the way, the holy
    way.

God bless the holy Vances—Rare are their wondrous kind;
When redeemed Heaven starts a parade—We expect them there
    to find.
For the Christ way they daily go whether rest comes on or no.

God bless the precious Vances—We can but love them still.
Where duty calls you'll find Vance there with dauntless heart
    and will.
Whether he's honored much or not, where duty calls he's on
    the spot.

God bless and keep the Vances—To God be all the glory;
To us be His salvation true; God help us tell the story.
May all the Word of God believe and then the Holy Ghost receive.
C. P. Jones

Eulogy in Memory of Elder John Vance

A life of service is at an end, and the prince of preachers gone;
O, our Father did His angels send, to call him to His throne.

His task complete, his work well done, no cause on earth to stay,
For God has claimed him as His own and kissed his soul away.

He worked until his day was done and then, to me it seems,
The battle fought, the victory won, lay down to pleasant dreams.

Indeed he lived a life sublime; a credit to his race;
Till he was called by Father Time to see his Father's face.

When God shall bid His saints arise in that Great Judgment Morn,
We'll meet again beyond the skies around the Master's Throne.
—Rev. Z. M. Winder, a Baptist Minister

Bishop Charles H. Mason

Elder C. H. Mason was the founder of church at Conway, Arkansas, and pastor of church at Lexington, Miss. He was founder of "Church of God in Christ" with headquarters in Memphis, Tennessee. Since he was an effective evangelist, he was able to make a great contribution to the beginning of the movement. He was one of the most daring and forceful preachers of the beginning of the church; and a most successful and persuasive street preacher. His dynamic manner of presentation drew crowds. His words were piercing like a dagger, and many who heard him, vowed never to return to hear him again; yet were back to hear him again at the very next meeting.

News of his presence in town was often sufficient announcement of a street meeting. At the beginning of the movement, street meetings were an effective medium of getting the good news over to the populace. The practice was much used in those early days of the movement.

Elder Mason, as he was then called, worked hand in hand for many years with Elder C. P. Jones bringing many to Christ and

50

Elder Henry R. McInnis

Bishop Charles H. Mason

Rev. Walter S. Pleasant

Elder Caleb D. Ratliff

51

awakening believers to the need of the Spirit filled life.

Questions of doctrine relative to the evidence of the presence of the Holy Spirit became the wedge which produced the gap and finally caused severance of relations between these two warriors for God.

Elder Henry R. McInnis

Elder Henry R. McInnis was born in Capiah County, Mississippi. He began his ministry in the Methodist Church; he entered the Holiness movement about 1900.

In the original records, the name of the fiery Elder H. R. McInnis does not appear because he was not in the conflict among the Baptists. It was from among the Methodists that Elder McInnis took his stand with the contenders of the new faith, not on the side line but in the front ranks. He was President of the Ministers' and Deacons' Institute of Utica and Hermansville District. He passed Dec. 6, 1956 at Utica, Mississippi.

Churches Rev. McInnis pastored: Little Zion, China Grove, Myles, Mississippi; Carlton Hill, White Rock, Third Temple, Jackson, Mississippi; Wolfe Lake, Yazoo, Mississippi; Christ Temple, Drew, Mississippi; Fairview, Carpenter, Mississippi; Lord's Tabernacle, Selma, Alabama; Sweet Rest, Pearson, Mississippi; Mt. Bethel, Jackson, Mississippi; Bethel, Sweet Home, Franklinton, Lousiana.

Rev. Walter S. Pleasant

Rev. W. S. Pleasant of Hazlehurst, Miss., was born at Utica, Miss., Oct. 24, 1853. He was affectionately called "Father Pleasant." He pastored two of the most important Baptist churches: White Oak at Carpenter and Damascus at Hazlehurst, Miss., where he was pastor for 40 years. He was courageous and persevering in character in the pursuit of that which he judged to be the right course of action, even in the face of seeming defeat.

He was one of the first to join with Elder C. P. Jones in the teaching of Holiness. He was the first president of the C. M. & I. College Trustee Board.

At the age of 21, he was married to Miss Frances Short. Ten children were born to them.

He died Feb. 7, 1935.

Elder Caleb D. Ratliff

Elder C. D. Ratliff, a good man and a great soul, was a capable administrator and a conscientious pastor. He was well respected, loved everybody and feared nobody, but trusted in his God. He studied documents and denominational literature widely to keep abreast of the times in which he lived.

At one time, as district assembly moderator, he ruled that as C. M. & I. College was undergoing a financial strain, his salaried officers would donate to that institution part of their pay for that convention and he led by turning over to that school nearly all of his meager pay. Like Barnabas, he was mighty in the Scriptures and his policy was to settle questions by the Book as he seemed to understand it, making his decisions, as he expressed it, "horse high, pig tight, and bull strong." With unimpeccable character, a remarkable memory and command of the Scriptures, he was elected District Instructor of the Bible. Often when he had no other way to meet his appointments promptly, he started far enough ahead of time and walked the distance rather than to arrive behind time.

At one time he saw a violent storm approaching and prayed for protection. The storm uprooted trees all about him but left him unharmed and his house untouched.

Rev. Alexander J. Scarborough

Rev. A. J. Scarborough, first pastor of Sweet Home Baptist Church, McComb, Mississippi, was one of original ministers in the New Church emerging from the Baptist Church. At that time, the Church as well as the Pastor affiliated with the New group.

In 1900 at McComb, Rev. Scarborough was present when three white bootleggers shot at Elder C. P. Jones five times trying to break up the meeting he was conducting. This incident inspired Elder Jones to write the song, "I Am Happy With Jesus Alone," in the home of Rev. Scarborough. Also another song appropriately written was "Give Me Grace to Die for Thee."

The scholarly Rev. Scarborough wrote the words to the song "I Will Trust Him Just The Same," (Matt. 16:24-26) and helped to organize the South Mississippi and East Louisiana District Assembly—the first organization of its kind in the movement. He served as its first president for many years, and was the first pastor of the church at McComb.

Rev. F. E. Williams

Rev. Frederick Ezekiel Williams was born August 3, 1877 in Gordonsville, Alabama. He studied at Calhoun Institute and Selma University in Alabama. He taught school in Lowndes County and at Luverne, Alabama.

In 1888 he joined the Boga Homer Baptist Church and served as church clerk and organist. In 1900 he was married to Miss Pinkie Caldwell, and to this union nine children were born.

In 1901 he was called to the ministry and was ordained in 1903 by the Church of Christ Holiness in Jackson, Mississippi. His first pastorage was at Calmel, Alabama, and Pensacola, Florida. Other churches pastored by Rev. Williams were: Cynthia at Jackson, Mississippi; Third Temple at Jackson, Mississippi; Tabernacle at Lucas, Mississippi; New Home at Jayess, Mississippi; Antioch at Bogalusa, Louisiana; Christ Temple at Birmingham, Alabama; Christ Temple at Chicago Heights; First Church at Indianapolis, Indiana; and Sweet Home at Franklinton, Louisiana.

For two years Rev. Williams worked with the Home Missionary Department of the Pilgrim Holiness Church. He was instrumental in affecting an affiliation between the Pilgrim Holiness Church and the Church of Christ Holiness, U.S.A.

He was stricken in the pulpit while conducting a service in Indianapolis, Indiana. He died November 14, 1943.

Rev. D. G. Spearman

Rev. D. G. Spearman pastored the Carlton Hill Church on Highway 18 southwest of Jackson, Mississippi, and the Cynthia Church on Highway 49 northwest of Jackson, Mississippi.

Rev. Spearman was a man of brilliant intellect, a deep thinker, an eloquent orator, a good singer, a diligent student, and could be ranked among the real forceful preachers of the land. He was gifted and a man admired and loved.

Rev. D. W. Welch

Rev. D. W. Welch of Pine Bluff, Arkansas, was a most daring and gifted pioneer preacher. He had a remarkable memory of the Scriptures. This gift seemed to have fallen on Rev. C. D. Ratliff whom he ordained, like Elijah's mantle fell on Elisha. Elder Welch was one of the first Holiness preachers to come to Dumas, Arkansas.

In his preaching he would often quote passages of Scripture from memory, and then have someone read the same passage from the Bible for verification of the fact that he was preaching from the Bible. To him a reference Bible was not a necessity.

Rev. John Day

Around Jackson, Mississippi, there was no question about the belief and sincerity of Rev. John Day. He was in the conflict in the beginning and remained until the end of his life.

Rev. G. H. Funches

The spirited fight seemed to have added to the length of life for Rev. G. H. Funches for he lived nearly 100 years.

Rev. John A. Jeter

The Rev. John A. Jeter, flanked by Elder C. P. Jones, took the initiative in the Arkansas insurgence with the assistance of Elder C. H. Mason who was pastoring a church at Conway, Arkansas, which he himself had established.

Rev. Willis J. Johnson
Rev. Thomas Sanders

Rev. Willis J. Johnson and Rev. Thomas Sanders were contemporaries of Elder Walter S. Pleasant.

Rev. Richard H. Morris

Rev. Morris became so supercharged with the new tenet that he gave land and built the church building for a place of worship for the adherents of the new faith. Like Elder Funches, he lived to be more than 90 years old without wavering in his conviction.

The Weekley Brothers

Eli, Lias, S. B. and Wash Weekley were in the main stream of the reactionaries throughout the transitory period.

Rev. Elias Weekley

Rev. E. L. Weekley was bold and daring when faced with religious persecution.

A mob came to Rev. Weekley's home to attack a minister who was stopping there when the persecution was at its zenith. Rev. Weekley placed himself in the door of his house facing the mob and challenged the mob to enter over his dead body. The mob did not cross his threshold. Such were the circumstances under which the Big Creek Church was established.

Rev. F. S. Sheriff

Rev. F. S. Sheriff was the pastor of Carlton Hill Church, Raymond Road, Jackson, Miss.

The First Sunday School Convention of the movement was organized in 1899 at Carlton Hill Baptist, and still affiliated with the Baptist Church. Rev. Sheriff was the pastor of Carlton Hill Baptist Church at this time. A Baptist Sunday School Convention was being held in a nearby Baptist Church when murder was planned in the S. S. Convention. The riot broke out before the supposed victim arrived. The adherents of the new movement left the scene. It appears to have been a brother E. L. Fizer who sped ahead of the others, met Brother C. P. Jones and told him of the riot. Faced with this kind of a predicament, Rev. Sheriff fearlessly opened his church where the first S. S. Convention was organized.

Rev. J. H. Green
Dr. Harry H. Jones
Rev. E. J. Lucas

These men were inspired to go into the foreign mission work and they went into areas in West Africa. Rev. Green, who had married a young woman from Arkansas, had been active in the

56

work of the church before going to Africa. He had been Sunday School superintendent, director of the choir, deacon, and printer of the magazine *Truth*.

EVANGELISM

My brethren, take me as it pleases you. Judge and regard me as the Spirit of Holiness may lead or permit you, but for many months my heart has ached for the lack of the spirit of evangelism among us. Many are willing to be named evangelists and to accept appointments at churches already established. But who will take the message to new fields or build the waste places? Who?

Solomon built Tadmor (I Kings 9:17-18) in the wilderness. He needed it as a frontier. Have we no more builders? Is there no more land to be possessed? May God clothe us with the whole armor and fill our hearts with valor to win souls. It will give us new zeal, a new faith, a new unity of love, a new vision of glory.

Brethren, we must not accept defeat. Jesus made the parable of the man who needed three loaves (Luke 11:1-13) and of the unjust judge (Luke 18:1-14) to teach us not to accept defeat. He is bound to supply our need. He is bound to defend us. We can make Him do it. In Isaiah 45:11 He says, "Ask of me concerning my sons and concerning the work of My hands, command ye Me". In the grace of the atonement He allows us to command Him. We have the divine message; let us not fail with it. Let us not take defeat. Let us not faint. Let us be unwilling to fail with it. Let us not loiter by the way.

—C. P. Jones

Obstacles Removed

Before there was organized mission endeavor in the movement, many independent workers started missions, some of whom became pastors of their stations.

It was near Jennings Crossing on the Fernwood and Gulf Railroad that Elder William E. Wellzey of the Mt. Olive Church of Christ (Holiness) in Magnolia, Mississippi, started a series of meetings and built a mission work.

As reported by Elder E. E. Sparkman: On one of his return visits, notices were posted about: "No Trespassing". He went a short distance up the railroad where a man gave him permission to conduct meetings at a different place near his home. Here the Elder started anew with boards nailed to wooden blocks as improvised seats. In his absence this man's wife had these seats taken to her home and used for firewood. But the pricks pierced her. (Acts 9:5) It's often dangerous to kick against the pricks.

The man who posted the notices lost his job and remained without work. In time, his conscience reminded him of his unprincipled deed and smote him until in desperation, he tore away all the notices and was given work that same day.

And the woman, Elder Sparkman says, while visiting in her home later, as they sat before the open fireplace, suddenly fell foremost and scarcely missed being severely burned as he helped her husband rescue her. This ended such obstacles at that pastorage.

Rev. C. C. Carhee

The ministry of Rev. Carhee is known throughout the United States. He is known among several Holiness groups as a chosen Evangelist of God.

Rev. Carhee has worked in sawmills at Monroe, Loring, and Bonning, Louisiana. During the early part of his ministry, offerings were not raised for his preaching. He has done other work such as fishing, etc. to support himself.

Rev. Carhee, in his early ministry, served as Moderator of a State Convention held in Gilford, La., in 1906, or 1907. This convention had been organized at Monroe, with Elder John Grewer, Elder E. W. Butler, Brother N. S. Cann, Brother W. H. Dunn, James Click, Elder Murray of Crockett, Arkansas. Elder Murray served as his secretary. Under Rev. Carhee's administration, the convention was brought into the National Convention about 1907.

Rev. Carhee was instrumental in organizing a Sunday School Convention with Sister E. D. Dixon Coffin of Los Angeles, California, as secretary.

Rev. Carhee has conducted evangelistic services throughout America. He has conducted meetings in Shreveport, La., in December 1909; in Swats, La., for Brother George King; in Belmont, La., December 1910 (3 souls saved); again, in Shreveport, La., for Elder E. W. Butler; in Hamburg, Ark. (7 baptized, 21 added to the church, offering raised was $28).

While Rev. Carhee conducted these meetings, he found a deal of opposition to his teachings of Holiness. Sometimes, he was put out of the church for his stand on Holiness. However, he would continue his preaching around the schools, bars, and sometimes, he would use tree stumps as a platform. Elder Carhee has done much "street preaching". He has been accused of breaking up churches with his preaching. His life has been threatened for his stand. However, he continued to preach. In Monroe, a group of Baptist and Methodist ministers met in Nebo, it is reported, to discuss the "Holiness Movement". About the close of Rev. Carhee's meeting at Monroe, five of these ministers were sent to inquire of Rev. Carhee about the Movement. One of the ministers carried a gun and was designated to stop him from preaching in the area. The nephew of this man was converted at one of the meetings. Rev. Carhee was cursed and reviled for his stand for Christ. Later, he was consoled by a Brother Davis, a dedicated Baptist Missionary. The people were fearful of continuing the meeting at the home of Mother Dunn and transferred to a park owned by a Mr. Richard. It was on this site that the Monroe church was organized by Elder Carhee.

While ministering in Crockett, Arkansas, Rev. Carhee heard of the Church of Christ Holiness in Jackson, Mississippi. He traveled to Jackson in August, 1906 to meet with brethren. In 1907, he united with the Church of Christ Holiness and entered C. M. and I. College. He then requested that Bishop Jones go to Louisiana and enlighten the people concerning the Holiness teaching. He remained at C. M. and I. College until 1910 and was ordained to the gospel ministry.

During Rev. Carhee's ministry, he has been instrumental in founding and organizing several churches. The following churches were organized, improved, or pastored by C. C. Carhee: Church at Monroe, La.; Church at Belmont, La. with Rev. Smith as Pastor; Church at Crockett, Arkansas; Church at Hamburg, Arkansas; New Lake Church in Mississippi; Anniecoco, Louisiana; Church at Leesville, Louisianna; Church at San Bernardino, California; Pilgrim Church at Los Angeles; Pilgrim Church at Las Vegas, Nevada; Church at Beaumont, Texas; and the Church at San Pedro, Calif.

THE EARLY HOME MISSIONARIES

It is interesting to note how ministers and missionaries were able to travel from place to place in the interest of the church work without travel allowances or travel conveniences.

Walking for miles over dusty roads or riding horse back, in buggy or open wagons were the customs and practices.

59

But like the United States mail, the Gospel Message had to go through and it did.

This Is Pioneer Rosa Daniels

A credit to the work and an outstanding Christian woman of her community was Sister Rosa Daniels of Lucas, near Silver Creek, Mississippi. The Bible was her guide.

In the early days of the Church of Christ (Holiness) movement, Sister Daniels traveled on horseback and on foot carrying on her mission work. She, with other women, would walk ten-mile distances to take the gospel light into new areas. She organized the Christian Women Willing Band in her local church (The Tabernacle Church of Christ Holiness) and the first such organization in the Lucas District; both of which she served as president for many years.

Sister Daniels was a living example to the end, for the women who knew her. All her seven children professed a hope in Christ.

Mother Louisa A. Mitchell.

Mother Louisa A. Mitchell was born in Marion County, Texas. Mother Mitchell was a pioneer missionary of the Church of Christ

(Holiness) U.S.A. for 37 years. She united with the church in 1904 in Monroe, Louisiana. She moved to Chicago, Illinois, in 1935 where she remained a faithful and loyal member until she became ill in 1941. She resided with her daughter, Mrs. Frances Mitchell Dunn in Chicago.

She was a Sunday School teacher, a deaconess, and served as secretary of the National Christian Women Willing Workers of the Church of Christ (Holiness).

Many souls have been led to Christ through the influence of this faithful mother. She died in 1947.

Sister Josephine Cann
Monroe, Louisiana

Mrs. Josephine Cann, the wife of Elder N. S. Cann, was one of the first national missionaries. She worked with the women throughout the church. She felt that all areas were her field: district, state or diocese, and the national.

But for the services of Sister Cann and the other good women who worked in the missionary field, many localities would not have had churches established.

Also, in communities where churches were already established, these missionary women have been instrumental in perpetuating the life of the church.

There is no attitude on the part of the hierarchy of the church to minimize the possibilities of the Women's Missionary Department of the Church.

Brother John Askerneese

Brother John Askerneese was born September 27, 1876, at Hazlehurst, Mississippi. He was converted under Rev. W. S. Pleasant of Hazlehurst, Mississippi. He and his family moved to Glendora, Mississippi, in 1913. Finding no Holiness Church there, he started a prayer band and Sunday School in his home. After it grew larger, he asked Rev. Smith Brown to come in and organize a church. The church was organized in his home, he went to his landlord and asked him to build a Holiness Church for his group. The landlord built the church and it was named Pilgrim Rest.

Brother Askerneese was a deacon in this church until 1918 when he and his family moved to Lambert, Mississippi. There he found no Holiness church and there again he started a prayer band and Sunday School in his home. Later they bought a tent and rented a lot on which to erect the tent. He was deacon there until 1922 when he left for Chicago. There he joined Christ Temple Church, and was made deacon and worked as such until his death May 7, 1941.

Missionary Dora Askerneese

Sister Dora Askerneese was born January 28, 1880 at Hazlehurst, Mississippi. She was converted under pastor W. S. Plesant.

In 1913 she moved to Glendora, Mississippi, with her husband and family. She soon began her community missionary work, and started a Sunday School and weekly prayer band in her home that grew into a church, named Pilgrim Rest, with Rev. H. R. Hicks as pastor in 1914. Her husband, Brother John Askerneese was the deacon.

In like manner soon afterward, a church was started in Sumner called Second Pilgrim Rest.

In 1919 the family moved to Lambert where she began her neighborhood missionary work. They rented some land, bought a tent, and began church services with Rev. A. G. Belton of Hollandale as minister.

In 1922 they moved to Chicago, Illinois, where she joined Christ Temple Church and the senior choir, and became a member of the deaconess board.

After the death of her husband, she went to live with her son, Pastor O. A. Askerneese in Omaha, Nebraska. She worked as missionary in his church until he was transferred to the church in Oakland, California, in 1943. After that she went to live with her daughter in New Jersey, joined Rev. Hemphill's church in New York, and worked with the missionary band there.

In 1951, she returned to Chicago, renewed her membership with Christ Temple Church under Bishop J. M. Haywood, worked with the deaconess board, and became president of the district foreign mission board. During the meantime, she lived with her son, Elihue Askerneese, until her death on February 19, 1958.

Missionary Eliza Thomas

Eliza Thomas was born June 9, 1874, Carpenter, Miss., to the union of Dan and Fannie Thomas. To this union 18 children were born. She became a Christian at an early age and joined Pine Grove Baptist Church. In 1888 she was married to Park McField. To this union six children were born; Nellie, Charles, Daniel, Nora, Cicero and Edward. Her husband and three of her children preceded her in death.

Missionary Dora Askerneese   Mrs. Eliza Thomas-McField

She joined Damascus church under the leadership of Rev. W. S.
Pleasant. In 1906 they moved to Jackson, Miss., and joined Christ
Temple under Rev. C. P. Jones. Later the family moved to St.
Louis, Mo., (1917). She served faithfully wherever she lived and
coming to St. Louis, she helped organize the church there. In 1922
she moved to Chicago and joined Christ Temple Church under the
pastorate of Rev. William Webb. She served as president of the
Missionary Board of the local church and of the district and diocese.

In 1924 she became seriously ill and gave up to die—eleven days
without food, water or sleep. She asked the Lord if there was anything He wanted her to do, to heal her and she would do it with all
her might and strength. A soft voice wispered to her *"You will
cheer thousands of souls."* Not knowing which way to go, she
prayed for guidance. She started out by going from door to door,
combing the neighborhood, consoling the sick, clothing the needy
and feeding the hungry—often out of her own pocket. Through this
activity many were brought to the Sunday School and Sunbeans
meetings.

Then she was directed to the county hospitals and jails for
thirty (30) years, then to Oak Forest hospital carrying 125 sand-
wiches, cookies and tiny bags of sugar to the old folks there.

63

Not only in Chicago, but she crossed towns, cities, and states, spreading cheer to the sick, consoling the shut-ins and bereaved. Since 1948 she served as National Missionary of the Christian Women Workers organization, spending much of her time in the field. She died in 1960.

Mother Josephine Harvey

Mother Josephine Harvey moved to Los Angeles, California, in 1943 from Mansfield, Louisiana. Since her arrival she has spent her entire life and energy doing missionary work among children. Because of her diligence and faithful service to the children she traveled up and down the Western Coast, helping the churches at Rose Hill, Pilgrim, Merced, Fresno, Faith Temple, Sacramento and wherever she could interest a group of Youngsters.

Hers was the Flannelboard method of teaching. While visiting Rev. C. B. Jordan, one day, she saw a group at play and called them together under a tree and taught them a Bible Lesson, a meeting which developed into a Bible Class, numbering 65. Many were the times she had no place to take and teach them but she continued her classes on the green grass. Her work here soon developed into the Faith Temple Church, founded by Rev. C. B. Jordan. She is now in her 70's but still finds the time and energy to teach children the Bible.

She is the mother of 11 children, five of whom are now active in various churches throughout the Western Diocese.

Missionary Amy Gordon and Others

Miss Amy Gordon was born and reared about Port Gibson, Mississippi. She literally left all to follow Jesus during the early days of the Church of Christ (Holiness) movement when she was a young woman. Often the Lord's first call to one is a call to consecration and preparation.

Miss Gordon said she had come down with tuberculosis; was given up to die, and was willing to go. The Lord had called her to His service, however, but she had not heeded his call. She said He promised her one more chance; that when she was emptied of every other ambition and abandoned to His mercy, He gave her life. Brought from the border-line of death, she began local Bible teaching and later started a work in Meridian, Mississippi. She kept this work flourishing under a Gospel tent until Elder John Vance went and, with members of that mission, built the first church of the movement in that city.

About 1923, her work ended in Meridian. Early in 1924 she came to Magnolia, Mississippi, where she made Elder Vance's home her headquarters and did itinerant mission work for a few years.

Sister Gordon trusted the Lord alone for her health as well as for the supply of her every other need, and many persons were healed through her gifts of healing; sometimes instantly, sometimes gradually.

Sister Gordon opened "Christ's Free Mission" in New Orleans, Louisiana, a home, as the name suggests, open to whoever of the Lord's people came to worship or conduct a series of meetings. One man who had held a series of meetings stated that the Lord sent him there from a distance of 500 miles to work in New Orleans at Christ's Free Mission. A Brother Ellis from the British West Indies described the mission as "the littlest" thing in New Orleans and the "biggest thing".

Sister Gordon said that it fell into her mind that the Lord gave to her as her field of labor first the largest city in Mississippi and now the largest city in the south. Her work through at the Christ's Free Mission in New Orleans, she did her last active work about Brookhaven, McComb, and Magnolia, Mississippi, before leaving out for her home eternal in May, 1938.

FOREIGN MISSION

The foreign mission work which is exhibited under the Name of This Church, was primarily the doings of the individuals who heard and answered the "Macedonian Call", "Come over into Macedonia and help us."

The Church itself has not had the personnel nor the resources to effectively spread its influence into foreign fields.

Beginning in 1902 and continuing until 1965, few names seem to have appeared in the record. They were Dr. Harry H. Jones, Brother and Sister J. H. Green, Bishop J. A. Jeter, Rev. Eli J. Lucas, Miss Estelle Russell, Miss Naomi Doles and Rev. Tyree Feltzs.

The general constituency of the church has had only limited knowledge of these foreign mission efforts. The correspondence to and from the missionaries gives some insight to the difficulties involved in the foreign mission efforts.

Dr. Harry H. Jones sailed for Congo Town, Monrovia, Liberia, West Africa, in 1902. He writes on Sept. 11, 1903:

I was about to take an evangelistic trip back into the country. I desire to take the Gospel to the regions beyond, (2 Cor. 10:16), that I may not build upon another's foundation. I was away about thirty-three days telling the story of the Cross, about sixty miles back, and told the Gospel story to hundreds. Some of them will never hear it again, I suppose. I will praise God and say "I have told them once on the mountain and down the valley." Wading in creeks and having to swim many, I'll risk my life to save a soul, for my soul and body are out at the stake for Jesus. "But he that glorieth, let him glory in the Lord." (2 Cor. 10:17.) I don't live any more for my own salvation (for my salvation is sure). I've prayed many a time that when I can't be used to save a soul, I may be allowed by Jesus to sleep.

Yours in Christ,
Harry H. Jones

In 1902, Brother J. H. Green, one of the early printers of the *Truth* magazine, the official organ of the movement, with his wife, went to Liberia, West Africa, with the hope of establishing a Christian colony there by 1904.

The record is not clear whether or not his plans of colonization materialized. Mr. Green did publish a paper, *The African League*. This paper was devoted to the material upbuilding of African society in the spirit of Christ.

Rev. E. (Eli) J. Lucas established the Lucas Tabernacle Church of Christ Holiness and pastored it while he remained in the state of Mississippi, sailed in 1902. He was engaged as a teacher in the Reeves Institute, Fortsville, Grand Bassa County, Liberia, West Africa.

The Reeves Institute was a school founded and run by the hard work and close management of a Mr. A. C. Reeves—not a rich man nor even an educated man, but a God-fearing man trying to civilize, christianize and educate the natives; some of whom he brought from slavery; keeping up the school with no help from abroad and scarcely any help from Liberia, was a significant job.

Congo Town
Monrovia
West Africa

Brother and Sister J. H. Green were well when I saw them. Thank God for the hope of seeing Brother J. A. Jeter from the United States.

Again he writes:

Heaven is sweet to me on earth. The Father yet gives to me health and strength and my soul He fills with heavenly vigor and still finds use for me in His service here. I glory in His works they are a pleasure. In June I made an 80-mile trip in five days in the regions beyond. How much I suffered bodily, I am able to tell. Scarcity of food, 25-mile points daily, a few poles and a rattan mat to sleep on at night, yet this was better than what my Master had. My body weary and worn but O how my spirit would leap for joy when I began to tell benighted souls of a Savior that had come!

The second day of my journey brought me to the town of a king who accepted me as a man sent from God. Again and again he and his subjects thanked me in their language (esei, esei). His island town was the scene of many battles—war is reported there now. Bidding the king farewell next day, I turned for my station in the midst of wild forest, spicy breezes welcoming me, greeted occasionally by wild animals, birds singing on every side, elephants plodding in rapid strides, and monkeys changing from limb to limb, seemed to welcome me to his forest home. I admired it, but my heart longed to reach another town.

Yours in Christ,
Harry H. Jones

Another Missionary Sent

In August of 1904, *Miss Estelle Russell,* one of the workers from the Christ Missionary and Industrial College at Jackson, Mississippi, was sent to join the missionaries already in Africa.

It appears that Miss Estelle Russell was from Selma, Alabama, and formerly a member of the church there once pastored by Elder C. P. Jones. She was the sister of Miss Luella Russell, a former matron at the Christ Missionary and Industrial College.

Pastor J. A. Jeter went to Africa in autumn of 1903 to ascertain and weigh the probability of establishing a full scale missionary work, in Liberia. He writes en route:

I'm now within a few miles of Liverpool, England. I hope to get a ship from that point to Monrovia, Liberia, West Africa. Our first day out from New York was sad indeed! We were caught in a gale about 5 p.m. It carried away the look-out bridge. One man and his wife died from the effects. Several first class passengers and three of four sailors were hurt. For two days and nights the ocean was rough. Sailors stated that there had been many years since they met with such occurrence. We happened to be one of the best ships. Above all Jesus was on board, and He will save the ship. That was His personal promise to me. His word is sure, Josh 1; Rom. 2:10. I beg your prayers that I have a safe journey to do His will.

Later he writes:

I'm now in Liverpool, England, safe in Jesus. I visited a Baptist Church and heard a good sermon from one of England's best preachers. I attended the Y. M. C. A., spoke and was invited to stay over. There are no colored churches here. This is a great country, but nothing to be compared with the heavenly.

Your brother in tribulation in Christ,

J. A. Jeter

On his return home in the spring of 1904, the Mission's Board President was accompanied by a native missionary, Miss Sumtumzi. She was to tour and study in this country preparatory to returning to help build Africa.

The Reorganization of the Foreign Mission Board

Excerpt from the President and Sr. Bishop's address. (Bishop M. R. Conic) 1956—Little Rock, Arkansas.

Foreign Mission

"The opportunity for Foreign Mission work is greatly upon us. For this we have cried for so long. Today we have a foreign Missionary stationed in Monrovia, Liberia, West Africa. Sister Naomi Doles of Norfolk, Va., informs us of the great door of opportunity now open in this area. We are asking that the C.W.W.W.s be given representation of the Foreign Mission Board and that their efforts be coordinated with the work of the Board."

The Nomination Committee of the parent body of the National Convention, recommended the following persons for members of the Foreign Mission Board: Chairman—Rev. J. C. Smith. Members—Rev. A. J. Torrey, Rev. Elmo Woods, Rev. L. D. Hughes, Rev. Tillman Broxton, Brother Jesse L. Doles, Brother Herman Session, Sister, Gladys M. Moore, Murle Bennett, B. T. Johnson, Eva Holt, Florence Johnson, and Pearle Lewis.

This Board met in this Convention for the first time, and elected as Vice Chairman: Rev. A. J. Torrey, Secretary: Sister G. A. Moore, Asst. Secretary: Sister H. Bennett, Treasurer: Brother Jesse L. Doles.

Thus the Foreign Mission Board of the Church of Christ (Holiness) USA, was reestablished. With the primary aim to support

68

Sister Naomi Doles, already on the field, which had been promised her in the 1955 convention in Chicago, Illinois, if she should undertake such a venture.

From information received from Rev. Montrose Waite, missionary of Monrovia, as to the required amount for support of a missionary in the field of Africa, we agreed to support Sister Doles with $1,800 annually, $150 per month, which we have done to this day. In these early days of the board the only monies available for this work was raised by the C.W.W.W. We shall be forever grateful to these noble women of our church whom for a number of years, under the able leadership of Sister Gladys Moore laid aside each year funds to foster a foreign mission program. We were able with this finance to support Sister Doles until we could get a financial program underway.

Chairman Smith appealed through the *Truth* to the ministers and deacons and during the session of the 1957 National Convention at St. Louis for donations and pledges for support of our missionary; also special offerings were raised and the continued support of the C.W.W.W.'s enabled us to build up a treasury to support the missionary through the year 1960.

In the 1958 National Convention, Rev. K. J. Samuels of Kumbonad, Kerala, India, was brought to and introduced to the national convention by Bishop A. B. Smith, of the Northwestern Diocese. Elder Samuels told us of his work in India and of the need of help there to reach the millions of people who knew not our Lord and Saviour Jesus Christ. He spoke of Hebron Bible Institute there, of which he was President, where native Christians were trained that they might carry the Gospel into the villages where Christ was not known. At this time there were 40 students at the Hebron Bible Institute.

Rev. Samuels, desired fellowship. He met with the fellowship committee of the National Convention and upon the recommendation of the committee, he was accepted as a member of the Convention and a Minister in the Church of Christ (Holiness) USA.

The Foreign Mission Board, Sunday School and H. Y. P. U. Congress, C.W.W.W.'s and the National Convention each gave him an offering to help him and his work.

The Foreign Mission Board in the 1959 Convention at Los Angeles, California, recommended that we support Rev. K. J. Samuels, as our Native Missionary in India at $25.00 per month for one year, also support three (3) native students at $10.00 per month

69

each, making a total support to India of $55.00 per month. The recommendation was adopted. This was done plus special donations and gifts until the 1960 Convention. Special donations are still being sent him from time to time through the Board.

Sister Naomi E. Doles, our Missionary, was home on furlough in 1960. She was with us in our National Convention. During her visitation to our churches, we were thrilled at what we saw and heard of her work in Monrovia, Liberia, West Africa, under the auspices of the Carver Foreign Missions Inc., of Atlanta, Georgia. We wondered why and questioned why she could not represent the Church of Christ (Holiness) USA. This is when we realized that we did not have what we wanted, a Foreign Mission post bearing our name with missionaries representative.

Sister Doles expressed a sincere desire to see the Church of Christ (Holiness) establish a work in Africa which she has repeatedly expressed across the years. She has also stated that if and when this desire is accomplished she is obligated to come to and work for the Foreign Mission effort of the Church of Christ (Holiness) USA. The Foreign Mission Board offered a resolution to the Convention that initial steps be taken toward raising finance for the purpose of establishing a Foreign Mission Post. We went on record as launching a $50,000.00 drive appealing to the members of the Church of Christ (Holiness) USA for $10.00 per member for the year for this purpose. This drive did not prove successful. However, it showed encouraging signs that we wanted a Foreign Mission Post. In this Convention we adopted a resolution to be sent to the chairman of the Foreign Mission Board and the vice-president of the National Convention, (Rev. J. C. Smith and Bishop O. W. McInnis) to Monrovia, Liberia, West Africa, at our earliest convenience to investigate the possibilities of establishing a work there. At this writing this mission has not been accomplished; not by neglect, but due to other developments. We are working toward having this mission accomplished by the Convention of 1966, by the help of the Lord. This year of 1960, being an election year, the following members were added to the board: Rev. O. C. Miller, Rev. J. L. Burris, Sister Rowenia Hannibal, Rev. Jess Auguerson, Rev. John Plummer, Asst. Secretary, and Rev. C. N. Ricks, Secretary.

In the 1961 National Convention the Foreign Mission Board recommended a resolution that $5.00 per capita be added to the Convention claims each year for Foreign Mission. This resolution

70

was adopted by the Convention.

1962 was an eventful year for the Foreign Mission Board in that the Rev. and Mrs. Cleatur Turner, Rev. O. O. Ross and Rev. Tyree Feltzs were led to go to Mexico. A mission venture was made at San Luis Rio, Colorado, Sonora, Mexico, of which Bishop Albert Hamilton, Jr., encouraged. The response in this venture was so exciting that Rev. Feltzs drove across the country stopping off at Jackson, Mississippi, to report this venture to the Senior Bishop M. R. Conic, then presiding over the South Central Diocese. Bishop Conic advised him to report the information and success to Foreign Mission Board Chairman, Rev. J. C. Smith. Rev. Feltzs proceeded on to Chicago, Illinois, and conveyed the same information to Bishop O. W. McInnis. The Chairman of the Church Extension Board was so elated over the information of the Mexico venture that he sent a special message to Chairman Smith by Rev. Feltzs. In April 1962 Rev. Feltzs finally arrived at Newport News, Virginia, and presented his information, maps, plot plans and legal deeds of two parcels of ground donated to the Church of Christ (Holiness) Mexico which was founded by the above named group of missionaries and organized by Rev. Feltzs. In as much as Rev. Feltzs was gifted to speak the Spanish language, he was the chief advisor and the missionary in charge. One thing worthy of note that some of these people who became members were old acquaintances of Rev. Feltzs whom he had not seen for over 12 years; namely the Carmelo Mendoza family. Brother Joaquin Castillon and Jesus Mendoza gave to the church the two lots above mentioned. Brother Carmelo Mendoza also gave two acres of a ranch site across the river known as "Colonia 10 de Mayo, Baja California, Mexico", and an option to buy the ranch and two adjoining properties which has a total area of over 135 acres. Chairman Smith did not have an opportunity to visit the Mexico Mission until September 1962. Missionary Feltzs brought and introduced to the Convention in 1962 two of his native missionaries from the Mexico Mission, Brother and Sister Jesus Ceballos, who were welcomed to the Convention by the delegates, also many contributions were given to our Mexican saints. The presence of these missionaries created such an excitement among the people that the Church Extension Board and the Foreign Mission Board had a joint meeting to discuss the possibilities of promoting a Post in Mexico. These boards agreed to send their chairmen to investigate this project. The name of Brother Jon Randall as Corresponding

71

Secretary was added in the 1962 Convention. On September 10, 1962, Rev. O. A. Askerneese, Secretary of the Church Extension Board, and Elder J. C. Smith, Chairman of the Foreign Mission Board, went to the Mexican Consulate at Washington, D.C., to obtain information as to the establishing of a Foreign Mission Post in Mexico. He informed us that a grant must be obtained from the Federal Government of Mexico and the post must operate under the supervision of a citizen of Mexico. He advised them to obtain a Federal Attorney down in Mexico. They visited Brother and Sister Ceballos in their little Jacalito on the ranch property, then traveled from there to the city of San Luis Rio Colorado, Sonora, Mexico, to the home of Brother Carmelo Mendoza. Brother Mendoza showed them the city and the two lots that were donated to the Church of Christ (Holiness) Mexico.

On October 1, the Trustee Board, Brothers C. Mendoza, Joaquin Castillon, Pablo Juarez and Jesus Ceballos, took the registered title holders to the State Department for the transferral of their rights to build on the property, over to the church. This being done, they were given proper papers. They took them back to the Judge at the county seat. He went out, saw the property, and informed them that before the transaction could be completed, the church would have to build an approved type of building on the property, so that they may have something on which they could be given title.

On October 2 we met once again in the home of Brother C. Mendoza with the trustees. Satisfied with the evidence we saw no reason for not going forward to establish a work in Mexico. A check for $800.00 was given by the Church Extension Board to pay title rights to build on one parcel of ground. The Foreign Mission Board paid $500.00 to Elder Feltzs to pay back monies he had borrowed to pay on another parcel of ground.

In June 1963 a request came to Chairman Smith from Elder K. J. Samuels of India to intercede with the American Consulate in India for a visa to come to the United States. Chairman Smith did so and permission was granted for Elder Samuels to visit the USA. The visa was later extended by Bishop Conic by writing the immigration authorities. Elder Samuels traveled extensively throughout our churches during his year stay in the USA.

In the 1963 national convention several special resolutions were offered to the body by the foreign mission board. Due to the immaturity of the board certain areas concerning the operation of the post in Mexico had not been specified until this time which had caused great hindrances in the growth of the work there. The first recommendation was that credentials be given to all foreign missionaries annually by the Foreign Mission Board Chairman. Secondly that the local trustees be allowed to cultivate the mission properties for two years and ten percent of profits be placed in the church treassury. Third that all matters concerning the mission post in Mexico be referred to the Foreign Mission Board (Western) consisting of Brother Jon Randall, Rev. L. D. Hughes, Brother Worlie Young, Sister Eva Holt with Rev. J. C. Smith, chairman.

Certain questions were raised in the convention relative to support of missionaries on the field, so Chairman Smith made extensive studies and brought forth documentary information and research of other foreign mission boards and organizations on record at Washington, D.C. These reports stated the amounts and conditions of support of various individuals and families throughout the world. The board concluded that upon review of this research the amounts of each board or organization varied but the amounts that we had designated were within reason; therefore the board recommended to the convention that no changes be made in our support of missionaries on the field. These recommendations were applauded and adopted by the convention of 1963.

On October 15, 1964 the first complete purchase of a foreign mission post in the domain of Mexico was made by the foreign mission board. A 135 acre parcel of land known as "lots twelve, thirteen and fourteen of the colony, May 10th, located in the delegation of Cuervos, Lower California, Municipality of Mexicali, Lower California" was purchased for the sum of $2,500 and donated to the *La Iglesia de Cristo (Santidad) de Mexico*" affiliated with the Church of Christ (Holiness) USA.

Soon after this land purchase a building program was undertaken and the foreign mission board provided means to begin construction of a permanent building 30 feet by 44 feet, to be built of concrete blocks upon that site. The week before the national convention in 1965 the foundation and floor of that building had been poured and a past dream was fast becoming a reality.

At this time we are happy to report this board has two American (Mexico) missionaries in the persons of Elder Feltzs and Elder Ross, one native Mexican missionary, Elder Pedro Viscarra, one American (Africa) missionary, Sister Naomi Doles, and one native India Missionary, Elder K. J. Samuels.

By the beginning of the year 1966, the foreign mission board has spent some $30,000 or more to bring the gospel to the heathens and enlighten a blighted people of the world. We pray God's blessings on this work that its talents may be increased ten fold and God may receive the glory throughout the world.

Elder J. C. Smith, Chairman
Jon A. Randall, Corresponding Secretary

Rev. Tyree Feltzs   Miss Naomi Doles

Miss Naomi Doles

Miss Naomi Doles of Surry, Virginia, is the most recent missionary from the church to Africa. She is stationed near Monrovia, Liberia, West Africa.

Miss Doles is well trained for her work. She has earned two degrees from two different institutions of learning, namely Carver Foreign Mission School at Atlanta, Ga. and the Prairie Bible Institute, Three Hills, Alberta, Canada.

In her work in Africa, she performs many services for the people teaching in many fields and on several educational levels. The scope of her work covers recreational, social, and religious in-

74

terests. To the natives she presents a living Christ, and she in turn, becomes the living Christ to the natives.

Rev. Tyree Feltzs

Rev. Tyree Feltzs, 242 East 2nd Street, San Bernardino, California, was born April 16, 1910. He has been in the ministry for 33 years. He organized the Christ Temple Church at San Bernardino.

He is one of the national evangelists. He has conducted many evangelistic meetings in various parts of the United States. Through his ministry, many hundreds have been brought to Christ. His knowledge and use of the Spanish language makes easier his ability to communicate with and establish churches in Mexico, referred to in the Foreign Mission report.

HEALINGS THROUGH FAITH AND PRAYERS
Father and Baby Healed by God's Power Alone

Dumas, Arkansas, 1-19-03. I wish to testify of the Lord's goodness to me. First, I'll say that from boyhood up to 1900, I was subject to the annoying disease called piles, suffering only 2 or 3 during the seasons. I spent several dollars trying different remedies, but all in vain. At last the truth was brought to this land and I readily accepted it. As I'd never belonged to any church at all, it wasn't hard for me to get saved. I'd seen different church members doing so many things I'd not do that I considered they were worse before God than I was according to Matt. 12:45. So on the last day of April, 1900, I accepted Him, praise His name. It seemed like because I'd left Satan, the Lord suffered him to touch me more severely than ever. I suffered continually April, May, June and part of July. I completely lost my crop, but during all my suffering I resorted to nothing but Jesus. So praise His name, He healed me completely and I've not been troubled since with that disease. We've a dear little babe, born April 20, 1901. It continued sick from its birth until about June, 1902. The world criticised and abused my wife and me to the lowest because we wouldn't take it to the

75

doctor, but praise His name, we had it on the altar before a Doctor who has never lost a case; so sometime in last June, I do not remember the date, it took with something like diarrhea and continued about 10 or 12 days. During this period it lost its appetite and couldn't eat anything for 6 or 7 days. When people came to see the baby they'd try to excite my wife by telling her the baby couldn't live much longer and she'd better take it to the doctor. She'd answer, "We've given it to the Lord and if it's His will for it to recover He'll raise it at His time; so we're willing for His will to be done." They kept saying the baby would be in its grave in a few days, but today it is a complete picture of health. They also said it would never walk. Now it is going from place to place by holding on to chairs, etc. It's improving so fast we keep eyes on it to keep it indoors. Sometime ago, Satan tried to discourage me by saying our baby would never be a well child. But my heart would leap for joy when I remembered Psa. 27:14, and to know that Jesus has already said He'll never leave me nor forsake me if I keep His sayings and do them.

Yours in Him,
Harry T. Terry

Sister Rachel Dees reports: In 1910, after I had been sick for some time, a sister wrote to Elders Elias Weekley and George Funches to pray for me. I was healed instantly. In 1954 when the doctor could neither diagnose my daughter's ailment nor give her relief from suffering, the Lord healed her instantly through the prayers of Elder Ben Aikens of Jackson, Mississippi. A Sister Cobbs of the community was healed of a broken arm through his prayers. I was healed instantly of a serious condition in my back through prayer by Elder Jenkins of Pearson, Mississippi. Many have been healed through the prayers of Elder G. H. Funches.

Mrs. Edna Brent of Pricedale, Mississippi, testifies to "Fruits of Faith" and prayers:

In the winter of 1937-38 *Sister A. M. Gordon,* one of our missionaries, held a 10-day meeting at Galilee Church of Christ (Holiness). During this time in a Bible lesson, she taught the young women to love their husbands, to be chaste, keepers at home, and to rear children. Then she asked all the barren women who desired to bear children to come to her to be anointed with oil and to be prayed for. My youngest child was 14 years old. I went forward. She anointed my head and prayed for me and in 1938 I conceived.

By faith my son was delivered from jail through Divine intervention. I was instantly healed of a sudden deathly attack of illness through the prayer of Elder H. J. Garner. In 1948 my little grandson was instantly healed of a hernia in one of Elder John Vance's healing meetings at New Home.

In 1949 I was hospitalized in New Orleans away from relatives and known friends, among strangers—French, German, and Jews. Mine was a serious case. I learned to trust the Lord more and more and He brought me through. A lady came from somewhere and said to me: "I can't go with you to the 12th floor but I will be waiting at your bedside when they bring you down." She was there when I awoke—a friend in need.

As I lay there after surgery, it seemed that I would die after all. Satan whispered, "You stood your operation but you are not healed. You have cancer." I gave up. I cried, prayed and asked the Lord to heal me and He did bring me through. I heard a voice say: "Look up and live". I looked up, as it seemed, into the sky and was healed that very hour. I know that was the fruit of faith. In 1954 I had boils—7 of them under my right arm and a large one on my hip. They began at once to heal in one of Elder Vance's healing meetings.

I could write a book on what the Lord has done through faith. My soul is a witness for my Lord.

Report is that during his last appearance in our National Convention, Bishop Jones gave his age as 77 years and stated that he'd not had a doctor for 51 years; that he'd learned to trust God alone for his health and that God will do as much for everybody if the life is right and filled with holy love and trust in God.

He said that once he hated the white race from what his grandparents said—how they were whipped till the blood ran down; but after he was saved, he loved that race as he loved others. See what happens when we get in God's way. He plead, *"Don't throw away divine healing."*

Sister Katie Lindsey who left this life a few years ago testified to the healing of her cow through his prayer, laying on of hands, and anointing with oil when the cow was past doctor's aid. In a few minutes the cow stood up and began to eat and lived a long time afterwards.

Yes, God's covenant covers all we can put under it. Israel's flocks and herds were included. Not a hoof be left behind. (Exodus 10:26) We are privileged to claim protection for our lives, our homes, and even our automobiles. Whether in Old Testament or New Testament, all the promises of God are in Him. Israel was promised all the land of Canaan, yet they only possessed all their feet trod upon.

Healings Through Faith and Prayers

Elder Vance held healing meetings at National Conventions and elsewhere and sent out anointed handkerchiefs to be applied to the sick for their physical healing. Elder Blackman, during his pastorate prayed for Sister Julia Frelicks—then a tumor dropped from the lower part of her body (into a slop jar).

Miraculous Deliverance of O. C. Miller

One Sunday Brother Spense Miller's 3-year-old son was seized with an attack of worms. His right side was dead, right eye closed and worms were choking him to death. A doctor came and stuck pins into him, but he didn't flinch. The doctor gave him up to die. The father held on in faith and urged the attendants and visiting saints to keep believing, and assured all that the child would recover. The mother was preparing dinner. He called all into prayer. First the family and then the pastor and Elder T. C. (Neal) Dyson prayed. The grandmother put the child into a tub with water in it. He was soon delivered of a ball of worms which then fell apart. They were about 8-inches long and the size of a pipe stem. In about an hour the child revived. He (Elder O. C. Miller) now lives at 7950 Pembroke, Baton Rouge, La., and pastors the Temple Church of Christ (Holiness), 8616 Cohn St., New Orleans, La.

TESTIMONIES OF HEALINGS THROUGH FAITH AND PRAYERS
by
Mrs. Coralani Flood of Los Angeles, California

I was born into the church invisible, the body of Christ in 1923. Coming out of the Catholic Church in which I grew up until I was grown, and then being born again, this message of salvation is very dear to my heart. The founder of this work was a prophet, a priest, and a prince among his own people, but somehow I do believe that had he been given to another race they would have esteemed and loved him more dearly. He was the greatest spiritual leader I have ever known or read of. They are singing his songs and hymns at my home in Honolulu, Hawaii. They are sung around the world.

I can only tell truthfully what I know and have seen. We have seen tumors removed, tubercular and heart patients healed, demon possessed, asthma, lame, deaf and many other diseases all healed by the power of the blessed Holy Spirit when Bishop Jones would anoint and pray for the sick in his wonderful, powerful Healing Services. I can witness to this truth as, I too, was healed many years ago. Two of my children are alive today healed after the doctors gave them up to die. After an illness of five years, Faith stepped in and God held death back because my beloved pastor refused to doubt God and instructed me to have faith and patience to wait on God. My daughter and son received their healing. Jas. 1:6-7 and Psa. 37:7)

A Child's Prayer Answered

An 8 year old girl's mother had not left her bed for months. Broken hearted, she read promises of answers to prayer from her New Testament, then asked, "Mother, can Jesus make you well?" "Yes, my child, but it's not His will. I'm in such agony I can't talk to you; go and play." The child went and thought and prayed, then returned with the words of assurance: "Mamma, I'm going to try Jesus once more. He says ask, and I'm going to ask Him. Now, Mamma, pray with me." Kneeling she prayed, "O Jesus, dear good Jesus, I have no happy days since Mamma has been sick these three months. She's so sick she can't talk to her little girl. She loves you and her little girl loves you." Suddenly she rose to her feet, and clapping her hands, cried, "He will, Mamma, He will." The lady had not moved her hands for months. Immediately she rose from her bed healed and able to go about and attend to her household duties, praising God.

The Community Life of Elder John Vance of Magnolia, Miss.
by Sister Edna C. Anderson

Elder John Vance moved here in December, 1920, with Mrs. Rosa L. Jones Vance, his wife by a second marriage, and his wife's seven daughters. The two sons still lived away.

Their coming here brought to this community one of its most highly respected citizens. He worked hard and reared and educated his children. Some of them after high school here, attended college in different parts of this State and in other States and are assets as citizens. Elder Vance proved to be a spiritual leader, giving whole-

79

some advice where needed, often going out of his way to encourage the discouraged and comfort those in distress and healing the sick by fervent prayer and faith in God. He was esteemed by white and colored, never seeming to tire of doing good. Words fail me to try to describe this wonderful life which many should emulate for it was indeed a blessing to mankind. Not many live such a long and useful life (85 years) as did he.

Many since his home-going have expressed their wish for such a leader in their community. Better that these words be spoken to one in one's life time. However, "They may rest from their labors; and their works do follow them." Rev. 14:13 I think we should ask God to give us more such men for our Christian Leadership.

Sister L. N. Burris, Mt. Hermon La., Route 1
Testifies of Salvation and Healing

I was already saved. About 1925 I become afflicted in my thighs and hips and unable to walk. A neighbor who had been afflicted as I was told me of a faith doctor who had rubbed her. My husband (Mr. Tate) got this doctor to come and rub me. He repeated the rubbings over and over with liniment which I think he himself made. It didn't help me so my husband sent me to the charity Hospital Clinic for examination. After I had taken part of the doctor's prescription with no results, I began to seek the Lorl, read my Bible and prayed. I read one day, "Is any sick among you, let him call for the elders of the church; and let them pray over him, anointing him with oil in the name of the Lord: And the prayer of faith shall save the sick and the Lord shall raise him up". (James 5:4-15) I sent for Elder Scarborough. He came and prayed. I didn't get well at once. It was hard for my people always got the doctor when one of us took sick. I had not been taught Divine healing nor had I been sick of account. I quit the medicine and prayed, yet for a whole year, I couldn't walk. I had to be helped —but I trusted the Lord. My husband left me. I lived with my parents and sometimes with my sister. They took me to church and after so long I got so I could walk with help, and then without the stick. Finally I could help on the farm, and made a bale of cotton. My husband then came home and rented some land and I kept working. But he kept worrying me and I tried to fight him. The Lord afflicted me again. I had nervous indigestion. My weight dropped from 200 to 160 pounds. Everybody thought I would die. Everything I ate hurt me. I was afraid to eat. For six months or more when I lay down at night, it seemed that I would die before daybreak; for six months or more. I made the Lord another promise; that I would do house to house work for Him and have prayer wherever I want.

The Lord healed me without the help of doctors or medicines. Since that time I've been telling all sick people how He healed me. I trust Him alone for my health and He has never failed me from that day. How I do thank and praise Him for it.

Miraculous Gift of Water

Sister Lillie Newsome, Route 1, Box 33, Pinola, Mississippi, reported that after eight vain attempts to get a well on her farm, the Holy Spirit urged her to go to her front porch one Saturday morning. Just then she saw Elder Vance passing on the highway. Said she to him: "The Lord says for you to pray that we get water." Meantime, she was directed to ask her husband to bring from town that same day a well bucket and a rope. On his return with these articles, she went to what had been the eighth dry hole in the ground and began to draw water and filled the vessel presently. (See II Kings 4:1-6)

People came from near and far to drink what she called holy water. Perhaps it was to prove her gratitude to the Lord, but for a long time the water did not clear in the well. During this time, Sister Vance visited in the home and found Sister Newsome rejoicing that whereas before this incident she had no water at all, now she had plenty of cool water that the Lord had miraculously provided. The water became clear even thought no curbing was in the well and it held up until there was blasting in the county for oil.

With the going down of the well, water systems were used so the family was provided with water by that process. Jesus never fails to help. Will we give Him an opportunity to supply our needs? He's waiting still.

The Stumbling Block Moved

I'm glad to say I'm saved in the blessed way of holiness and sanctification and kept from sin by the power of God. I do thank the Lord for sparing me to see the day when I can live happy in my home.

I prayed to the Lord to move the stumbling block although I didn't know what the stumbling block was. On the fourth Sunday in August the Lord filled me with the Holy Ghost. Two days later my husband was saved and ever since that time my home has been happy.

Truly I believe I was the stumbling block. But I praise the Lord that we both are now saved and "rejoicing night and day as we walk the narrow way; for he washed our sins away. Hallelujah!" O that I may learn to do His will forever. "For I am not ashamed of the gospel of Christ, for it is the power of God unto salvation to every one that believeth." (Romans 1:16)

Mrs. Lucy Smith
518 Cedar Street
Pine Bluff, Arkansas
January 11, 1905

From a married woman and the mother of a daughter: "My son has fought in three wars across the ocean on bloody battlefields where his face was shot away by the blast of enemy guns, But God once more held back death and bade him live on. We praise His holy name and thank Him for His mercy."

Sister Ellen McLelland testifies: "When I was living in Pike County, Mississippi, in 1911 there came a great storm through our community. It blew down the nearby church house, uprooted trees, and destroyed many houses.

"Meanwhile I was in my room praying. At the same time my oldest daughter saw an angel standing in a corner of her room. I know he was watching over us and our home for there was no harm done to our place."

Sister Sarah Vernon's testimony from her own lips is that from her conversion as a young mother she has been a missionary. She works with children, in prisons, and elsewhere in communities. Her version of "Happy Birthday" runs: "Happy birthday to you, just one will not do, Take the gift of salvation, And you will have two".

She states that through her bi-weekly visits to a prison, reading and explaining the Scriptures, praying and testifying, and having prisoners give their testimonies, one young man was saved and a woman living out of wedlock was converted and came out to live for the Lord. At one time and place some began to see their conditions and requested that Sister Vernon come weekly instead of bi-weekly. Whether she is in her former home in Louisiana, in

California, or in Washington, she goes alone when there is no
one to accompany her and works on her mission. (Luke 10:37b)

Gulfport, Mississippi
February 12, 1946

Beloved Daddy Jones:

Just received Brother Strong's letter yesterday announcing your
departure for various points. May God's presence be real to you all
along the trip and may He uphold you by His mighty power. I
know you will be a blessing to the church and all who love your
God. I hope, by God's grace, to see your face once more and hear
the sound of your voice.

How Satan hates God's anointed! I am praying for you and the
faithful Brother Strong. What a blessing you will be to Him. What
a blessing you have been to me. I have faith in you.

Enclosed please find an offering from the Lord whose treasure
you are. With a heart full of Christian love and gratitude for your
prayers.

Your devoted daughter in the gospel,
Louise Cotten

1201—36 Ave.

*   *   *

ARTICLES OF FAITH AS TAKEN FROM THE MANUAL

Chapter I—Articles of Faith
Article I.   God

We believe in one God, and that He only is God, and that as
God, He is Triune, being revealed as Father, Son and Holy Spirit.

Article II.   The Son of God

We believe that the Son of God is the Second Person of the
Holy Trinity, and as The Son of God, He became incarnate by
The Holy Spirit, and being born of the Virgin Mary, united with
Himself the divinely begotten Son of Man, called Jesus, thus
uniting in one person God and man.

Article III.   The Holy Spirit

We believe that the Holy Spirit is the third person of the God-
head, and is ever present, and active in and with the Church of
Christ, convicting, and regenerating those who believe and sanctifying believers, and guiding into all truth as it is in Jesus.

83

Article IV.   The Holy Bible

We believe that the Holy Bible is composed of sixty-six books, commonly known as the Old and New Testaments, and that they are the revealed Words of God written by Holy men as they were moved by the Holy Ghost.

Article V.   Original Sin

We believe that original sin is that corruption of the nature of all offsprings of Adam, by which we all are separated from original righteousness and that in the Scriptures it is described as "the carnal mind," "the flesh," "sin that dwelleth in me," and such like. It continues to exist until eradicated or destroyed by the Holy Ghost, through the blood of Christ. I John 1: 6-10; Rom. 7; Heb. 9:11 (9-11-14)14; 10:29; 13:12.

Article VI. Atonement

We believe that the atonement made by Jesus Christ through the shedding of His blood for the remission of sins, is for the whole human race; and that whosoever repents and believes on the Lord Jesus Christ is justified and regenerated and saved from the dominion of sin. Rom. 3:22-26; 5:9; Heb. 2:9.

Article VII.   Repentance

We believe that repentance is a sincere change of the mind, involving a sense of personal guilt of sin, and a turning away from same. And that the penitent heart is graciously helped by the Spirit of God. Acts 2:38; 26:18; Acts 3:19.

Articles VIII.   Justification

We believe that justification is God's word done for us, by which full pardon is granted to all who believe and receive Jesus Christ as Savior and Lord. Rom. 3:24; Acts 10:43.

Article IX.   Regeneration

We believe that regeneration is the new birth, that is, God's work done in us, by which the believer is given a Spiritual life, and rectifying the attitude of the will toward God and Holy things, John 3:6; Titus 3:5.

Article X.   Sanctification

We believe that sanctification is that act of Divine grace whereby we are made holy. In justification, the guilt of sin is removed; in regeneration, the love of sin is removed; in sanctification, the inclination to sin is removed. Sanctification must be definitely experienced to fit us to see the Lord. I Thes. 5:23; Heb. 10:14; John 17:17; Heb. 12:1-14.

Article XI.   Resurrection
We believe that Christ truly rose from the dead, and ascended into heaven, and is now sitting at the right hand of God The Father making intercession for us. I Cor. 15:14-20.

Article XII.   The Second Coming
We believe the Lord Jesus Christ will return to judge the quick and the dead; and that we who are alive at His coming shall not precede them that are asleep in Christ Jesus. I Thes. 4:13-18.

Article XIII.   Baptism
We believe that Baptism is commanded of Our Lord and that it belongs to the believer of the Gospel, "not infants who cannot believe," and that the Bible way of administering it is by immersion. Matt. 28:19-20; Mark 16:14-16; Rom. 6:1-7.

Article XIV.   The Lord's Supper
We believe that The Lord's Supper is a New Testament Ordinance, and that it was instituted when our Lord celebrated His last Passover with His disciples, and that it consists of bread and wine, and that as often as we take it we show forth the Lord's death till He comes again. Matt. 26:26-29; Mark 12:22-25; Luke 22:19-20; I Cor. 5; 11:23-24.

Article XV.   The Gift of the Holy Ghost
Section 1. We believe that every true believer is heir to the gift of the Holy Ghost. Gal. 4:6-7.

Section 2. We believe that He is the gift of God in Christ Jesus to the children of God, sanctifying, quickening, guiding into all truth, and giving power to obey and witness God's Word. John 14:16-26; Acts 1:8.

Section 3. We believe that the receiving of the Holy Ghost is subsequent to conversion. Acts 8:14-16; 19-14.

Section 4. We believe that a backslider must be reclaimed before he or she can receive the Holy Ghost.

Section 5. We believe that the Holy Ghost baptized the whole church on the Day of Pentecost because of the Jewish nation, and the whole Church in Cornelius' house because of the gentile nation;

and that always thereafter, He is referred to as a gift. Acts 2:38-39; a receiving, Acts 19:1-2; a filling, Eph. 5:18; an anointing, I John 2:27; II Cor. 1:21. He is never again referred to as a baptism for there is but one baptism. Eph. 4:1-5.

Article XVI. Footwashing

We believe in footwashing as an act of obedience in following the example given by our Lord Jesus Christ. (Not practiced by many of the churches)

Article XVII. Spiritual Gifts

We believe that spiritual gifts are set forth in the 12th, 13th and 14th chapters of First Corinthians.

Section 1. That no one gift is the specific sign or evidence of the Holy Spirit's presence, but faith (Heb. 11:1) and Love (I Cor. 13; John 13:35) are the evidences; not even power alone is the evidence for that may be of Satan.

Section 2. That these gifts, though they may be of use to edification, may be counterfeited and are not to be trusted as evidence. II Thes. 2:7-12; II Tim. 3:8.

Section 3. That there are three essential evidences of true religion. Faith, Hope, and Love. I Cor. 13:13.

Section 4. That the Bible endorses speaking in tongues, or a gift of tongues but that no one really speaks in tongues unless he speaks a language understood by men, as in Acts 2.

Section 5. That though one speak with tongues, it is no evidence of the Holy Ghost at all, but merely a sign.

Article XVIII. Divine Healing

Section 1. We do not condemn physicians and medicines because the Bible does not. Prov. 17:22; Ezek. 47:12; Col. 4:14; Matt. 9:12.

Section 2. We believe and teach Divine Healing according to the Scriptures. Isa. 8:20.

Section 3. We believe that it is a gift set in the Church and that the prayer of faith will save the sick and The Lord will raise them up. James 5:15.

CHAPTER IV

THE CONVENTIONS

OFFICERS OF THE NATIONAL CONVENTION, 1945-1946

Bishop C. P. Jones, D.D. LL.D., President Senior Bishop
   1327 E. 42nd St., Los Angeles 11, Calif.
Bishop Wm. A. Washington, D.D., Executive Vice President
   Presiding Bishop of the Western Diocese
   826 E. 32nd St., Los Angeles 11, Calif.
Bishop E. W. Butler, Presiding Bishop, Southwestern Diocese
   812 Izard St., Little Rock, Ark.
Bishop Wm. Mitchell, Presiding Bishop, North Central Diocese
   4737 Newberry Terrace St., St. Louis 13, Mo.
Bishop W. E. Holman, Presiding Bishop, Eastern Diocese
   736—4th Street, S E, Washington 3, D. C.
Bishop J. M. Haywood, Presiding Bishop, Northern Diocese
   6657 S. Wabash Ave., Chicago, Ill.
Bishop Gordon Hay, Presiding Bishop, Southeastern Diocese
   4618 Champlain Ave., Chicago, Ill.
Bishop O. B. Cobbins, Presiding Bishop, South Central Diocese
   248 East Ash St., Jackson 17, Miss.
Bishop J. A. Jeter (Retired)
   1807 W. 32nd St., Little Rack, Ark.
Rev. M. R. Conic, Recording Secretary
   862 E. Princess Anne Road, Norfolk, Va.
Bishop O. B. Cobbins, Corresponding and Statistical Secretary,
   248 East Ash St., Jackson 17, Miss.
Rev. L. M. Relf, Financial Secretary
   6246 S. Park Ave., Apt. 202, Chicago 37, Ill.
Brother Walter Moore, Treasurer
   6219 South Park Ave., Chicago, Ill.

GENERAL BOARDS 1945-46

BOARD OF CLAIMANTS

Brother T. H. Smith	Brother William Hines
Bishop W. E. Holman, Chairman	Rev. L. A. Cruise
Rev. P. H. Curry, Secretary	Rev. William M. Acty
Deacon E. T. Johnson, Treasurer	Rev. B. T. Johnson
Brother A. W. Adams	

87

PUBLISHING BOARD 1945-46

Bishop J. M. Haywood, Chairman Rev. G. A. Thomas
Dr. S. J. Anderson, Executive Sec. Rev. J. W. Gilbert
Rev. L. D. Polk, Treasurer Rev. C. L. Carhee
Bishop William Mitchell Sister M. M. Adams
Bishop J. Gordon Hay

Prof. W. H. Howard, Editor-in-Chief, Truth
Messenger
Dr. O. D. Henry, Secretary of Publication

CHURCH EXTENSION—MISSION BOARD 1945-46

Bishop William Mitchell, Chairman Rev. J. D. Gordon
Dr. S. J. Anderson, Secretary Rev. L. Randall
Rev. Ellwood Rector, Treasurer Brother E. L. Fizer
Rev. O. A. Askerneese, Field Agent Brother Ed Smith
Rev. Ben Aikens

BOARD OF EDUCATION 1945-46
(For one year)

Bishop O. B. Cobbins
Prof. R. C. Cook Rev. D. S. Michael
Rev. E. L. Fizer Sister C. B. Spruille
Brother A. Hamilton, Sr. Bishop E. W. Butler
Rev. L. J. Jackson Rev. J. R. Perkins

(For two years)

Rev. O. D. Henry Prof. W. H. Howard
Mrs. G. G. Brinkley Rev. G. A. Thomas
Sister Pearl Clarke Rev. S. B. Thomas
Brother E. L. Hall Bishop William A. Washington
Bishop W. E. Holman Bishop William Mitchell

(For three years)

Brother Jesse Bell Rev. F. A. Boyd
Brother F. E. Dyson Brother Q. M. Green
Rev. L. M. Relf Mrs. T. M. Washington
Mrs. R. C. Lee Rev. H. R. McInnis
Bishop J. M. Haywood Prof. Myrtis Amacker

88

BISHOP M. R. CONIC
PRESIDENT, NATIONAL CONVENTION
CHURCH OF CHRIST (HOLINESS) U.S.A.

Rev. E. K. Bethel, 1807½ W. 35th Pl.,
Los Angeles, Calif.
Rev. L. P. Johnson, Detroit, Michigan
Rev. P. H. Curry, Missionary, 2492 Alabama Ave.,
S.E. Washington, D.C.
Rev. S. L. Jordan, Missionary

This national convention was organized 69 years ago at Jackson, Mississippi, its present headquarters, by the late Senior Bishop Charles Price Jones who held leadership of the group until his passing, January 19, 1949. (While the call was made in 1896, the first convocation was actually held in June 1897.)

From this group have sprung several Holiness bodies* all of whom owe much to the religious zeal and spiritual insight and inspiration of Bishop Jones whom God used mightily.

By Bishop M. R. Conic

August, 1954

*See Chapter 12, "The Expanding Perimeter".

National Convention Officers
1964-65

PRESIDENT	Bishop M. R. Conic
VICE PRESIDENT	Bishop O. W. McInnis
RECORDING SECRETARY	Rev. L. P. Camper
FINANCIAL SECRETARY	Rev. J. C. Smith
TREASURER	Brother Walter Moore
STATISTICAL SECRETARY	Brother Leonard Moore
CORR. SECRETARY	Rev. A. J. Perkins

Bishops' Council
1964-65

Bishop M. R. Conic, Chm. National Publishing Board, General Chairman
Bishop O. W. McInnis, Editor of Truth, Vice Chairman
Bishop A. J. Torrey, Chm. National Education-Trustee Board
Bishop Clifton Goodloe, Chm. National Trustee Board
Bishop A. D. Williams, Chm. Church Extension Board
Bishop David P. McPherson, Chm. Board of Claiments

The National Convention (1943)

National Executive Council
1964-65

Bishop M. R. Conic, 4852 Victoria Ave., Los Angeles, California
　　Presiding Bishop, Western and North Western Dioceses
Bishop O. W. McInnis, 8321 So. Calumet Ave., Chicago, Illinois
　　Presiding Bishop, Northern and South Eastern Dioceses
Rev. Maurice D. Bingham, President National S.S. & H.Y.P.U.
　　Congress
Rev. John Sanders, Dr. W. H. Howard, Rev. G. A. Thomas,
Rev. L. M. Relf, Brother Fred Brown, Rev. O. A. Askerneese,
Brother J. C. Smith, Rev. J. Augurson, Rev. J. Plummer Jr. Rev.
C. N. Ricks, Brother Jesse Doles.

Bishop David P. McPherson, 862 E. Princess Anne Rd., Norfolk
　　Virginia
　　Presiding Bishop, Eastern Diocese
Bishop Clifton Goodloe, R.1, Box 186, Canton, Mississippi
　　Presiding Bishop, South Western Diocese
Bishop A. D. Williams, 4864 Fountain Ave., St. Louis, Mo.
　　Presiding Bishop, North Central Diocese
Bishop A. J. Torrey, 4305 O'Bannon Drive, Jackson, Mississippi
　　Presiding Bishop, South Central Diocese

National Education—Trustee Board
1964-65

Chairman Bishop A. J. Torrey, Jackson, Miss.
Executive Secretary Rev. John Sanders, Jackson, Miss.
Recording Secretary Brother W. H. Castilla, Jackson, Miss.
Ass't. Rec. Secretary, Brother Wilber Robinson, Canton, Miss.
Treasurer Rev. G. A. Thomas, Canton, Miss.

Board Members

Bishop M. R. Conic	Brother Willis J. Burris
Bishop Clifton Goodloe	Brother Bernard O'Neal
Rev. Maurice Bingham	Rev. L. M. Relf
Brother William Callion	Brother W. L. Sutton
Brother Ernest White	Brother Willie Davis

92

93

Brother James Smith   Treasurer
Rev. Carl Austin   Brother Rayford Lee, Jr.
Rev. Joseph Holland   Rev. A. J. Perkins
Rev. Samuel Ballard

Staff

Bishop O. W. McInnis   Editor of *Truth*
Brother Victor Smith   Manager of Publishing House

Foreign Mission Board
1964-65

Rev. J. C. Smith   Chairman
Bishop A. J. Torrey   Vice Chairman
Rev. C. N. Ricks   Recording Secretary
Brother Jon A. Randall   Corresponding Secretary
Brother Jesse Doles   Treasurer
Rev. L. D. Hughes

Rev. Jesse Augurson   Brother Cruz Juarez
Brother Worlie Young   Sister L. K. O'Neal
Mrs. Anna Willis   Mrs. E. M. Holt
Mrs. Lillie Wilson   Rev. James Stuart, Jr.
Rev. Robert Keetch   Brother E. McField
Rev. J. L. Burris   Miss C. B. Kimbrough
Mrs. B. T. Johnson   Mrs. Gladys Moore
Rev. O. C. Miller   Mrs. M. Bennett
Mrs. Rowenia Hannibal   Rev. Tyree Feltzs

DIRECTORY OF CHURCHES AND MINISTERS
EASTERN DIOCESE
CHURCHES AND PASTORS

Northern District

FIRST CHURCH OF CHRIST
1935 Madison Ave.
New York, N.Y.
Rev. W. L. Jerome, Pastor
40 W. 135th St. #2P
New York, N. Y.

FIRST CHURCH OF CHRIST
1219 Hamlin St. N. W.
Washington, D. C.
Rev. C. P. Jones, Jr., Pastor
621 Quincy, N. W.
Washington, D. C.

ZION CHAPEL CHURCH OF CHRIST
732 Webster St. N. W.
Washington, D. C.
Rev. Albert Green, Pastor
1401 Fairmount St. N. W.
Washington, D. C.

FIRST CHURCH OF CHRIST
Freeman, Virginia
Rev. Joe N. Hutchinson, Pastor
624 Day St.
Hampton, Virginia

CHURCH OF CHRIST
Surry, Virginia
Rev. W. H. Reddick, Pastor
381 Hobson St.
Hampton, Virginia
Southern District

FIRST CHURCH OF CHRIST
862 E. Princess Anne Road
Norfolk, Virginia
Bishop David P. McPherson,
  Pastor
2720 Chesterfield Blvd.
Norfolk, Virginia

ST. TIMOTHY CHURCH
OF CHRIST
1715 Madison Ave.
Newport News, Virginia
Rev. J. C. Smith, Pastor
1711 Madison Ave.
Newport News, Virginia
IMMANUEL CHAPEL
536 South Street
Hampton, Virginia
Rev. S. G. Winston, Pastor
1519 Glasgow St.
Portsmouth, Virginia
MT. OLIVE CHURCH
OF CHRIST
Portsmouth, Virginia
Rev. John Stith, Pastor
3022 Salter St.
Newport News, Virginia

ORDAINED MINISTERS

Northern District:
Rev. Vattel Jackson
2523 N. Capitol St.
Washington, D. C.
Rev E. Campbell
1611 Forest Ave. #E
Medley Heights,
Fort George Meade, Md.
Rev. C. P. Jones
621 Quincy St, N. W.
Washington, D. C.
Rev. S. Pyes
2107 12th Street, N. W.
Washington, D. C.
Rev. O. A. Askerneese
536 Riggs Rd., N. E.
Washington, D. C.
Rev. J. B. McGarrah
728 Underwood Street
Washington, D. C.
Rev. Albert Green
1401 Fairmount Street, N. W.
Washington, D. C.

Rev. W. L. Jerome
40 West 135th St., #2P
New York, N. Y.
Rev. B. Robinson
105 73 Remington St.,
Jamaica, New York
Rev. W. Blount
177 28 Troutville Rd.,
St. Albans, New York
Rev. James Carter
2488 7th Avenue,
New York, N. Y.
Rev. Walter Smith
17 W. 125th St.,
New York, N. Y.

Southern
Bishop David McPherson
2720 Chesterfield Blvd.,
Norfolk, Virginia
Rev. S. G. Winston
1519 Glasgow St.,
Portsmouth, Virginia

Rev. John H. Stith
3022 Salters St.,
Newport News, Virginia

Rev. J. C. Smith
1711 Madison Street
Newport News, Virginia

Rev. William H. Riddick
381 Hobson Street
Hampton, Va.

Rev. Joe N. Hutcheson
624 Day Street
Hampton, Va.

NORTH CENTRAL DIOCESE
Churches and Pastors

MISSOURI DISTRICT
CHRIST TEMPLE CATHEDRAL
4301 Page Blvd.
St. Louis, Mo.
*Bishop A. D. Williams, Pastor
4864 Fountain Avenue
St. Louis, Mo.

BETHEL TEMPLE
3314 Hickory Street
St. Louis, Mo.
*Elder James Stuart Sr.,
1717 Marcus Avenue
St. Louis, Mo.

MIDWEST DISTRICT
CHRIST TEMPLE CHURCH
2124 N. 26th Street
Omaha, Nebraska
*Elder Carl Austin, Pastor
2122 N. 26th Street
Omaha, Nebraska

CHURCH OF CHRIST
Denver, Colorado
*Elder J. H. Manley, Pastor
4115 N. 21st Street
Omaha, Nebraska

CHURCH OF CHRIST
1322 N. Greenwood Blvd.,
Tulsa, Oklahoma
*Rev. Arnold Goodlett, Pastor
1322 N. Greenwood Blvd.
Tulsa, Oklahoma

CHRIST TEMPLE
702 Oakland Street
Kansas City, Kansas
*Elder Maurice Austin, Pastor
702 A Oakland Street
Kansas City, Kansas
TENNESSEE — KENTUCKY
    DISTRICT
CHRIST TEMPLE CHURCH
907 South Lauderdale
Memphis, Tenn.
*Elder James Stuart, Jr., Pastor
907 South Lauderdale
Memphis, Tenn.
CHRIST TEMPLE CHURCH
211 Eastern Avenue
Jackson, Tenn.
*Elder Claudius Ricks, Pastor
213 Eastern Avenue
Jackson, Tenn.
FIRST HOLINESS CHURCH
205 East Jefferson St.
Brownsville, Tenn.
*Elder C. H. Harris, Pastor
1949 Hunter Avenue
Memphis, Tenn.
CHRIST TEMPLE CHURCH
Fulton, Kentucky
*Elder F. L. Lawrence, Pastor
207 Taylor Street
Fulton, Kentucky
CHURCH OF CHRIST
Hickman, Kentucky
*Elder F. L. Lawrence, Pastor
207 S. Taylor Street
Fulton. Kentucky

SEATS CHAPEL
Cedar Grove, Tenn.
*Elder C. H. Morris, Pastor
607 Wells Street
Memphis, Tenn.

CHURCH OF CHRIST
Huntington, Tenn.
*Elder A. C. Flakes, Pastor
RFD 1 Cedar Grove, Tenn.

ORDAINED MINISTERS

Bishop A. D. Williams
4864 Fountain Avenue
St. Louis, Mo.

Elder James Stuart, Jr.
907 S. Lauderdale Street
Memphis, Tenn.

Elder Hugh Jarmon
3928 A Cook Avenue
St. Louis, Mo.

Elder Abner Koehn
110 Lundy Lane
Jackson, Tenn.

Elder James Stuart, Sr.
1717 Marcus Avenue
St. Louis, Mo.

Elder Jesse Manley
4115 W. 21st Street
Omaha, Nebraska

Elder Fred. A. Hobbs
2086 Farrington Street
Memphis, Tenn.

Elder Carl Austin
2122 N. 26th Street
Omaha, Nebraska

Elder Maurice Austin
702 Oakland Street
Kansas City, Kansas

Elder Arnold Goodlett
1322 N. Greenwood Blvd.,
Tulsa, Oklahoma

Elder C. H. Morris
607 Wells Street
Memphis, Tenn.

Elder C. H. Harris
1949 Hunter Street
Memphis, Tenn.

Elder L. Berry
913 Mississippi Street
Memphis, Tenn.

Elder Robert Davis
Tulsa, Oklahoma

Elder F. L. Lawrence
207 Taylor Street
Fulton, Kentucky

Elder Herley Pearson
Rt. 1, Box 88
Hickman, Kentucky

LICENSED MINISTERS

Elder Raymond Warren
3314 W. 27th
Kansas City, Kansas
Elder E. Moore
Jackson, Tenn.

Elder Lem Johnson
4846 A Hammett Pl.
St. Louis, Mo.

ILLINOIS
CHRIST TEMPLE
 CATHEDRAL
552 E. 44th Street
Chicago, Illinois
*Bishop O. W. McInnis, Pastor
8321 S. Calumet Ave.,
Chicago 19, Illinois

SECOND TEMPLE
234 West 69th Street
Chicago, Illinois
*Elder C. L. Flakes, Pastor
9546 South Prairie
Chicago, Illinois

BETHEL TEMPLE
1442 S. Pulaski Rd.,
Chicago, Illinois
*Elder A. J. Olive, Pastor
6345 South Green Street
Chicago, Illinois

CHRIST TEMPLE
1610 Shields Avenue
Chicago Heights, Illinois
*Elder M. F. Brown, Pastor
1612 Shields Avenue
Chicago Heights, Illinois

CHRIST TEMPLE #2
1427 Ellis Avenue
E. Chicago Heights, Illinois
*Elder Marcus Irons, Pastor
1332 Werline
E. Chicago Heights, Illinois

CHRIST TEMPLE
Maywood, Illinois
809 9th Avenue
*Elder Ernest Williams
1431 Greenwood Avenue
E. Chicago Heights, Illinois

INDIANA
FIRST CHURCH
789 Edgemont
Indianapolis, Indiana
*Elder J. E. Holland, Pastor
4110 N. Capitol Avenue
Indianapolis, Indiana

CHRIST TEMPLE
2472 Pierce Street
Gary, Indiana
*Rev. L. M. Relf, Pastor
2464 Pierce Street
Gary, Indiana

MICHIGAN
ZION CHAPEL
3000 24th Street
Detroit, Michigan
*Rev. A. J. Perkins, Pastor
360 East Boston Blvd.
Detroit, Michigan

SECOND TEMPLE
4831 Scottern Street
Detroit, Michigan
*Elder J. A. McKanders, Pastor
5275 Pacific Avenue
Detroit, Michigan

CHRIST TEMPLE
27035 Colgate
Inkster, Michigan
*Elder Samuel Kendrick, Pastor
29444 Alan Street
Inkster, Michigan

OHIO
BETHEL CHURCH
11624 Kinsman
Cleveland, Ohio
*Elder James Robinson, Pastor
11804 Avon Avenue
Cleveland, Ohio

GLENVILLE CHURCH
9009 Wade Park Avenue
Cleveland, Ohio
*Elder M. D. McGee, Pastor
10317 Yale Avenue
Cleveland, Ohio
MT. ZION CHURCH
620 Fernwood
Toledo, Ohio
*Elder Morris Robinson, Pastor
837 Palmwood
Toledo, Ohio

FIRST CHURCH

786 South Rhodes

Akron, Ohio

*Rev. Percy Dixon, Pastor

3235 East 118th Street

Cleveland, Ohio

ORDAINED MINISTERS

ILLINOIS

Bishop O. W. McInnis
8321 S. Calumet Avenue
Chicago 19, Illinois

Elder J. S. Allen
6330 S. Throop Avenue
Chicago, Illinois

Elder M. F. Brown
1612 Shields Avenue
Chicago Heights, Illinois

Elder O. B. Cobbins
810 E. 51st Street #812
Chicago, Illinois

Elder Lorenze Drakes
1421 14th Place
E. Chicago Heights, Ill.

Elder C. L. Flakes
9546 South Prairie Avenue
Chicago, Illinois

Elder Marcus Irons
1332 Werline
E. Chicago Heights, Ill.

Elder A. J. Olive
6345 S. Green Street
Chicago, Illinois

Elder G. W. Revel
6836 St. Lawrence
Chicago, Illinois

Elder Booker Rogers
1416 Greenwood Ave.
E. Chicago Heights, Ill.

Elder Ernest Williams
1431 Greenwood Ave.
E. Chicago Heights, Ill.

Elder Horace Wilson
1508 Ellis Ave.
E. Chicago Heights, Ill.

INDIANA

Elder Willie Dean
2608 Polk Place
Gary, Indiana

Elder J. E. Holland
4110 N. Capitol
Indianapolis, Indiana

Elder Fred Moseley
2467 Pierce Street
Gary, Indiana

Elder A. J. Myers
6534 Oakview Drive
New Augusta, Ind.

Elder Russell Rayburn
2264 Taft Street
Gary, Indiana

Elder L. M. Relf
2464 Pierce Street
Gary, Indiana

MICHIGAN

Elder A. J. Criss
4223 Riopelle Street
Detroit, Michigan

Elder Luther Jenkins
2975 Webb Street
Detroit, Michigan

Elder Samuel Kendrick
29444 Alan Street
Inkster, Michigan

Elder A. J. Perkins
360 E. Boston Blvd.
Detroit, Michigan

Elder J. A. McKanders
5275 Pacific
Detroit, Michigan

Elder J. C. Tyner
601 College S. E.
Grand Rapids, Michigan

OHIO

Elder Thomas Johnson
11410 Hazeldale Avenue
Cleveland, Ohio

Elder M. D. McGee
10317 Yale Avenue
Cleveland, Ohio

Elder James Robinson
11804 Avon Avenue
Cleveland, Ohio

Elder Morris Robinson
837 Palmwood
Toledo, Ohio

LICENSED MINISTERS

Rev. L. Block
2436 Adams Street
Gary, Indiana

Rev. Joseph Criss
4203 Crane
Detroit, Michigan

Rev. Percy Dixon
3235 E. 118th Street
Cleveland, Ohio

Rev. James Mitchell
2101 E. 21st Avenue
Gary, Indiana

Rev. Marion Wolfe
3342 W. Chicago #D4
Detroit, Michigan

Rev. Leroy White
263 W. Hampton Drive
Indianapolis, Indiana

Rev. Elbert Watts
2607 N. Central Avenue
Indianapolis, Indiana

SOUTH EASTERN DIOCESE
Churches and Pastors

SUTTER STREET CHURCH
735 Sutter Street
Montgomery, Alabama
*Rev. Samuel McGee, Pastor
3211 Mobile Drive
Montgomery, Alabama

BEULAH CHURCH
845 Harwell Street
Atlanta, Ga.
*Elder W. S. Kilgore, Pastor
2097 Verbena Street N. W.
Atlanta, Ga.

FIRST CHURCH
2529 Central Avenue
Birmingham, Alabama
*Rev. J. S. Kirkland, Pastor
2928-34th Street N.
Birmingham, Alabama

LORD'S TABERNACLE
CHURCH
807 Minter Street
Selma, Alabama
*Rev. Arthur Green, Pastor
1611 Church Street
Selma, Alabama

ORDAINED MINISTERS

Rev. A. Banks
205 W. Fair
Atlanta, Ga.

Rev. J. S. Kirkland
2938-35th Street N.
Birmingham, Ala.

ORDAINED MINISTERS

Rev. Arthur Green
1611 Church St.
Selma, Ala.
Rev. W. S. Kilgore
2097 Verbena
Atlanta, Ga.

Rev. Samuel McGee, Jr.
3211 Mobile Drive
Montgomery, Ala.

SOUTH CENTRAL DIOCESE

CHURCHES AND PASTORS
1964-1965

CHRIST TEMPLE CHURCH
329 E. Monument Street
Jackson, Mississippi
*Bishop A. J. Torrey, Pastor
4305 O'Bannon Drive
Jackson, Mississippi

CYNTHIA CHURCH
Highway 49 North
Jackson, Mississippi
*Rev. Edgar Callaway, Pastor
3910 Main Street
Jackson, Mississippi

SECOND TEMPLE
2916 Lilly Street
Jackson, Mississippi
*Rev. L. P. Camper, Pastor
3652 Westchester Drive
Jackson, Mississippi

NEW LAKE CHURCH
Livingston & Beasley Rd.
Jackson, Mississippi
*Rev. J. L. I. Graham, Pastor
3449 Oakland Street
Jackson, Mississippi

THIRD TEMPLE
1405 Morehouse Street
Jackson, Mississippi
Rev. L. P. Bearden, Pastor
1725 Topp Street
Jackson, Mississippi

MOUNT BETHEL CHURCH
1756 S. Gallatin
Jackson, Mississippi
*Rev. J. T. Hill, Pastor
316 Monticello
Hazlehurst, Mississippi

SWEET REST CHURCH
RFD 6, Box 58
Jackson, Mississippi
*Rev. J. T. Hill, Pastor
316 Monticello
Hazlehurst, Mississippi

SWEET HOME CHURCH
RFD 4, Box 126
Jackson, Mississippi
*Rev. J. T. Hill, Pastor
316 Monticello Street
Hazlehurst, Mississippi

WOLFE LAKE CHURCH
RFD 4
Yazoo City, Mississippi
*Rev. Willie Jenkins, Pastor
RFD 6, Box 30
Jackson, Mississippi

MT. ZION CHURCH
1930 Wilton Street
Jackson, Mississippi
*Rev. Willie Jenkins, Pastor
RFD 6, Box 30
Jackson, Mississippi

COLLIS HILL CHURCH
Terry, Mississippi
*Rev. George A. Thomas, Pastor
232 E. Cohea Street
Jackson, Mississippi

TOUGALOO CHURCH
Tougaloo, Mississippi
*Rev. Willie Kendrick, Pastor
RFD 2, Box 269
Jackson, Mississippi

MT. OLIVE CHURCH
Highway 18 West
Jackson, Mississippi
*Rev. L. D. Webb, Pastor
P. O. Box 102
Hazlehurst, Mississippi

BEREAN CHURCH
Lexington, Mississippi
*Rev. L. D. Webb, Pastor
P. O. Box 102
Hazlehurst, Mississippi

MT. PEREA CHURCH
Lexington, Mississippi
*Rev. W. H. Hollins, Pastor
P. O. Box 173
Folsom, La.

PLEASANT GREEN CHURCH
Railroad Avenue
Canton, Mississippi
*Rev. J. B. Burley, Pastor
232 Roosevelt Street
Jackson, Mississippi

SWEET HOME CHURCH
Pelahatchie, Mississippi
*Rev. Willie Bingham, Pastor
1221 Florence Street
Jackson, Mississippi

C. M. & I. CHAPEL
3910 Main Street
Jackson, Mississippi
*Rev. J. L. I. Graham, Pastor
3449 Oakland Street
Jackson, Mississippi

CHURCH OF CHRIST
Greenville, Mississippi
*Rev. W. D. Roberts, Pastor
RFD 1, Box 121
Shaw, Mississippi

CHURCH OF CHRIST
Leland, Mississippi
*Rev. B. T. Jones, Pastor
RFD 1
Cleveland, Mississippi

CHURCH OF CHRIST
1419 Roosevelt Street
Clarksdale, Mississippi
*Rev. B. T. Jones, Pastor
Route 1
Cleveland, Mississippi

CHURCH OF CHRIST
Drew, Mississippi
*Rev. Eddie Jones, Pastor
P. O. Box 5523
Jackson, Mississippi

TEMPLE CHURCH OF CHRIST
Ruleville, Mississippi
*Rev. W. H. Hollins, Pastor
P. O. Box 173
Folsom, La.

CHRIST TEMPLE CHURCH
1010 Chrisman Avenue
Cleveland, Mississippi
*Rev. J. B. Burley, Pastor
232 Roosevelt Street
Jackson, Mississippi

GALILEE CHURCH
McComb, Mississippi
*Rev. E. E. Sparkman, Pastor
130 Mississippi Street
McComb, Miss.

STARR HILL CHURCH
Fernwood, Mississippi
*Rev. E. E. Sparkman, Pastor
130 Mississippi Street
McComb, Miss.

NEW HOME CHURCH
Jayess, Mississippi
*Rev. W. H. Hollins, Pastor
P. O. Box 173
Folsom, La.

SPRING BEULAH CHURCH
Ruth, Mississippi
*Rev. John Sanders, Pastor
3432 Livingston Road
Jackson, Mississippi

MT. OLIVE CHURCH
Magnolia, Mississippi
*Rev. Maurice D. Bingham,
  Pastor
215 Denwiddie Street
McComb, Mississippi

SPRING HILL CHURCH
Tylertown, Mississippi
*Rev. J. L. I. Graham, Pastor
3449 Oakland St.
Jackson, Mississippi

CHRIST TEMPLE CHURCH
Oakvale, Mississippi
*Rev. John Roberts, Pastor
Box 816
East Mulga, Alabama

CHRIST TEMPLE CHURCH
Summit & Denwiddie Streets
McComb, Mississippi
*Rev. Maurice D. Bingham,
  Pastor
215 Denwiddie Street
McComb, Mississippi

FIRST CHURCH OF CHRIST
  (HOL) USA
Gillespie Street
Starksville, Mississippi
*Rev. W. H. Hollins, Pastor
P. O. Box 173
Folsom, La.

MT. OLIVE CHURCH
714 Short 9th Street
Hattiesburg, Mississippi
*Rev. Edgar Callaway, Pastor
3910 Main Street
Jackson, Mississippi

ROSE HILL CHURCH
Pinola, Mississippi
*Rev. J. B. Burley, Pastor
232 Roosevelt Street
Jackson, Mississippi

MORAL GROVE CHURCH
Byram, Mississippi
*Rev. Willie Bingham, Pastor
1221 Florence Street
Jackson, Mississippi

ALSTON FIRST CHURCH
Sessums, Mississippi
*Rev. John Roberts, Pastor
Box 816
East Mulga, Alabama

PINE GROVE CHURCH
Starkville, Mississippi
*Rev. John Roberts, Pastor
Box 816
East Mulga, Alabama

WEST POINT CHURCH
West Point, Mississippi
*Rev. Irving Harris, Pastor
Sessums, Mississippi

CHRIST TEMPLE CHURCH
Port Gibson, Mississippi
*Rev. J. B. Burley, Pastor
232 Roosevelt Street
Jackson, Mississippi

WHITE OAK CHURCH
Highway 18-2½ Miles S. E.
Carpenter, Mississippi
*Rev. Willie Bingham, Pastor
1221 Florence Street
Jackson, Mississippi

FAIRVIEW CHURCH
7½ Miles from Carpenter
*Rev. Willie Jenkins, Pastor
RFD 6 Box 30
Jackson, Mississippi

LITTLE ZION CHURCH
3½ Miles from Carpenter
Hermanville, Mississippi
*Rev. M. T. Newsome, Pastor
Lermann, Mississippi

LUCAS CHURCH
Lucas, Mississippi
*Rev. Edgar Callaway, Pastor
3910 Main Street
Jackson, Mississippi

CHURCH OF CHRIST
Shaw, Mississippi
*Rev. W. D. Roberts, Pastor
RFD 1, Box 121
Shaw, Mississippi

BETHEL CHURCH
Indianola, Mississippi
*Rev. W. D. Roberts, Pastor
RFD 1, Box 121
Shaw, Mississippi

CHURCH OF CHRIST
Crystal Springs, Miss.
*Rev. E. C. Duncan, Pastor
McComb, Mississippi

TEMPLE CHURCH
Old Highway 51
Brookhaven, Miss.
*Rev. Willie Bingham, Pastor
1221 Florence Street

ST. PETER CHURCH
3 Miles E. of Hazlehurst
Hazlehurst, Mississippi
*Rev. W. H. Hollins, Pastor
P. O. Box 102,
Folsom, La.

WILDERNESS OF JUDEA
Hazlehurst, Mississippi
*Rev. L. D. Webb, Pastor
Box 102
Hazlehurst, Mississippi

GALILEE CHURCH
Hazlehurst, Mississippi
*Rev. Eddie Jones, Pastor
P. O. Box 5523
Jackson, Mississippi

DAMASCUS CHURCH
Hazlehurst, Mississippi
*Rev. George A. Thomas, Pastor
232 E. Cohea Street
Jackson, Mississippi

CANEY CREEK CHURCH
Old Highway 51 South
Jackson, Mississippi
*Rev. Eddie Jones, Pastor
Box 5523
Jackson, Mississippi

ROCK HILL CHURCH
Mt. Olive, Miss.
*Rev. Robert Durr, Pastor
Prentiss, Mississippi

CHRIST TEMPLE CHURCH
Prentiss, Mississippi
*Rev. Robert Durr
Prentiss, Mississippi

CLARK CREEK CHURCH
Patterson, Mississippi
*Rev. M. T. Newsome, Pastor
Lorman, Mississippi

THOMAS CHAPEL
Prentiss, Mississippi
*Rev. G. A. Thomas, Pastor
232 E. Cohea Street

ORDAINED MINISTERS

Bishop A. J. Torrey
4305 O' Bannon Drive
Jackson, Mississippi

Rev. L. P. Camper
3652 Westchester Drive
Jackson, Mississippi

Rev. J. E. Bearden
1725 Topp Street
Jackson, Mississippi

Rev. Edgar Callaway
3910 Main Street
Jackson, Mississippi

Rev. J. L. I. Graham
3449 Oakland Street
Jackson, Mississippi

Rev. J. T. Hill
316 Monticello Street
Hazlehurst, Mississippi

Rev. Willie Jenkins
RFD 6, Bo 30
Jackson, Mississippi

Rev. G. A. Thomas
232 E. Cohea St.
Jackson, Mississippi

Rev. Willie Kendrick
RFD 2 Box 269
Jackson, Mississippi

Rev. L. D. Webb
P. O. Box 102
Hazlehurst, Mississippi

Rev. W. H. Hollins
P. O. Box 173
Folsom, La.

Rev. J. B. Burley
232 Roosevelt St.
Jackson, Mississippi

Rev. E. N. Haggans
Box 14
Starkville, Mississippi

Rev. B. N. McGowen
Jayes, Mississippi

Rev. Willie Bingham
1221 Florence Street
Jackson, Mississippi

Rev. W. D. Roberts
RFD 1, Box 121
Shaw, Mississippi

Rev. B. T. Jones
Rt. 1
Cleveland, Mississippi

Rev. Eddie Jones
P. O. Box 5523
Jackson, Mississippi

Rev. E. E. Sparkman
130 Mississippi Street
McComb, Mississippi

Rev. John Sanders
3432 Livingston Road
Jackson, Mississippi

Rev. Maurice Bingham
215 Denwiddie Street
McComb, Mississippi

Rev. John Roberts
Box 816
East Mulga, Alabama

Rev. Irving Harris
RFD 1, Box 248
Sessums, Mississippi

Rev. M. T. Newsome
Lerman, Mississippi

Rev. E. C. Duncan
McComb, Mississippi

Rev. Robert Durr
Prentiss, Mississippi

Rev. D. L. Dyson
1705 Barrett Street
Jackson, Mississippi

Rev. J. E. Graham
3341 Edwards Street
Jackson, Mississippi

Rev. O. L. Williams
Rt. 1, Box 75
Silver Creek, Mississippi

Rev. Jacob Hunter
211 Ruby Street
Hattiesburg, Mississippi

Rev. Frank Jordan
1227 E. 2nd Street
Clarksdale, Mississippi

Rev. W. M. Barnes
Moseley Street
Jackson, Mississippi

Rev. Josh Carey
345 Jullienne Street
Jackson, Mississippi

Rev. M. Robinson
Ruleville, Mississippi

Rev. Andrew Mitchell
1420 Collier Street
Jackson, Mississippi

Rev. M. H. McGee
Tylertown, Mississippi

106

SOUTH CENTRAL DIOCESE CONVENTION—1946

Christ Temple Church, Jackson, Mississippi

O. B. Cobbins, Presiding Bishop

Front row seated:

Eight from the left: Bishop E. W. Butler, Bishop O. B. Cobbins

SOUTH WESTERN DIOCESE
CHURCHES AND PASTORS

District No. 1
CHIRST TEMPLE CHURCH
812 Izard Street
Little Rock, Arkansas
*Rev. J. L. Burris, Pastor
4309 W. 5th Street
Pine Bluff, Arkansas

CHRIST TEMPLE CHURCH
4309 W. 5th Street
Pine Pine Bluff, Arkansas
*Rev. J. L. Burris, Pastor

CHRIST TEMPLE CHURCH
Clayton & Willow Sts.
Conway, Arkansas
*Rev. A. J. Parish, Pastor
1600 Pine Street
Arkadelphia, Arkansas

CHRIST TEMPLE CHURCH
West Pleasure Street
Searcy, Arkansas
*Rev. Fred A. Hobbs, Pastor

CHRIST TEMPLE CHURCH
927 W. 17th Street
Texarkana, Texas (No Pastor)
District No. 2

ST. MATTHEW CHURCH
901 Louise Anne Ave.
Monroe, La.
*Rev. Jesse Augurson, Pastor

CHRIST TEMPLE CHURCH
Hamburg, Ark.
*Rev. Jesse Augurson, Pastor

CHRIST TEMPLE CHURCH
Lake Providence, La.
*Rev. Jesse Augurson, Pastor

STAR LIGHT CHURCH
200 Miss. Street
Mansfield, La.
*Rev. Jesse Augurson, Pastor

CHRIST TEMPLE CHURCH
1406 Jordan Street
Shreveport, La.
*Rev. John Sanders, Jr.

WALNUT GROVE CHURCH
Homer, La.
*Rev. Henry Ward, Pastor

ST. PETER'S CHURCH
Wisner, La.

ZION TEMPLE CHURCH
RFD 1 Box 1A
Gilbert, La.
*Elder Bennie Lee, Pastor

CHRIST TEMPLE CHURCH
P. O. Box 613
Leesville, La.
*Elder Samuel Murray, Pastor
District No. 3

ANTIOCH CHURCH
461 First Street
Bogalusa, La.
*Rev. John Sanders, Jr. Pastor

SWEET HOME CHURCH
Franklinton, La.
*Bishop Clifton Goodlee, Pastor

PLAINVIEW CHURCH
Rt. 1
Mt. Hermon, La.

BETHEL CHURCH
Franklinton, La.
*Rev. Bennie Lee, Pastor

MIDWAY CHURCH
Folsom, La.
*Elder Samuel Murray, Pastor

CHRIST TEMPLE CHURCH
8616 Cohn Street
New Orleans, La.
*Rev. O. C. Miller, Pastor
7950 Pembroke
Baton Rouge, La.

PLAINVIEW CHURCH
Baton Rouge, La.
*Rev. O. C. Miller, Pastor
NEW SALEM CHURCH
Mansfield St.
Marrero, La.
*Rev. J. D. Washington, Pastor
OAK GROVE CHURCH
RFD 1 Box 127
Tickfaw, La.
*Elder Willie Dyson, Pastor

NEW JERUSALEM MISSION
Gratna, La.
*Elder James Lee, Pastor

MT. ZION MISSION
Hackley Road
Franklinton, La.
*Elder Willie Magee, Pastor

ORDAINED MINISTERS

Bishop Clifton Goodloe
RFD 1 Box 186
Canton, Mississippi

Elder John Sanders, Jr.
3432 Livingston Road
Jackson, Mississippi

Elder Bennie Lee
Rt. 1
Mt. Hermon, Louisiana

Elder Samuel Murray
Box 66
Folsom, Louisiana

Elder Willie E. Dyson
1029 17th Avenue
Franklinton, La.

Elder Joseph Thompson
2622 S. Derbigny Street
New Orleans, La.

Elder Willie J. Magee
1428 Dobson Street
Franklinton, La.

Elder James Lee
1229 Marshall Street
Marrero, La.

Elder Fred A. Hobbs
2086 Farrington Street
Memphis, Tenn.

Elder J. L. Burris
4307 West 5th Avenue
Pine Bluff, Arkansas

Elder J. A. Allen
1641 Charlevoix Street
Bogalusa, La.

Elder George Conerly
Route 1
Mt. Hermon, La.

Elder J. D. Washington
Rt. 3 Box 208
Prentiss, Mississippi

Elder Jesse Augurson
605 Dixie Street
Monroe, La.

Elder Henry Ward
P.O. Box 223
Winnsboro, La.

Elder A. J. Parish, Sr.
2705 West 27th Street
Pine Bluff, Arkansas

LICENSED MINISTER
Brother W. M. Malone
1824 Valentine Street
Little Rock, Arkansas

BISHOP A. HAMILTON, JR. AND MINISTERS OF THE
NORTHERN DISTRICT—WESTERN DIOCESE

Front Row, from left to right: Rev. Elmo Ollison, Rev. M. D. McGee,
Bishop Albert Hamilton, Jr. Rev. Lester D. Hughes, Rev. C. B. Jor-
dan. Back Row, from left to right: Rev. R. Luster, Rev. Swift, Rev.
Anthony, and Rev. Samuel Smith.

WESTERN DIOCESE

Names and location (address) of each Church in the Diocese. Included are the names and addresses of the pastors of these churches.

Southern District

ANTIOCH CHURCH
245 East Walnut Avenue
Monrovia, Calif.
*Rev. A. M. Hall, Pastor
1425 So. California Avenue
Monrovia, Calif.

CALVARY CHURCH
7191 Cypress Street
Fontana, Calif.
*Rev. Clarence Goodwin, Pastor
1452 West 16th St.,
San Bernardino, Calif.

CHRIST TEMPLE CHURCH
1275 East 54th Street
Los Angeles 11, Calif.
*Bishop M. R. Conic, Pastor
4852 Victoria Avenue
Los Angeles 43, Calif.

CHRIST TEMPLE CHURCH
1040 Winston Drive
San Diego, Calif.
*Rev. Samuel Ballard, Pastor
601 West 52nd Place
Los Angeles, Calif.

110

FAITH TEMPLE CHURCH
10107 Grape Street
Los Angeles 2, Calif.
*Rev. C. B. Jordan, Pastor
10107 S. Grape Street
Los Angeles 2, Calif.

NEW TESTAMENT CHURCH
1847 W. Florence Ave.
  (Box 47674)
Los Angeles 47, Calif.
*Rev. John Plummer, Jr., Pastor
352 West 88th Place
Los Angeles 3, Calif.

CHRIST TEMPLE CHURCH
San Bernardino, Calif.
1442 West 11th Street
*Rev. Willie Richards, Pastor
1700 West Claude
Compton, Calif.

PASADENA CHURCH— Christ
  Temple
211 Glorieta St.,
Pasadena, Calif.
*Rev. Timothy Burr, Pastor
1720 East 23rd Street
Los Angeles 58, Calif.

PILGRIM CHURCH
13722 South Avalon Ave.,
Los Angeles 59, Calif.
*Rev. R. L. Bradley, Pastor
2033 North Corlette Avenue
Los Angeles 59, Calif.

PILGRIM CHURCH
1515 North "D" Street
Las Vegas, Nevada
*Rev. George L. Harris, Pastor
412 Van Buren Avenue
Las Vegas, Nevada

SECOND TEMPLE CHURCH
4414 South Hoover Avenue
Los Angeles 37, Calif.
*Rev. A. L. Ballard, Pastor
1754 East 43rd Street
Los Angeles 58, Calif.

TABERNACLE CHURCH
24356 East Central Avenue
San Bernardino, Calif.
*Rev. W. M. Harris, Pastor
139 South Waterman
San Bernardino, Calif.

NEW HOPE CHURCH
1119 Rhea Street
Long Beach, Calif.
*Rev. L. J. May, Pastor
901 West Magnolia St.,
Compton, Calif.

GOOD NEWS CHURCH
1467 Lincoln Avenue
Pasadena, Calif.
*Rev. Carlos D. Caldwell,
1528 Navarro
Pasadena, Calif.

Northern District

ALL NATIONS CHURCH
2003 Woolsey Street
Berkeley 3, Calif.
*Rev. Eugene Brown, Pastor
2001 Woolsey Street
Berkeley 3, Calif.

FIRST CHURCH
509 "J" Street
Merced, Calif.

GOLDEN GATE CHURCH
2201—19th Street
San Francisco, Calif.
*Rev. Samuel Smith, Pastor
300 Salinas Avenue
San Francisco, Calif.

111

BETHEL CHURCH
2119 Eunice Avenue
Fresno, Calif.
*Rev. Samuel Seals, Pastor
511½ San Juan Avenue
Venice, Calif.
EMMANUEL CHURCH
839-13th Street
Oakland, Calif.
*Rev. L. D. Hughes, Pastor
839—13th Street
Oakland, Calif.

ZION TEMPLE CHURCH

6325 Sunriver Drive

Sacramento, Calif.

*Rev. Elmo Ollison, Pastor

1057 Vasco Road

Livermore, Calif., 94550

WESTERN DIOCESE—CHURCH OF CHRIST (HOLINESS) U.S.A.
ORDAINED MINISTERS

Rev. A. M. Hall
1425 S. California Avenue
Monrovia, Calif.

Rev. Estell McLaurin
747 East 94th Street
Los Angeles 2, Calif.

Bishop M. R. Conic
4852 Victoria Avenue
Los Angeles, Calif. 90043

Rev. James Reece
775 West Harriet
Altadena, Calif.

Rev. John Jeter, Jr.
414 E. Imperial Highway, Apt. 2
Los Angeles, Calif. 90059

Rev. C. C. Carhee
1832 East 41st Place
Los Angeles, Calif. 90058

Rev. Samuel Ballard
601 W. 52nd Place
Los Angeles 37, Calif.

Rev. Charles Gorman
9909 S. Figueroa
Los Angeles 3, Calif.

Rev. Ezekiel Moore
830 West 138th Street
Compton, Calif.

Rev. Carlos D. Caldwell
1528 Navarro
Pasadena, Calif.

Rev. James Thrash
7718 Halldale
Los Angeles, Calif. 90047

Rev. W. E. Bingham
132 S. Towne Ave.
Los Angeles, Calif. 90061

Rev. A. L. Ballard
1754 East 43rd Street
Los Angeles, Calif.

Rev. C. B. Jordan
10107 Grape Street
Los Angeles, Calif. 90002

Rev. Willie Calhoun
1224 East 120th Street
Los Angeles, Calif. 90059

Rev. R. L. Bradley
2033 North Corlette
Los Angeles, Calif. 90059

Rev. Donald Brown
10432 Mary Street
Los Angeles, Calif. 90002

Rev. J. B. Bass
1200 West 55th Street
Los Angeles, Calif. 90037

Rev. W. M. Harris
139 S. Waterman
San Bernardino, Calif.

Rev. Tyree Feltzs
242 East 2nd Street
San Bernardino, Calif.

Rev. W. H. Howard
750 East 46th Street
Los Angeles, Calif. 90011

Rev. G. L. Harris
412 Van Buren Street
Las Vegas, Nevada

Rev. Lester D. Hughes
839—13th Street
Oakland 7, Calif.

Rev. Samuel Smith
300 Salinas Avenue
San Francisco, Calif.

Rev. William Pope
1224 Francisco Street
Oakland, Calif.

Rev. Willie Richards
1700 West Claude St.,
Compton, Calif.

Rev. O. O. Ross
500 Vermont
Altadena, Calif.

Rev. G. L. Walker
2043 E. 115th St., Unit 135
Los Angeles, Calif. 90035

Rev. W. E. Jones
1275 E. 54th Street
Los Angeles, Calif. 90011

Rev. Timothy Burr
1720 East 23rd Street
Los Angeles, Calif. 90058

Rev. L. J. May
901 W. Magnolia
Compton, Calif.

Rev. D. M. Drough
10522 S. Wilmington
Los Angeles, Calif. 90002

Rev. John Plummer, Jr.
352 West 88th Place
Los Angeles, Calif. 90003

Rev. J. H. Young
1351½ East 49th Street
Los Angeles, Calif. 90011

Rev. Elmo Ollison
1057 Vasco Road
Livermore, Calif.

Rev. Eugene Brown
2001 Woolsey Street
Berkeley 3, Calif.

Rev. Samuel Seals
511½ San Juan Ave.
Venice, Calif.

LICENSED MINISTERS

South District

Rev. Timothy Seals
8912 South Andrews Place St.
Los Angeles 47, Calif.

Rev. Elton Herring
2001 Easy Street
Long Beach, Calif.

Rev. Orie Benjamin
326 E. 118th Street
Los Angeles 59, Calif.

Rev. R. Benjamin
1020 South Harlan
Compton, Calif.

Rev. C. R. Goodwin
1452 West 16th Street
San Bernardino, Calif

Rev. Washington Drake
6723—2nd Avenue
Los Angeles 47, Calif.

Rev. Huey P. Sheriff
1343 W. 96th Street Apt. #6
Los Angeles 46, Calif.

Rev. Robert Keetch
604 South 45th Street
San Diego, Calif.

Rev. Verdie Calhoun
Los Angeles, Calif.
Northern District

Rev. Judas Stevenson
4210 Potrero Avenue
Richmond, Calif.

Rev. Edgar Ward
Rev. W. A. Baggett
1935 Stuart Street
Berkeley, Calif.

Rev. Nathaniel Winn

NORTHWESTERN DIOCESE

CHURCHES AND PASTORS
CHRIST TEMPLE CHURCH
Rev. C. L. Carhee, Pastor
317—20th Avenue
Seattle, Washington 98122

MORNING STAR CHURCH
Rev. Eugene J. Williams, Pastor
901 South 7th Street
Yakima, Washington

ORDAINED MINISTERS
Rev. C. L. Carhee
317—20th Avenue
Seattle, Washington 98122

Rev. R. Luster
341—29th Avenue
Seattle, Washington

Rev. E. J. Williams
903 S. 7th Street
Yakima, Washington

LICENSED MINISTER
Elder W. Elam
3110 Cherry Street
Seattle, Washington

MINISTERS UNION OF THE SOUTHERN DISTRICT,
OF THE WESTERN DIOCESE
REV. JOHN PLUMMER, JR. PRESIDENT
BISHOP M. R. CONIC, PRESIDING BISHOP

Seated from left to right: Rev. J. Plummer, Jr. President; Bishop
M. R. Conic, Presiding Bishop; Rev. R. L. Bradley, District Chairman;
Rev. C. B Jordan, President of the Mission Board
Standing from left to right: Rev. J. D. Manley, Rev. W. E. Drake,
Rev. Donald Brown, Rev. Foe, Rev. O. Benjamin, Rev. E. Moore,
Treasurer, Rev. V. Calhoun, **Standing in back row from left to
right:** Rev. E. Herring, Rev. J. Jeter, Jr., Rev. H. P. Sheriff,
Rev. L. J. May, and Rev. G. L. Walker.

The Ministers Union of the Southern District

in the Western Diocese

Rev. J. Plummer, Jr. President

The Ministers Union of the Southern District in the Western
Diocese was organized by the late Bishop A. Hamilton, Jr. January 26, 1957. This body of ministers were to study and discuss
ways and means of improving the effectiveness of the Ministers
and the work of the Churches. They were also to study and discuss ways and means of attacking and solving the problems con-
fronting Ministers in their Church work.

Past Presidents—Rev. A. M. Hall, 1957-59; Rev. C. P. Jones,
Jr. 1960-62; Rev. C. B. Jordan, 1962-63; Rev. J. Plummer,
Jr., 1964—.

SWEET REST CHURCH
Jackson, Mississippi

CHRIST TEMPLE CHURCH
814 Izard Street
Little Rock, Arkansas

116

CHAPTER FIVE

THE LOCAL CHURCHES

THE EARLY CHURCHES
1895-1904

The Rising of Churches

In the beginning, there was no thought of building a new church as a distinct Christian movement. But as Luther's and Wesley's teachings were in advance of the theology of their day, so far in advance were the teachings of the pioneers in this movement that they were forced out of the church too which they belonged. Therefore, they were forced to build another church.

The first entirely independent church was built at Lexington, Mississippi, where Elder C. H. Mason was pastor.

The Sweet Rest Church was organized in 1898 under the leadership of Elder C. P. Jones before the withdrawal from the Jackson Missionary Baptist Association in December, 1900.

In the new organization, the services were held under a brush arbor with Elder Jones serving as pastor from 1903-1912.

Land for an edifice was purchased from Brother Willie Bibb for the amount of $50.00. The deacons were: Brother John Jackson, Brother L. L. Garrison; Brother George Wright and Brother E. L. Curry. The Trustees were: Brother Mack Jenkins, Sr., Brother George Wright and Brother Richard Manuel.

The Church has since been under the leadership of the following ministers: Rev. A. T. Rucker, Rev. John Day, Rev. H. R. McInnis, Rev. John Sanders. A new edifice was constructed in 1958 under the leadership of the present Pastor, Rev. J. T. Hill. The Deacons are Brother L. L. Garrison, Brother Anglon Dillions, Brother Mack Jenkins, Jr., and Brother Willie Jenkins, Jr. The Trustees were: Brother Robert Thompson, Brother Robert Bibb, Brother Frank Johnson, Brother Obidiah Jenkins, and Brother Robert McLaurin.

117

Some of the first members were: Deacon John Jackson, Sister Addie Jackson, Brother George Wright, Sister Susie Wright, Sister Mary Daniel, Sister Susie Keats, Brother Reuben Keats, Deacon Luther Garrison, Sister Leona Garrison, Brother Quitman Baton. In 1885 a church was organized in the Sons of Ham Hall on Broadway near Ninth Street in Little Rock, Arkansas. The church was named St. Paul Baptist Church. The first pastor Rev. C. P. Hughes was followed by Rev. Talley.

When Rev. C. P. Jones was elected pastor of St. Paul Baptist Church, Rev. John A. Jeter was one of the deacons.

Rev. Jeter succeeded Rev. C. P. Jones as pastor of the church, and remained pastor until 1921. He was the pastor when the church moved to a frame building at 814 Izard St. This church burned down and a small church was erected on the rear of the lot for use until the present brick building was erected and completed in 1899.

In 1898 a controversy arose between the Baptist leaders and Rev. C. P. Jones about the preaching of Sanctification and Holiness. Rev. J. A. Jeter, the pastor of St. Paul Baptist Church, became involved in the same controversy, and shared with Rev. Jones the persecution which followed. They were brought to trial in a Baptist conference in a building on the campus of Arkansas Baptist College. For the trial a white minister, Rev. Ben Cox was called in to help make the decision. His decision was: "Be careful with the brethren". The right hand of fellowship was withdrawn from both Rev. C. P. Jones and Rev. John A. Jeter. Rev. Jeter still held the pastorate of the new St. Paul Baptist Church which was then being completed. The corner stone was changed to read: "Holy Ghost Church of God", and the name of the church was changed likewise.

With the Little Rock Church securely in hand, the church at Pine Bluff, also pastored by Rev. Jeter, became the next Focal Point where a consolidated campaign was of utmost importance.

The persecution had created a great fervor in the midst of the adherents of the new movement. A zealous band of "Crusaders" walked the 45 mile distance from Little Rock to Pine Bluff, and returned, to surmount whatever suppression there was to the spreading of the new teaching through the new church at Pine Bluff, Ark. Some of the first members of the church were J. F. Hurd, Deacon E. M. Johnson, Sisters Anna Johnson, Elvie Pitts, Maggie Baylor, Synora Handy, Bassal Lee, Irene Boley, Monroe

Lee, Brother Esau and Mary Brown, Georgia Morris, Brother and Sister Locket, Susie Howard, Sister Martin, Rev. William Banner and wife Lillie, Rev. E. W. Green, Brother and Sister Harry Elam, Rev. J. D. Gordon.

The pastors were Reverends J. A. Jeter, William Mitchell, O. L. Mitchell, E. W. Butler, O. D. Henry, F. A. Boyd, A. J. Parrish, and J. L Burris.

Bethel Church
Franklinton, La.

There were about twelve members in the organization: Brothers and Sisters Hamp Bickham, Isem Wilson, John Wilson, Sisters Emma Harvey and Lucinda Bell and Brother William Burton, who served as first deacon. He was known as a "Father Burton" and was a faithful leader. He could neither read or write when the church was organized but later he learned both. His home was the minister's home. His and Sister Emma Burton's lives were of service and he could always be depended upon.

After the church was established a large number of members of Jerusalem Baptist Church came down and joined Bethel. The present membership is about 230. These auxiliaries are functioning: S. S., C.W.W.W., Standard Bearers, Sunbeams, H.Y.P.U. The S.S, H.Y.P.U. and C.W.W.W. were organized by Pastor Brunson.

The pastors of the church have been Reverends L. J. Brunson, Joe King, John Vance, J. L. I. Conic, H. R. McInnis, Robert R. Sears, William Mitchell, F. E. Williams, B. T. Johnson, and W. H. Hallins.

The C.W.W.W. looks after the sick and needy. They have a sick committee and a good works committee. These committees seek to save the lost ones. They keep a storage chest in which they keep supplies donated by the sisters to be given to the less fortunate, according to their need.

Berean Church, Lexington, Miss.

The fire that burned the girls' dormitory at Natchez College (Baptist) Natchez, Miss., may have produced the sparks that set aflame the light which caused the church at Lexington, Miss., to come into existence.

Miss Margaret Lee (Washington) was attending Natchez College when the girls' dormitory was burned. The dormitory girls were sent home. They were to begin raising money to rebuild the dormitory. Miss Margaret Lee, a member of ASIA Baptist Church in Lexington, got permission from the pastor to get Elder C. P. Jones to run a week meeting to help her raise some money. He came, and was asked to return again but could not. Elder C. H. Mason was sent. The effect of preaching Sanctification and Holiness caused the door of the church to be closed, and Elder Mason had to find another place. Prof. John A. Lee permitted his home to be used, but it was too small. Elder Jones from Jackson and Elder W. S. Pleasant from Hazlehurst had come up to help. The use of an old abandoned gin house belonging to Mr. Watkins (white) was granted. The group formally accepted the new faith and teaching and elected Elder C. H. Mason for their first pastor. This was the first entirely independent church of the new movement.

When the dissension arose over the "speaking in tongues" and "the dance" was introduced as a part of the doctrine of the new movement Elder Mason was still pastoring at the Lexington Church. It was not until 1910 that this church was definitely separated from the main body of the new movement. At this time the element which remained with the main body of the new movement had to get out.

In the course of years, the new group had had many pastors, some of whom were Reverend J. A. Jeter, J. L. I. Conic (H.

Blackman and W. A. Thurmond lived there) J. T. Woodson, H. B. Johnson, L. D. Webb, H. Bailey, and John Sanders.

Some of the first members were Brother John and Rosa Lee, Mrs. Margaret Lee-Washington, the Blackman Family, Rev. Noah Smith, the W. A. Thurmond Family, Sister Rosa Head, Brother John Davis, and the Golden Family.

Christ Temple Church
Corner Willow and Clayton Sts., Conway, Ark.

The Church at Conway, Ark., was founded in 1899 by Elder Charles H. Mason. He was the noted and effective street preacher. The first meeting place of the church was a dance hall. The first building was erected on the corner of Willow and Clayton Streets. The edifice was rebuilt in 1948 under the pastorate of Rev. J. Gordon.

Some of the first members were Rev. C. H. Mason, Brother G. G. Matthia, Sister Addie Matthia, Brother Jospes Jones, Sister Catherine Jones, Brother Jim Perry, Sister Ada Perry, Brother R. M. Manley, Sister Leona Moore, Brother M. Manley, Sister Fannie Manley, Brother James Manley, Sister Lucy Looper, 1259 Harrison St., Brother John Dorman, Sister Rosa Nichols-Wallace (90), Brother D. O. Hill (89), Sister Anna Hill (86).

The pastors have been Reverends C. H. Mason, Roscoe, J. A. Jeter, William Mitchell, E. W. Butler, Tolbert, Dan Washington, J. D. Gordon, O. L. Mitchell, C. L. Carhee, and J. L. Burris.

Antioch Church of Christ (1950)
Bogalusa, La

The Church of Christ Holiness, U.S.A. in Bogalusa, La., was started in an old K.P. Hall in the southern part of Bogalusa. Later a three room house on the north avenue was rented. After that Brother R. C. Cook, an undertaker, negotiated for a lot, and built the first church edifice. In 1950 the church was rebuilt on the same sight by Rev. Gordon.

The church was started by Rev. J. E. Burris and Brother Harness. (For 1 year Brother R. C. Cook acted as pastor.) The succeeding pastors were Reverends John Vance, Pounds, H. B. Johnson, L. J. Brunson, Wm. Mitahe II, F. E. Williams, B. T. Johnson, J. B. Burley, John Sanders, and Bishop Clifton Goodloe.

Christt Temple Church
1409 W. 5th Ave.
Pine Bluff, Ark.

The Christ Temple Church, Pine Bluff, Ark., was founded in 1899 by Elder J. A. Jeter. The unique incident in connection with the establishment of this church was the daring 45-mile walk of the "Crusaders". From Little Rock to Pine Bluff and from Pine Bluff back to Little Rock, Ark. That was their demonstration of their faith in the "new movement", and their demonstration to continue in the "WAY" in the face of inpending perils.

A brush arbor was used as the first meeting place. Some of the first members were Dr. M. J. Hollis, Sister Martha (95), Sister S. S. Hampton, Sister Rebecca Means (died in 1964, age 83), Brother and Sister R. M. Manley and Rev. D. W. Welch.

The pastors have been Reverends J. A. Jeter, O. L. Mitchell, J. L. I. Conic, A. J. Williams, R. L. McAlister, Roscoe, E. W. Butler, Dan Washington, J. D. Gordon, J. L. Burris. The church was rebuilt by Rev. J. L. Burris.

Soon after the church was established in Little Rock, Pastor Jeter came to Pine Bluff and started a mission on the corner of 5th and Spruce under a brush arbor. Here Elder A. J. Williams, one of the early ministers, helped to organize the church and on this site the house was later built. Among the earliest members were the Patterson Family, Elder A. J. Williams and wife Sarah, Brother and Sister Claiborne, Brother Matthews, Sisters Harriet (Ellis) Poole, Mary Smith, Floretta Thomas, Lydia McNeal, and Barbara Mosby. All of these with others of that noble band have braved life's stormy sea and made their landing and have left others here to carry on.

Elder Williams built up churches and held pastorates on the Cotton Belt, R.R. Sister Williams was a dutiful worker in what ever phase of the Christian cause it was her lot to be chosen. Report is that she stated that the Lord gave her the name "Willing Workers Organization" for the sisters' Christian band. Here originated what we now know as the "Christian Women's Willing Workers Organization." In this movement, Sister H. Poole, persevering C.W.W.W. local and state president, usually led her group, as she was accustomed to say, "over the top" at the general convocation. For the saints here worked as a unit in their endeavors. Sister Maggie Patterson was a prominent leader and

Antioch Church

Christ Temple Church
Pine Bluff, Ark.

bible teacher and the Patterson home was early recognized as a
home for pastor and other onsitting ministers and Christian workers, for the church parsonage was not built until years later under the pastorage and guidance of the dynamic J.L.I. Conic.

123

New Home Church of Christ
Jayess, Miss.

The New Home Church of Christ Holiness U.S.A. had its beginning in 1900 at Jayess, Miss. This church was in the south Mississippi and East Louisiana District Assembly organized by Rev. A. J. Scarborough.

For a while this church reported the largest membership of any church in the South. And probably the only exception for the demonstration as a whole were Los Angeles, California and Chicago, Illinois.

Some of the first members of the church were: Ben Manning, Emma Manning, York Ratliff, C. D. Ratliff, Victoria Ratliff, Charles Sibley, Ollie Sibley, Calvin Carney, Phyllis Carney, and the Lenoir Family. Mother Lenoir was 110 years old when she died two decades ago.

The church has had the following named pastors; Reverends Charley Forest, L. J. Brunson, William Webb, J. L. I. Conic, Brumfield, John Vance, William Mitchell, F. E. William, M. W. Wilson, W. A. Nolley, Benjamin Akins, Clifton Goodloe, and W. H. Hollins.

The Rose Hill Church of Christ Holiness
Pinola, Miss.

The Spring Valley Church near Mendenhall, Miss. had been organized and the following two ministers had presumably been working there when one of our missionaries, a Sister Jane Grubbs, brought down from her home in Mendenhall, Elder Stewart and

Elder G. W. Cooper, both of Jackson, Miss. in 1900. They taught Bible lessons from house to house and later set up a Gospel tent in an oak grove. Here within about 6 months the Rose Hill Church of Christ Holiness was organized with above a dozen members in 1902. Brethren often went in buggies and wagons before daylight to bring the preachers in time for the Sunday morning meetings. At times the ministers walked the 14 miles distance from Mendenhall. Attendance was good and the Lord blessed their efforts, some opposing, notwithstanding. Of that number was a (white) man who struck one of the ministers, Elder E. H. Thomas and the white man died within three weeks. Among the early members was Brother Ephraim Neusome, who has been faithful in every department of the church work throughout these years. Sister Celie Steels, through whose prayers of faith the Lord gave a son to a barren woman. Sister Addie Comper and Mattie Brench, who gave the church site for as long a time as the building would be used for church purposes. Among the contributions for the building was a donation of $25 given to Sister Steels by white friends. In general it can be said that the white people favored the work as a contribution to the communities wherever it was established, and they backed it with their good will through kind words and otherwise.

The pastors have been Reverends G. W. Cooper, C. D. Ratliff, Enoch Thomas, T. J. Hardy, John Vance, W. H. Hollins, John Nichols and Ezra Berry.

Mt. Perea Church
Carroll County, Mississippi

The Mt. Perea Church of Christ Holiness U.S.A. was established in 1900 according to the most reliable sources available.

This effort was spearheaded by Reverends Lee Porter Cobbins, Westly Moore, B. Tolbert and Brother James Washington. Rev. L. P. Cobbins was the first in the county to accept the teaching of sanctification and holiness, and thus he became the leader of his group.

Like other groups they faced the housing problems, for the brush arbor could only be used during the summer months.

The community had built a house for the public school. The church was allowed to use the school house for a few years until they were able to build an edifice of their own. The process became reciprocal for soon the schoolhouse had deteriorated to the extent that the school had to move to the church edifice. It was not many years before the community got together and had a Rosenwald School built. Then the church and the school were separated again. But for how long? Across the years the necessary repairs were not made but the church services were again carried on in the schoolhouse, and there remained for 20 and more years. Before the 20 year period expired the school was consolidated with other schools in another district. Thus the church was left alone in a deteriorating building in an undesirable location.

Thomas and Elizabeth Townsend

Many of the older members had died or moved away. The picture shown here is that of the chairman of the Senior deacon board, Thomas Townsend and his wife, Elizabeth Townsend, the leader of the Sisters Work, who with their large family moved from the community.

Another location for the church was found and purchased near the county public road.

With some aid from the National Church Extension Board a new church has been erected after 60 years of reciprocity.

In addition to the ministers mentioned above, the following ministers have pastored the church: Reverends G. L. Bogan, John Vance, W. A. Thurmond, W. H. Hollins, H. Bradley, J. T. Woodson, and George Durr.

Some of the first members of the church were: Deacon Thomas and Sister Townsend, Rev. L. P. and Martha Cobbins, Deacon Jeff and Sister Cornelia Dixion, Deacon George and Sister Sallie Townsend, Rev. H. M. and Mattie Cobbins, Sister L. Hudson, Sister Lillie Potts, Brother Jacob Nichols, and Mother Charlotte Washington.

Spring Beulah Church
of Christ (Holiness) U.S.A.
Ruth, Miss.

In 1901 an unlicensed preacher, Emanuel M. Huey, began preaching in a schoolhouse on the property of a generous man near Ruth, Miss., whose name was Gus Jackson. Improvised seats were made of boards nailed atop wooden blocks. In the same year P. L. Brent, M. M. Manning, H. J. Garner, Sam Moss, E. Montgomery and L. Haynes started a prayer meeting and kindled a spiritual fire in the neighborhood. This fire burned on until 1905 when Elder C. P. Jones came down from Jackson and held a revival meeting at Mt. Zion Baptist Church at about a five mile distance. Among those who accepted the preaching as truth were the above named persons and Wallace and Wm. Manning.

In 1906 Elder E. M. Huey organized the church with these charter members. Elder G. L. Hutchins, a Baptist minister, assisting, at a place in a grove where they used water from a cool spring; so they named the church *Spring Leaf.* Mr. Jackson sold the site for as long a time as a building on it should be used for church purposes and permitted the brethren to take the lumber away when they no longer worshipped there. In August of that year (1906) Elders W. S. Pleasant and W. J. Johnson of Hazlehurst, L. W. Lee of Lexington and A. J. Scarborough of McComb came and organized the South Miss. District Assembly, with Elder Scarborough as its first moderator. As the work grew and expanded this organization became known by its present name, the South Miss. and East La. District Assembly.

Christ Temple Church
The Mother Church
Jackson, Miss.

The Christ Temple Church, The Mother Church, 329 E. Monument St., Jackson, Miss., was conceived in tribulation and born in adversity in an atmosphere of religious bigotry.

The Church began in 1902 with a band of believers in Christ Jesus under the leadership of Elder C. P. Jones. The band had been ruled out of the Mt. Helm Baptist Church through a decision of the Miss. Supreme Court. The decision involved the church property holdings and changing of the denominational name of the church.

In 1902 when the expulsion notice was served, Elder C. P. Jones walked out of the Mt. Helm Baptist Church with his adherents and shortly convened the followers in a special service in the Benevolent Hall. Here a committee was appointed to find a location for a new church. All six members of the committee went out on the appointed day and converged on the same location almost within an hour. The uniformity of actions caused the members of the committee to feel that the Lord had led them to that location. The report was made to and accepted by the assembly. On the next Sunday a service was held on the vacant lot with Elder Jones speaking while standing in a wagon. $1200 was raised that day to pay for the lot at the corner of E. Monument and North Lamar Streets.

Plans were made to immediately begin the edifice. The plans had already been given to Elder Jones; 60 ft. wide, 90 ft. long and 30 ft. high. The brethren were not able to visualize such massive plans which the Lord had revealed to Elder Jones. So they proceeded to plan for and build a unique frame edifice, but less spacious than the former plan. This frame church was known as "Christ's Tabernacle" Church. This building did not stand for more than three years.

(The compiling committee failed to find a picture of the frame edifice.)

During the time that Vardaman was governor of Mississippi, one night a mob was chasing a Negro who they claimed had committed an offense against a white woman, and charged that the Negro hid in the Church; the mob set fire to the church and would not allow the fire department to extinguish the conflagration.

By 1906 the burned frame tabernacle was replaced with the "First Temple" a brick structure erected according to the first plan revealed to Elder C. P. Jones; 60 ft. wide, 90 ft. long, 30 ft. high. This building stood for 50 years.

The ground floor was used for mid-week services, the Sunday School and the Parochial school which developed into what became known as Christ Missionary and Industrial College. The printing establishment was also housed on the ground floor. The pastor's study, the secretarial offices, and the choir rooms were on the main floor. The large choir stand and the pipe organ were located in the balcony over the pulpit. The building had a total seating capacity of more than 2,000.

The Sunday services had an aggregate of 800 to 1000 in attendance. Both day and night services were well attended in those days. People walked from two to five miles to get to the services. People drove; came in buggies; came by wagon; and rode on horse back from miles around; and would come early in order to get seats, in probably one of the largest church sanctuaries in the state.

For the first 22 years, 1897-1919, the Christ Temple Church was the seat of the annual sessions of the National Convention. Often the crowds grew beyond the seating capacity during the National Conventions. Later, the convention was made up of elected delegates. This tended to reduce the attendance.

During the first two or more decades of the conventions, room and meals were furnished free to delegates. The local members of Christ Temple Church took the delegate into their homes without charge. The food was donated and prepared in the kitchen and served in the dining room at the church free. All gave of their provisions and services as unto the Lord.

There was something sentimental about the Old Christ Temple Church—THE MOTHER CHURCH—The First Temple. The knowledge of the razing of the old "First Temple" edifice was a disheartening omen. It had become endeared to thousands. Many had entered her doors laden with sin and broken hearts, but left sweetly saved and washed in the blood of the Lamb. Within her four walls, many had been healed of their physical infirmities through faith in the hand working of God. Beneath her roof many had been filled with the glorious infilling of the Holy Spirit.

Many are they who had praised God and shouted for joy upon the bosom of her floors. Some even walked upon those sacred barren grounds, shedding tears of sorrow from their eyes.

Alas, she is razed to the ground; and who shall raise another steeple with tapering spire skyward in her stead?

Today, it would cost approximately $500,000.00 to build and equip the equivalent of such commodious plant.

A remnant lingered after the benediction at Christ Temple Church, Jackson, Miss., during the pastorate of Elder C. P. Jones.

Temple Church Just Before Demolition

Benediction time at Christ Temple

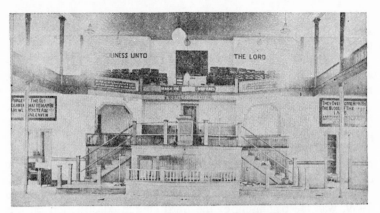

The Spacious Sanctuary of Old Christ

New Educational Building
Christ Temple Church

He had just pronounced the benediction and was still at the stand in the pulpit. With such a large crowd it took some time to clear the sanctuary.

The vacated interior before razing, Christ Temple Church, Jackson, Miss. The front interior of the sanctuary gives a view of the pulpit and surroundings.

The lower platform in front of the pulpit opened into the baptistery. The door in the rear of the pulpit led down into the pastor's study.

The balcony was rectangular and contained seats for several hundreds. The dimensions were; 60 ft. by 90 ft. That was the same dimension, but divided into several service departments.

The education building of Christ Temple Church erected in 1959, was the beginning of the third church construction on this corner since 1900. The first was the frame construction in 1902. The second, and the "First Temple", just recently demolished, was erected in 1906. The third construction was planned to be in two units. The education unit, the side entrance of which is here shown with the membership group, erected in 1959. The sanctuary was intended to have been erected ere this time.

Christ Temple Church officers; L to R. Front row: Deacon James Polk; Trustee John P. Younger, Asst. Pastor, Rev. William Barnes; Pastor Bishop A. J. Torrey; Deacon Cleveland Younger; Deacon Frank A. Moore; L. to R. 2nd row; Trustee Huertu White; Jr. Deacon William Barnes; Jr. Deacon Clifford Holloway; Jr. Deacon Samuel Polk; Jr. Deacon Willie Earl Washington; Deacon Jonas Moore Sr.; Trustee A. N. Jackson-chair; Trustee Willie Nath Hamilton; Trustee Oscar White; Jr. Deacon McArthur Torrey; Deacon W. T. Daves-chair.

The *Young Peoples Choir* of Christ Temple Church, Jackson, Miss.

As the choir appeared on W. J. T. V., Channel 12, Jackson, Miss., from 8:30 A. M. to 9:00 A. M. September 13, 1964.

L. to R. Row 1 *Mrs. Minnie Biggs Porter, Sponsor,* Bettye McGlother, Phillis Hamilton, Barbara Barnes, Vivian Hamilton, Lauretta S. May, Charlotte Shinault. Row 2. Louis Polk, Gertrude Speech, Miriam Torrey, Agertha Barnes, Mary Nell Barnes, Linda Hamilton, Doris Curry. Row 3. McAuthur Torrey, Samuel Polk, Faye Richard Speech, Willie Earl Washington, Benjamin Torrey, Roosevelt McNeil, Merril Torrey. Choir members not on picture: Willie Johnson, William Barnes, Jr. Marion Roots.

132

Officers: Christ Temple Church

Choir: Young People

A service group, the *Ushers* of Christ Temple Church, Jackson, Miss. under the leadership of Brother Essex McNeamer (1931) They are:

L. to R. Row 1. Brother Essex McNeamer, President, Miss Mable Jackson, Miss. Ethel Thomas, Mrs. Eliza Gobson, Miss Evelyn Thomas, Miss Martha Ann Holmes-Miller.

Row 2. Miss Genola Sims, Mrs. Genova Spencer-Christian, Mrs. Mattie Seaton-Bailey, Brother John Gordon.

Row 3. Miss Alma White, Miss Cosmos McGhee, Mrs. Bessie Patton, Miss Fannie Mae Luckett, Mrs. Bessie White, Brother Burbon Rhone, Miss Beatrice Michael, Mrs. Lula Riley Boone.

Some of the first members were: the Hyram Wright Family, the Henry Moore Family, Sister Lizzie Wilson, Sister Williams, Sister Mary Stewart Johnson, Brother Tom Malone, Mrs. Maude Simon, Sister Matilla Kimbrough, Sister Fannie Burrel Jones, the Bettie Dorsey Family, Brother E. McNeamer, Sister Sarah J. Thomas Land, the Fannie Seaton Family, W. S. Keys and wife, George A. Thomas, the Eddie Crane Family, Tom Grant and wife, G. W. Cooker and wife, Tom Davis and wife, the Willie Farnish Family, the Jeff Robinson Family, the Wm. Seaton Family, the Maria Postum Family, the William Butler Family, Sister Elviria Thomas.

PASTORS: Reverends C. P. Jones, Sr., Dr. Morris. R. L. McAllister, L. J. Brunson, O. B. Cobbins, E. W. Butler, J. L. I. Conic, J. D. King, acting, W. A. Thurmond, L. P. Johnson, M. R. Conic, Albert Hamilton, Jr., David McPherson, and A. J. Torrey.

Spring Beulah Church of Christ Holiness, U.S.A.
Ruth, Mississippi

Monthly pastoral Sundays, Sunday School, Wednesday night services with much prayer and Bible study, and Sunday morning sunrise prayer meeting were regular features. So hungry were hearts for the living word that the saints here as throughout the movement took their Bibles with them wherever they went daily. TRIBULATION: The doctrine was misunderstood and often the adherents were persecuted by many. On their way to sunrise prayer meeting one Sunday morning; L. Haynes, H. J. Garner, Wm. Manning, Frank Palmer, G. W. Manning, E. E. Manning, and possibly a few others saw a crowd of white men on the road side gambling. Frank accosted them: "You shouldn't be gambling, come to prayer meeting". They did come. And with them came others also and demanded that Frank be turned over to them,

Miss. Alexandria Joycelyn Holloway
Pianist

Miss Lois Roots
Organist

Ushers

135

against the pleadings of the rest of the Brethren. But Frank begged so as he caught hold of Wm. Manning and L. Haynes when they were dragging him out. These two men were allowed to go with the crowd into the woods. There they laid Frank across a log and whipped him severely. He finally had to leave that part of the country.

Johnny Brent was the first Church clerk and served capably and dutifully for about twenty years. Elder E. M. Huey was the first pastor and served in the capacity of pastor till his death in 1942.

The New Spring Beulah Church

The New Spring Beulah Church of Christ Holiness, U.S.A., Ruth, Mississippi, was organized by Elder Caleb D. Ratliff who had accepted the doctrine of the Church in 1906 and served as its first pastor until he resigned. After World War I when shifting residents scattered families of both churches from near the Gulf to Canada, membership in each of the two churches became so small that the two chose to unite into one body. This they did in 1935 and built a church more centrally located and named the new church Spring Beulah. Elder John Vance held the last revival in Spring Leaf that year and the first revival meeting in Spring Beulah the same year in the fall. After Elder Huey's death, Elder Bert N. McGowen carried out his unexpired term. He was succeeded by Elder John Vance, the present pastor in 1955.

DAMASCUS CHURCH OF CHRIST HOLINESS

Hazlehurst, Mississippi

The Damascus Church grew out of the white Damascus Baptist Church, during slavery, built in 1855. The slaves used the balcony of the white church. Later, the Negroes built a brush arbor on the grounds of the white church and held services for themselves using Rev. Henry Askerneese as the first pastor of the colored Damascus Baptist Church until 1881. During the meantime, a frame edifice was erected to replace the use of the temporary brush arbor. Elder W. S. Pleasant was pastor from 1881 to 1900, when the church changed to the new denomination "Holiness" Church. Elder W. S. Pleasant continued his pastorate of the changed denomination from 1900-21, the picture (p. 138) showing the church membership in front of the church was taken in 1945.

In 1921, Rev. Louis J. Brunson succeeded Rev. W. S. Pleasant as pastor and remained pastor until Jan. 27, 1931

On Jan. 27, 1931, the third pastor of the new denominational church, Rev. Geo. A. Thomas, was elected.

The Damascus Church of Christ Holiness, U.S.A. broadcasts each First Sunday at 7:00 A. M. over station WMDC.

The Sunday School, C. W. W., and youth programs are functioning in the church. These auxiliaries help to demonstrate the realities of the joy of life when lived according to the will of God. The happy ushers shown here perform a part of the services that the church gives to its members and communion.

Plans have been projected to erect a new edifice in the near future.

Some of the first members of the church were Rev. and Sister W. S. Pleasant, Brother Wm. Handy, Sister T. J. Handy, Sister Lula Tannly, Sister Vinly Parker, and Sister Estell Jefferson.

This special call was made to pastors and deacons to meet at Terry, Miss.

"In the name of the Most High God, we beg that every pastor and deacon composing the Jackson Baptist Association will meet at Collis Hill Baptist Church, Terry, Miss. at 10:00 A.M., Friday October 26, 1900, for the purpose of prayerfully considering what we shall do about the unchristian way our church affairs are carried on by those who are leaders, and who will not allow us to consider it in the association. Let every one come who believes that the "Word of God is right." (Ps.3:4) Let everyone come who believes that "the man shall not live by bread alone, but by every word that proceedeth out of the mouth of God." (Matt. 4:4) Let every one come who believes in "one God, one faith, and one baptism." (Eph. 4:5) Come praying that the Lord's will be done.

Yours in the name of Jesus Christ;

ELDERS

W. J. Johnson	H. Diggs	F. S. Sheriff
R. Thompson	A. Brown	T. Sanders
W. S. Pleasant	E. M. Bennett	H. Dees
R. B. Brown	S. A. Jordan	E. J. Lucas

Damascus Church of Christ Holiness

Usher Board
Damascus Church of Christ

Collis Hill Baptist Church
Terry Mississippi

138

The special called meeting met at the time and place so designated, and functioned in accordance with the call. "Now we command you brethren, in the name of our Lord Jesus Christ, *That ye withdraw* yourselves from every brother that walketh disorderly, and not after the tradition which he revealed from us" (2 Thess. 3:6)

"Therefore in obedience to the word of God, and in consideration of the fact that the association will not desist but persistently insist upon their disorderly way, we hereby in the name of Christ Jesus, renounce our allegiance to the Jackson Baptist Association to lift up the standard of Christ among his people, as baptized believers in Christ.

"We, therefore, now and hereby resolve ourselves into an Association of baptized believers in Christ to be known as 'Christ's Association of Mississippi', of baptized believers, and that our cause for so doing, as here set forth, be submitted to the people at large for their prayerful consideration of the justice of our cause."

"We also commend that the churches, all baptized believers in Christ, be and are called to meet and permanently organize this association, Friday Dec. 28, 1900, at China Grove church at Miles Station, Miss.

Respectfully Submitted
W. S. Pleasant, Committee chairman
J. H. Green, Committee secretary

R. Thompson	F. S. Sheriff
S. B. Weekley	Frank Sutton
Spencer Parker	P. M. Wiggins
T. A. Fields	S. A. Jordan
W. J. Johnson	

Brother Charles Kendrick was the delegate from the Collis Hill Baptist Church to the Dec. 28, 1900 meeting at the China Grove Church, Miles Station, Miss., and was chairman of the committee on permanent organization.

NOTE: The above extracts were taken from the minutes of the meeting indicated. Since this date the name of the association and the name of the denomination have undergone changes.

The Collis Hill Church of Christ Holiness, U.S.A. had its beginning with the new movement in December 1900.

The church edifice was rebuilt in 1931, and was remodeled at a later date.

Elder C. P. Jones may be considered as the first pastor of the new Church. Some of the pastors since then were Reverends L. J. Brunson, G. A. Thomas, M. W. Wilson, W. A. Thurmond, J. T. Woodson, E. N. Haggans, J. B. Burley, and G. A. Thomas at present time, 1965.

Among the earlier families of the church were the Kendricks, Binghams, Fields, and Graysons.

The pictures shown here were taken in 1964 about 60 years after the church was established, but show some of the children, grand children, and great grand children of those original families. The community was fairly well settled in the beginning and has remained a community of responsible citizens.

The church broadcasts each Sunday at 7:00 A.M. over station WMDC.

Midway Church of Christ (Holiness) Folsom, La. 1902.

Elder J. E. Burris, of Franklinton, La. was invited by Brother Monroe Andrews to come and take charge of a meeting being held under a turpentine shed here. Elder Burris came, and held meetings first in vacant houses then in private homes. Also services were held under a brush arbor and in the store of a white man who gave an old house for a church building. The members brought additional lumber and an acre of land on which they built the first Holiness Church in this community and after drifting about a year, named the church *Midway*.

Elder Burris organized the church the previous year, 1909, under the brush arbor with ten members. Among these were *Brother Monroe Andrews, Deacon A. J. Garrett,* and *Brother and Sister Cyprion*. Pastor Burris built the second church on the highway in 1904 and was privileged to serve here until he left this life in 1946.

During these early years the pioneers searched the scriptures and trusted the Lord more fully in the affairs of their lives. Brother Charlie Weary's daughter had been sick for some time and was now dying-cold up to her knees and her eyes set in death. Her father spread the word; the saints came and prayed. In about 15 minutes the girl revived and went to church that day, Today, May, 1957 she is a living testimony to the miracle wrought in her case.

Assistant pastor Jule Richard's small daughter (3 or 4 years old) had never walked; her limbs were weak. One Sunday after

A Choral Group
Collis Hill Church 1950

Collis Hill Church—Pastor—
Officers—Choir: Terry, Miss. 1964

First Church of Christ, Holiness, U.S.A.
Brownsville, Tenn.

141

preaching her mother brought her to the altar and Pastor Burris prayed for her. She soon started walking, and 20 years later she is a healthy mother of children.

It was about 1925 or 1926 that National Missionary Miss Amy Gordon, visiting in this community, set up the C. W. W. organization in this church. Later the H. Y. P. U. was organized, both during the administration of the first pastor.

Pastors in order: Elders J. E. Burris, E. Davis, A. J. Allen, and W. H. Hollins, present minister, 1957.

First Church of Christ (Holiness) U.S.A., Brownsville, Tennessee

About 60 years ago the First Church of Christ (Holiness) U.S.A., located on East Jefferson Street, Brownsville, Tennessee, was founded under the administration of Rev. J. C. Copeland, and the following Founding Fathers; Brother George Morton, Brother Men Shaw, Brother Charlie Bradford, Brother Andrew Loving, Brother Peter Wiley, and Brother George Hill, on the 14th day of December, 1903. The church still remains on the same site, and is pastored by the Elder C. H. Harris. Sister Edna Mae Willis, Clerk.

The Tabernacle Church of Christ—Lucas, Miss.

As reported by the members W. L. Sutton, Mary Hall, E. L. Hall, L. D. Armstrong, V. T. Sutton and Pastor John Vance.

In the early days of the movement Elder C. P. Jones came to Lucas, an all Negro town in south-east Mississippi, to attend a Baptist Association and preach standing on a wagon as pulpit. Many were turned out of the church as a result of an upstir made by some of the members. Among those turned out were Brother and Sister Sutton and their family.

Elder Ely J. Lucas came from Arkansas and preached in private homes for about one year. At a meeting in the home of a Mr. Henry White, somebody shot into the house but nobody was hurt. The band later held services in the schoolhouse until the door was closed against them. There upon they built a little church and named it the Lucas Tabernacle Church of Christ. Elder Lucas left to go to Africa. Some time after he left Elder John Vance came and held services and was assisted by "Father" W. S. Pleasant and one of the Weekley brothers. Sisters A. R. L. Lucas, Annie Armstrong and Viola Lee organized the Sisters work, perhaps about 1907. These sisters walked ten miles and took the

142

message of the Word of Life to the regions boyond where others were hungering for a closer walk with God.

Elder John Vance Reports: One morning while I was plowing in the field I was impressed to go to Lucas and preach. I had never been to Lucas. I quit plowing and rode in my buggy to Hazlehurst, a 21 mile distance, and on the J. C. train to Brookhaven thence to Monticello in a log train. Finding Pearl River one mile out of its banks a ferry man rowed me across to his home, from whence I walked a distance of ten miles to Silver Creek and two miles further to the home of Brother Tom J. Hardy. Brother Hardy who was also plowing in his field, later became one of our most capable pastors. When I told him that the Lord sent me to the church at Lucas he replied that the church had been fasting and praying for the Lord to send them a pastor, and that if the Lord sent me I was the one to pastor them.

The church had been left orphan by its founder and former pastor, Elder J. Lucas, for whose family the town was named. Elder Lucas was one of our foreign missionaries and among our first missionaries to Liberia, West Africa. I accepted that pastorate and served the church nearly 18 years. During this time, perhaps about 1906, the first church was burned down allegedly by a man incensed by the pastor's denunciations against remarriage of a divorced person having a living husband or wife. This man threatened to whip the pastor with a rawhide whip he used in driving a 3-yoke ox team. Often when he didn't come to church and disturbed the services he sent his two sons who would put out the lights, etc.. But the way of the transgressor is hard.

So the church fasted and prayed. "Vengeance is mine: I will repay saith the Lord."

Then one day when the desperate man left his team harnessed at his syrup making and went into the woods one of his nephews shot him to death. We rebuilt where the church now stands.

The pastors have been as follows: Rev. Eli J. Lucas; Rev. John Vance; Rev. Cabel D. Ratliff; Rev. Fredrick Ezekiel Williams; Rev. S. T. Cobbins; Rev. Willie A. Thurmond; Rev. Joe D. King; and Rev. W. H. Hillins.

Christ Temple Church, Tougaloo, Miss.

The Christ Temple Church of Tougaloo, Miss., was founded in 1901, in the Tougaloo College community.

The young Rev. William A. Washington seems to have been the

first pastor. The succeeding pastors have been Rev. H. Blackman, Rev. G. A. Thomas, Rev. W. A. Nolley, Rev. J. E. Graham, Rev. Willie Kendrick.

Some of the first members were Brother and Sister Pat Smith, Brother and Sister Vinson and family, Brother and Sister Dawson, Brother Scot Wilson, Sister Slaughter, Sister Gladys Wilson, and Sister Monan.

The church has a good location in an enlightened community.

Mt. Bethel Church of Christ (Holiness) U.S.A.
Jackson, Miss.

Mt. Bethel Church was organized in the home of Brother Andrew and Sister Henrietta Young in 1902. It was the National Convention of the Church of God. on August 21-27, 1922 at Montgomery, Ala. that the name was changed to the Church of Christ (Holiness) U.S.A.

The trustees were (1). Andrew Young, (2). Joshua Garey and (3). Ed Myles.

The first building was built under the pastorate of Rev. John Vance. His successors were Rev. John Hardy, Rev. George Thomas, Rev. M. R. McInnis, Bishop W. A. Thurmon, Rev. J. T. Woodson and Rev. J. T. Hill.

The church was rebuilt by Elder J. T. Hill in March 1953. The trustees were (1). Joshua Garey, (2) Luster Osborne and (3) Ollie Thomas.

Big Creek Church of Christ Holiness, U.S.A.
Sister Rachel Dees, Reporter

Elder C. P. Jones preached at Big Creek Baptist Church near Jackson, Mississippi, in 1896 and 1897, trying to show the people the true light of the Gospel. Some accepted some others rejected. In this community lived the Weekley brothers, Elias (E. L.) and Wash, both ministers of the Gospel.

Finally an angry mob came to Elder E. L. Weekley's home to beat the new preacher. The host stood in his door, as the angel stood in Lot's door and prevented them, declaring: "You can't come in unless you walk in over my dead body. They didn't go in. After the truth spread and many persons came into the knowledge of Bible religion, the band was put out of the Baptist Church with the pastor, Elder Tom (T. M.) Sanders in 1903.

During this period of years, Sister Wash Weekley was healed of a tumor by faith and prayer—Jas. 5:14-15. A brother Willie

Christ Temple Church
Tougaloo, Mississippi

Mt. Bethel Church of Christ, Holiness, U.S.A.
So. Gallatin St., Jackson, Mississippi

145

Johnson of the community visited in the home of a neighbor family, members of the Baptist Church, whose daughter was suffering from toothache. The daughter reported this conversation: "Do you believe in prayer?" "Yes," "If you believe in prayer, I'll pray for you. Prayer will help you." The daughter testified to the truth of his words and that he rubbed her jaw and prayed for her and stated after prayer that she would never again have a toothache nor would she ever have to go to a dentist to get her teeth pulled; that she could pull her own teeth. This she did.

The effects of that prayer lasted as long as she lived, above 60 years of age. The work goes on.

The Big Creek Church was among one of the first churches to be established. (The church had previously been a Baptist Church). The effort to establish the church was met with much opposition.

The Tabernacle at Dumas, Ark.

In Autumn of 1899 two men, J. A. Witherspoon, an influential member of the M. E. Church and John Burns, a Baptist deacon got some holiness preacher to come here and conduct some preaching services. Elders D. W. Welch, J. A. Jeter and A. J. Williams, C. H. Mason, J L. I. Conic and L. W. Lee and Elder Hoard were among the first. They preached in the churches and in the school house and on the street corners. (Street corners were Elder Mason's favorite parishes through the years.) To learn that Elder Mason was in town was sufficient announcement that a street meeting was on.

Sinners were converted, spiritual life was deepened in christians and interest ran high. Souls were saved. So greatly did hearts thirst for the living God that attendance seemed as large during hard, cold weather as at other times; nor did rain seem to hinder the gathering. Meantime, the enemy of all righteousness was not idle.

Dissension was manifested where it was usually found. One of the greatest showers of blessings known to this compiler fell one night during a meeting in a school building in Dumas, Arkansas. Next day news spread that a minister who had started on the journey but was unable to go all the way with the Saviour, stated that he had purposed to rout the worshipers, to murder and to burn the building. But that as he and his band neared the house the earth shook and they were frightened and fled. That ended that sort of persecution. But as light shone on more and more Christians found the way to happy and victorious living through the

Spirit of Promise of whom Jesus said "He dwelleth with you and shall be in you" (Jno. 14:17) and "He shall guide you into all truth" (Jno. 16:13)

"There signs shall follow them that believe" were our Savior's words after He had conquered death, hell and the grave (Mark 16:17). This statement promise, "in My name they shall cast out devils," has been fulfilled repeatedly and variously through the years and the countries. There was in this congregation a Sister Mary Simpson, a very devout saint. One Sunday morning her baby daughter had a disturbing crying spell in the services. The mother stated that this child was cheerful and loving at home, had these outbursts only at church, and requested prayer that the Lord cast the devil out of her. The church knelt in prayer. The child became attractive, grew into a modest young woman and was a chief Bible Reader in the public services.

Two incidents might well be mentioned here: One concerning the use of tobacco, the other a physical healing. Sister Bettie Gaiter had listened to the teaching but no one could find the word "Tobacco" in the Bible. So she decided to prove the teaching either valid or invalid by this test: Anything on the end of the mantel near her front door met her view as she walked in. Right on the end of the mantel toward the door she laid her smoking pipe and tobacco, saying, "Lord, if you don't want me to smoke, you are able to take away the taste for smoking. Now if you don't take the taste away I'm going to smoke." She stated that from that moment, she had no longer a taste for tobacco.

Sister Vance and Rosa Lee Jones had studied books by moonlight. Her sight became poor, her eyes pained. She committed the matter to the Lord. He remedied the trouble. For some years, her teeth had ached and she had used remedies. One morning after the above experience, it seemed that a tooth would never quit aching. She sat before the fire somehow holding creosote and cotton instead of putting it into the tooth. Finally, it seemed as if someone kept saying to her. "Trust the Lord for one thing, trust him for another." The thought deepened; faith entered. Into the fire went the creosote and away went all other medical remedies that she found about the house, the tooth ceased ahcing. This is how Sister Vance was led into the faith of Divine healing without medical aid.

Christ Temple Church
McComb, Mississippi

The Christ Temple Church in McComb, Miss. was organized in 1898. This was one of the first churches organized in the beginning of the movement. The church is valued at $12,000 with about 50 members.

The list of former pastors follows:

Rev. A. J. Scarborough   Rev. E. N. Haggins
Rev. L. J. Brunson   Rev. F. A. Boyd
Bishop W. A. Thurmond   Bishop A. J. Torrey
Rev. W. A. Nolley   Rev. Maurice D. Bingham

Rev. Maurice Bingham

Pastor of the Christ Temple Church in McComb. He formerly pastored the church at Hattiesburg, Miss. He also was a former teacher at C. M. & I. College.

Christ Temple
Memphis, Tennessee

In 1899, Brothers Will, Nathaniel and Sister Laura Stuart taught Holiness at Whitehaven, Tennessee, at the home of Brother and Sister Sam Davis at which time Brother Sam and Hannah Davis were saved under Brother Robert Booker and Brother Sanders.

Later, the mission moved to the old Hammon Taylor school under the leadership of Brother D. W. Welch. Brother R. J. Davis was saved under him in 1899.

This mission went down and in 1903, Brother C. H. Mason built a church on South Wellington Street. Then all the Saints from the mission went to the church on Wellington Street. We carried on with Brother Mason until 1906.

Brother C. P. Jones and Brother C. H. Mason had many discussions on this matter of "Tongues." They could not work together any longer. Brother Jones told the saints all that believed as Brother Mason did and wanted to follow him, go with him. But those that believed as he did, to stay with him.

The church went to court to try to get the building on Wellington Street. The court here decreed in favor of the church, but Brother C. P. Jones could not be there on Sunday, so he gave the church up. Brother C. H. Mason appealed to the higher court in Jackson, Tennessee. This court gave the building back to Brother C. H. Mason.

149

At this time, about 1907, the church had to get a new name in order to get the church chartered.

In about 1915, we held service at Brother Franklin's church on Mississippi Avenue and Brother C. P. Jones was pastor. Brother Jones could not be there on Sunday, so he gave the church up. Elder Daniel J. Washington was appointed pastor. The Church was unable to support a minister and Elder Washington had to resign.

Finally, a lot was found at Iowa and Lauderdale. The Church went on for a while paying notes as agreed, but because of some disagreement, the church went to court again and lost. Brother S. L. Jordan got a lawyer to re-open the case and the church compromised for about $250. Before the church left Iowa and Lauderdale Street, it called Brother Freeman as pastor of the church. Elder I. L. Jordan was the next pastor. He advanced money to complete the church, but because of some dissatisfaction between the group and Elder I. L. Jordan, he was forced out of the church building. Later, the church bought a lot at the present address 907 S. Lauderdale Street. Elder S. L. Jordan remained the pastor. At this time, Bishop J. L. I. Conic sent Elder J. Y. Herd to oversee the church. Elder Mosby, Brother George King, Elder B. A. Jordan, Elder L. D. Berry were very active members. Later, Elder J. L. I. Conic was sent as pastor. Following him, Bishop W. M. Mitchell came but stayed only a short time. The Lord sent Elder J. L. I. Conic back to us. He then had to leave and he sent his son, Elder M. R. Conic as pastor. He was a great help to us. He served us until March 1939 when he left to take a job in Washington, D. C. Then came one of our own young men Elder L. P. Johnson, a dynamic preacher. After him came, Elder M. F. Brown. Elder O. A. Askerneese then came to the church Oct. 15, 1957. He is responsible for the present church building.

After Elder Askerneese left came Elder C. L. Carhee. In October 6, 1960 Elder James C. Stuart, Jr., from Kansas City, Kansas was transferred here by Bishop M. R. Conic. We thank God for his leading us up to now and under his administration progress is being made spiritually, materially; and financially. The Church property is valued as $40,000.00 and there are 110 members.

Galilee Church of Christ Holiness, U.S.A.
Hazlehurst, Mississippi

Galilee Church of Christ Holiness is located nine miles West of Hazlehurst, Mississippi, on the Hazlehurst and Port Gibson Road. In 1898, Andrew Winston sold one-half acre of land to the Baptists for a church. The Church was built because Hall Hill, the main church which is four and one-half miles West of this church was unable to accommodate its large membership of 600. The Trustees were Brothers Tom Berkley, Henry Henly and C. D. DeMyles, and Rev. John DeMyles, Pastor. This church remained a Baptist church for approximately five years. After which the members decided to change to the Holiness movement. The Trustees, Brothers Ben Austin, James Farley, Frank Rockingham, Henry Henly and E. R. Winston purchased the church and land from the Baptists for the sum of $50.00. The Church was later remodeled. Brother Austin gave enough logs to remodel the building. The Deacons came together, floored and made new seats for the church. The floor was of rough lumber and the seats were very crude shaped. The officers of this church were Brothers Ben Austin, Tom Berkley, and James Farley, Deacons: Brother E. R. Winston, Clerk; Rev. S. B. Brown, Pastor. This church served as a place to worship as well as a community school. It burned down March, 1913. A community school was later built which too served as a place to worship.

Three years later the previous church was erected. The first officers of this church were Brothers Ben Austin and S. B. Davis,

Deacons; Brother E. R. Winston, Clerk; Rev. Jodia King, Pastor. Brother Dave Smith was appointed Deacon after Brother S. B. Davis' health failed.

IN 1933, Brothers Cleo Virgil, Clarence Virgil, Timothy Winston and Willie T. Davis were ordained deacons by Rev. J. E. Bearden. Sister Lurlean Davis was Clerk. Brother Virgil who was a member of the Wilderness of Judah was appointed head Deacon because the deacons were quite young. He served until 1955. His youngest son, Brother Cleo Virgil was appointed head deacon. He passed away September 6, 1964 at the age of 98. About the same time Rev. J. E. Bearden appointed Brother D. M. Winston for a deacon.

The present edifice was begun May 9, 1963 and dedicated October 12, 1963, under the pastorate of Rev. Eddie Jones.

THE FOLLOWING MINISTERS PASTORED GALILEE CHURCH

Rev. S. B. Brown	3 years
Rev. Jodia King	3 years
Rev. Emanuel Greenfield	7 years
Rev. Sylvester Davis	3 years
Rev. Leon Beasley	1 year
Rev. George Mason	3 years
Rev. J. E. Bearden	13 years
Rev. W. H. Hollins	12 years
Rev. Eddie Jones	Present Pastor

Three of these ministers still live: Rev. J. E. Bearden, Rev. W. H. Hollins and Rev. Eddie Jones. All others have gone to be with the Lord.

The present deacons are: Brothers Cleo Virgil, Clarence Virgil, Timothy and D. M. Winston. Sister Melinda Winston, Clerk; Sister Rubye W. Anderson, Assistant Clerk; Brother Clarence Virgil, Treasurer and Rev. Eddie Jones, Pastor.

The oldest person who was among the first to be baptised at this church is Sister Carrie Singleton who is 88 years old. The first member to be funeralized from the new edifice was Sister Thelma Virgil, the wife of Brother Cleo Virgil, who passed away February 5, 1964.

PINE GROVE FIRST CHURCH OF CHRIST
Starkville, Mississippi

The Pine Grove First Church of Christ (Holiness) U.S.A. was established in the year of 1900 in a little church. The first minister to preach holiness here was the late Reverend L. A. Bell. Others are as follows: Reverend James Elliot, and the late Reverends Noah Smith, Elam Shoves and G. L. Bogan who served as pastor for 35 years until his death in the year of 1930. After him came Rev. E. N. Haggans who was elected in the year of 1950. Reverend John Roberts was elected in the year of 1951 and is still serving to this day. Elder Andrew Brown, Elder Ed Smith and Elder Green Henderson contributed great service to the church. All are deceased except Elder Andrew Brown who later joined the Church of God in Christ.

Deacons of the church have been Gus Sharp, Brother Monk Henderson, Brother Sam Sharp, and Brother Ed Smith (who later was called into the ministry) all deceased.

Presently serving as deacons of the church are Brother Ike Harris, Brother Percy Bell, Brother Finnal Jordon and Brother Tom Jones.

The Sutter Street Church of Christ Holiness, U.S.A.
Montgomery, Alabama

In July 1904, Rev. William A. Washington, of Jackson, Mississippi, came to Montgomery, Alabama, preaching 'Holiness on the streets of the city.' The first meeting as remembered by some was held on the corner of Day and Holt Street. The Street meetings were wonderful and from time to time other ministers and co-workers of the faith would come to Montgomery and help carry on the powerful fiery meetings. After a length of time, this group decided that they needed a permanent place to worship and be sheltered from the rain and cold so that the meetings could still go no.

The first occasion was on Holt Street in a building facing Grady Street. After having meetings in this building for quite awhile, the church was then organized. Rev. Washington was its first pastor. Later, the members of the church moved into a hall on Magnolia Street where the present Azell Baptist Church now stands.

With Rev. Washington as pastor and a faithful group of brothers on the deacon board, the meetings were very spirited, and fire seemed to come from on high. The membership grew fast and later a building site was purchased at 735 West Sutter Street for a Church. Soon the first building, a frame one, went up for service. Everyone was happy, as the meetings continued, the church membership also grew.

Then under the leadership of the second pastor, Rev. J. L. I. Conic, a brick building went up around the frame one. Different brothers would come and give a day's work or more as long as the building was being constructed. The sisters would send dinner to the working brothers in the day time. To those who worked on the building at night, the sisters would send supper. There would be singing and working at the same time praising the name of the Lord.

Some of the brothers, among the first, that helped with organizing and building of both churches were; Rev. J. L. Conic, Brother Sandy Smith, Brother Samuel Martin, Brother Frank Carson, Brother James Mills, Brother Obie Thomas, Brother James Cook, Brother Eddie Relf, Brother L. Goldsmith, Brother Anon Nickerson, Brother B. M. Draugh, Rev. Caesar Banon, Rev. Rance Allen, Rev. Wm. Mitchell and Brother L. M. Lanton.

These brothers and others with the help of friends had a part in the work and building of this church. Before the completion of the brick church around the frame one, a Kindergarten was opened with a lively group of small children with Sister Lizzie Thorn as teacher, A few years later, school was taught here from the first through the sixth grade with Miss Ethel Lee of Salem as teacher, and one co-worker later. Rev. J. L. I. Conic was pastor. The present Bishop M. R. Conic was the little Major Conic in the first grade.

Around 1912 or 1914 an organ was purchased and a choir was organized under the direction of Brother Gibson. Its first organist was Miss O. C. Taylor. From this time on different ministers pastored the church. Then there would be times when it had no pastor at all.

In 1920, Rev. W. H. Dunn, a pastor, and builder remodeled the inside of the church by building a choir room, a pastor's study, a new choir stand and a baptismal pool under the pulpit. The Church is valued at $45,000.00.

Since the church was organized in 1904, there have been twenty pastors; four of whom became Bishops. Some being ordained in the church. The ministers who have served as pastors are:

Rev. A. T. Rucker	Rev. L. P. Johnson
Rev. Frank Christian	Rev. Willie Kilgore
Rev. L. M. Relf	Rev. O. C. Burns
Rev. Sam J. Anderson	Rev. W. M. Acty

Rev. J. M. Hodges
Rev. Samuel McGee (1963-
Rev. W. A. Washington
Rev. J. L. I. Conic
Rev. Eugene Haggans
Rev. Lyons

Rev. W. M. Mitchell
Rev. Frank Williams
Rev. Hence Johnson
Rev. W. H. Dunn
Rev. W. A. Carter
Rev. H. A. Marangeopha

The Caney Creek Church of Christ (Holiness)
Jackson, Mississippi
as reported by Sister Rachel Dees

In 1901 Elder G. H. Funches was called to pastor Caney Creek Baptist Church near Jackson, Mississippi, in the earlier days of the movement. When the greater gospel light dawned upon his vision he began preaching holy living to his congregation, but his deacons and many of his members were hostile to the new preaching. In 1903 the officers and deacons told the pastor to get out and that if he didn't get out on the square he would get out by the muzzle of the gun.

The pastor advised "all who believe the word of the Lord is right come, and we will hold services under this nearby tree." The deacons drove them from that place also. They then worshiped for a while in the home of a Mr. Murray and settled finally under a brush arbor by the roadside. Here they remained until they built a new church, the Caney Creek Church of Christ in May, 1904, having been put out of the Baptist Church in April, 1903. For the dedication service Elder Wash Weekley brought the morning message and Elder John Vance, the afternoon message. The house was dedicated to the service of God *only*. From that time the work has been going on. Elder G. H. Funches pastored for seven years; Elder Wash Weekley for two years, Elder Thomas Sanders two years. Elder G. H. Funches returned and pastored until 1931.

Following Elder Funches, Elder Daniel Mitchell was elected pastor. He served faithfully for seven years. During his administration the church was repaired.

Rev. Willie Jenkins Sr. came to Caney Creek about 1941. He served for seven years.

Rev. J. T. Hill was elected. He built the church with inspiration.

A very young man and in his early ministry came to Caney Creek, the beloved Rev. Camper. He was spiritually strong and steadfast.

Rev. Eddie Jones was elected in 1955 and has been faithful ever since. His greatest desire is to save souls for the master, visit the sick and carry his corner in every respect. Thanks to the Lord for such a man. Rev. Jones has been with us for nine years.

In 1900 when Elder C. P. Jones came here and began preaching holiness, people were hungry for the Word of Life that many of them walked barefoot for miles, putting their shoes on just before reaching the place of worship; such as schoolhouses and private homes. Yet there was much opposition manifested in various ways; for some ignored the gospel as heretical. But as time went on people accepted the word as preached and taught and began to testify, shout and sing and many were healed of various ailments through his prayers, according to scriptures. These healings before the eyes of the people caused them to believe more and more in the new teaching and the Word of God as they read it for themselves.

After many decided to accept the teaching as Bible doctrine, the church was organized in the schoolhouse under the leadership of A. J. Scarborough. They were moved to a new location in 1908. Among the earliest workers from the beginning were Elder A. J. Scarborough, Elder T. C. Dyson and Brother (John) J. E. Burris, who were later ordained to the ministry and held several pastorates. These brethren fasted and prayed in their secret places and recommended prayer against every obstacle and for saving souls and for healing of bodies. Others early members were Brothers John Taylor, Eldridge Magee, James Magee, Walter Langson, William Dyson, and Almos (A.) Amacker, a pillar in the church. From the beginning of this church to the end of his earthly life it was never too hot or too cold, never too wet for A. Amacker to be at his post of duty. He was the first Sunday School superintendent and was at prayer meeting every week, among other services for the good of the church. The first choir was organized by Brother Ernest Sims. Later, Brother Willie Crain assumed leadership of the chair.

It was 1900 that a number of the brethren went up to a Baptist Association in Mississippi and testified. They were insulted and put out and ordered not to return. But they were undaunted. Stir-

The Sweet Home Church of Christ (Holiness) at Franklinton, Louisiana.

ring times were these. On their way home Elder Scarborough, the first pastor of the church for 20 years, until 1919, composed the symn "I'll Trust Him Just the Same" inspired from Job 13:15.

In a meeting in McComb, Mississippi, a man shot at Elder C. P. Jones. Out of this tragic experience, he was inspired to write, "Grace to Die," composed from Matt. 16:24-26. Read it. "Whosoever shall lose his life for my sake shall find it." Report is that after Elder Jones held meetings in homes many accepted the preaching and made confessions to the effect. Even in individual homes and while working in the fields the people would begin to sing and shout and praise God for what they had heard. Once when Elder Jones returned to Franklinton to run a ten days meeting, a tent was set up in front of the church house, for the building was too small to accommodate the crowd attending, which included whites as well as colored. Often the gatherings were so large that Elder Scarborough adopted his practice of holding "Grove Meetings"— preaching under the shade of nearby trees. After one of Elder Jones' services hard rain continued. He prayed for the rain to stop so the people could go home. The rain ceased and the sun came out. The Second Pastor, Elder H. R. McInnis, who pastored the church for thirty years from 1919 to 1949.

Among the devout women of this church were Sisters Norah Thompson, Mary (Dale) Dyson, Endia Long. These women went from house to house and even along the roadside, praying and talking and reading the scriptures to old and young and did much good. Sister Thompson was the first president of the Christian Women Willing Workers' organization here. She held that office until after she became physically disabled. Organizations now functioning in this church are the Sunday School and C. W. W. W. Standard Bearers, Sunbeams, H. Y. P. U. Ushers, Deacons, and Trustee Boards, Pastor's Aid and Sr. and Jr. Choirs. Some of these met monthly, some semi-monthly and some weekly.

The first Deacons were T. C. (Neal) Dyson, Almore Amacker, Oscar Brock, Walter Langston, Hampton, Bickham, Gean McGee, John Burris and Elridge McGee. Some additional first workers were E. McGee, J. Taylor, J. McGee, Green McGee, Wm. Dyson, Fletcher Dyson and Noah Thompson. Rev. John Sanders the third pastor served 12 years and was followed by Bishop Clifton Goodloe our present pastor. The Church was rebuilt in 1958.

The Church of Christ
Brookhaven, Miss.

Sister Mattie Hare testifies.

Elder John Vance was a real man of God—an out and out Christian gentleman. He rebuilt the church and we organized the church in my house. The Lord blessed us in that place. It seems that while I now write I can see him leaping and preaching the word and telling about the kingdom of God and its righteousness.

Now that he is gone to get his reward, may the church live on till Jesus comes.

It appears that someone had started a work there about 1903 which had run down. For Elder John Vance reported that there were six women standing when he began preaching there in 1905. They first held meetings in a vacant house owned by a Mrs. Mattie (Cotton) Hare. There they organized the church when the attendance grew too large for that house Mr. Dove Coleman opened to the band the doors of his big house. The members gave of their money, solicited help and gave rallies until they built the present church on the land given by "Granny" Milton. On the corner stone of the present church are engraved the names of Elder John Vance and a few others.

Among early members were Sisters Granny Milton, Mattie (Cotton) Hare, Belle Dixion, Missouri (Campbell) Turner, Frances Carter, Emma Gaines, Dave Coleman, Lulu Cotton, Brother Cotton, Sister Pinkie Phillip, Rev. and Sister John Vance, Brother and Sister Wells, Ann Perkins and Frankie Perkins; Brethren Willie Ford, one of first deacons and Sunday School superintendent, who served faithfully and efficiently in every department of the local.

The pastors have been Reverends Wash Weekley, John Vance, H. Blackman, and Willie Bingham, Sr.

THE SPREAD OF CHURCHES 1905-1919
Hamburg, Arkansas

The Church of Christ Holiness, U.S.A. was established in 1912 under the threats of expulsion from the city because of their religious contention. A group under the leadership of Brother Sam Harris, marched to the Mayor's office singing, "We are marching to War," and valiantly defended their stand for the cause of Christ.

The present church edifice was built in 1926 by Rev. N. S. Cann.

Data on Churches 1895-1904

Church Name and Location	Date founded	Founder or First Pastor	Succeeding Pastors	First Members
Cynthia Jackson, Miss.		D. G. Sparkman	F. E. William E. W. Butler W. Kendrick	A. Hamilton Sr.
Mt. Olive Jackson, Miss.		J. L. I. Conic	G. A. Thomas J. T. Woodson L. D. Webb	Brother and Sister E. Fizer
White Rock Jackson, Miss.		C. P. Jones	John Vance E. Owens Judge Hayes H. R. McInnis Willie Bingham A. Green	Matthew Chase S. Arcora Chase Eddie Walton Annie Walton John Wilcher Fannie Wilcher Brother and Sister Ben Watkins Brother and Sister Will Thompson
Carlton Hill on Raymond Road near Jackson	1899	F. S. Sheriff	H. R. McInnis	L. J. Jackson Sister Ford

Data on Churches 1895-1904

Church Name and Location	Date founded	Founder or First Pastor	Succeeding Pastors	First Members
First Church of Christ, Starkville, Miss., 613 Gillespie St.	1899	R. H. I. Clark	James Elliott Eli J. Lucas Wash Weekley J. L. I. Conic G. L. Bogan J. D. King J. W. Dudley H. B. Johnson E. N. Haggans	Deacon and Sister Jesse Bell Brothers A. L. and K. Bell Rev. and Sister Mose Minor Henry McCall J. P. Hardy Viney Pierce Ned Joiner Sister E. Montgomery Sister D. Lindsay Brother and Sister H. Watts Sister Maria, Margarett and Annie Murdock Brother and Sister J. Livingston Brother Conner

Data on Churches   1895-1904

Church Name and Location	Date founded	Founder or First Pastor	Succeeding Pastors	First Members
St. Peter, Wisner L. A. Holy Grove Road met in home to organize	1923	Henry Ward	Jesse Augurson Eddie Jones	The Augurson Family Sister Vinia Gilbert Penman Swazer Luke Hilliard
Christ Temple Indianola, Miss.	1900	L. W. Capshaw	Tolbert E. R. Driver J. Waddell H. Blackman Lucas John Vance W. A. Thurmond W. H. Dunn Nichols Thomas E. N. Hogans F. A. Boyd Ross W. D. Roberts	C. C. Phillips Susie Phillips L. W. Capshaw Rachel Capshaw T. Mabley Hannah Mabley J. H. Marcus Lillie Marcus Agusta Bliss

162

Data on Churches   1895-1904

Church Name and Location	Date founded	Founder or First Pastor	Succeeding Pastors	First Members
Christ Temple Greenville, Miss.	1903	J. C. Cartwright	N. Sanders W. H. Dunn J. E. Bearden J. W. Coleman W. J. Nixon L. J. Brunson W. A. Nolley W. H. Ross W. D. Roberts B. T. Jones	
Moral Groal Byram, Miss.	1902	G. H. Funches	A. Hamilton W. A. Nolley Willie Bingham	Brother and Sister Lum White Brother and Sister Will McGee Brother and Sister John Brinson Brother John Gain
Pleasant Green Canton, Miss.	1902	J. Clark	H. Blackman C. Goodloe W. Jenkins L. B. Camper J. B. Burley	

163

Data on Churches 1895-1904

Church Name and Location	Date Founded	Founder or First Pastor	Succeeding Pastors	First Members
White Oak Carpenter, Miss.	1900	W. J. Johnson	W. S. Pleasant J. D. King John Vance Charles Lynch Felix Lennis W. H. Hollins J. D. Webb	Brother and Sister Ezekiel Virgie Brother L. Williams Sister Cora Williams Sister M. Rhymes Brother J. H. Smith
St. Peter Hazlehurst, Miss.		S. Minor	H. Blackman W. A. Thurmond J. D. King John Vance A. J. Torry	

Data on Churches   1895-1904

Church Name and Location	Date Founded	Founder or First Pastor	Succeeding Pastors	First Members
The Lord's Tabernacle 809 Minter Ave. Selma, Ala. Rebuilt in 1904	1902	Wm. A. Washington	C. P. Jones Hicks J. L. I. Conic A. B. Bryant W. H. Dunn A. T. Rucker H. R. McInnis W. M. Mitchell S. J. Anderson Dave Wallace John Vance H. B. Johnson J. Kirkland Samuel Kendrick Arthur Green	Annie R. Hines A. B. Bryant Charley Cole John Jackson Hecter Jones Lucy Ford Mary Elleby Jim Reed Luetta Russell Emma Williams Jeff Lakes Elex Russell Jake Williams Phillips Braxton
Pine Green Acona, Miss.	1902	H. Blackman	Rev. Hicks	The Spurlin Family Father Randall Louis Randall Sam Randall Rev. and Sister Head

165

The pastors have been Reverends Murrel, N. S. Cann, Jesse Augurson.

Some of the first members were Brother Sam Harris, Sister Annie Hanes, (96), Brother Elex Johnson, Sister Ellen Johnson, Sister Ada Kittrell, Brother Shede Colbert, Sister Lottie Worthy-Thomas, Deacon Kelsey, Sister Amanda Brannon, Brother Mack Collins, Sister Bettie Collins, Brother Dan Gilliam, Brother Wyart Black, Sister Bettie Harris, and Brother Dave Neighbors.

Rev. Judge E. Hayes

Lilly St., Jackson, Miss.
The Second Temple Church 2916

Organized in 1911 by Rev. Judge E. Hayes. The first edifice was erected by Rev. Hayes on Brown Street.

Some of the officers then were Brother S. Thornton, Brother Will Smith, Brother Jack Ford, Sister Bettie Dorsey, and Sister Julia Hays-Cook.

Rev. George A. Thomas and Rev. Willie Kendrick pastored the church after Rev. Hayes died.

In 1958 under the pastorage of Rev. Lee P. Camper, additional property was purchased and the present edifice was erected.

Christ Temple Church of Christ (Holiness) U.S.A.
Cleveland, Mississippi

Founded by Brother Elex McClure and Brother Ben J. Simmon in private home.

The church was organized by the late Rev. Novell Sanders in 1907 in a Masonic Hall. The church edifice was erected in 1908. Reverend Sanders pastored the church from 1907 to 1927. Brother Michael Sanders was the first deacon. Some of the first members were the following:

Brother Michael Sanders and Family
Brother B. J. Simmons and family
Brother Champ Holmes and family
Brother Major Williams and family
Brother Hank Jones and family
Mother Mary Holmes and family
Brother L. K. Neal and family
Brother A. W. Adams and family
Brother John Crawford and family
Brother W. O. Sanders
Brother Alex Matthews and family
Brother I. J. Smith and family
Brother Jim Hicks and family
Sister Annie Keys
Brother C. Norm and family
Brother W. C. Holmes and family

167

The deacon board;

Brother Michael Sanders   Brother Ollie Sanders
Brother Major Williams   Brother Alex Matthews
Brother Alex McClure   Brother John Crawford
Brother B. J. Simmons   Brother Melvin Thomas
Brother George Holmes

The only charter member living now is Sister Mary Holmes. Our first revival in 1907 for one week added 40 members to the church. The church grew rapidly.

Christ Temple, the Mother of the Greenville Dist., has made history in honorable leadership and has had only 4 pastors since organized. Namely the Rev. N. Sanders, Rev. J. E. Bearden 28 years, Rev. F. A. Boyd, Rev. J. B. Burley, the present pastor.

Brother Michael Sanders

Wolfe Lake Church of Christ (Holiness)
Yazoo City, Mississippi

Christ Temple Church of Christ (Holiness) U.S.A., Yazoo City, Miss. was founded in 1908 under the leadership of Rev. C. C. Carhee. In Brother Carhee's travels he wandered upon the home of Brother and Sister George Taylor, Sr. He discussed the possibility of organizing an inter-denominational prayer band, which they did. The response and success was astounding. This mixed group conducted their meetings in an abandoned hall about six miles north of Yazoo City, Miss. Then came a Rev. Eugene Hagan, who possessed an unusual talent for captivating audiences in song and in words. This combination set the community on fire and paved the ways for a brighter future.

168

The next minister, Rev. Anthony Rucker, was a carpenter and an excellent organizer, as well. In 1910 he bagan the task of organizing this group. He was really the first to organize this group as a church. His first deacons were: Brother Hilliard Jackson, George Taylor, Sr., Isiah Roots, Sr., William Buton, Charley Bunton, and Joseph Roots. Sr.

The happiest time in the lives of these early believers was the spring of 1912, when with Pastor Rucker as head carpenter, they built their first church. With approximately $125.00 they bought all lumber and materials necessary to build a reasonably large church with the exception of the shingles from a huge cypress tree donated by a white land owner.

Among the first faithful families were: Fisher Johnson, Henry Johnson, Isaac Litman Johnson, Reaver Brown, Wade Byrd, Pansie Carter and Sister Lou Love.

The pastors through the years were: Reverends C. C. Carhee, Eugene Hagan, Anthony Rucker, H. R. McInnis, J. L. I. Conic, Novel Sanders, J. E. Bearden, Benjamin Akins and Willie Jenkins, Sr.

The church was rebuilt in the late thirties and again in the spring of 1963 under the pastorate of Rev. Willie Jenkins, Sr.

Those serving presently as deacons are: Brothers Curley Wilson, Ernest White, Raymond Brown, William Trotter and Emmanuel Taylor.

Serving faithfully as trustees are Brothers Raymond Brown and Milton Byrd.

Sweet Home Church, Pelahatchie, Mississippi
by Elder John Vance

I was invited to come and preach at a sawmill commissary at Pelahatchie, Mississippi, during a noon hour in 1910. White people, informed that I was preaching a heretical doctrine, came out in great numbers with guns, intending to run me away. They came again with guns that night, where I was preaching in the community hall, and lay around on the ground.

However, after their arrival, they understood differently about my preaching. I announced that I would preach the next day in a pine thicket near the hall. They came to the thicket meeting and gave into the offering after the sermon. The amount raised was fifty dollars with which we began to build our first Holiness Church at Pelahatchie, Mississippi.

169

Often when the house was filled so that entrance through the door was impossible, the deacons and their brethren would let white women and children inside to hear the preaching, and raised the windows while their men outside stood near by and listened, attentively, to the services.

The following ministers have pastored the church: Reverends John Vance, Sears, J. D. Hardy, L. J. Jackson, and Willie Bingham.

Some of the first members were: Sister Ida Fletcher, Sister Lizzie Wilson, Sister Julia Watts, Brother Brown Fletcher, and Brother Clark Robinson.

Christ Temple Church
Los Angeles, California

Christ Temple Church was organized October 17, 1917, Elder C. P. Jones Pastor, in the home of Brother and Sister Isaiah Myles on East 23rd Street, Los Angeles, Calif. Elder C. P. Jones had conducted a tent service for Pastors of all denominations and revival for Rev. J. D. Gordon of the Tabernacle Baptist Church at 12th and Hemlock Streets. Some had accepted the truth as Elder Jones preached it, and came in with the organizing of the church.

Brother and Sister Isaiah Myles, Brother and Sister Isaiah French, Sister Lucy Dixon and Family, Brother F. P. Shaw, Brother Sweeney, Sister Julia Shakelford, Elder R. A. Garrison, Mrs. Brooks, Mr. and Mrs. Frank Harris. In a short time other Saints

170

joined us: Brother T. H. Smith, Brother Sherman Chisley, Brother W. B. Smith, Brother J. H. Young and their families. Brother W. B. Woodman and family, Sister L. D. Pruitt, Sister E. L. Graves and others.

We worshiped in different places: a store on Central Ave., between 14th and 15th Street, The Washington and Central Ave. Hall and the Y. M. C. A. on East 9th St.

On January 1918 Elder Jones married Miss Pearl Reed of the 2nd Baptist Church. The church property at 37th and Naomi Sts. was purchased in 1921. Here many other saints, coming to Los Angeles, joined with us in the work. In 1926, finding the church inadequate, our present place at 54th and Hooper Avenue was purchased. It took hard work and sacrifice to liquidate the debt. The Lord gave us a friend in Mr. Alfred Mitchell of Long Beach, Calif., who helped us greatly. Rev. George Strong came to us and was much help to the Pastor and also the church. Some improvements were made while he was with us. After many years of hard work our Pastor's health began to fail. Rev. S. J. Anderson was called as assistant pastor. During his stay we were blessed with improvements. In 1947 Elder C. L. Carhee was called to help Bishop Jones carry on the work of the church. Bishop Jones passed on to be with the Lord January 19th 1949, during the So. California Convention. The other pastors serving Christ Temple were Bishop Andrew White, Elder J. C. Smith, Bishop S. Hamilton Jr., Rev. C. P. Jones Jr., and Bishop M. R. Conic.

Deacon Board, 1965
Christ Temple Church—1965

Seated L. to R. W. Young, O. Farmer, Chm., Pastor M. R. Conic, S. Mitchell, A. Carr.

Standing: E. McDaniel, C. Juarez, H. Hopkins, W. W. Drake, H. Brown, A. Wellington, Sec. J. Robinson, J. Randall.

171

Trustee Board, 1965

Seated: Left to Right: Brother Emmett White; Bishop M. R. Conic, Pastor; Brother Garfield Tucker, Chairman.

Standing: Brother Charles Hines; Brother Douglas Williams; Brother Abe Haynes; Brother Darrell Mitchell; Brother James Hart; Brother Samuel Bingham; Brother Tony Carr.

Missing: Brother W. E. Drake.

C.W.W.W. No. 1

Front row, Left to right: Sister E. Coffin, Sister A. Haynes, Sister C. C. Carhee, Sister M. Farmer, Sister. V. Jones, President S. James, F. Johnson.

Second row; Sisters H Garden, V. Carr, A. Young, Sec'y.

Third row: Sisters B. Harper, L. Golden, E. Hightower, T. Smith, E. Moore, Z. Marbury.

Fourth row: Sisters C. V. Johnson, R. E. Mickey, E. Lee, J. M. Helton.

Fifth row: Sisters A. Hamilton, E. L. Dunn, M. McCuien, H. Bass, A. Juarez and D. M. Draugh

172

Deaconess Board, 1965

Seated, left to right: Sister I. Draugh, Sister S. Boyd, Sister S. B. Ballard.

Standing: S. T. Smith; Sister M. Farmer, Sister B. Harper, Pastor M. R. Conic, Sister M. McCuien, Chairman, Sister O. McDaniel

Women's Auxiliary 1965

Front row, left to right: Mrs. Lula Grayson, Sec'y, Mrs. Elizabeth Johnson, Financial Sec'y Mrs. Amanda Smith, Treas., Mrs. Mary Crute, Vice president, Mrs. Maude L. Conic, President.

Second row: Mrs. Mary Ann Wells, Mrs. Ruby Butler, Mrs. Emma Robinson, Mrs. Dollye Terrell, Mrs. Faye Knott.

Third row: Mrs. Elise Williams, Mrs. Gladys Parks, Mrs. Grace Willis, Mrs. Otha M. Taylor.

Fourth row: Mrs. Ruby Mitchell, Mrs. Joe Lillie Weakley, Mrs. Zulu M. Marbury, Mrs. Eva Vaughn, Mrs. Martha Rice.

Senior Choir, Christ Temple Church 1965

Front Row: Left to Right. Sisters Elizabeth Moore; Mary Wells; Anna Johnson; Ethel Hightower; Carlotta C. Randall, Organist;

Second Row: Sisters Elizabeth Johnson, Financial Secretary; Elise Williams; Ethel Moore; Secretary; Bessie Moore, Emma Robinson.

Third Row: Sisters Ruby S. Mitchell; Lora Drake; Emma Drake; Lois Jane Hamilton, Pianist.

Fourth Row: Sister Bessie Robinson; Annie Tarvin; Blanch Harper; Ethel Tucker, Treasurer.

Fifth Row: Brothers Harry Brown; Johnny Robinson, Chaplin; Hobard Hopkins, Vice President; Samuel Bingham; Garfield Tucker, Minister of Music; Douglas Williams; Tony Carr.

Youth Choir, 1965

Front row: Jerry Drake, Harry Jones, Sis Bessie Moore, Directress Ruth Moore, Vice President, Catherine Drake, Joyce Bass, Al Haper

Second row: Kathleen Moore, Synrve Drake, Lestine Drake

Third row: Gwendolyn Farmer, Sec'y J. Moore, George Jones, Pres.

Fourth row: Lloyd Moore, Frances Moore, Sister Walter Harper, II

Christ Temple Cathedral, Church of Christ (Holiness) U.S.A.
Chicago, Illinois

In the year of 1917, during World War I, there was a great
exodus of our people from the South to Chicago in search of
better economic conditions, among whom were many members
of the well established Holiness movement, founded by the late
Bishop C. P. Jones. Among the first arrivals of this group was
Brother E. T. Johnson of Hattiesburg, Miss., who began immediately in search of a group of his faith. Failing to find a group of
the Holiness Faith, he wrote to Jackson, Miss., headquarters, and
inquired if there was a mission of the faith in Chicago. He received
an answer from Rev. Wm. Knox, an assistant to Elder Jones of
the Temple of Jackson, that there was no Holiness Church in
Chicago.

On receipt of this information, Brother Johnson called together
the following persons whom he had been able to contact: Brothers
Simms, Holloway, Hines, Thomas, Sisters Holloway and Solomon.
At the home of Brother Holloway 3737 Federal St. a prayer meeting was conducted. This group prayed and fasted earnestly and
asked God for a work in Chicago.

In the fall of the year prayer was answered when Rev. C. E.
Owens came from Jackson, to work with them. He taught Bible
lessons every Tuesday night. A few weeks later the Methodist
Mission at 568 E. 35th St. opened their doors to them. They held
meetings there every Sunday at 3 o'clock in the afternoon. The

175

meeting there was a great success for the Band steadily increased in number. It was there that Christ Temple Church was organized with about 30 members. The Deacons and Trustees combined were Brothers Mack Jordan, Chairman; Walter Wright: E. T. Johnson: Moses Phillips. George Holloway, Matthew Thomas: George Hines: and Walter Moore, Treasurer. Rev. C. E. Owens was elected pastor. Among the charter members were Brother and Sister George Holloway, the families of Brothers E. T. Johnson, Moses Phillips, Matthew Thomas, Walter Wright, George Hines, Walter Moore, Jerry Johnson, and Thurmond Matthews.

They were not content with only one service a week. The greatest number of the members had children and the children were in need of spiritual training. They made an appeal to the church for more time, but the church was also struggling to better its condition and the appeal was turned down. Further up the street was another Mission at 520 E. 35th Str. which they rented. There, they organized the Christ Temple Sunday School, Brother E. T. Johnson, Superintendent, Mrs. Alice Wright, Secretary.

In the summer of 1918 the Church moved to 3243 Cottage Ave. Brother John Leggett and his family united with the Church and Brother Leggett was elected Superintendent of the Sunday School. Seeing the need of a choir, Brother McGee called together a few singers to furnish music for the services. Among these were Sisters Allan, Susie Phillips, Susie Henry, and Annie M. Hall (née Phillips) who was only ten years old, the youngest in the group.

"Blessed are they which do hunger and thirst after righteous, for they shall be filled." This scripture was fulfilled upon the arrival of Rev. Wm. Webb from Magnolia, Miss. in May 1919. Rev. Webb was invited to Chicago to conduct a 30 day revival He preached the unadulterated gospel which tore up the evil roots of the hearts of men and women causing them to stop and examine themselves. The revival was not without its effect for in October 1919 the Church elected Rev. Webb as Pastor. More souls gradually came into the fold, so much so that the need for a larger place was urgent. Accordingly, they set forth and purchased a building at 3848 Langley Ave. at a cost of $3,000. It was here that the first Christian Willing Workers was organized. Originating from a prayer band of women who met at the home of Sister Nettie Phillips. Sister J. E. Johnson was the first President. They formerly met once a week in the afternoon but at the suggestion of Sister Nettie Phillips their meeting time was changed to Tuesday

176

night and this has been their weekly meeting night up to the present time. The works of the following sisters who are all deceased shall never be forgotten: Sisters Dora Webb, Susie Jordan, Lovie Barnes, Sophie Martin, J. E. Johnson, Susie Phillips, Louise Coleman, Leanna Moore, Louise Mitchell, Rosa Chandler, and many others who have gone to be with their maker. They worked faithfully and willingly.

In 1919 Brother William L. Johnson united with the Church and became intensely interested in the welfare of the choir. In the home of Brother J. E. Johnson the Senior Choir of Christ Temple was organized with three sopranos, one alto, one tenor, and one bass. Brother W. L. Johnson was elected director and Miss Dora King, pianist. New members were so rapidly coming into the Church that the house was too small to hold them, again search was made for a larger place. The members wanted a Church this time, not a store front or a house. After a thorough search of a few months this church at 44th St. and St. Lawrence was selected, inspected, and finally purchased for $55,000 in the spring of 1927.

Several years of successful work was experienced at this place under the leadership of Rev. Webb. Early in the year of 1937 Rev. Wm. Webb relinquished his pastorate. The next pastor was the late Bishop Henry L. Carver who came to Christ Temple in the spring of 1937, In 1938 he was made Bishop and placed over the Northern Diocese. Under his pastorate the Deaconess Board and Missionaries were organized, a beautiful Wurlitzer Pipe Organ was installed and new pulpit furniture was purchased. He paid the church debt from $15,000 to $7,000. Bishop Carver will be long remembered for his sacrifices and faithful service among us. He labored untiringly until he died in March 1944.

Rev. Jesse McGarrah is due creditable mention here, having served as Pastor from March through August of 1944. He did a wonderful work in these few short months.

In August of 1944 the National Convention sent Bishop J. M. Haywood to pastor the church and preside over the Northern Diocese. Under his administration the church debt was paid off. and new lighting system was installed and a parsonage was purchased. Many souls were added to the church.

In January, 1953 the National Convention appointed Bishop M. R. Conic as pastor of the Christ Temple Church at Chicago, Illinois, and presiding Bishop of the Northern Diocese, after the former pastor, Bishop J. M. Haywood, severed his connections with the Church of Christ (Holiness) U.S.A. by written resignation, January 16th, 1953. This action was confirmed by the National Convention in August of 1953 in Detroit, Michigan.

Prior to his coming, Christ Temple Cathedral had accepted a remodeling program at a cost of approximately $93,000. A few of the major accomplishments under him were as follows: seats and book pockets, $9,300; rebuilding organ, $2,000; parsonage, $22,000; garage at parsonage, $1,100; boiler and stoker at the

Christ Temple Deacon Board—1955

Row 1—Deacon Liston Wilson, Church Treas., Deacon E. T. Johnson. Chairman, Deacon J. D. Ware. Row 2—Deacon Euel Bunton, Sec., Deacon Hugh N. May, Deacon James Smith. Row 3—Deacon Willie Taylor, Deacon Willie Little.

church, $2,800; making a grand total of $130,000. He was a young man with a heart after God, who like Solomon of old, desired God to lead him in all of his undertakings, The Lord blessed the church spiritually as well as financially. His rich sermons and seasoned Bible lessons were a source of inspiration to all. The membership grew from about 200 to approximately 350. Before leaving Chicago the church debt was reduced from $130,000 to less than $9,000.

In August, 1961, the National Convention sent Bishop O. W. McInnis, Vice President of the National Convention, to pastor the Cathedral Church of Chicago, Ill. and to preside over the Northern Diocese.

In November 1961, he moved to Chicago with his family and began to serve as pastor of the church.

He began on a journey of his ministerial life by preaching from the depths of his soul, doing the only thing he knew best—to

Trustee Board—1955

179

preach God's word to men and women in all walks of life. Through his dynamic and soul-saving messages, approximately 100 were added to the church.

Under his leadership, the church department has raised approximately $85,000. One of the most outstanding achievements of his pastorate was the building at 548-50 East 44th Street that was purchased for $16,000. We are happy to report that it is paid for in full. This building is to be converted into an educational center which is very much needed in Chicago. He has helped the church in making improvements in the property and has served faithfully and untiringly.

Pastors

Rev. C. E. Owens, 1917-19
Rev. Wm. Webb, 1919-37
Bishop Henry L. Carver, 1937-44
Rev. Jesse McGarrah, Mar-Aug, 1944

Bishop Jacob M. Haywood, 1944-53

Bishop M. R. Conic, 1953-61
Bishop O. W. McInnis, 1961-

Deaconess Board—1955

Row 1—Sister Dora Askerneese, Sister Nettie Phillips, Sister Florence Johnson—President, Sister Mary Burney, Sister Bessie Ware, Row 2 —Sister Bessie May, Sister Annie Taylor, Sister Onie Flakes, Sister Ernestine Smith.

Class No. 3, Christ Temple
Sunday School

I Row—From left to right seated
1. Mrs. Sarah Williams, Organizer and First Teacher
2. Mrs. Gladys Moore, Teacher
3. Mrs. Frances M. Dunn
4. Mrs. Catherine Nolan
5. Mrs. Elva Cobbins
6. Mrs. Senora Jackson
7. Mr. Rainer B. Wilson, S. S.
   Supt.

II Row—Reading from left to
   right seated
1. Miss Evelyn Spruille
2. Mrs. Beulah Conic
3. Mrs. Irma Lee
4. Mrs. Madera Rice
5. Mrs. Novella Jackson
6. Mrs. Arlee Olive
7. Mrs. Julia McInnis
8. Mrs. Ellee Johnson

III Row—Left to right standing
1. Mrs. Onie Flakes
2. Mrs. Geneva McField
3. Mrs. Miss Bessie Ware
4. Mrs. Lillie Wilson

5. Mrs. Nellie Green
6. Mrs. Mildred Johnson
7. Mrs. Ruth Glaspie
8. Mrs. Amanda Rudd
9. Miss Susie B. Jones

181

The Women's Auxiliary—1955

Left to right. Row 1—Sisters Nadie White, Lois Cotton, Maude Conic, Willette McGee, Ruth Taylor.

Row 2—Sister Anoceal Conley, Brother Frank Ross, Sisters Mildred Sanders, Noble Perrell.

Row 3—Sisters Lena Baker, Mollie Hughes, Dorothy Snipes, Lurlene Moore.

Row 4—Sisters Ruby Jordan, Christola Jenkins, Carrie Peters, Ruth Glaspie.

Row 5—Sisters Ardella Robinson, Bettie Neal, Susie B. Jones.

E. T. Johnson, Chairman-Emeritus Deacon Board
Walter Moore, Chairman Trustee Board

The pair has worked together through the years to safely steer the ship of state of the Christ Temple Church 552 E. 44th Street, Chicago 53, Illinois.

Christian Women Willing Workers—1955

Left to right. Row 1—Sisters Dora Askerneese, Catherine Nolan, Jessie Mae Phillips (President), Eddie Mae Taylor, Ella M. Johnson (Secretary).
Row 2—Sisters Frances M. Dunn, Nettie Phillips, Mary Burney, Bessie Ware, Novella L. Jackson.
Row 3—Sisters N. Williams, Gladys Moore, Mary Lee, P. Ross.
Row 4—Sisters Senora Jackson, W. Wilson Sara Williams, Myrabell **Baker.**
Standing—Sister D. L. Fields.

Sunday School Officers—1955

Left to right. Row 1—Brother Rainer Wilson, Mrs. Synolve Flakes-Moore, Supt. Hugh N. May, Miss Mildred Jones, Mrs. Nadie White.
Row 2—Mrs. Bessie May, Mrs. Myra Bell Baker, Mrs. Sarah Williams, Rev. A. J. Oliver (Associate Pastor), Brother Willie Little.
Row 3—Miss Mollie Hughes, Mrs. Ruth Glaspie, Mrs. Christola Jenkins.

Deacon Elliot Talmas Johnson
Charter Member, Christ Temple Church, Chicago, Illinois
Chairman-Emeritus of Deacon Board

184

Elliot Talmas Johnson was born November 23, 1892 in Bolden, Mississippi, the thirteenth child of Arthur and Sarah Johnson. When he was five years old, he was taken by his parents to live in Rankin, Mississippi. His father was a blacksmith by trade.

Elliot's father died when he was six years old leaving his mother with great responsibility trying to finish paying for a home site and rearing her children. At the age of seven years, he decided he wanted to become a Christian, and was baptized by the late Bishop C. P. Jones, Sr. At the age of nine, he was taken from school to help support his mother. In 1905, his mother died and he was left alone.

In 1911, he was ordained a deacon by Rev. S. T. Cobbins and others. In this office, he has proven faithful. In 1918, he was married to Miss Elizabeth Hines, a God-fearing woman, and to this union four children were born. In 1917, he was impressed to move to Chicago seeking better wages. In this, he was successful. Having become satisfactorily situated, he began to look for a church home. He visited many missions and churches, and finding none of his faith, he wrote to the Headquarters in Jackson, Mississippi, and was informed there was none. This prompted him to begin a prayer meeting and Bible study in the home of Brother George Holloway, who was a kind and faithful servant of God. Aiding him were Brothers E. Sims, Matthew Thomas, George Hines, Sister Holloway and Brother and Sister Solomon. This group fasted and prayed and asked God for a work in Chicago. Out of the prayer meeting grew Christ Temple Cathedral, 552 East 44th Street.

Brother Walter Moore

About 1890 Walter Moore, the son of the late Henry Moore, was born in Jackson, Mississippi.

At the age of eight years he became helpful around the church and parsonage, especially running errands and doing chores for Elder C. P. Jones.

He was a charter member of the mother church at Jackson.

He moved to Chicago and participated in establishing the Christ Temple Church here. He was a charter member, a member of the first trustee board and the first treasurer. He has been with the

Rev. C. E. Owens

Brother Walter Moore

Sister Julia McInnis

Rev. William Webb

church continuously since the church was organized 48 years ago in 1917. He, like Deacon E. T. Johnson, has worked with each pastor of the church.

The indications are that every person who has ever been a member of the Christ Temple Church knew Brother Walter Moore.

As chairman of the trustee board for more than 30 years, he has directed much of the business affairs of the church.

He is a member of the National Education-Trustee Board, and Treasurer of the National Convention.

Sister Julia McInnis

Sister Julia McInnis, born in Carpenter, Mississippi, attended Chapel Hill Baptist Church, during the early years of her life. She received her academic education at Utica Institute, Utica, Mississippi and Lanier High School at Jackson, Mississippi.

Following her marriage to Bishop O. W. McInnis of the Christ Temple Church, she became a member of the Holiness Church. A family of six children blessed this union.

Throughout the years of Bishop McInnis' many pastorates, Sister McInnis, in her quiet, unassuming manner, worked faithfully, cooperatively and effectively with the women's department and with the primary children in the local district, diocese, and national churches.

Rev. C. E. Owens

Rev. C. E. Owens, the first pastor of Christ Temple Church, was reared in Hattiesburg, Mississippi. When a student at C. M.. and I. College, he was observed to be steadfast in his religious contentions. It took a "C. E. Owens" to make a break through in establishing a church where he pastored for two years; and then pastored the church in St. Louis, Missouri.

Rev. William Webb

The late Rev. William Webb, the second pastor of Christ Temple Church in Chicago, was born in Magnolia, Mississippi. He grew up and was converted to the doctrine of the Church of Christ Holiness, U.S.A. at Fernwood, Miss. under Elders W. S. Pleasant and Dr. C. P. Jones, Sr.

Shortly after his conversions, he was called to the ministry. He was ordained by Elders W. J. Pleasant and W. J. Johnson to take care of the church at Fernwood. Later, he started a church at Magnolia. His life as a minister was one of fruitfulness and

187

service for the Lord and Saviour.

He built four churches and pastored six.

In May, 1919, he went to Chicago on a vacation trip. While there, Pastor C. E. Owens asked him to conduct a revival for the church, and forty members were added to the church. In October of the same year, the church called him back to Chicago to take charge of the church as pastor, and he remained as such until January 1937.

During the time Elder Webb was pastor, the church moved from 3243 Cottage Grove to 3848 Langley Avenue (at a cost of $9,000). In 1927, the church moved into the $55,000 church at 552 East 44th St. Elder Webb led the church to success during this period.

JONES TEMPLE—CHICAGO

During 1926, Christ Temple Church at Chicago, Illinois, found within its ranks those saints who desired to establish a second church and seek another place of worship.

Approximately one hundred twenty members were involved including the following and their families: Brother L. F. Dunn, Brother Walter Wright, Brother Walter Moore, Brother W. L. Johnson, Brother Anderson, Brother Washington, Brother F.F. Rudd, Brother Walter Pleasant, Brother P. McField, Brother R. J. Burgess and many others.

To accomplish this end and save this remnant, General Overseer C. P. Jones ordered Overseer J. L. I. Conic to come to Chicago to establish another congregation. It fell to Elder Conic's lot to become the first pastor. This group purchased a building at 43rd Street and Champlain Avenue.

In 1930, Elder W. H. Dunn of Norfolk, Va., succeeded Elder Conic as pastor. During Elder Dunn's administration, the name of the church was changed from Jones Temple to First Church.

After three years of service Elder Dunn returned to Norfolk. He was followed by Elder Conic for a very short period. Elder L. M. Relf was transferred from Indianapolis to First Church where he remained until 1936 when the two congregations were re-united at Christ Temple Church at 44th and St. Lawrence under the pastorate of Elder Wm. Webb.

Sister Ella James

Sister Ella M. James was the niece of Brother James Brewer of Searcy, Arkansas, and the wife of Trustee O. H. James, Christ

Brother Hiram Wright, Sr.   Sister Ella James

Temple, Chicago, Illinois. She was a devout Christian and was one of the first to introduce the work of Child Evangelism in the Christ Temple Church, Chicago, Illinois. In 1949, with the aid of Moody Bible Institute, she began a Bible Class in her home, with a group of children, ages 5-12. Her last meeting was held the third Friday in December, 1951. She passed from this life January 9, 1952: leaving her work as a memorial.

Deacon Hiram Wright, Sr.

Among the early members of the Mother Church at Jackson was a devout Deacon, Hiram Wright. A Charter member, he and his wife, Sister Fannie Wright served faithfully under Pastor C. P. Jones. He was the father of Walter S. Wright Sr., Hiram Wright Jr., and Sister Mary E. Owens.

Mrs. Fannie Mae McFerren

Mrs. Fannie Mae McFerren is the granddaughter of Deacon Hiram Wright—one of the first deacons of Christ Temple, the Mother Church, Jackson, Miss., and the niece of Mrs. Mary Wright Owens, the widow of Rev. C. E. Owens, the first pastor of Christ Temple Church, Chicago, Illinois.

Mrs. Fannie Mae McFerren   Rev. Alonzo J. Olive
1955

Mrs. McFerren is a graduate of Chicago-Land Laboratory School of Leadership Education, Naperville, Illinois. She studied at Moody Bible Institute. She was general superintendent of Coppin A.M.E. Church School.

The Christ Temple Church, Chicago, Illinois, was very grateful to Mrs. McFerren for her most helpful service to the Child Evangelism Program carried on at the Christ Temple Church. She became the motivating leadership spirit in the program.

Rev. Alonzo J. Olive

Rev. Alonzo J. Olive of Chicago, Illinois, pastor of Bethel Church of Christ (Holiness), U.S.A. and former Associate Minister of Christ Temple Cathedral Church of Christ Holiness, U.S.A.

Rev. Tom C. Toliver

Rev. Tom C. Toliver of Chicago, Illinois, works with the Bethel Church, Chicago, Illinois. He is known for his remarkable memory of the Scriptures, and can quote the book, chapter and verse with exceeding clearness.

Rev. Tom C. Toliver
Bethel Church of Christ

Bethel Church of Christ Holiness, 1442 South Pulaski Road, Chicago, Illinois, was organized in September, 1954. Rev. O. C. Burns, Pastor; Rev. Joseph Allen, Co-Pastor; Rev. Willie Osborne, Assistant. The membership group picture was taken in 1955. Rev. A. J. Olive is the present pastor. Rev. Tom C. Toliver, Associate Minister.

Brother John Askerneese

Brother John Askerneese was born September 27, 1876 at Hazlehurst, Mississippi. He was converted under W. S. Pleasant of Hazlehurst. He and his family moved to Glendora, Miss., in 1913. Finding no Holiness Church there, he started a prayer band and Sunday School in his home. After the group became too large, he asked Rev. Smith Brown to come in and organize a church. The church was organized in his home. After it grew too large for the house, he went to the land owner and asked him to build a church for the group. This the man did and the church was named Pilgrim Rest Holiness Church. He was a deacon in this church until 1918 when he and his family moved to Lambert, Miss.

There he found no Holiness Church and again he started a prayer band and Sunday School in his home. This time the group purchased a tent and rented a lot on which to erect it. He was deacon of this church until 1922 when he left for Chicago. There he joined Christ Temple and was made a deacon where he worked as such until his death on May 7, 1941.

191

Third Temple Church
1405 Morehouse St.
Jackson, Mississippi

In 1913 a group of inspired women started a prayer meeting in Washington Addition, a sub-division of Jackson, Mississippi. They found they needed a shepherd for their flock. This band of saints called the Rev. H. R. McInnis as their minister and leader. In seeking for a place to worship, the home of Mr. Moses Phillips was opened to them for their accommodation. In February of 1913 this band was organized into a church by Rev. McInnis. When the growth of the church became too large for the home of Mr. Phillips, the congregation, being unable to purchase a building at that time, used a tent for the time being.

The church was organized with the following persons as charter members: Brother and Sister Moses Phillips, Brother and Sister John Leggett, Brother and Sister Joseph Harding, Brother Lennie Wright, Sisters Sidney Austin, Mary Boyd, Annie Harding and Nila Campbell. Others who came later were Rev. and Sister Jacob Nichols, Rev. George Walker, Brother Charlie Lee, Sisters Annie Nelson, Mamie Haywood, E. Hayes and Caldwell. Many of these have gone to be with the Lord.

When this congregation was ready to build, a building site was purchased from Mr. Charlie Henry at the corner of Dalton and Barrett Streets for the sum of sixty dollars. When enough funds had been raised the church hired Mr. Robert Dorsey to build the first edifice of the Third Temple Church of Christ (Holiness) U.S.A., at a cost of four hundred dollars.

It was pastored by Elder H. R. McInnis, Elder F. E. Williams and Bishop E. W. Butler. In 1928 the frame building was condemned on the corner of Dalton and Barrett Streets, and Third Temple Church decided to buy the Evening Light Church on Morehouse Street for $14,000. The Rev. George Thomas was assigned as pastor, and served for a number of years. Rev. Joe King was elected as pastor and served until his death. Rev. L. J. Brunson was elected as pastor and served for a short time. Elder Jesse McGarrah was elected pastor and served about four years. Elder J. B. Burley was elected as pastor and served about nine years.

The First Temple Church of Christ (Holiness) was under construction and Bishop David McPherson pastored both churches until their church was rebuilt. Rev. J. E. Bearden was elected as

192

pastor and has served more than four years. As of now he is still pastor. The church property is evaluated at $40,000 and has a membership of about 150.

Third Temple Church of Christ (Holiness) U.S.A.
Jackson, Miss.

Shown in this group along with the Pastor, Rev. J. E. Bearden of Third Temple Church of Christ (Holiness) are reading from left to right, front row: Deacon Joshua Horton, Deacon Andrew Johnson, Deacon Jerome Nelson, Pastor Bearden, Deacon Arthur Pepper, Deacon Robert Vaughns and Deacon James Ward. Back row: Rev. Willie Bingham, Sister Emma Carpenter, Sister Sidney Austin, age 91, oldest living member and one of the organizers of Third Temple Church, Sister Naomi Holloway, Church Building Fund Worker and Rev. D. L. Dyson.

Church of Christ (Holiness) U.S.A.
St. Louis, Missouri

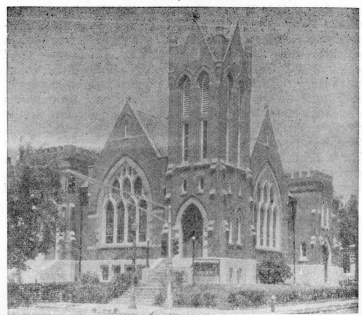

During the Convocation of 1916 held at Jackson, Mississippi, the late Bishop C. P. Jones related how ripe the harvest fields were in the North, and how few reapers were available. He expressed the hope that more laborers would heed the call. The pastor at Mt. Olive, the late Elder Enoch Thomas, decided to heed this call to help spread the Gospel. He discussed the matter with his congregation of 10 families, and it was agreed that he should go to St. Louis, Missouri, and that 3 other families would join him. In February, 1917, Elder Thomas, his wife, Mary and children, Charity, Robert Lee and Evelyn arrived in St. Louis, taking up residence at 3029 Semple Avenue. Deacon Marshall Ellison, his wife, Lily and children, Minnie, James, Abraham, and Virginia came in March; Brother Lewis McKinnis, his wife, Ella, and daughters Sally and Elizabeth joined the group in April: Brother Stafford Newsome, Virginia Belle, his wife, and their children, Honor, Virginia and Ceetee arrived in May. All these families found homes in the 3000 block of Semple Avenue. This group used several temporary places of worship, including a Baptist Church nearby on Semple Avenue and a mission conducted by Brother Charles Thomas at 5467 St. Louis Avenue, Bishop Jones had told Elder Thomas of a mission conducted by Rev. Willie Stuart and his brother, Rev. James Stuart, Sr. We communed with them for a period of time, but later sought a location of our own.

The search for a suitable place of worship led us to a house at 4126a Finney Avenue, which was rented for $8.00 per month, where services were held in one room. Thus, on September 30, 1917, the Church of Christ (Holiness), at St. Louis was organized. Later, in the year, by the help of God, a lady proprietor of a flower shop at 4144 Finney quit business, and offered the premises to Elder Thomas. He being a carpenter by trade, erected a rostrum in the largest room and the 4 families worshipped there. In short time, many souls were added. Elder O. C. Burns assisted the Pastor and contributed much to the growth of the group. During this period Elder Park McField and his family united with us; "Father" Calhoun, a teacher of children, came with us from the mission of St. Louis Avenue and became our first Sunday School teacher; Brother Allen Mosley, his wife, Lula and daughter, Clara, joined us. (Sister Clara Mosley was our first organist,) Elder L. E. Chavrias, Elder Jackson and Brother J. A. Irving also joined us. When Rev. Thomas was called to a church in Virginia, Elder Jackson succeeded him. By this time, our little place could no longer hold us comfortably, so we sought larger quarters. The Church moved to a more suitable place on the Hodiamont Line near Sarah Street. There, under our new Pastor, Elder Jackson, we continued our services.

Two members who voted against moving, Deacon Calhoun and Elder Chavrias, re-rented the residence that the congregation had vacated and resumed services there. In time, Rev. A. J. Rucker came to the city, and was asked to preach for them. He readily agreed to do so. Many members of the main body, being hungry for real Gospel Truth, returned to the old place, solely to be under the ministry of Elder Rucker. Those who felt they could live and grow under the ministry of Rev. Jackson, remained. Thus, we were divided. The group, under the leadership of Elder Rucker, took "Deep root," and began to work with amazing zeal and enthusiasm. The part of the congregation that remained with Elder Jackson bought a little residence on Fairfax Avenue for a place of worship. Thus, it seemed, we were hopelessly divided. But the Lord impressed and inspired Bishop J. A. Jeter to come to the city and work for our re-union. And so, after a series of lessons and sermons, special lectures or exhortations, he succeeded in bringing us together again. This breach was so completely closed that the congregation went ahead with unbroken solidarity. It was an occasion of great rejoicing when these bodies re-united.

In time, our growth made another re-location necessary. Elder Rucker negotiated to purchase a church at 4200 Finney Avenue and the Officers were successful in making arrangements for the purchase of the property and the fast growing little group cheerfully made the necessary financial sacrifices.

After the purchase of Mt. Olivet Chapel, there was steady growth in membership. Elder Rucker resigned as pastor in 1922 and Elder McClure was appointed temporary pastor. Bishop J. L. I. Conic was instrumental in getting Dr. H. L. Caver to come to St. Louis as pastor. He was received most wholeheartedly. The Church expanded numerically and financially. It must be said also, that among the members were some noble, church living workers whome God used effectively in establishing the Church. Among these were: Deacon Jesse Bell and family, Elder W. M. Ward and family, "Father Calhoun," Deacon W. H. Johnson and family, Elder O. C. Burns and wife, the Bruce family, the Wells family, the Picket families and a large number of others whose names are in the "Lamb's Book of Life."

But, one morning, those who lived in the immediate vicinity of the Church were startled to see our little church building being consumed by flames! As discouraging as this seemed, it proved to be the opening of another door to further expansion. Though out-of-doors, and worshipping here and there, the majority of the group stuck together, believing firmly that He who inspired the beginning and growth of the work, was fully able to bring victory out of apparent defeat, and help us in still greater effort. Thereafter, we made the best we could of these adverse conditions until our opportunity came for another and higher step. The insurance we carried netted us $900.00 This enabled the officers to begin arrangements for the erection of the little brick church building at 4200 Finney Avenue. Mr. Charles J. Gates, owner of Gates Funeral Home, graciously extended us the privilege to use the basement of his establishment, thereby making it possible for us to continue our services. Later, a lodge hall was rented so that we were able to meet regularly during the re-building period. On April 10, 1924, a very happy, zealous little group dedicated this little brick church at 4200 Finney, Bishop H. L. Caver, Pastor.

After we were happily settled in our new little home on Finney Avenue, the National Convention saw fit to assign Dr. Caver to the Presidency of our Boydton, Virginia, School. This proved a heavy blow to our local cause, as many members of the group could not adjust themselves to such sudden, serious changes and so were quite discouraged. A ray of hope was given to us, however, when Bishop J. L. I. Conic came to us. His ministry seemed to be healing the wounds caused by Dr. Caver's departure, when suddenly, at the Convention, he, too, was taken from us and sent to Chicago.

We were blessed, fortunately, with a young minister of our group, Rev. J. L. Brown. Rev. Brown's splendid sermons were highly beneficial to us. Also, our own good, old veteran, and Assistant Pastor, Rev. W. M. Ward, gave us timely and helpful exhortation. Eventually, Rev. Owen of Chicago, was called and served a year. The vacancy caused by his departure was filled, most of the time, by our blessed old father in the work, Dr. J. A. Jeter. We can never forget the sweetness of that fatherly administration. Undoubtedly, Dr. Jeter was clothed with Divine Love and kindness for God's people.

The mortgage on the church was paid off during his administration. He remained with us until the re-call of Dr. Caver, who resigned the presidency of Boydton College. In time Bishop Conic replaced Bishop Caver as Pastor. The coming of Bishop W. M. Mitchell, as pastor, through appointment by the National Convention, opened a new era in the history of this chuch.

In the Spring of 1938, the church building located at Pendleton Avenue and Page Boulevard was placed on the market for sale. When the suggestion was made to the congregation to purchase this edifice, many of the members thought the idea ridiculous and felt it too great a task, under our system of collecting funds, for our small group. But we must pay tribute to Bishop Conic for his prayers and encouragement that led us into this transaction, Mother Bland, who prayed and prodded the men to act, and the Trustees, Samuel Hill and Herman Bell, who persistently insisted that we could handle the transactions. Ultimately, the building was purchased for the sum of $20,000.00. The coming of Bishop Mitchell to us, proved to be the "spark-plug", as it were, to our "machine", and it immediately started. His sincere, unselfish preaching of Truth, and his uncompromising stand for God's plan for the support of His House, "tithing," has proven, and will prove successful.

A list of the officers who served this church up to the acquisition of this edifice includes Brothers F. Calhoun, Ross Pickett, J. Ward, Jesse A. Bell, A. W. Adams, Julius Irving, Samuel Hill, John T. Spriggs, Marshall Ellison, W. M. Fort, George W. Bruce, Calvin Weaver, J. Herman Bell, Edwin Hill, Robert Carter and George Avery.

The pastors who have served this congregation include: Elder Enoch Thomas (1917-18), Elder Jackson (1918), Elder Park McFeild (1919), Elder A. J. Rucker (1919-22), Elder McClure (1922), Bishop H. L. Caver (1922-24), Bishop J. L. I. Conic (1924), Elder Owens (1925), Bishop J. A. Jeter (1925-29), Bishop Caver (1929-34), Bishop J. L. I. Conic (1934-38), Bishop W. M. Mitchell (1938-51), Elder Frank A. Boyd (1951), Elder Millard F. Brown (1951-57) and Bishop A. D. Williams (1957-present). The Associate Ministers included Elder O. C. Burns, Elder A. H. Bostic, Elder W. M. Ward and J. L. Brown. The present Assistant Pastor, Elder Hugh W. Jarmon, was ordained by Bishop Mitchell in 1947, and has served in this position, most faithfully and graciously, since 1951, under 3 pastors.

Three of the original members of the 1917 group remain with us in the persons of Brother and Sister Lewis McKinnis and Sister

Virginia Newsome Jarmon. Sister Hattie Lumpkins, one of our first Mothers, is still with us and will soon observe her 102nd birthday.

Like the acorn that "fell on the lea" and grew into a mighty oak; like the "Mustard Seed" in the Messiah's parable that became a tree; so from 8 persons, who felt divinely impressed to begin a church for God in St. Louis, has come our present, progressive group at Pendleton Avenue and Page Boulevard.

Christ Temple Church (Holiness), U.S.A.
Chicago Heights, Illinois

In 1919, Christ Temple was organized at Wentworth Avenue and Fifteenth Street in Chicago Heights by Brothers Anthony Prowell, Marcus Irons, Ulus Irons, and Brother J. J. Peterson. In that same year, the church prospered, the group was forced to secure a large building and they moved to Fifth Avenue and Sixteenth Streets. Under the leadership of Elder Gus Mitchum, they began to raise money to purchase a church. A lot was secured on Fourteenth Street and Fifth Avenue, however an injunction prevented them from building a church on that site. Finally, they were able to purchase a lot at 1610 Shields Avenue and they moved to the basement. It was at this location that the present edifice was constructed.

They had no pastor at this time, however, the members carried on until Rev. Webb, the pastor of Christ Temple Cathedral in

Chicago, sent the Rev. C. E. Owens to be their pastor. After serving them for a short time, he resigned in favor of Elder Billie Smith. Later, the Rev. Cain became our next pastor.

By this time, Elder J. J. Peterson had begun preaching and Rev. Webb requested that he carry on until the Rev. F. E. Williams was sent as psstor. After serving there for a short time, Bishop J. L. I. Conic was called to take the leadership. The church prospered, and during his administration, Bishop Conic sent Rev. M. Irons to East Chicago Heights, Illinois and Rev. J. J. Peterson to Gary, Indiana. These missions grew and later churches were erected on both of the sites.

After leaving the church, Bishop Conic was followed by a series of ministers, including: Rev. Daniel Washington, Bishop J. Jeter, Bishop J. G. Hay, Rev. C. S. Cooke, Rev. Richard Martin, and Rev. L. M. Relf. The latter, Rev. Relf, served successfully for sixteen years until he resigned in 1957, and Rev. M. F. Brown was called from St. Louis to pastor the Church.

Founding members and those who stood by the church in its struggle: Sister Elizabeth Willis, Sister Fields, Sister Thomas, Sister J. Irons, Sister Melvine Holmes, Sister M. Gordon, Brother L. Wells, Brother M. Irons, Brother J. J. Peterson, Brother Ulus Irons, Brother Henry Corbins, Brother C. F. Davis, 22 years Supt. of Sunday School, Elder Cain.

Glenville Church of Christ (Holiness) U.S.A.

The Glenville Church of Christ (Holiness) U.S.A. in Cleveland, Ohio, was founded by its former pastor, Elder Ezekiel Moore, in September 1946. (Picture in upper left is of Elder Moore.) He started Sunday services and mid-week Bible lessons is his home at 10705 Earle Avenue. On the first Sunday, the congregation consisted of his family and few neighboring children. Neighbors donated and loaned chairs to seat the congregation. His home caught fire and for a while services were not held.

One of the members, Brother Claudius Ricks, opened his home on East 82nd Street to the church. Some of his neighbors made complaints about the services in the home so we left there. In 1948 we rented the gymnasium in the Phyllis Wheatley Building on the corner of East 46th Street and Cedar Avenue. At the end of 1948, the church again moved into the home of its pastor, Elder Moore. We met there until 1952.

Glenville Church of Christ (Holiness) U.S.A.

In 1952 we rented a hall at the corner of East 105th Street and St. Clair Avenue. At first we had only Sunday services there. We had weekly Bible lessons and prayer meeting at the homes of members and others who invited us in. We referred to these as our 'cottage meetings.' Later we held mid-week services at Standard Hall, also.

We began a Building Fund while at Standard Hall. In July 1955 we moved to our present location, 909 Wade Avenue. The church was dedicated in October of that year.

In January 1961 our Pastor was led of the Lord to California. Rev. Tillman Broxton served as interim pastor until October 1961 when Elder M. D. McGee, our present pastor, arrived from the Golden Gate Church of Christ (Holiness) U.S.A. in San Francisco California. (Photo in upper right is Elder McGee).

First Church of Christ (Holiness) U.S.A.
862 East Princess Anne Road
Norfolk, Virginia

"Go up to the mountain, and bring wood, and build the house; and I will take pleasure in it, and I will be glorified, saith the Lord."—Haggai 1:8.

The history of Christianity is, in a sense, the history of buildings. The course of Christianity across the ages, may be traced by the buldings erected as the result of Christian influence and testimony.

Primarily, the building, like any other material structure, is created for people. The way in which a structure is scaled, and oriented to human need, detrmines the degree of its success or failure, as a functional tool.

The visible church as the instrument of Christ, must express His redemptive purpose. The word of God must be faithfully preached, and the sacraments duly administered, thus nurturing and developing the family of God.

In the Grace and providence of God, we are blessed to set apart a house for the glory of the Creator and the good of His Creation.

This task has been accomplished, through the cooperative efforts, of the boards, the committees and members of the First Church of Christ and of our community.

In memory of those who labored with us, who saw the vision, but failed to see its fulfillment. They are resting from their labours and their works do follow them.

Bishop David P. McPherson, Pastor

The Church And The Educational Buildings

The First Church of Christ (Holiness) was erected on the present site in 1922. Although the building was by no means old as church buildings go, it had deteriorated to the point where a new church edifice was a necessity.

The trustees of the church envisioned the idea of setting up a junior trustee board. This junior trustee board was organized with the idea of acquainting a few of the young men of the church with the physical as well as the spiritual operations of the church. It was from this group of young men that the idea of a building fund to erect a new church or to completely renovate the existing one was born. The idea of establishing a building fund was accepted wholeheartedly by the congregation. When the building fund was a success, ground was broken for the educational building July, 1963.

The educational building was completed in August of 1963. The congregation then began to worship in the educational building, while the sanctuary was under construction.

Mrs. David McPherson

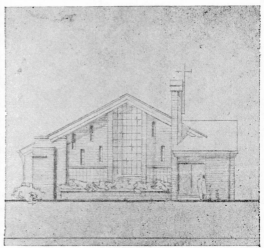

First Church of Christ (Holiness) U.S.A.
June 1964

The front view of the church. The side view (not shown) would show the education building.

The educational building has provisions for five class rooms, ladies' and men's lounges, the kitchen, the church office, and an assembly hall which can be used as a dining room. The air-conditioned sanctuary includes the pastor's study, choir rooms, consultation room and lavatories.

The Church Progress Through the Years

Except the Lord build the house, they labour in vain that build it; except the Lord keep the city, the watchman waketh but in vain. Psalms 127.

Like all spiritually inspired organizations success and progress were inevitable. The history of the First Church dates back as far as 1897 when Reverend Parker Williams of Langley, South Carolina, held meetings in the homes of Sisters Mary Morris,

203

Grant St. Church

Emma Jackson, Lucy Cox Adline Walton, Emma Jenkins, Louise Whitehurst and Mary Lee. As the Lord added souls it became necessary to seek a definite place of worship. The first such place was the Edward Funeral Home on Queen Street. Frequently street meetings were held in different parts of the city on Sundays.

As of August 1961, there were only two surviving members of this early beginning. One was former deacon Wm. T. McDonald (92) of Norfolk, Va., and his sister, Mrs. Emma Jackson of New York City.

In 1900, the first pastor, Rev. Samuel Jackson, two deacons, Wm. T. McDonald and Edward Cox, joined with the group to help in the determined efforts to organize a body of believers in Christ. Under their guidance a house on Grant Street was secured, which became known as "Grant Street Holiness Church," in 1902, and remained there until 1923.

Following Pastor Samuel Jackson were Rev. Venerable and Rev. Humphrey. They knew of the holiness movement in the far south under the leadership of Elder Charles Price Jones of Jackson, Mississippi, and sought affiliation with that movement. Elder K. H. Burress of Atlanta, Ga., one of the general overseers of the Church of Christ Holiness, was sent by Elder C. P. Jones to Norfolk to give further advice and guidance to the church effort there.

The next two pastors were Rev. Enoch Thomas and Rev. Tom Simmons. Following them was Elder J. A. Jeter of Little Rock, Ark. The rate of growth in membership necessitated a larger place of worship.

In 1922, the 862 Princess Road location was purchased, and here the "First Church of Christ Holiness" was erected under the leadership of Pastor J. A. Jeter.

204

First Church of Christ Holiness

Elder William Hudson Dunn was pastor of the church from 1925 to 1930, and from 1933 until his death in 1942. During the interim, 1930-1933, Rev. L. J. Brunson of Mississippi, was the pastor.

Bishop Major Rudd Conic was pastor from 1943 to Feb. 1947. The church building-debt was liquidated.

Bishop Obadiah Wesley McInnis was pastor from 1947 to Oct. 1961. The plans for a new church edifice and education building progressed to an advanced stage during his pastorate.

By vote of the National Convention in Norfolk in August 1961, Bishop O. W. McInnis was transferred to Chicago, Illinois, and Bishop David P. McPherson of Jackson, Miss., was transferred to the Norfolk, Virginia church pastorate.

Some of the First Members

Brother Alex McNeal
Brother J. E. Delk
Brother Tucker
Sister Lucy McNeal
Brother Geo. Morris
Sister Lula Young
Sister Emma Jackson

Sister Mary Morris
Sister Anna Stevens
Sister Lucy Cox
Sister Emma McDonald
  Jackson
Sister Addie Wilson
Sister Melissa Epps

205

Deacon William T.
  McDonald
Sister Louise Whitehurst
Sister Annie Young
Sister Viola Young
Sister Annie De Vaughan
Sister Mary Braye

Sister Adline Walters
Sister Luvenia McDonald
Sister Della Young (Deaf
  & Dumb)
Sister Emma Jenkins
Sister Mary Lee

THE CHAIRMEN

J. A. Howard, Chairamn of Trustee Board and Building Committee;
Harley Robinson, Chairman of Deacon Board Emeritus; R. T. Alex
Chairman of Deacon Board

206

OFFICIAL STAFF OF THE CHURCH

Deacons: R. T. Alex, Harley Robinson, Milton F. Gay, Sr., Willie Cobb, Lewis Harrell, Jesse Doles, Johnny Lewis, Lee Bonds, Geo. Thompson, James Howard. **Trustees:** A. Drew, Eddie Hicks, Cecil McIver, (not shown) Albert Dunn. **Jr. Trustees:** Ralston McInnis, James F. Gay, Edward R. Hicks, (not shown) J. H. Newby

Pastor: Bishop David P. McPherson

SUNDAY SCHOOL OFFICIAL STAFF

Supt. R. T. Alex, Asst. Supt. Frank Brown, Sec'y Ruthie Benyard, (Sitting, Left to right) Sister Mildred Howard, Sister Elaine Malloy, Building Fund Committee: Bertha Hightower, Josephine Alston. Teachers: E. Malloy, E. Bazemore, Lenell Dunn, Jesse Doles, Bishop McPherson, James Howard.

The Senior Choir

(Sitting, left to right) Sister Mildred Howard, Sister Elaine Malloy, Sister Thelma Gay, Sister Clara Saunders, Sister Edna Bazemore. (Standing, 2nd row) Sister Vivian Griffin, Sister Elzena Newby, Sister Fannie Taylor, Sister Mary Lewis, Sister Erma Craft, Sister Iris McPherson, Organist. (3rd row) Sister Edna Goldwire, Sister Louise Hicks, Sister Jennie Norwood, Sister Mardessie Holloway (back row) Brother Joseph Morris, Jr., Director; Brother Harry Riddick, Brother William Parker, Brother Howard Taylor. (Members not in photo) Sister Marie Demary, Sister Josephine Austin, Sister Ugertha Doles, Brother James Brown, Brother Lee Bonds.

THE GOSPEL CHOIR

(Sitting left to right) Sis. Cozette Drew, Lula Hill, Rosa Jackson Cora Walton, Rae Brown, Organist; Fannie White, L. Pledger, Sarah Hassle, Josephine Alston, Elouise Lee, Marie Patterson, Marie Demary, Kenneth White, Herbert Brown.

JUNIOR CHOIR

Mildred Howard, Sponsor; Leser Howell, Organist; Ruthie Benyard, President; Paulette Williams, Juliette Taylor, Ida Mason, Deborah Garrett, Helen Benyard, Joyce Speller, Ruthie Benyard, Mason, David McPherson, Elmore Brown, Clarence McPherson, Frank Brown.

THE HELPING HAND COMMITTEE

Sister Josephine Alston, Mary Lewis, Mary Cobb, Iris McPherson, Lena Filhoil, Virginia Walton, Lenell Dunn, Ray Brown, Lottie Williams, Louise Hicks (not shown) President Cozette Drew.

USHER BOARD I

Lena Filhoil, Mildred Evans, Lena Edmonds, Beulah Faine, Winnie
Moore, Georgia Sykes, Captoria Alex, Dora Jordan, Chairman; C.
Alex.

USHER BOARD II

Lucy Brookins, Mary Lewis, Lottie Williams, Josephine Alston, Lenell Dunn, Roberta Birdsong, Louis White, Dorothy Overton, Sarah Brown, Chairman Louise White.

Data on Churches 1905-1919

Church Name and Location	Date Founded	Founder or First Pastor	Succeeding Pastors	First Members
CHRIST TEMPLE Ruleville, Miss. 766 Lafayette St.			G. W. Cole N. Sanders I. E. Bearden E. W. Butler J. B. Keys A. J. Torrey	
CHRIST TEMPLE Belmont, L. A.	1912	C. C. Carhee Geo. Fletcher	C. C. Carhee W. M. Cephus K. H. Burris O. L. Mitchel E. W. Butler R. L. McAllister N. S. Cann A. Ragland Bennie Lee F. A. Boyd Mose Fay J. F. Harris Ed. Glen Sam Murray	E. P. Bass Rosa Bass Cassie Woods Octavia Wilkins Ben J. Smith Pearl Smith A. B. Smith Sallie Smith Lavel Lewis Lolla Williams Georgia Glover

Data on Churches 1905-1919

Church Name and Location	Date Founded	Founder or First Pastor	Succeeding Pastors	First Members
CHRIST TEMPLE Tchula, Miss. in Deacon Geo. A. Freeman's home.		C. P. Jones C. H. Mason	L. P. Cobbins	Deacon Geo. A. Freeman
CHRIST TEMPLE Oakvale, Miss. under brush arbor	1905	T. Hardy S. Daniel A. Blackwell John Michels	C. D. Ratliff John Vance W. A. Thurmond J. D. King H. Garner W. H. Hollins O. L. Williams John Roberts	
MIDWAY Folsom, L. A.	1909	J. E. Burris	E. Davis A. J. Allen	Deacon A. J. Garrett Brother Monroe A. Andrews

216

Data on Churches 1905-1919

Church Name and Location	Date Founded	Founder or First Pastor	Succeeding Pastors	First Members
CHRIST TEMPLE New Orleans, L. A.	1914	James S. Plain	James S. Plain John Boatner O. C. Miller	Matilda Lee Geo. Coleman Eugene Thompson Mother J. Thompson James Stewart Janie Plains Octavio Manual Beulah Coleman
CHRIST TEMPLE Leland, Miss.	1917	W. H. Dunn	J. W. Coleman W. J. Mixon F. A. Boyd W. D. Roberts B. T. Jones	Calvin Lumpkins Mattie Lumpkins Aaron Barron Ruth Hopkins
CHRIST TEMPLE Leesville, La. Home of O. L. Mitchel		C. C. Carhee O. L. Mitchel	O. L. Mitchel R. L. McAlister A. J. Parrish B. J. Smith Brother Rials F. A. Boyd Sam Murray	O. L. Mitchel, & wife J. Porter & wife Albert Brown A. B. Smith Joe Lewis

Data on Churches 1905-1919

Church Name and Location	Date Founded	Founder or First Pastor	Succeeding Pastors	First Members
WALNUT GROVE Homer, La.	1915	N. S. Cann	N. S. Cann B. T. Johnson Henry Ward	A. Z. Johnson Elex Crue Cronie Seals Arzella Ward Beulah Jones
MT. ZION, Gilbert, La. Hwy 15		N. S. Cann	N. S. Cann A. J. Parrish Wm. Felton D. J. Washington	Sister L. V. Nicholson Jim Winn Van Thomas, Sr. Van Thomas, Jr. Lee Pierce & wife David Winn Dan Ward Nancy Thomas Deacon C. E. Neals Professor Ernest

218

Data on Churches 1905-1919

Church Name and Location	Date Founded	Founder or First Pastor	Succeeding Pastors	First Members
SEARCY, Ark.	1910		O. L. Mitchel Robert Ravis E. W. Butler Link Williams J. D. Gordon Carl Austin	Rilla Snike Brother Spearman James Brewer Jack Snike
TEXARKANA, Texas			A. Ragland W. H. Dunn E. W. Butler Browns family	Henry Holt Brother McIntyre A. J. Parrish
MT. OLIVE Hattiesburg, Miss. Short 9th St.	1911	S. T. Cobbins	E. N. Haggans John Vance R. H. Hines M. D. Bingham A .D. Mitchel	S. T. Cobbins & wife E. T. Johnson & wife G. B. Hines & wife Mat. Thomas Geo. Holloway A. Wiggins & wife O. B. Cobbins Nettie Sims

Data on Churches 1905-1919

Church Name and Location	Date Founded	Founder or First Pastor	Succeeding Pastors	First Members
CHRIST TEMPLE Arkadelphia, Ark.		J. A. Jeter Brown Welch	J. L. I. Conic D. J. Washington Wm. Polk Joe Covington A. J. Parrish A. D. Williams Carl Austin	
BEULAH Atlanta, Ga.		K. H. Burris H. J. Blakley	Harvey Jackson W. Hemphill W. S. Kilgore S. J. Anderson J. H. Haywood L. P. Johnson H. B. Johnson Garrett Wilks H. M. Wofford W. S. Kilgore	O. W. Owens H. M. Wofford H. J. Blakley A. Banks John Robinson

Data on Churches 1905-1919

Church Name and Location	Date Founded	Founder or First Pastor	Succeeding Pastors	First Members
STARLIGHT Mansfield, La. So. Washington Ave.	1916	N. S. Cann B. F. Furry Frank Hall Brother Street	N. S. Cann Ed. Sweet B. J. Smith Edgar Glenn Jesse Augurson F. A. Boyd Sam Murray	B. F. Furry Carry Furry Ida Rowe Josephine Harvey E. Glenn Beulah Glenn Frank Hall Nettie Hall
ZION TEMPLE Robeline, La.	1915	A. D. Abbot C. C. Carhee Sam Morris	W. M. Cephus B. J. Smith E. Glenn A. D. Abbot F. A. Boyd Bennie Lee Samuel Murray	Sam Morris & wife A. D. Abbot T. Davis & wife E. Washington & wife Geo. Brown Sister Florence Washington Sister Mary Washington Sister Annie Washington

Data on Churches 1905-1919

Church Name and Location	Date Founded	Founder or First Pastor	Succeeding Pastors	First Members
CHRIST TEMPLE Shreveport, La. 1406 Jordan St.	1907	E. W. Cole John T. Brown	E. W. Butler R. L. McAllister Hall C. L. Carhee A. J. Parrish B. T. Johnson F. A. Boyd Jesse Augurson	J. S. Williams & wife Brother & Sister Chavis John Terry & wife Armstrong family Sister Chaney Ruffins Sister Ida Rose John Lover Brother Blackman
FAIRVIEW Carpenter, Miss.	1935	Annie Wince Milsie Reed H. R. McInnis	Geo. Henley A. J. Torrey W. Jenkins	Annie Wince Milsie Reed Deacon P. T. Torrey Joel Bradley I. W. Bradley

Data on Churches 1905-1919

Church Name and Location	Date Founded	Founder or First Pastor	Succeeding Pastors	First Members
CHURCH OF CHRIST Birmingham, Ala.	1913	F. E. Williams	Steve Moody W. A. Carter L. M. Relf S. J. Anderson Bennie Lewis John Roberts C. C. Casey	Mamie Reed Wilda Atchinson Bennie Lewis
GLENVILLE Cleveland, Ohio 9009 Wade Park	1946	Ezekiel Moore	M. D. McGee	E. Moore & family Lillian Golden Geraldine Golden T. Broxton A. Childress & wife Many Jones Virginia Burney Joseph Golden C. N. Ricks
CHRIST TEMPLE Tulsa, Okla. 1322 N. Greenwood St.	1942	A. B. Smith	B. F. Hill Robert J. Davis A. Goodlett	Sister Lizzie Harris

223

Data on Churches 1905-1919

Church Name and Location	Date Founded	Founder or First Pastor	Succeeding Pastors	First Members
CALVARY Fontana, Calif.	1953	Mission Bd. & Rev. J. C. Smith	J. C. Smith Estell McLaurin C. R. Goodwin	Georgia Abernathy J. C. Smith & wife Victor Smith Pearl Clayor Doris Mulley McLaurin Family Silas Smith Lucille Smith
CHRIST TEMPLE Port Gibson, Miss.	1957	A. J. Torrey	M. T. Newsome J. B. Burley	M. T. Newsome & wife Delois Dorsay Lillie May Douglas
CHRIST TEMPLE San Bernardino, Calif. 1442 W. 11th St.	1960	Tyree Feltz	Tyree Feltzs W. Richards	C. Cain and family Geo. Smith and family Jolita Feltz

Data on Churches 1905-1919

Church Name and Location	Date Founded	Founder or First Pastor	Succeeding Pastors	First Members
CHRIST TEMPLE San Diego, Calif.	1958	Tyree Feltzs	Willie Calhoun Charles German Samuel Ballard	Sister Falconer Robert Keetch & family Sister J. Matthews C. R. Goodwin & fam. Sister N. Scott Mendenhall family Sister A. Samuels Sister Seals Sister Tucker Sister Johnson Sistre Young Sister Brown Sister Jackson Brother Ronnie Eckles
TALLULAH, LA. Mission 239 South St.	1959		O. L. Williams	Sister L. Cann Sister Mary Jenkins Brother Hanking

Data on Churches 1905-1919

Church Name and Location	Date Founded	Founder or First Pastor	Succeeding Pastors	First Members
MT. ZION, Toledo, Ohio 620 Fernwood.	1934	J. L. I. Conic L. Randall	Wm. Hicks Albert Criss M. Robinson	Wm. Taylor Flossy Wade H. R. Hicks Sarah Hicks Hattie Campers Willie Mae Hicks
NEW SALEM Marrero, La. 1540 Mansfield St.	1956	Bennie Lee	Bennie Lee	Rubie Davis Dora Vance Ella Torry Frances Craft Elihu Watts James Lee Oda Mae Lee Carrie Jean Tell David Torry Bettie Lee Davis Jimmie Lee Watts

The First Church of Christ, 1219 Hamlin Street North East, Washington, D. C., was organized in 1920 by Elder Conic. The present $90,000 edifice was erected during the pastorate of Elder O. A. Askerneese.

The ministers who have pastored the Church were Reverends J. L. I. Conic, K. H. Burris, H. B. Johnson, Coleman, Henry Holt, O. D. Henry, W. M. Acty, W. E. Holman, A. J. Perkins, A. M. White, C. L. Carhee, O. A. Askerneese, C. P. Jones Jr.

Some of the first members were Brother and Sister J. C. Cook, Brother and Sister Charles Price, Brother and Sister William Harris, Sister Sophonia Richardson, Rev. C. R. Price (one of the founders,) Sister Inez Cook, Sister Pearl Clark.

The Sweet Home Church of Christ
R, 4, Box 126, Jackson, Mississippi

The Sweet Home Church was started by Sister Viola Jones in August 1930, by starting Prayer Meetings in her home. A prayer band was organized and through this organization, a brush arbor was built. A church was organized in November, 1942, by Rev. Albert Hamilton, Jr. The church building materials and a part of the land were given by Deacon Mack Jenkins. At the time the deacons were West Taylor, and Mack Jenkins.

In 1944 Bishop O. B. Cobbins appointed Rev. J. T. Hill as pastor to succeed Rev. Albert Hamilton, Jr., under the leadership of Rev. Hill.

Zion Chapel Church
Detroit, Michigan
Rev. A. J. Perkins, Pastor

Deacon Mack Jenkins

The members are planning to build a new edifice in the near future.

The present Deacons are Deacons Mack Jenkins, Eddie Jones, and L. V. Jones. The trustees are brothers Julius Harris and George Garner, Turner Jenkins and Nilon Seals.

Golden Gate Church, San Francisco

The Golden Gate Church had its beginning in October 1943 in the home of the late Bishop A. B. Smith, 1743 Laguna Street. Some of the first members were Sister A. B. Smith, Elder and Sister A. D. Williams and children, I. G. Iris and Dewelene; Elder A. B. Smith's children Samuel, Joseph, Benjamin, Magnolia and Oliver; Sister Frankie Benefield, Brother Elbert Bass and Sister Cora Rucker.

The Lord blessed us to open a new place of worship at Baker and Pine Streets, June 18, 1944. New members added were Elder Elmo Ollison, Brother Roscoe Smith and family, Brother and Sister S. Neal, Brother and Sister Charles Ligons, Brother Jerry Ollison and Brother John E. Porter.

Elder A. B. Smith moved to Merced, Calif., leaving Elder A. D. Williams as our pastor. Following Elder Williams, Elder Ollison served as pastor. when we worshipped in the home of Brother Roscoe Smith. From there we went to the home of Brother Joseph T. Smith.

In September 1948 we bought and moved into our buiding at 1369 Ellis Street. Following Elder Ollison came Elder M. D. McGee of Indiana as pastor. In 1960 we were informed that our property would be bought to make way for redevelopment. From here we bought the property we now have at 704 Vermont Street.

Elder M. D. McGee was called to pastor the Glenville Church in Cleveland, Ohio, in September 1961 after which Elder Samuel Smith became our pastor. Church Officers: Brother K. D. Benefield, Church Deacon Board, Deacons Jerry Ollison, Abraham Speech, Roscoe Smith, Joseph Smith and Quinnie York. Trustees, Brothers Roscoe Smith, Chairman, Jerry Ollison, Ivory Speech, Abraham Speech, Quinnie York, Treasurer, and Joseph T. Smith, Secretary.

C.W.W.W. President Sister Addie Lee; Sister Cula May Smith, Vice President; Sister Dolores Ollison, Secretary; Sister Juanita York, Treasurer; Deaconesses Sister Helen Lover, Chairman; Sister Cora Rucker, Sister Nattie Burton, Sister Addie Lee, Sister

Frankie Benefield, Sister Beatrice Walker. Sunday School Superintendent Brother Abraham Speech, Secretary Angela Smith.

Emmanuel Church of Christ Holiness, U.S.A.
Oakland, California

The Emmanuel Church was organized by Rev. W. J. Sims in his home under the direction of Bishop William A. Washington in 1944. The following persons were present: Rev. and Sister W. J. Sims and family; Brother and Sister Terry, Sr. and family; Sister Martha Lewis; Sister L. Lewis and family; and Sister Cleopatra Sims; Brother and Sister Willis Cole and Sister Mary Prentice joined the church later. The Congregation moved into its new church in Oct. 1944.

At the February 18, 1945 meeting, three trustees were elected. They were: Brother John Terry, Brother W. J. Sims and Brother Willis Cole.

On February 25th, 1945, a special meeting was called by the Pastor, Elder W. J. Sims, to approve the necessary resolutions, by laws and constitution for the Emmanuel Church of Christ, (Holiness), required by the State of California to have the church incorporated.

The Deacon Board, 1946-1953

Brother E. C. Cromwell, Chairman

Willis Cole

Garman Marshall

Manuel Kemp

The Trustee Board, 1946-1953

Brother Willis Cole, Chairman

Sister O. A. Askerneese

Ollie Cole

E. B. Goodwin

Gladys Williams

The Church Clerks, 1944-1964

Sister W. J. Sims

Sister Bernice Hall

Brother Alfred Sims

Sister Edith Searcy

Sister O. A. Askerneese

Sister E. B. Goodwin

Brother I. G. Williams (now acting)

Sister Mary Prentis

Sister Mary Louise McGee

The Sunday School Superintendents

Sister W. J. Sims

Sister Pearline Lewis

Sister Ollie Cole

Sister Edith Searcy

Brother Walter Jackson

Sister E. B. Goodwin

Brother Ray Goodwin

Brother R. Luster

Sister D. McPherson

Brother Lucious Winn

Brother Snyder Winn

The C. W. W. Presidents, 1945-1964

Sister W. J. Simms

Sister E. B. Goodwin

Sister Mary Winn

August, 1945, the SUNBEAM was organized by Sister Austin with,

Sister Betty Joe. Sims — President,

Sister Barbara J. Sims — Secretary,

Brother Demetrick Sims — Treasurer,

Sister Ollie Cole — Supervisor and

Sister Edith Searcy — Assistant-Supervisor

Emmanuel Church Pastors, 1944-1964

Elder W. J. Sims 1944-1946

Elder O. A. Askerneese 1946-1951

Elder W. Jackson 1952-1953

Elder A. D. Williams 1953-1957

Elder L. D. Hughes (1957)

First Church of Christ (Holiness) U.S.A., New York City
(New York Merger—November 2, 1963)

The merger of the First Church of Christ (Holiness) U.S.A., 352 Lenox Ave., with the First Church of Christ Incorporated took place on November 2, 1963 under the auspices of Bishop O. W. McInnis, Bishop David McPherson and the newly elected pastor Rev. William L. Jerome. The Mission on Lenox Ave. moved to the premises of 1935 Madison Ave., the present Church Home of the Church of Christ (Holiness) U.S.A. The Lord has marvelously blessed in the work. Every Auxiliary of the Churches of Christ (Holiness) U.S.A. has been set up and working in Love and Spirit. The Lord has constantly added to the church numerically and has blessed financially. The edifice has been improved and an organ has been installed. Although death has called some of the old warriors such as Sister Annie Cook, wife of the late Bishop Cook, Sister Jessie Johnson, formerly of St. Louis, Deacon Holloway and others, God has given to the Church a wonderful young minister, Rev. James Carter and his entire family to be an asset to the entire Church. The assistant pastor, Rev. Booker Robinson and the associate ministers, Rev. Blount, and Rev. Walter Smith are of great assistance to Pastor Jerome in the two year period of the merger. Tribute is given to our organists, Sister Lena Smith and Brother Cooleridge Huey for their splendid work with the choirs: junior and senior. Other officers are to be commended for their endeavors in each department of the Church. The Pastor highly appreciates the cooperation of all officials and laymen for their endeavors during the two years he has labored in this phase of the vineyard for Jesus Christ our Lord.   Rev. William L. Jerome, Pastor

Mount Zion Church of Christ (Holiness) U.S.A.
Jackson, Miss.

The Mt. Zion Church of Christ (Holiness) U.S.A. began in 1926 as a mission in a Blacksmith Shop on the corner of Raymond Road and Midway St., with Elder Brumfield, Brother William Jackson, Brother Woodall, Sister Annie Reed, and Sister Singleton. Elder Brumfield being of a different faith moved out. These Saints held on, and together went to the home of Sister Reed, where they sang songs and prayed to God. Elder Lonnie Jackson was called to them to preach the word of God. Leaving this dear sister's home, they went to a brush Arbor, where they praised God in the highest and thanked him for his many blessings.

Elder Willie Jenkins, Sr., a very young man called to preach God's Holy Word was invited out to preach to the precious Saints there. They were encouraged and led to believe that he, Elder Jenkins, was God's chosen one to lead them forward.

The weather caused them to return to different homes for service. The Lord added one every now and then. During this time money was being raised and saved to buy a plot of land to build a place of worship, with Elder Jenkins still preaching the word and encouraging them to go forward. In 1939 a small plot of land was purchased and a small church was built, with Brothers William Jackson, Richard Thomas, and Samuel Walker serving as trustees.

The late Father Henry R. McInnis was invited to preach a special message and name the church. In 1948 the church was enlarged. Elder Jenkins has served faithful for 26 years. The Lord has saved a large number of people during his administration, bodies have been healed, lame made to walk, and souls encouraged to stay with the Lord. All of the old patriarchs have gone on, but the Lord still has a faithful few, yet carrying on, raising funds for a modern edfice.

Pilgrim Church of Christ (Holiness)

1515 North "D" Street

Las Vegas, Nevada

Rev. G. L. Harris, Pastor

Pilgrim Church of Christ (Holiness), U.S.A., Las Vegas, Nevada was organized as a mission in 1929 by Elder B. F. Armstrong and Brother Dan Washington. Our first place of worship was a tent at the same location where the present building was later built. The church was built through the untiring efforts of Elder Armstrong. It was the first church built on the Westside where most of the colored people lived at that time. Many people who were originally Baptist and Methodist joined the church. Some of them left to join their own denominations, but some of them remained.

Elder Armstrong served until 1939 at which time Elder George Strong was appointed pastor. Elder Strong served for one year. Rev. L. A. Cruise was appointed pastor in 1940. Rev. Cruise served as pastor until 1951 when he returned to Los Angeles. Elder George L. Harris who was serving as assistant pastor then served as pastor and was appointed as pastor in 1952 by Bishop

233

Massengale. The church is presently under the pastorship of Rev. G. L. Harris.

Members, passed on to glory, who contributed much to the growth and welfare of the church: Brother Leroy Christenson, Sister Elvessie Johnson, Sister Willie A. Mishey, and Sister Maude Harris.

All Nations Church of Christ (Holiness) U.S.A.
Berkeley, Calif.

During the war years 1944-1945 many people migrated from the south to the west coast seeking a better way of life. Many of them came to the Bay Area.

Being conscientious Christians they searched for the church of their choice where they could worship God in the manner they were accustomed to. Eventually they found a Mission in Oakland pastored by Elder Sims. As some or most of the transplanted members lived in Richmond and Berkeley, they began to look for a place in Berkeley. Brother and Sister John Terry who had lately arrived from Shreveport, La., graciously opened their home at 1400 67th Street.

At this time Elder David McPherson was the pastor. He remained with us until 1948. Officers of the church were as follows: Chairman of Deacon Board, Brother Louis Foy, (Deceased), Chairman of Trustees, Brother David Winn; Church Clerk, Sister Ola M. Lewis; Treasurer, Brother John Terry; Sunday School Superintendent, Brother Isaiah Winn; President C.W.-W.W., Sister Levell Lewis; President of Busybee, Sister Johnnie P. Terry; Charter Members: Brother John Terry, Sister Ola Debose, Sister Lue Mitchell, Brother Isaiah Winn.

In 1948 the members found a church for sale which they purchased. In order to make the $7,000.00 down payment loans were made from many members and friends. The membership moved into the building on Jan. 1, 1949. The church began to grow spiritually and numerically. Elder A. D. Williams served us until 1953 when he was succeeded by Elder Elmo Ollison under whose administration the building was entirely remodeled, an organ was purchased and the church generally began to expand. Under Elder Ollison the Church was re-admitted to the convention and more members were added. From September 1961 when Elder Ollison resigned until March 1962 Elder William Pope served as pastor. At this point Presiding Bishop A. Hamilton Jr., appointed Rev. Eugene Brown as pastor. Under his leadership the church is progressing splendidly.

Church of Christ, Crystal Springs, Miss.

The Church of Christ was founded in Crystal Springs, Miss., by Rev. Benjamin Akines in 1932. Rev. Akines preached to two members. They were Sister Polly Stevenson and Brother Porter Sibbie. The Sibbie family joined the Church of Christ in November 1933. Later in December of the same year Brother A. C. Catching and the Jones family joined the Church.

In 1935, the Carter family and Brother James May joined the Church of Christ. We were worshiping the Lord in a Tabernacle in Free Town. The tabernacle was taken away from us, and the Lord blessed us to have our meeting in Brother and Sister Sibbie's home one (1) year and six months.

The Lord blessed us to raise money to buy a piece of land on highway 51, and there we built a small Church. The Church grew with the few members until we were able to add more to the Church.

Rev. Akines became very ill. The Church had $250 in the treasury which was turned over to his wife to help with Rev. Akines' illness.

In April 1957, Rev. John Sanders came to the Church of Christ with 16 members who joined the Church. The Church of Christ raised $600 for building fund, along with the help of Rev. E. C. Duncans.

Rev. Eddie Jones came to the Church of Christ in Sept. 1964 on the First Sunday in November. The Church of Christ raised $168 for the building fund.

Some of the first members of the Church were: Sister Polly Adams, Brother Porter Sibbie, Sister Sora Sibbie, Sister Rosie Leesibbie, Sister Ethel Jones, Brother James May, Brother Annais Catchings, Sister Lois Sibbie, Sister Mozella Jones, and Sister Annie Bell Jones.

Christ Temple Number 2
East Chicago Heights, Illinois

Christ Temple Church Number 2 was organized, September 1935, with Reverend Marcus Irons as pastor and the following members:

Mrs. O. Broden and Mrs. Ben Bridgewater as deacons and Mrs. Bertha Hall, Mrs. Kate Williams, Mrs. Ernie Walker and Mrs. Lula Dokes. This organized group had no place to worship and Mrs. Lula Dokes opened her home to them to hold services. The Sunday School was made up of the above named families. Rev. Ernest Williams, pastor of Christ Temple of Hazelcrest, Illinois, the son of Mrs. Katie Williams was reared up in Christ Temple No. 2. The church began to grow. The group had to move in larger quarters. The only church in the village was the Christ Baptist (white) and they let Christ Temple Number 2 worship in the afternoon in their church.

Rev Irons, seeing the need of a building, began to build a church. The building was completed in less than a year. In 1943 the building burned down. A new one was started. Many of the members had become discouraged and ceased attending. Rev. Irons and a few members continued. They had a new church but no choir. Mrs. Alberta Armstrong made a canvass of the Village getting old members back into the church and new members organized a choir. Rev. Irons has served this church twenty-seven years. The church has a membership of 22, a thirty voice male choir, three local ministers. New improvements have been made on the building.

236

Christ Temple Church No. 2
East Chicago Heights, Illinois

Christ Temple Church of Christ
(Holiness), Omaha, Neb.

237

Christ Temple Church of Christ

The Christ Temple Church of Omaha, Nebr. was organized in 1922 by Elder A. T. Rucker. Some of the first members were: Brother Fredrick Clark, Brother John Anderson, Brother Frazier Huntley, Brother Henry G. Anderson, his wife Mrs. Armelia Gaines Anderson, Mother Clara Anderson, Sister Mattie Middleton, Sister Lula Redd, Rev. O. J. Burkhart, Brother Singleton, Brother Eunice Butler, Sister Mildred West, and Bertha Mallory. The Pastors of the Church have been: Rev. J. T. Brown, Rev. A. T. Rucker, Rev. O. J. Burkhart, Rev. O. A. Askerneese, Rev. L. M. Relf, Rev. William Acty, Rev. J. W. Goodwin, Rev. James Stewart, Sr., Rev. C. N. Ricks, Rev. C. N. Austin.

St. Timothy Church of Christ

The St. Timothy Church of Christ, 1711 Madison Avenue, Newport News, Va. was organized in 1903 by Elder Joseph Ely. Later by Elder John F. Morrison. The church had previously been with another church fellowship. When Elder Morrison came to this brotherhood, he brought the church with him. The other pastors who followed him were Reverends W. H. Dunn, L. P. Johnson, E. K. McFadden, O. D. Henry, David P. McPherson and J. C. Smith.

New Hope Church
The New Hope Mission, Church of Christ (Holiness) U.S.A.

238

St. Timothy Church of Christ
Newport News, Va.

was organized in 1948 at 15th and Fashion Street, Long Beach
California by Elder L. J. May and a company of men and women,
including Sister Elizabeth May, Mrs. Henrietta May, Sister Donie
Reed, Sister Leora Johnson, Sister G. Carroll and Elder and
Sister B. M. Draugh.

The New Hope Mission was opened June 27, 1948 by Rev.
I. L. Craft and congregation. The first sermon was preached by
Rev. Craft. At first the work was mostly with children. After
much hard labor, the Lord sent us two young men in the persons
of Brother Verdie Calhoun and his brother Willie Calhoun, who
later were called to the ministry. Through their preaching and
witnessing, most of the adult members were added to the church.
May God continue to bless their labor in the gospel.

In the year, 1950, we bought a piece of property at 1119 Rhea
Street on the east side of Long Beach, where the church is now
located as shown above.

A list of its pastors includes: Rev. Eugene Brown of Los Angeles, Elder Ezekiel Moore of Cleveland, hio, and Elder L. J.
May, founder and present pastor.

Bethel Church of Christ (Holiness) U.S.A.

Bethel Church of Christ Holiness started from a small mission with just a few members under the leadership of our late Bishop Albert Hamilton, who worked faithfully with the church here until he became pastor of the Mother Church in Jackson, Mississippi.

Rev. James Robinson, who is the present pastor had the foresight and vision that Bethel should move forward. He worked prayerfully to lead Bethel Church to purchase, beautify and dedicate a place of worship which is located at 11624 Kinsman Road, Cleveland, Ohio.

New Testament Church of Christ (Holiness) U.S.A.
Rev. John Plummer, Jr., Pastor and Founder
The Church grew out of a "Cottage Bible Class" conducted by

240

Pastor John Plummer. This class was an inspiration to all who attended. In 1957, Rev. Plummer saw the need of a new work on the South-West side of Los Angeles. The Pastor then went into fasting and prayer for the leading and guidance of God for this new venture. After receiving the "go ahead" from the Lord, and upon receiving permission from the late Presiding Bishop Albert Hamilton, Jr., the Pastor founded and organized the New Testament Church, December 31, 1960 with eight charter members:

Brother T. Seals	Brother J. Sutton
Brother K. White	Sister Patricia Plummer
Brother C. R. Goodwin	Sister E. Goodwin
Brother S. E. Sutton	Sister Q. E. Sutton

The first services were held January 1, 1961, in a small rennovated building seating capacity of 50 persons at 7404 South Western Avenue with approximately 20 persons present.

The late Presiding Bishop Albert Hamilton, Jr., was a great source of inspiration and encouragement to the members. He encouraged them to canvass the neighborhood for all people regardless of race or church affiliation.

Since this small beginning, the membership has increased seven times its original membership. We praise God that nearly half of this number were new converts and found Christ at this church.

The Church moved to a larger building seating 110. A new Church is in the offing for the near future.

The Church has an Evangelistic program which has been the key to the rapid growth in membership. The canvassing program is geared toward surveying the area and inviting people to church. The pastor has laid the example by leading in this endeavor. The visitation team calls on persons who are interested in uniting with the church or who desire additional information about the church.

The Personal Workers and Altar Workers are trained to lead men to Christ. The pastor makes home calls of the membership, especially, the sick and shut-in, and the inactive members. The Church publishes a monthly paper which circulates in some 25 states, foreign countries and to service men on the bases.

The pastor has attended Biola Bible College, a graduate of Los Angeles City College and a graduate of California State College at Los Angeles. He is a writer, counselor, soul winner and is on call to speak throughout the Los Angeles area by various groups. Our pastor conducts a weekly Bible Class at the church, and discusses several major Bible themes.

Several of the members hold office in the convention. The pastor is a member of the National Executive Board and Nat. S.S. and H.Y.P.U. Congress.

The membership is made up primarily of young adults, "sprinkled" by a few "seasoned" adults. The average age of the membership is 28. The oldest is in her eighties. The membership is made up of 60 per cent women and 40 per cent men.

The Church has a Sunday School, Holiness Young People's Union, Deacon Board, Trustee Board, Fisherman's Club, Christian Women Willing Workers, Three Choirs, Male Quartette, Usher Board and Courtesy Committee.

The Church holds a fellowship dinner for new members. The purpose is to get better acquainted with the new members. At our beginning, we received aid from several Sister Churches who loaned chairs: Pilgrim Church and Christ Temple Church, L.A.

The Church's membership is still increasing. The key to its rapid growth is its Christ-centered program, Christ-centered sermons, and emphasis on Evangelism.

Pilgrim Church of Christ (Holiness), U.S.A.
Los Angeles, Calif.

The Pilgrim Church of Christ (Holiness) was started from a club of neighborhood children by Sister Sarah Harris and family. From this club, a Sunday School class and House-to-House Prayer band were organized.

Sister Emma Lewis requested if a mission could be started in Watts, California. Everyone was in harmony. In starting, Sister

242

Bembo and her husband gave use of their lot on 105th Street for as long as it was needed.

The latter part of January, 1923, Elder Henry Clay Holt was given permission to begin a mission in Watts, California, now known as South Los Angeles, by the late Bishop C. P. Jones, Pastor of Christ Temple Church of Christ (Holiness), at that time located at 37th Street and Naomi.

Elder Holt and Elder Saunders began by holding prayer meeting in the home of Brother and Sister Horace Brown, located on 113th Street, Watts, California. Present at that first meeting were: Brother and Sister Horace Brown, Mother Owens, Sister Spencer, Sister Novella Johnson, and Sister Eva Bingham.

July 16, 1923, Eva Bingham became the bride of Elder Holt. At this time, the attendance had increased to the point that a larger place for Worship had to be obtained. Elder and Sis Holt personally purchased a house and lot on 112th Street, making a down payment of three hundred fifty dollars ($350.00).

Approximately two years later, another mission was organized from the late Bishop William A. Washington's Church, located on 103rd Street. It was later disbanded and the members united with Elder Holt and members on 112th Street. The building on 103rd Street was moved on 112th Street lot; and the building on 112th Street which was being worshiped in by Elder Holt and members was moved to the rear of the lot and used as a Parsonage. The new members that united were Sister Blue and family, Brother Harris and family, and Elder Draught. A name for the church was appropriated at this time. It was suggested and named "Union Mission."

In 1927, Elder and Sister Holt went on the mission field. The mission was then turned over to Bishop William A. Washintgon, being the presiding Bishop of the Western Diocese, which he appointed Elder Lewis Pastor. After the tragic death of Elder Lewis' wife, the property was sold and a church site was purchased at 106th and Compton Ave. Rev. G. B. Washington was sent to pastor the mission. Through the trick of the enemy, this church was burned down.

After an elapse of time, Rev. D. J. Washington and wife canvassed the neighborhood and gathered children and organized a Sunday School. Sister Edna Peoples was Superintendent and Rev. C. C. Carhee became pastor for a while. Elder Caldwell became the Pastor and later a church was built on the site at 106th

Street and Compton Ave., and named Pilgrim Church of Christ (Holiness), Rev. Caldwell was the pastor and builder. The building was beautiful and was dedicated. Rev. Caldwell did a wonderful work. Elder W. M. Harris and family was still faithful workers. Brother C. J. Tique came to help in the Sunday School and church. He helped purchased seats for Pilgrim. Elder Caldwell was later sent to Fresno, California, to pastor.

Elder Bethel then pastored for a while. Bishop William A. Washington, presiding Bishop of the Western Diocese, sent Rev. I. L. Craft as pastor in 1942. He remained there until August 1953. Elder L. D. Hughes was appointed pastor by Bishop A. M. White.

The Board of Education purchased the church property on 106th Street and Compton Ave. The church later bought and paid for the property at 11909 So. Main Street where Pilgrim was moved. After pastoring a few years, Rev. L. D. Hughes was sent to Emmanuel Church of Christ (Holiness) in Oakland, California by Bishop A. Hamilton, Jr.

Rev. R. L. Bradley, Pastor of New Hope Church of Christ (Holiness), and congregation combined with Pilgrim and Bishop A. Hamilton appointed Rev. Bradley, Pastor. On December 6, 1959, Pilgrim moved into a new edifice on 13722 So. Avalon Blvd. where Rev. Bradley and congregation are still worshipping and serving the Lord.

Faith Temple Church of Christ Holiness, U.S.A.

Brother C. B. Jordan was praying to God to grant him a place to start a Mission. One night, he had a dream and in the dream he saw a house which was empty; he said that God had showed him the place that he could start a Mission, but he was going to wait on God. So he kept these things in his heart. Several months after the vision, Brother Jordan was driving by with his eldest son, and when he arrived at 102 Grape Street, he looked and saw people moving out of the house on the corner. Brother Jordan was able to rent the house for $40.00 a month. He prepared the house for worship. Brother Jordan said that he prayed for a name and the Lord led him to the name "Mission Faith Temple." On the third Sunday, January 15, 1956, Faith Temple Mission had their first service. Brother Jordan's wife and family

244

and Brother A. L. Jordan and wife and family, Mother Harvey and one visitor were present in the first Service. Mother Harvey acted as Secretary in the first Sunday School.

At one point, it seemed as if the Mission would fail to materialize. After an investigation, Bishop M. R. Conic consented for the mission to continue. The Lord added to the Mission as time went on. In June of 1956, the mission board paid $500.00 down payment on the lot where Faith Temple Mission was located. The full price was $4,500.00.

On the 28th of January, 1959, Faith Temple Mission moved to 10103 Grape Street. They demolished the house at 102nd and Grape Street and the house on the second lot. On March 14, 1959, Faith Temple Mission had their Ground-Breaking Service. Finally, on October 5, 1960, the construction of the new church started. After all improvements are made and evaluation of the development is completed, the cost will exceed $90,000.00.

Christ Temple Church of Christ, (Holiness) U.S.A.
Gary, Indiana

The church was organized in 1932 by Reverend J. J. Peterson, who remained pastor of the church for 30 years. The church was being enlarged at the time of his death in 1962.

Reverend L. M. Relf was appointed pastor to succeed Rev. Peterson.

The Zion Chapel Church of Christ (Holiness) U.S.A., presently located at 732 Webster Street N.W., Washington, D.C., 20011, was founded November 2, 1952, by pastor, William Lloyd Jerome, who was ordained at the same time of the Founding Service of the church by the presiding Bishop of this Diocese, Bishop O. W. McInnis. God had shown Pastor Jerome in a vision the entrance to an auditorium. He began looking for a place to worship and was led to the sixteen hundred block of R Street N.W. There he found the auditorium he had foreseen. After contacting Mr. Leslie Williams, director of the Capital Music School, the auditorium was sub-rented for the beginning services of Zion Chapel.

The service was conducted by Rev. C. L. Carhee, the District Chairman of the Northern District of the Eastern Diocese. The meeting was attended by the members of First Church and well wishers and friends. When the invitation was extended following the sermon by Rev. Carhee, Rev. Jerome, Sister Virginia Jerome, Sister Angeline Coleman and Sister Elsie Smith took their stand as Charter Members of the church. Services were conducted at 2:30 each Sunday thereafter until the church began to increase in membership. In the immediate locality which was canvassed by the charter members, we gained the fellowship of the Broadwater family. Through the children we gained the parents. Deacon Hoke Smith was the only deacon. Faithful supporters such as Sister Anne Robinson, Sister Vera Dixon and families of each, Sister Maria Hackett who joined the church in its infancy,

Rev. Albert A. Green, Sr., Pastor
Zion Chapel

Sister Erma Thornton more recent in coming from West Virginia, Mother Coleman, Mother Ford and others who joined in the more recent years have carried on to date.

The church moved from the auditorium after a brief period of six months to a basement where we stayed for a two year period. There we doubled our efforts to secure a place where we could wholly hallow it to the glory of God. The basement belonged to the Capital School of Music and they had the right to use it for other purposes at will. Struggling in the basement until God blessed financially with donations from friends and well wishers, we accumulated enough money with the assistance of the Church Extension to purchase a house on 13th Street N.W., which was the home of Zion Chapel for a period of years. At 13th Street, Sister Christine Hodges and eventually Rev. Hodges came to worship with us. Sister Hodges was an asset to the church with the gift God gave her to teach; also Rev. Hodges, who was a talented musician. The Sunday School and Choir was organized before the church left the basement. The choir was under the leadership of Sister Virginia Jerome. The pastor encouraged the youth to further their study of music which resulted in Sister Carolyn Smith becoming the musician for the church. The C.W.W.W.'s were immediately in effect. Later on the W.A.C.'s were organized. As we expanded we availed ourselves of every opportunity for service and auxiliaries.

Special donations came into the services by friends such as Mrs. Sarah Thomas, Mrs. Lucy Ford who shared their tithes con-

247

sistently with the church although they were non-members but honorary; the Federal Life Insurance Co., Boyd's Beauty House, Chistley's Florist also made donations. Solicitations from members of our sister churches across the country helped us raise enough money to begin purchasing the church edifice located at 732 Webster Street N.W. The National Convention was approached and gave assistance. The building was bought, our goal had been won. The church moved forward by the help of God. Rev. Jerome was called to New York to pastor Lenox Avenue Mission one Sunday per month at the death of Rev. William Acty which divided his time between the two churches. Finally at the merger of the group on Madison Avenue and Lenox Avenue Mission, Rev. Jerome accepted full time pastorate.

Following the resignation of our Founder and Pastor, Rev. Jerome, which was regretfully accepted on August 14, 1961, the church prayerfully considered Rev. Vattel Jackson as Acting Pastor. On September 7, 1961, Rev. J. C. Smith, District Chairman of the Eastern Diocese, instructed us relative to selecting a pastor. The church unanimously voted to accept Rev. Vattel Jackson as Interim Pastor. During the administration of Rev. Jackson the membership prayed and worked together. On July 10, 1962, a business session was called by the District Chairman, Rev. J. C. Smith. At this meeting it was unanimously voted that Rev. Albert A. Green, Sr., become pastor. This was confirmed by the presiding Bishop of the Eastern Diocese, Bishop David Mc-Pherson of Norfolk, Virginia.

Rev. Green is a graduate of the Washington Baptist Seminary and has studied at American University. The church is growing spiritually. Thirteen new members have united, five by Baptism. Among the souls added was Sister Ellen Gibson and four of her children. God has blessed them with wonderful talents. Sister Gibson is the Directress of the Youth Choir. Brother Frank Dixon was not only saved but healed of cancer. Brother Rufus Smith has been called into the Ministry, having preached his trial sermon on December 13, 1964. He is now doing a wonderful job as Sunday School Superintendent. Under the Spirit-led leadership of Rev. Green, souls are continuing to be blessed. We are very grateful for his faithful wife, Sister Elisabeth Green, who is an inspiration to us, and a wonderful servant of God, taking her place in the choir and doing whatever her hands find to do.

The church is growing financially, due to the complete reorganization of the membership and reactivation of the committees.

During this administration alterations have been made on the church building. A choir stand has been added. This project was sponsored by the Senior Choir, under the direction of Sister Erma Thornton. It was through the leadership of Sister Thornton and continuous prayer by the choir for a pianist after Sister Carolyn Smith left the church to become pianist of the First Church of Christ (Holiness) U.S.A., that God blessed us with a very fine Spirit-filled musician in the person of Brother Alphonzo E. Jackson. The choir is progressing in a marvelous way. New carpet has been purchased for the auditorium by the C.W.W.W.'s, under the leadership of Sister Elsie Smith. The project now being sponsored by the Sunday School is the purchase of a Station Wagon proposed by Deacon L. H. Smith, and executed jointly by Deacon Smith and Brother Rufus Smith. This project is expected to become a reality in the very near future. We believe that many souls will be won through this effort and Personal Evangelism.

God blessed us with one deacon until the ordination of Brother Joe B. Willis during the 1963 Diocese Session. The church is not only reaching the community with the Gospel but is taking its place in helping to alleviate the poverty problems that exist, by collecting clothing for the needy which is distributed through the various organizations.

Thus Zion Chapel marches on through love, faith, prayer and victory in Jesus Christ.

Inkster Church of Christ

249

The Christ Temple Church at 27035 Colgate Street, Inkster, Michigan, opened on the first Sunday in January, 1956, with Rev. Samuel Kendrick, the founder, as pastor.

A lot was purchased and a new edifice was erected thereon. The architecture of the church is unique among other churches of the denomination.

Some of the first members were Brother Isaac Jonson, Sister Nartickle E. Kendrick, Sister Lucile Hopkins, Brother Hobard Hopkins, Brother Isaac Roats, Sister Lillian Roats, and Sister Etta Flucker.

SECOND TEMPLE CHURCH 1965, LOS ANGELES, CALIF.
Standing: Left to right, Reverend Charles Ligons—Associate Minister; Elder A. L. Ballard—Pastor; Reverend Huey P. Sheriff—Associate; Seated: Rear left, Deacon John Plummer, Sr. Inset: Reverend H. C. Thompson.

Second Temple Church of Christ (Holiness)
Los Angeles, California

On March 12, 1958 the Second Temple Church of Christ (Holiness) U.S.A. was organized at the home of Elder (see picture) Henry C. Thompson, 1236 E. 99th St. Los Angeles, Calif.

The meeting was call to Order by Bishop Albert Hamilton Jr. Open Song, Near the Cross. Prayer. Elder Henry C. Thompson.

Roll of Members:

Rev. A. L. Ballard,
Rev. James Thrash,
Rev. Henry C. Thompson,
Deacon John Plummer,
Deaconess Odessie Plummer,
Brother Clifton Plummer,
Brother James Plummer,
Sister Wilhelmina Foster,

Sister Annie B. Thrash,
Sister Gussie Clark,
    (see picture);
Sister Yvonne Plummer,
Sister Evelyn Plummer,
Sister Vivian Thrash,
Sister Pauline Clark,
Sister Peggie William.

Rev. A. L. Ballard was placed in charge as Pastor; Rev. James Thrash Assistant. Bishop Albert Hamilton Jr. encouraged the Church to go forward in the Lord. He explained the Manual to the Members concerning the Bible Doctrine, of the Church of Christ (Holiness) U.S.A. which is the principle of Christian Living based on the Word of God, with those encouraging words our Faith was strengthened to stand in these trying times.

Our first service was held in the home of Rev. and Mrs. James Thrash, 909 East 73rd Street. On April 6, 1958, we moved to a new location, address: 4131 South Hoover, Los Angeles, California. At this address the following persons united with us. The Mose Walter Family united on March 15, 1960. These are the names, Juleann Walter, Rosetta Walter, Jessie Walter and Robert Walter. They remain with us, until they move from the city. Sister Clestine Hurley and Sister Maxine Moore also unite with Second Temple Church of Christ (Holiness) U.S.A. in 1960. On April 30, 1961, Sister Evelyn Moore and family united with Second Temple Church of Christ (Holiness) U.S.A. They were Faithful Workers in the Lord. They united their hearts in Prayer and we all received a Blessing.

Elder Huey Sheriff came to help us in Nov. 1961 and has been a source of inspiration to us, and now superintendent of the Sunday School.

251

We were encouraged and inspired by Rev. Charles Price Jones and Christ Temple Church of Christ (Holiness) and Members. He encouraged us to go forward for the Lord.

There were added to the Church four members who came into the Church of Christ (Holiness) U.S.A. Namely:

Sister Ida Bennett and family, Sister Barbara Ross united with Second Temple Church of Christ (Holiness) U.S.A., and was a loyal member of the Church.

Elder Vaugn united with Second Temple Church of Christ (Holiness) U.S.A. in 1958. He is gone to be with the Lord.

Sister Bertha Ford from Memphis, Tenn., came to help us in June 1963. Sister Georgie M. Kidd from Texas united with us in July of 1963. Sister Gloria Mae Sheriff from the Olive Missionary Baptist Church of New Orleans, Louisiana, united in November 22, 1963.

These are new members which were added to the Church in the year of 1964. There were seven that were baptized. These are the ones: Larry Banks, Barbara Thrash, Sylvia Clark, Michael Banks, Emily Ballard, Gloria Gatlin and Yvonne Gatlin.

The Rev. and Mrs. Charles Ligons and family came to us from Christ Temple Church of Christ (Holiness) U.S.A. at 1275 E. 54th St., Los Angeles, California. They have been very helpful and a great blessing to us.

In the month of October of 1964, Sister Dorothy Golden, Sister Shirley Wynne and Sister Oletta Murphy. New members that were added in the same month of October: Charlette Wynne, John Allen Wynne and Shiela Wynne. God has nicely blessed us in every way both spiritual and financial.

First Officers
Trustees

Elder James Thrash .... Chairman
Elder Henry C. Thompson .... Treasurer
Deacon John Plummer
Clerk
Sister Annie B. Thrash .... Church Clerk
Sister Wilhelmina Foster .... Treasurer
Sister Gussie Clark .... Pianist
Deaconess
Sister Oddessie Plummer
Sister Evelyn Moore who was consecrated as a deaconess un-

252

der the leadership of Bishop Albert Hamilton Jr. Place Second
Temple Church of Christ (Holiness) U.S.A., Rev. A. L. Ballard,
Pastor.

Our Pastor encouraged the Members to maintain Fellowship and
Brethren love and let nothing separate us from the love of God.

Rev. A. L. Ballard, Pastor

Rev. Huey Sheriff, Church Clerk

Rev. James Thrash, Treasurer

SECOND TEMPLE CHURCH OF CHRIST
(HOLINESS), U.S.A.
234 W. 69th ST., CHICAGO 21, ILL.

The church was started in 1961 with Rev. C. L. Flakes as
pastor and assisted by Rev. Samuel McGee with presiding Bishop
M. R. Conic officiating.

The church has grown to a membership of about 40 within
the four years under the pastorage of Rev. Flakes. Rev. Samuel
McGee was sent elsewhere after the first year.

In designating the personnel of the Second Temple Church picture the names of the 21 children shown in the picture are not
given. Reading from left to right, *First row seated*: Herman S.
Nichols, Chairman of Deacon Board; Thomas Jefferson, Rev.

253

C. L. Flakes, Pastor; Mrs. Onie Flakes, Pastor's wife; Squire C. Baker, Chairman Trustee Board, Bertram Holmes, Trustee. *Second row seated*: W.A.C.C., Mrs. Nadie White, Pres.; Mrs. Mary Brown, Sec.; Mrs. Lela Bunton, Mrs. Ruth Glaspie, Treas. C.W.W.W., Mrs. Clara Denham, Mrs. Myrabell Baker, Mrs Ruth Sheffer, Pres.; Mrs. Thelma Jefferson, Sec.; Standing Choir, *First Row*: Cynthia Morris, F. Morris, Myra Baker, Beverly Jefferson, Sec.; Desaree Baker, Dorotheus Schaffers, Mrs. Jettie Smith, Mrs. Agnes Collins, Treas.; Mrs. Iris Watson, Pianist. *Second row*: John Schaffers, Freddie Morris, Tony Williams, Alvin Morris, Lavel Watson, Pres.

PLAIN VIEW NO. 2 CHURCH

The Plain View No. 2 Church was organized, May 11, 1947, at Baton Rouge, Louisiana. Officiating organizing officials were: Rev. O. C. Miller, Rev. John Boatner, and Rev. Neal Dyson.

The church property is valued at $30,000. The dedication service for this new edifice was held June 7, 1964 with eighteen adult members. Some of the first members of the church were: Sister Jessie Miller, Sister Eva Vernon, Sister Ortee Williams, Sister Willie Ree Burkhalter, Sister Evie Harvey, and Sister Ollie Mae Miller. Rev. Otis C. Miller is pastor.

EMMANUEL CHAPEL, HAMPTON, VA.

About twenty-seven years ago, the Lord impressed one of His followers, Sister Blanch D. Lloyd of Phoebus, Va., to have her neighbors to come in to her home for Bible Study and prayer. Her aim was to get the word of God to those who were unchurched; feeling that they would come to a home more readily than to church.

She went about her mission by contacting many of the neighbors and people of that community, prepared her first Bible lesson and trusted God to do the rest.

On the appointed Friday night many of those contacted showed up; this was the beginning of the Prayer Circle. To encourage those who attended and others to attend, a delicious repast was served each Friday night and the word of God was taught in its fullness. Many for the first time realized what real salvation meant. The Lord blessed Sister Lloyd's efforts, in that souls were saved and believers baptized.

The members decided to bring an offering to help the underprivileged, the old folks home which was in existence at that time and to support a native preacher in Liberia, West Africa. Many families were blessed through the members of the Prayer Circle, both spiritually and materially.

On Wednesday nights we held prayer and praise services, on Friday nights Bible study and on Sunday afternoon Sunday School.

After meeting from house to house for a number of years, the membership grew to the extent it demanded a larger place of worship. The members were faithful in making financial pledges to purchase a lot to erect a building that would accommodate the growing membership.

The Lord miraculously supplied the needs. The lot was purchased on 536 South St., Hampton, Va., and the building was erected.

In the course of three and one half years, with a few faithful saints the debt of over $10,000 dollars was cleared and the mortgage burned.

A bus was purchased to transport the members of the Sunday School. What a mighty God we serve! After hearing the then Elder David McPherson preach at St. Timothy Church of Christ Holiness at Newport News, Va., we became interested and were blessed to have him preach for us each Sunday afternoon at 3:00 o'clock. His ministry was such a blessing that members who were

255

unchurched desired a church home and plans were made to become a Chartered Church.

On March 30th, 1951, under the supervision of Bishop O. W. McInnis we were organized as a Chartered Church and the then Elder D. McPherson was appointed to serve us each Sunday evening and Wednesday nights. We were blessed to have fellowship with the churches in the Eastern Diocese and to have many of the ministers of the Gospel such as Elders J. T. Hill, O. W. McInnis, A. D. Williams, A. M. White, and L. Randall to render services at Emmanuel Chapel. It proved such a blessing we decided to become affiliated with the Church of Christ Holiness, U.S.A. On Jan. 25th, 1957, we became affiliated and the Elder S. G. Winston was appointed to that charge.

—Sister Margaret B. Jones, Historian

First Church of Christ (Holiness) U.S.A.
Merced, California
509 J. Street,

In 1944 the late Bishop A. B. Smith, then known as Elder A. B. Smith, organized First Church, in the home of Brother Lee Yokley and worshiped in Brother Eugene Williams house.

A broad hearted Methodist minister, Rev. Samuel Perry allowed the worship to be held in his church for some time. Then a faithful sister who came to Merced from Louisiana, Sister Octavie Porter (a widow), loaned the church ($800) eight hundred dollars to begin buying lumber to build. Then a brush arbor was built to worship in for a period of time. The church and parsonage was built on the lot purchased. The church was incorporated on May 16, 1945. The trustees, Brother E. P. Bass Sr., Brother Eugene Williams, Brother Lee Yokley. Members as follows: Brother L. W. Wilkins, Sister L. W. Wilkins, Sister E. P. Bass, Sister Octavia Porter, Sister A. B. Smith, Sister Mammie Yokley, Sister Velma Bass and many others who were added to the church.

Church of Christ (Holiness), U.S.A.
Sacramento, California

In March 1951, Brother Joseph Roots, Sr., was moving from Jackson, Mississippi, to Sacramento, California, he heard that there was no Church of Christ Holiness in Sacramento, so he stopped in Los Angeles and talked to Bishop A. White and told him they wanted to start a church in Sacramento.

A few months later Bishop White sent Brother Frank Barber, Brother Lester Hughes, and Brother Charles P. Jones, Jr., to be in service.

Brother Frank Barber was chosen to be the pastor. He was very faithful and came from Los Angeles to Sacramento for service every 1st and 3rd Sunday. During this time the name Zion Temple was chosen for the church.

Services were being held in the home of Brother J. Roots until land was purchased and the church built. In November 1954 the church was completed and then dedicated. In October 1955 Brother James Thrash became the pastor. He also came from Los Angeles on 1st and 3rd Sunday and a few months later Brother Donald Brown started assisting him by coming on the 2nd and 4th Sunday. In 1956 we were blessed to purchase the house next door for the church parsonage.

In 1958 Brother Samuel Smith became the pastor. He came from San Francisco and later moved his family to Sacramento and he resided in the parsonage.

In 1962 Brother E. Ollison became our pastor and a few months later Brother E. Ward began to assist him. Brother Ollison came on 1st and 3rd Sunday, Brother Ward came on 2nd and 4th Sunday.

Brother E. Ollison and Brother E. Ward are very faithful.

St. Matthew Church of Christ
Monroe, La.

The St. Matthew Church of Christ, Monroe, La., first met in Mother Dunn's home. They then met in a building in a park near present site, 801 Louisan Ave., Monroe, La. The church was first started April, 1906, by Rev. C. C. Carhee and Judge King as Christ's Holy Sanctified Church.

The value of the church property is about $12,000. The number of members including children is about 75. The names of pastors in the order of their service are: Rev. N. S. Cann, Rev. W. H. Dunn, Rev. A. J. Parrish, Rev. A. Ragland, Rev. Jesse Augerson.

The names of some of the first members of the church: Mother Lizzie Dunn, Rev. N. S. Cann, Sister Josephine Cann, Rev. and Sister Israel Overton, Sister Mary Fairchild, Sister Emma Lowe, Sister Ida Williams, Sister Beatrice Mitchel, Sister L. A. Mitchel, Sister Florence Lee, Sister Nancy Henderson, Sister Mattie Bunton, Brother John Mitchel, Sister Riley Mitchel, Sister Eddie Jackson.

CHURCH OF CHRIST (HOLINESS), U.S.A.
DREW, MISS.

Brother Robert Jackson, who was a member of a Holiness church elsewhere, moved here and started holding meetings in his home.

In 1913, Elder N. Sanders, father of many Holiness churches in the Mississippi Delta, preached here under a tent with some degree of success. Also services were held under a sawmill shed and in an empty 2-room house. Later in 1914, Elder Sanders, the first pastor, organized the church in 1914 with 18 members. Mr. George Stakly, a white man gave material for framing a church house and the members were assessed and gave the money for the building. Elder A. G. Belton of Mound Bayou, erected the first and present building in 1916. Elder C. C. Carhee, then of Shaw and later moved to Los Angeles, painted the church.

Elder N. Sanders pastored the church until his death in 1927. Then followed Elders J. E. Bearden, William Mitchell, H. R. McInnis, Clifton Goodloe, and A. J. Torrey, L. P. Camper, William Jones, M. T. Newsome.

Some of the first members were Brother Robert Jackson, Brother J. S. Farley, Sister Emma Farley, Sister Demeris Farley Sanders, Brother Jimmy Corbett, Sister Emma Corbett, Brother Joe Redmond, Brother Elex Barber, Brother Elex Wince, Brother Will Wiggins, Brother Elex Mays, Brother Andrew White, Brother S. M. Mamie Mitchner and Sister Hattie Leggett.

THE ROCK HILL CHURCH OF CHRIST (HOLINESS)
NEAR MT. OLIVE, MISSISSIPPI

This church was established in 1905 by Elder A. C. Camper. The work began under a brush arbor 14 miles north of Prentiss, Miss., with 8 members: Elder I. M. Smith, Brothers Robert Shivers, Isaac Brunson, Mack Thompson, Sisters Louise Shivers, Annie Smith, A. Gowns and Deacon George A. Durr.

Brother Mack Thompson gave the church site and Elder Enoch Thomas, the first pastor, built the church and remained pastor for several years. The members suffered much persecution, the common lot of pioneers. Elder Enoch Thomas resigned and moved to St. Louis Mo., in Feb. 1917. After he left, the church was without a pastor for about four years. During this time different ministers preached for the church occasionally. Sister Jane Johnson, first missionary of this district, came down from Jackson and taught Bible lessons from house to house, which helped to keep the spiritual fires aglow, while Deacons Madison White and George Durr taught Bible lessons weekly and the church kept up her Wednesday night prayer meetings, Sunday School and services Sundays and Sunday nights. The sisters walked ten miles taking the Gospel to others hungering for more spiritual light.

The second pastor, Elder Ezra Berry, was followed by Elders T. J. Hardy and Albert Myers, respectively, each of whom served the church two years. Elder Hardy often remarked, "I have not much time; I must hurry." Surely enough, his time proved short but his race was well run. Elder E. D. Tyner came and served the church one year. Then came Elder John Vance and rebuilt the church house and remained pastor for twenty-eight years, till his last illness in 1955. Rev. Vance was followed by Rev. W. H. Hollins. At this time the deacons were: Deacon Madison White, Deacon Elijah Lockhart. There are about 75 members.

THE PLAIN VIEW CHURCH OF CHRIST (HOLINESS) U.S.A.
NEAR MT. HERMON, LA.
ORGANIZED JANUARY, 1905

Elder A. J. Scarborough was pastoring a Baptist Church nearby. He began to preach holiness, which preaching split the church. Brother Anderson Brumfield then invited Elder L. J. Brunson of McComb, Miss., to come and preach in this community. He came, and he and his band held meetings in an old barn in a swamp, belonging to Mr. F. M. Brown (white), until they built the first church. They organized the church on the 2nd Saturday in January 1905, in the home of Brother Dave Slocum with Deacon William Webb of Fernwood, Miss., assisting. Elder Brunson had the people to bring their Bibles to the services and read for themselves, so nobody could refute the doctrine. At this time Deacon Webb was illiterate. But through the efforts of his devout Christian wife and with a desire to study he learned to read and write. He was ordained to the ministry and became an organizer of churches and a builder of lives. He was one of the most capable, pastors of the movement; one of the most influential and best loved. Pastor Webb was not a great pulpit orator but his messages carried great weight. He was magnetic, drawing men to him. His smiling face and friendly manners found friends for him in all denominations—he was pastor of all men. Sinners most pro-

259

foundly respected him. He lived among his members; learned their problems, prayed daily for them and ministered to their sundry needs and his membership followed him whenever he moved and wherever. He went from church to church.

After organizing the church they bought an old school building from the local school board and built the church house on the site of the old barn given by Mr. Brown. Later on Brother Marshall Brumfield gave a church site on the highway during the first pastorate of Elder J. E. Burris. Here they built the 2nd church and Brother Anderson Brumfield named the new church Plain View.

Among the original members were Deacons Anderson Brumfield, Arthur Brumfield, Dave Slocum, Brothers King Brumfield, Morgan Reed, John Wilson, Marvin Slocum; Sisters Corine Brumfield, Emma Corine Slocum, Sarena Brumfield, Luna Miller, Lucy Dawson, Modessa Dawson, Fannie Dawson. Among those considered pillars in this church, some of whom are gone from this life, while others are yet carrying on might be mentioned Brother Marshall (M.M.) Brumfield, Sisters Sarah Vernon, Ollie Vernon, Marry Miller, Stella Harvey, L. N. Burris, Denie Burkhalter—laborers to help keep spiritual fires aglow as well as carry on the material part of the work.

Pastors in order: Elders L. J. Brunson, George Brumfield, John Vance, J. E. Burris, John Vance, J. E. Burris until he left this life, B. T. Johnson the present pastor (in 1957, but died in 1960) through whose planning, supervision and labor the present church was built, modern even to a shower bath—on the same site as the second church. Functioning organizations in this church are Sunday School, C.W.W.W., H.Y.P.U.

The New Lake Church of Christ (Holiness) U.S.A.
Jackson, Mississippi

In the early years of the work after a group of members were put out of Hope Spring Baptist and other churches near by, they came together and began meeting under a brush arbor. Elder Tom Sanders, the first pastor, walked 10 miles every Sunday and held services in the home of Mrs. Nancy McCoy, meeting on the ground until they built the church after some 10 months.

In this home or on this ground they organized with about 25 members and named the church New Lake. Among the original members were Brothers Pete Silas, Eddie Silas, Patrick, Frank

The New Lake Church

Berry, Thomas Roach, and Sisters Nancy McCoy, Ada Warren, Laura Patrick, Emma Jones, Sarah Roach, Ella Commander and Elmyra Castilla.

"Father" Sanders remained pastor till his death. Then came Elder J. D. King and did likewise, serving 29 years. He organized four auxiliaries in the church in addition to the already live choir and prayer band and left the church in a new building process. Third pastor, Elder Clifton Goodloe, wonderfully supervised the building project, baptized several converts and with all auxiliaries alive, left of his own accord. Fourth pastor, Elder Leo Butler served well for a short time. Fifth pastor, Elder L. P. Camper, energetic and courageous, stepped up the Sunday School hour from 10 a.m. to 9:30 a.m., added the Pastor's Aid Club and water system, baptized three new converts and left of his own accord after a rather short but pleasant stay. Sixth pastor, Elder William Jones is a warm hearted man of understanding. His motto is "The church and its belongings kept at their best." Under his leadership we've got our power mower, another piano and five new members and all auxiliaries are moving forward.

Present value of church property including parsonage $6,000. Number of members including children 40.

THE MT. OLIVE CHURCH OF CHRIST (HOLINESS) U.S.A.
MAGNOLIA, MISSISSIPPI

About 1901 Elder William Webb, the first pastor held meetings first in his own home and from house to house by requests. Later the meetings extended to the streets, school house, and brush arbor and finally settled under a shed. Here they held meetings for a year. And here was organized the Mt. Olive church, with above two dozen members. Among the charter members were Brothers William Ellzey, Jim Simmons, James Harrington, Caleb Hill and (Father) Peter Hill and Sisters Rachel Warren, Janie Harrington, Dora Webb, Maggie Webb, Hannah Ross, Lucy Hill, Catherine Cockerham, Ella Ellzey, Ella Simmons, Bertha Graham and Mother (Mary) Hill. Elder L. J. Brunson had organized the Star Hill Church at Fernwood, four miles north of Magnolia and lent his efforts toward strengthening this work.

Early organizations in the church were regular services one Sunday, Sunday School Young People's meeting Sundays P.M. and Women's Willing Workers, Mondays P.M. The Women's Willing Workers was an outgrowth of what in the beginning of the work was called women's or sisters' meetings. These meetings were attended by women of all ages and even girls. Often women brought their little children along, numbers of whom were converted as a result of the deep spirituality of these meetings. There were Bible teachers among the women and the pastor, other ministers and visitors came in and usually added zest to the services.

Elder Webb set the willing workers to raising money to help finance the building of a church house. This they did and thus provided recreation for young and old by giving suppers—selling eatables generally on Saturday nights at the individual homes. Additionally other individuals gave money to help on the building fund.

The pastor exhibited such keen devotion to visiting, counseling and comforting his members that at one time when he returned home following a 3 weeks leave of absence, they gave him a surprising reception. As to praying, miraculous, Divine manifestations accompanied prayer in those days of believing prayers.

Sister Ella Ellzey suffered from a painful rising on her breast which the doctor had said it would require an operation to remove. She went to the home of Sister Bell Ross. After prayer together, the rising burst, the lump came off and Sister Ellzey reached home, instantly healed on the way. "I will show thee great and mighty things which thou knowest not" (Jer. 33:3 was literally fulfilled.)

Among well-known ministers who have served this congregation were Elders William Webb, A. J. Scarborough, L. J. Brunson, John Vance, and J. E. Burris—all now "serving in another room."

Elder Sparkman reports that during Elder C. D. Ratliffs' last illness, Elder L. J. Brunson, on a visit and regretting that he was taking nothing, said that in front of him flew up a drove of partridges. One struck against a building and fell dead on the ground. "This is just what I wanted," were the sick man's words, as he learned how his craving was surprisingly met (Pro. 10:24b).

CHURCH OF CHRIST (HOLINESS) U.S.A.

The Church of Christ (Holiness) U.S.A. of 789 Edgemont, Indianapolis, Ind., was organized about the year of 1922 by Bishop H. L. Caver of Little Rock, Ark., on Ogden and 12th Sts. with about twenty members.

Among the first members were, Ministers: Rev. William Webb, Rev. Jackson, Rev. Knox and Rev. F. E. Williams; Deacons: Brother Steven Lewis, Chairman, Brother Henry White, Brother Jeff Davis, Brother Israel Willis and Brother Jeff Williams. The sisters of the church were: Sister P. Castian, Sister Ella Coleman, Sister Ollie King, Sister Minnie Jones, Sister Hallie England, Sister Emma Lewis Lewis, Sister Jenney Davis, Sister Armanda Willis, Sister Carey Williams, Sister Rachel Washington, Sister

Maggie Vell, Sister Hattie White, Sister Mattie Paste and Sister Nettie Anderson.

Rev. F. E. Williams of Birmingham, Ala., began pastoring about the year of 1924 until 1930. During his pastorate the church was relocated on North and Blackford Sts. and finally moved to 522 Patterson St. The latter part of 1930 he resigned. He was then succeeded by Rev. David Caldwell of Georgia. His pastorate lasted about 9 months. Beginning in 1931 Rev. G. W. Hemphill of Virginia pastored the church for about 3 years. He was succeeded by Rev. L. M. Relf who pastored the church for about 3 years.

Abraham, a Man of Faith and a Friend of God

By faith Elder Randall, when he was called to go out into a place which he should after receive for an inheritance, obeyed: and he went out not knowing whether he went. By faith he sojourned in the land of promises, as in a strange country. He assumed the pastorate of this church on October 3, 1938, located at that time on Patterson Street. If an attempt was made to describe it, it would rightly be called a "store front" church. Things both spiritually and financially were at a rather low ebb. Being a man of faith, he was undaunted by these conditions, so we pressed on. He asked the church to cooperate with him two years and he promised that working together they would be able to accomplish things of which they would not be ashamed.

Shortly after this time he began to look around for a place where they might build a church. One day he met a strange man who asked him if he were looking for a place to build a church. Overjoyed, he immediately replied, "Yes." The stranger then told him about Mr. Taylor who had land on Edgemont Street that he wanted to sell. These incidents happened when Elder Randall was a stranger in the town. So it is apparent that this was a plan of God.

It is characteristic throughout the ages that men have not always immediately followed their leaders. A small minority of the members refused to come. It looked as though their struggles had just begun. To their great dismay came opposition from without; neighbors petitioned the zoning board in protest against the building of a church at this location. The zoning board refused to issue a permit.

264

This move brought additional turmoil—this time within the group. Elder Randall doubled his determination to carry out what he believed was God's plan for him and the membership while some in the group sought legal help. But he still had to depend on the Lord to fight the battle. Finally through faith and prayer the zoning board relented and gave permission to build.

Many still remembered when they were dwelling in the tabernacle or tent, how the neighbors again petitioned the zoning board, which ordered the tent taken down. Only a few were willing to sit in the open basement, referred to as the open "hole" with newspapers and umbrellas over heads—protecting them from the weather as services were conducted.

Before long the basement was completed. Soon came on the war which temporarily brought the building activities to a halt; for government restrictions made it extremely difficult to get building materials. After searching in this city and in other cities, the pastor obtained the necessary material to complete the building. Finally people caught the vision and rallied with their financial support. God blessed spiritually and financially so much so that the building was paid for on its completion. These experiences brought the group closer together, on a high spiritual level and gave greater unity. From this man of faith and courage have gone forth spiritual sons who have accepted the ministry and are carrying out God's work and plans in various sections of the country. Evidence of this is the church plant, the market value of which is $40,000; the effect of their work is being felt by the community; the neighbors who at first bitterly opposed them have become their staunch friends. In these particulars they see the visions of the man of faith become realities. And now understand more clearly that "Faith is the substance of things hoped for, the evidence of things not seen." By it Elder Randall obtained a good report. "Wherefore God is not ashamed to be called his God."

He was pastor until his death on 12th Jan. 1956. Rev. A. Beasley was acting pastor until October 1956. Then Rev. J. E. Bearden assumed the pastorate until December 1959, at which time he resigned.

In January of 1960 Rev. J. E. Holland the present leader, was appointed acting pastor until the meeting of the national Convention after which he was elected pastor.

MORNING STAR CHURCH OF CHRIST, (HOLINESS), U.S.A.

The history of the Morning Star Church of Christ, (Holiness), U.S.A. of Yakima, Washington, had its beginning in 1946. When Brother and Sister Elmer Woods were given the vision to build a holiness mission here in Yakima.

They started saving their tithe money, and in 1948 they purchased a corner lot on South Seventh Street and Pacific Avenue, at a cost of $775.

By now Brother Woods and Sister Woods needed money and manpower to continue their work. Brother Tom and Sister Lela Longmire at this beginning agreed to give their support in this great project of building a house for the Lord. Also at this time the late Bishop A. B. Smith and his loving wife came into this northwestern area. Bishop Smith brought along with him his wife, Elder Craft, Elder Clarence Carhee and Deacon T. H. Smith.

At this meeting the church was organized and Elder Elmer Woods was ordained as a minister of God and pastor of the Morning Star Church of Christ, Holiness, with Brother Tom Longmire as deacon. These two brothers and their wives were the only members at this time. Church construction began May 1st, 1953.

The saints had a mind to work, but they needed money to put up a place of worship.

266

Bishop A. B. Smith came to their aid with $100 from the Mission Board of the Church of Christ, Holiness, plus the Extension Board gave the Church $500. With this money, the basement was dug and construction began, but the $600 soon ran out. Then Elder Woods and Brother Tom Longmire got acquainted with some saints of the Nazarene Church. After these saints heard these brothers' requests, they personally loaned them $600 which came close to completing the basement of our church. The church was blessed in having certain men of our community to devote some labor in the building of our basement. Namely a contractor loaned Elder Woods a mixer and gave some cement and sand, also the Black Masons gave the church their labor. May the Lord reward each one for his labors.

The basement is now complete and now we look back and see how far the Lord has brought our church, through the fruitful service and labors of many of the saints. We must mention the late Bishop A. B. Smith and Sister A. B. Smith, the faithful of God, who gave up the comforts of their home in California to come and labor untiringly with great faith, patience and love. God bless them. Also, our church remembers the great missionary zeal of Mother Prentiss, a wonderful saint of God. Many of the other saints of God have been of great blessing unto the church. Saints such as Mother Vernon, Sister Hawkins, Sister Harvey and Sister G. Moore. Later, the Church was blessed with the dynamic Bible teaching of Sister Holt, Sister Gatling and Sister Naomi Doles. The church has been blessed by these men and women of God: Brother Carhee (the Evangelist), Elder Tyree Feltzs, of whom God caused souls to be added unto the Church. God bless them.

Since the church began, it has been blessed by many, many saints of God, of whom space and memory won't permit me to record. After Bishop Smith passed, God blessed us to come under the leadership of Bishop A. Hamilton, a great teacher sent of God. He and his loveable wife, Sister Hamilton, also Sister Dunn, and Sister Graves would usually accompany him to Yakima and Seattle. The church profited greatly from each of these soldiers of the Cross.

Our Bishops, evangelists and missionaries would only be here once or twice a year, so our church had need of pastors from its beginning up until now. Elder Woods pastored our church from its beginning in 1950 until he retired in June, 1952. Several were added to the church in this period.

Elder Zed Crowley succeeded Brother Wood. In his ministry, several families joined the church. The church's very first candidate for baptism was Brother Lloyd Mitchell, who is now serving in the U. S. Airforce in South Vietnam. Pray for him.

Elder Samuel Kendricks pastored our Church after Brother Zed left. He (Elder Kendricks) and his wife were a blessing unto our community. Many souls were blessed through him.

Next we had Elder Ruben Davis who worked hard for the Church. God bless him.

Elder Rufus Luster and family, pastored us for a period in which some of the believers were sanctified through the sound teachings of the word of God.

Elder Luster resigned in 1959 as pastor. Elder Emmanuel Campbell and family were fellowshipped into our church on November 27, 1960. He then took over as pastor and served the church faithfully until he was transferred to Alaska in the U.S. Air Force in July of 1963.

During his ministry here, the interior of the church was completed with new lighting, the ceiling covered with sheet rock and painted. New lawns around church plus a retaining wall around the church property. May the Lord ever bless all of our past ministers for their contributions.

Presently, our church is laboring under the leadership of Elder E. J. Williams. As you look around the church you can see many new improvements and additions that our pastor has contributed to the church. Also, some souls being added unto the church.

We look back to our beginning with 4 souls. Now we have about 40 members in church and 62 in Sunday School, yet we feel that there is much toil that we have not trod as yet. We know God is able to give us the City if we remain steadfast and unmoveable, always abounding in the Word of the Lord. We are still in the basement and we have hoped to take our building on up this year. Pray much for us.

—Brother Henry Beauchamp (History Reporter)

—Elder E. J. Williams (Pastor)

CHAPTER VI

THE MINISTRY

BISHOPS OF THE CHURCH 1927—1965

In 1927, at Norfolk, Virginia, Elder C. P. Jones was impressed to make a change in the title of his ministry after thirty two years as the General President and Overseer of the National Convention.

He felt led to have the National Convention create the office of Bishop, but there was a bit of reluctance on his part of allowing himself to be set apart as the only Bishop, without similar recognition extended to the other ministers in their jurisdictions. After prayerful consideration, five of them were designated as Bishops with C. P. Jones as the Senior Bishop. The

The first bishops of the Church of Christ Holiness (U.S.A.) were elected in August, 1927, at the National Convention in Norfolk, Virginia. Charles Price Jones, Senior Bishop and President; John F. Morrison, Junior Bishop; James L. I. Conic, Junior Bishop and Vice-President; William A. Washington, Junior Bishop; Edward W. Butler, Junior Bishop.

other four were, namely: J. L. I. Conic, Vice-President; E. W. Butler; J. F. Morrison and William A. Washington. They served as Junior Bishops and overseers of their respective areas.

BISHOP JOHN F. MORRISON

Bishop J. F. Morrison was an able, consecrated man of God. He was one of the most popular, and most beloved overseers of the church. He left behind an enviable record as a pastor and a tried friend of every institution the church attempted to sponsor. He was most zealous in the cause of soul-saving. His devoted prayer life enhanced his service as a soul saver.

An evangelist who conducted a meeting for Elder Morrison said that any time he would wake up at night he would hear this saintly man praying. He died in 1935.

BISHOP J. L. I. CONIC

Bishop J. L. I. Conic was born at Lexington, Mississippi, October 15, 1876. He was married to Miss Louise Virginia of Jackson, Mississippi. Three children were born to this union: James, Alma and Major Rudd.

Bishop J. L. I. Conic   Bishop William A. Washington

He was an early convert to the new faith, licensed to preach in 1892, and ordained in 1898. He established the church at Arkadelphia, Arkansas, the Mt. Olive Church at Jackson, and the Green Hill Church at Adams, Mississippi. He pastored churches at Selma, and Montgomery, Alabama, Jayess, Starksville, and Yazoo, Mississippi, Franklinton, La.; Pinebluff, Ark.; Memphis, Tenn.; Chicago Heights, Illinois; Chicago, Illinois; Washington, D. C.; St. Louis, Missouri; and Christ Temple, Jackson.

He was chairman of Publishing Board; President of C.M. and I. College, Vice-President of the National Convention for 17 years; Bishop of the Northern Diocese; and, finally, Presiding Bishop of the Southeastern Diocese. He died May, 1939 at Jackson Mississippi.

BISHOP WILLIAM A. WASHINGTON

Bishop William A. Washington was born in 1886 in Carroll County, near Black Hawk, Mississippi. His mother, Mrs. Charlotte Washington, was the mother of seven sons who became

271

ministers, three of whom became pastors in the Churches of Christ, Holiness, U.S.A.

His first Church Pastorates were Tougaloo and Adams, Mississippi; Selma and Montgomery, Alabama. He later went West and became a builder and pulpiteer and "carved a diocese out of the Rockies," as it were!

His chief cornerstone was the establishment of the Bethel Church of Christ, Holiness, Corner East Adams and Hooper Avenues, Los Angeles, California. Under his Pastorate, Bethel Church grew to over 1200 in membership. Many other churches were established in the West under his administration. He was the first Presiding Bishop of the Western Diocese. He was Chairman of the Publishing Board; Member of the National Educational-Trustee Board of C.M. and I. College; Vice-President of the National Convention; and Chairman of the National Executive Board.

He was the Chairman of the Editing and Revision Committees of the 1926, 1936, and 1945 Edition of the Church Manuals. He died May, 1949, at Los Angeles, California.

BISHOP EDWARD W. BUTLER

Bishop Edward W. Butler was born 1870 in Jackson, Mississippi. His parents were members of Mt. Helm Baptist Church and were put out with the group led by Elder C. P. Jones in 1902.

He later moved to Shreveport, La. It was from here that his development in the ministry took place.

He pastored Conway, Little Rock, Pine Bluff, and Searcy, Arkansas; Shreveport and Belmont, Louisiana; Ruleville, Mississippi, Cynthia and Christ Temple, Jackson.

He was Presiding Bishop of the Southern Diocese and later the Southwestern Diocese. He was secretary of the C.M. and I. College Board, Secretary of the Board of Bishops, and Vice-President of the National Convention. He died August 1953.

THE OTHER BISHOPS OF THE CHURCH 1928-1965

BISHOP H. L. CAVER

Bishop H. L. Caver was born Feb. 14, 1880, in Monroe, La. After receiving his early education in his hometown, he felt the call to the ministry. Having a desire to better prepare himself for the Lord's work, he secured permission from his parents to attend college. While in school, he sought the Lord for a companion. He was married to Miss Sarah Crawford in 1913. To this union, 9 children were born.

He graduated from Philander Smith College in Little Rock, Ark., and later taught there for four years.

He was licensed to preach in 1916 and was ordained in 1917.

Bishop H. L. Caver

Bishop Edward W. Butler

He toiled at C.M. and I. College and at the school in Boydton, Va. He pastored in St. Louis and Chicago, Ill. He was elected Bishop in 1938 over the Northern Diocese. He was faithful until his death on March 16, 1944.

Sister Sarah Caver, the widow of Bishop Henry L. Caver resides in Detroit, Mich. She was a Vice-President of the Michigan-Ohio District.

She is a cheerful, faithful worker, filled with the Spirit. She was a great help-meet to her husband through out his many and varied endeavors.

BISHOP WILLIAM H. DUNN

Bishop William Hudson Dunn was born in Monroe, La. on April 28, 1879.

He was baptized at the age of 10 years in the New Hope Baptist Church. His early education was at the Industrial High School at Monroe, La., and he attended college at Leland University, New Orleans, La.

In 1907, he accepted the life of holiness.

In the same year, he was ordained to preach, and received his first pastorate in Crossett, Ark. Bishop Dunn pastored at the following places: Garyville, Monroe, Baton Rouge, La.; Greenville, Hollandale and Indianola, Miss., Selma and Montgomery, Ala. From 1925 to 1930, he pastored the First Church in Norfolk, Va., and from 1930 to 1933 he pastored First Church in Chicago, Illinois. Afterwards, he returned to Norfolk and pastored there from 1933 until his death October 29, 1942. Bishop Dunn was consecrated to the office of Bishop in 1933. He was over the Eastern Diocese. He also served as a member of the Trustee Board of C.M. and I., Secretary of C.M. and I College from 1915 to 1922. He was business manager of the paper *Truth* and served as Secretary of the National Convention of Church of Christ (Holiness) U.S.A. from 1912 to 1935.

BISHOP WILLIAM MITCHELL

Bishop William Mitchell was born Feb. 20th, 1874 in La Pine, Ala.

He was converted and joined the church at Montgomery, Ala., during the pastorate of Rev. William A. Washington. He pastored at Crossett, Conway and Little Rock, Ark., Jayess, Miss., Bogalusa, La., Portsmouth, Va., and St. Louis, Mo.

He was elected a Bishop in 1938 and was assigned Presiding Bishop of the North Central Diocese. He was pastor of the Christ

Bishop William H. Dunn

Bishop William Mitchell

Bishop O. L. Mitchell

Bishop J. A. Jeter

Temple Church at St. Louis, Mo., at the time of his death on February 21, 1951.

BISHOP O. L. MITCHELL

It was in the home of Brother and Sister O. L. Mitchell that Rev. C. C. Carhee called the meeting for the purpose of starting a church which became the church now located at Leesville, La. Rev. Mitchell was the first pastor. Other churches pastored by him were at Tallulah, La., Searcy, Pine Bluff, and Little Rock, Ark.

BISHOP J. A. JETER

Bishop J. A. Jeter was born in 1854 in Ottoway County, Va. He died in Little Rock, Arkansas, September 15, 1945, in his early nineties. He was one of the pioneer workers with Bishop C. P. Jones and established many churches throughout the work.

Writes Mr. R. L. Cotton (white): "Pastor J. A. Jeter, Sr., was a venerable teacher of rare ability, possessor of love and tenderness and of the gift of giving bitter medicine in sugar-coated pills. Above a blameless character, he was an illustrious Christian personage; enterprising, successful and prosperous businessman, always his presence graced the National Convention group."

As president of the Foreign Missions Board, in 1903, he went to Monrovia, Liberia, West Africa, to review the work of the missionaries of the movement and to weigh the possibilities of establishing a full scale work in Africa.

On returning in the spring of 1904, he was accompanied by Miss Sumtumzi, a native Christian Missionary. Miss Sumtumzi came here to visit among the churches and to learn more about the methods employed in Missionary work in the United States, as a further preparation in her work to help build a better Africa. "Go and do thou likewise," says the Master to his followers today.

In 1929, he was elected to the Bishopric and assigned to the States of Arkansas and Missouri as his diocese.

BISHOP W. E. HOLMAN

Bishop W. E. Holman came into the fellowship of the brotherhood about the time that the Episcopal Polity was promulgated. He was accepted with his present "Bishop" title.

He worked with a group in Wisconsin.

For several years he solicited funds for C.M. and I. College. He was equipped and adapted for that kind of work with a good

276

Bishop Jacob M. Haywood   Bishop J. Gordon Hay

prospective field. For a while he was president of the school.

In 1942 he was assigned presiding bishop of the newly-created Northeastern Diocese.

In 1943, when the Northeastern Diocese was again brought back into the Eastern Diocese, Bishop Holman was assigned presiding bishop of the Eastern Diocese, following the death of Bishop W. H. Dunn.

BISHOP JACOB M. HAYWOOD

Bishop Jacob M. Haywood came to the fellowship in 1941 from the Church of God in Christ and was made overseer of the Southeastern Diocese. In August 1942, he was elected to the Bishopric and assigned presiding bishop of the Southeastern Diocese. In 1944, he was assigned to presiding bishop of the Northern Diocese and pastored the Christ Temple Church in Chicago, Ill. He resigned in January, 1953.

BISHOP J. GORDON HAY

Bishop J. Gordon Hay came to America from one of the islands of the British West Indies. He soon entered into the fellow-

277

ship of the brotherhood. In 1942 he was consecrated to the bishopric and made co-adjutant with Bishop W. E. Holman in the Northeastern Diocese with headquarters in New York. In 1944 he was assigned to Presiding Bishop of Southeastern Diocese. He died in 1946.

BISHOP O. B. COBBINS

Reverend Otho Beale Cobbins was born seven miles south of Lexington, Mississippi, in Holmes County, in October 21, 1895. He was reared as an orphan, who knew neither father nor mother. His different relatives took care of him until he was "on his own" early in life. Though shifted from hand to hand, he was never bereft of a religious climate. At the age of 16, he was converted, joined the Christ Temple Church of Jackson, Mississippi, and was baptized by Pastor C. P. Jones. He was licensed to preach by Elder C. P. Jones in 1916, and was ordained in 1921.

He had a ministerial ancestry. For over 100 years the gospel had been carried by ministers in the direct lineage of the Cobbins family.

In October 1943, Rev. O. B. Cobbins was appointed Adjutant-Bishop of the South Central Diocese. He was succeeded in 1947 by Bishop M. R. Conic.

BISHOP ALBERT HAMILTON, JR.

Bishop Albert Hamilton Jr., was born September 22nd, 1903 at Pocahontas, Miss. He became a Christian at the age of 13 and joined the Cynthia Church under the pastorate of Rev. F. E. Williams. He attended school at Utica Institute, Miss.

In 1926, at the age of 23, he married Miss Alice Harris of Greenwood, Miss.

He served as president of the Jackson and the Terry S. S. Convention. In 1927 he accepted the call to the ministry, and in 1939 was ordained by Rev. H. R. McInnis, Rev. George A. Thomas, Rev. O. B. Cobbins, Rev. L. W. Sheriff, and Rev. F. E. Williams. His first sermon was delivered at the Christian Church of Greenwood, Miss. His first pastoral appointment was to the Moral Grove Church at Byran, Miss., by Bishop J. L. I. Conic. From there he was sent to Jackson, Tennessee, and thence to Cleveland, Ohio. In 1953 he was sent to the Mother Church at Jackson, Miss.

In 1956, at the National Convention at Little Rock, Ark., he was elevated to the Bishopric and assigned to the Western Diocese,

Bishop B. Cook, Jr.   Bishop A. Hamilton, Jr.

succeeding the late Bishop A. M. White.

He was stricken December 11, 1961 and died June 18th, 1962 while pastoring Christ Temple Church, Los Angeles, Calif.

BISHOP B. COOK, JR.

Bishop B. Cook, Jr. established the first church of the Holiness Movement in New York City.

He was made Co-adjutant Bishop of the Eastern Diocese.

The Eastern Diocese has been a fertile field, and has produced many personalities of worth. Bishop Cook died in 1940.

BISHOP A. B. SMITH

Bishop A. B. Smith was born in Arkansas. He moved to Louisiana and later married Miss Sally Porter. While in Louisiana, he heard the gospel as preached by Elder C. C. Carhee and accepted Christ as Saviour. He later accepted the call to the Gospel Ministry.

Bishop Smith moved to Tulsa, Oklahoma, and there founded and built a Church of Christ Holiness, U.S.A.

Bishop Smith moved to San Francisco, California, during the Second World War and founded the Golden Gate Church. Bishop

279

Smith, during the latter part of 1945 moved to Merced, California, and founded and built the Merced Church.

In 1956 at Little Rock, Arkansas, he was consecrated to the Bishopric and sent to preside over the Northwestern Diocese. He was also the founder of the Churches at Seattle and Yakima, Washington, along with Elder C. C. Carhee.

Bishop Smith was called from labor to reward in 1959. Truly, Bishop Smith was a missionary for Christ. His widow resides in Merced.

BISHOP WILLIE THURMOND

It is not certain that Bishop Thurmond was present in the meeting in Lexington, Miss., in 1902 conducted by Elders C. H. Mason, W. S. Pleasant, and C. P. Jones, when five gunshots were fired into the meeting. No one was killed.

Whatever the perils may have been, Willie A. Thurmond lived to later become pastor of that church.

Other churches he pastored were: Mt. Perea in Carroll County, Indianola, Miss., McComb, Miss., and Christ Temple Church, Jackson, Miss. He later became chairman of C.M. and I. College Trustee Board, Second Vice-President of the National Convention and Bishop of the South Central Diocese. He died in 1944 in Jackson. His widow, Mrs. Dora Riley Thurmond, now resides in Los Angeles, Calif.

BISHOP C. A. TWINE

The elderly sage C. A. Twine of Tidewater area was born about 1859, during the latter period of slavery.

He was made Adjutant-Bishop for the Eastern Diocese in 1938. The witty, hoary sage could hold the attention of this audience with ease. The venerable Bishop C. A. Twine was about 104 years old when he died in 1963.

BISHOP ANDREW WHITE

Bishop White was born to Mr. Field White and Mrs. Maggie White on July 13, 1913 at Yazoo City, Mississippi. In 1932 he united with the home church, pastored by the Rev. J. E. Bearden and later by Rev. F. E. Williams.

He attended high school at Yazoo City, Alcorn, and Jackson Colleges. He later attended Butler University's School of Theology in Indianapolis, Indiana. He taught school in Mississippi

Bishop A. B. Smith   Bishop Willie Thurmond

Bishop C. A. Twine   Bishop Andrew White

before moving to Indianapolis in 1938. On October 10, 1939 he was married to Miss Lilly White. He joined the First Church of Christ (Holiness) in Indianapolis pastored by Rev. Louis Randall. He received much of his spiritual inspiration and guidance from Pastors Bearden and Randall. His labors in the church included singing in the choir, Superintendent of Sunday School, and Deacon. He acknowledged his call to the ministry in 1945 and was ordained in 1946.

In January 1949 he was called to the First Church of Christ (Holiness) in Washington, D.C., where he remained until August 1951 when he was consecrated to the bishopric and sent to preside over the Western Diocese and pastor the Christ Temple Church of Los Angeles, California.

Bishop White passed away on September 22, 1955. His favorite saying was, "What I do, I have to do it quickly for I have only a short time."

BISHOPS OF THE CHURCH 1927-1965

1927-1949	Charles Price Jones	*
1927-1939	James L. I. Conic	*
1927-1953	Edward W. Butler	*
1927-1947	William Alexander Washington	*
1927-1935	J. F. Morrison	*
1927-1940	G. A. Goings	*
1927-1940	H. H. Moody	*
1928-1947	W. E. Holman	
1929-1945	J. A. Jeter	*
1935-1942	William Hudson Dunn	*
1936-1938	O. L. Mitchell (Adjutant)	*
1937-1944	Willie A. Thurmond (Adjutant)	*
1938-1944	Henry L. Caver	*
1938-1951	William Mitchell	*
1938-1940	B. Cook, Jr. (Adjutant)	*
1942-1953	Jacob M. Haywood	
1942-1946	J. Gordon Hay	*
1938-1942	C. A. Twine (Adjutant)	*
1945-1947	O. B. Cobbins (Adjutant) to C. P. Jones (1943-45)	
1947-1965	M. R. Conic	
1951-1955	Andrew M. White	*
1956-1965	Obadiah Wesley McInnis	
1956-1959	A. B. Smith	*
1956-1965	David McPherson	

1956-1965   Clifton Goodloe
1956-1962   Albert Hamilton, Jr.   *
1961-1965   A. D. Williams
1962-1965   Allan J. Torry

PRESIDING BISHOPS 1964-1965

Northwestern Diocese, Bishop M. R. Conic
    4852 Victoria Ave., Los Angeles, Calif.
Northern Diocese, Bishop O. W. McInnis
    8321 South Calumet Ave., Chicago, Ill.
Southwestern Diocese, Bishop Clifton Goodloe
    Rte. 1, Box 186, Canton, Miss.
Eastern Diocese, Bishop David McPherson
    2720 Chesterfield Blvd., Norfolk, Va.
North Central Diocese, Bishop A. D. Williams
    4864 Fountain Ave., St. Louis, Mo.
South Central Diocese, Bishop A. J. Torry
    4305 O'Bannon Drive Jackson, Miss.
Western Diocese, Bishop M. R. Conic
    4852 Victoria Ave., Los Angeles, Calif.
Southeastern Diocese, Bishop O. W. McInnis
    8321 South Calumet Ave., Chicago, Ill.

BISHOP M. R. CONIC

On December 22, 1909 at Jackson, Mississippi, a child was born to the late Bishop J. L. I. and Mrs. Louise Virginia Crawford Conic, whom they named Major Rudd. His early childhood was spent in several cities, namely: Jackson, Mississippi, Pine Bluff, Arkansas, and Montgomery, Alabama.

At the age of 8 in 1917, while attending C.M. and I. College he accepted Christ as his personal Saviour. When he was 11 years of age the family moved to St. Louis, Missouri, where he spent one year. Returning to Washington in 1925 he remained there until 1928 when he graduated from Dunbar High School.

In 1929 he went to C.M. and I. College for a two year period as a teacher. Following a year's absence, he returned to C. M. and I. College, Jackson, Mississippi, in September 1932 and spent four years as President of the school.

Christmas of 1933 he was married to Miss Maude L. Sallis of Little Rock, Arkansas. To this union four children were born, namely: Major Rudd, Junior Frances Carlotta, Bettye Ruth, and

Elizabeth Maude. He was ordained at Jackson, by Bishop E. W. Butler, Bishop J. L. I. Conic, Elder O. B. Cobbins, and Rev. F. E. Williams. He began his pastoral activities in Memphis and Jackson, Tennessee, in the spring of 1937 where he spent two years. In September, 1940 after an absence of 18 months from the pastorate, which time was spent in Washington, D.C., he returned as full time pastor to Christ Temple Church at Jackson, Tenn., where he remained three years. During this pastorate in Jackson the church secured valuable property, on a part of which, a new edifice, is now located. In September 1943 he accepted the pastorate of First Church of Christ (Holiness) U.S.A. Norfolk, Va., where he remained until February, 1947.

During his first 20 months in Norfolk, a debt of 20,000 dollars was liquidated, clearing the church of all indebtedness.

In 1947, he was appointed pastor of the Christ Temple Church, the Mother Church, Jackson, Miss., by Presiding Bishop O. B. Cobbins of the South Central Diocese.

In May 1947 he succeeded Bishop O. B. Cobbins as executive Secretary of the Trustee Board of C.M. and I. College which position he held until March 1953.

In 1947 there was an insurrection in the church. An extra session of the National Convention was called in May 1947 in Jackson, Mississippi, by Bishop E. W. Butler as ordered by Bishop C. P. Jones. The regular session of the National Convention was changed from Los Angeles, California to Chicago, Illinois. Rev. M. R. Conic was made Bishop and placed over the South Central Diocese succeeding Bishop O. B. Cobbins.

In August, 1948 he was made First Vice-President of the National Convention succeeding Bishop E. W. Butler. In 1949 after the passing of Bishop C. P. Jones he was made President of the National Convention and Senior Bishop of the church.

After his arrival in Jackson, to begin his administration, Bishop Conic saw the dire need of improvements in and around the church. A beautiful Hammond Organ and a grand piano were purchased. One of his main objectives was to pay off a church debt of several thousand dollars.

In January, 1953 the National Executive Council appointed Bishop M. R. Conic as pastor of the Christ Temple Church at Chicago, Illinois and presiding Bishop of the Northern Diocese, after the former pastor, Bishop J. M. Haywood severed his connections with the Church of Christ (Holiness) U.S.A. by written

284

resignation, January 16, 1953. This action was confirmed by the National Convention in August of 1953 in Detroit, Michigan.

Prior to his coming, Christ Temple Cathedral had accepted a remodeling program at a cost of approximately $93,000. A few of the major accomplishments under him were as follows: seats and book pockets, $9,300; rebuilding organ, $2,000; parsonage, $22,000; garage at parsonage, $1,100; boiler and stoker at the church, $2,800; making a grand total of $130,100. He was a young man with a heart after God, who, like Solomon of old, desired God to lead him in all of his undertakings. The Lord blessed the church spiritually as well as financially. His rich sermons and seasoned Bible lessons were a source of inspiration to all. The membership grew from about two hundred (200) to approximately three hundred fifty (350). Before leaving Chicago the church debt was reduced from $130,100 to less than $9,000.

In August, 1961, the Convention again sent Bishop Conic to Jackson, Mississippi. He was there only a short time, but he was instrumental in purchasing the McGhee home. In August of 1962 Bishop Conic was transferred to Los Angeles, California, by the National Convention as pastor of the local church and Bishop of the Western Diocese. He went with a mind to do the will of God. He has worked very hard since he has been there and as this book goes to press that church is in the process of securing a new edifice.

Throughout the national work of the Churches of Christ Holiness the laity found the following qualities typical of Bishop Conic that made him one of the most respected ministers in the Holiness movement. When all around him was disappointment, he was patient and long-suffering. When success smiled on him it was merely material for thankfulness. When there was suspense, he prayed for perseverance. When dangers arose, he had faith and courage. When praise was heaped upon him, he was a servant of humility.

BISHOP O. W. McINNIS

Vice President of The National Convention 1956, Chairman of the National Church Extension Board 1959-1964, Editor of *Compass,* Editor of *Truth,* The Official Organ of The Church.

Bishop O. W. McInnis was born December 24, 1909, in Myles, Mississippi. He attended school at the Utica Institute, Utica,

Miss.; Rust College, Holy Springs, Miss.; and Jackson College in Jackson, Miss. Later he taught in the Hinds County Elementary schools.

In May, 1936 he was married to Miss Julia Broome. They were the parents of six children: three girls and three boys.

It was in 1936 that he also accepted the Lord as his personal Saviour and was converted and united with the Christ Temple Church in Utica, Miss. He was called to the ministry the same year. Being a young man, full of zeal, he did not stop until he preached his trial sermon on the first Sunday in November, 1939. In August, 1943 he was ordained and placed as pastor of the Christ Temple Church in Kansas City, Kansas, in the Western Diocese while Bishop William A. Washington was presiding.

In March, 1947 he was called to pastor at the Cathedral Church of the Eastern Diocese in Norfolk, Va. His works at the local church and the diocese were fruitful in the area.

In August, 1961, the National Convention sent Bishop O. W. McInnis, Vice-President of the National Convention, to pastor the Cathedral Church of Chicago, Illinois, and to preside over the Northern Diocese. In November, 1961, he moved to Chicago with his family and began to serve as pastor of the church. He began on a journey of his ministerial life by preaching from the depths of his soul, doing the only thing he knew best—to preach God's word to men and women in all walks of life. Through his dynamic and soul saving messages, approximately 100 were added to the church. Under his leadership, the church department has raised approximately $85,000. One of the most outstanding achievements of his pastorate was the building at 548-50 East 44th Street, purchased for $16,500.

We are happy to report that it is paid for in full. This building to be converted into an educational center which is very much needed in Chicago. He has helped the church in making improvements in the property and has served faithfully and untiringly.

A Tribute to Bishop McInnis
Faith is the path to power divine,
The Christian way to truth sublime.
It is our anchor in the storm,
It is our promise of a brighter morn.
It is our strength in time of sin,
He cares for them who trust in him.

286

Bishop O. W. McInnis   Bishop David P. McPherson

Hope is the vision of faith's success,
The Christian Way from life's distress.
It is the anchor of the soul.
It is the grace that makes us bold.

It is the rainbow in our sky,
Promise of sunshine bye and bye.
Love in the world is the greatest thing,
The Christian way to bless the king;
It is the mainspring of the life;
It is the way from earthly strife;
It is a balm for every pain.
Who knows its joys, has every gain.

BISHOP DAVID P. McPHERSON

Bishop David McPherson, Norfolk, Virginia, was one of the
five bishops elected by the National Convention in 1956, at Little
Rock, Arkansas. He was placed over the South Central Diocese,
and pastor of the Christ Temple (Mother Church) at Jackson,
Mississippi. His other pastorates were All Nations Church, Berkeley, California; Saint Timothy, Newport News, Virginia; and

Third Temple, Jackson, Miss. In 1961, he was transferred to Norfolk, Virginia, as presiding Bishop of the Eastern Diocese, and pastor of the First Church in Norfolk, Virginia. He is a member of the Church Extension Board, and Chairman of the Board of Claimants.

BISHOP A. D. WILLIAMS

Bishop A. D. Williams, St. Louis, Mo., was elected to the Bishopric in 1961. He and Sister Williams are blessed to have three children. One daughter is the wife of Bishop David McPherson, of Norfolk, Va.

He has pastored churches in Pine Bluff, Ark.; All Nations, Berkeley, California; Golden Gate, San Francisco, Calif.; Emmanuel, Oakland, Calif. He is the Presiding Bishop of the North Central Diocese and pastors the Christ Temple Church, in St. Louis, Mo.

BISHOP ALLEN JOSEPH TORREY

Bishop A. J. Torrey was born February 29, 1904, in Copiah County, Mississippi, to the late Perry and Martha Ann Torrey. He accepted Christ in 1917. He was called to the ministry in 1936, ordained in 1943 and consecrated to the Bishopric in 1962. He has held the following positions: President of the Utica and Hermanville District H.Y.P.U. and Sunday School Convention, recording secretary for the National Education Trustee Board, member of the Board of Education, and President of the Diocese H.Y.P.U. and Sunday School Convention. Bishop Torrey served as District President of the following districts: Utica and Hermanville, Greenville and the South Mississippi District.

He pastored and rebuilt a church at Hermanville, McComb, Fairview, Carpenter, Miss. and founded the church in Port Gibson, Mississippi. He pastored and repaired Clark Creek Church in Patterson, Mississippi, and St. Peter Church in Hazlehurst, Mississippi. An annex was added to the church in Ruleville, Mississippi, under his administration. He left in the treasury $1,100.00 for a new church when he pastored the church in Drew, Miss. He is chairman of the Board of Education and acting president of C.M. and I. College. He is currently Bishop of the South Central Diocese and pastor of hte Mother Church, Jackson, Miss.

Bishop A. D. Williams

Bishop Allen Joseph Torrey

Bishop Clifton Goodloe

BISHOP CLIFTON GOODLOE

Bishop Clifton Goodloe began his ministry in 1940 as assistant pastor of Pleasant Green Church of Christ (Holiness,) U.S.A., 215 Walnut Street, Canton, Mississippi, under the administration of Rev. Blackman. He held this post for three years. He was appointed pastor at Canton, Mississippi, in 1945 by Bishop O. B. Cobbins. In 1947 he pastored New Lake Church of Christ (Holiness), Jackson, Miss. He pastored the following churches at Drew, Miss., Bogalusa, La., Shaw, Miss. and New Home Church, Jayess, Miss., where he built a church. He also pastored for 6 years in Franklinton, La. and built a new church. He is now at Sweet Home, Franklinton, La. and Plain View Church at Mt. Hermon, La. He has been Supervisor and Presiding Bishop over the South Western Diocese for the past 12 years.

PASTORS

Rev. J. E. Bearden

Rev. J. E. Bearden was born in Jefferson County, Fayette, Mississippi, March 7, 1893. When about seventeen years of age he moved to Webb, Mississippi, for a short time and from there he went to Helena, Arkansas. From Helena, he went to Boyle, Mississippi, and at the age of eighteen, was converted and baptized in the Damascus Missionary Baptist Church where he served until Rev. Black of Greenville, Mississippi, came along and taught and preached Holiness. It was then that he realized what it meant to be saved and so cast his lot with the Holiness movement.

On November 28, 1912 he was married to Miss Beulah Taylor at Boyle, Mississippi. Later, he was called into the United States Army and served until the Armistice was signed and was honorably discharged on December 12, 1918. In 1920 he was called to the ministry and ordained, June 20, 1924. He began his pastoral work at Yazoo City, Mississippi, and went from there to Glendora. He pastored, and built, a church at Clarksdale, Mississippi, for about ten years and at Wolfe Lake for nine years. He also pastored at Galilee Holiness Church, west of Hazlehurst for about eleven years.

He pastored for a few years at Drew, Mississippi, and built and pastored at Cleveland for twenty-nine years and four months, moving from there to Indianapolis, Indiana, and was pastor of the Holiness Church there for three years.

Rev. J. E. Bearden

He is presently serving as pastor of Third Temple Church of Christ, Holiness in Jackson, Mississippi, and has been serving here since December, 1959.

Rev. Bearden is also president of the Diocese Mission Board for the South-Central Diocese. For about twenty years he served as president of the Church work of the Greenville District.

Elder J. B. Burley

Elder Burley joined the Church of Christ Holiness in 1945. His first pastoral work was at Terry, Mississippi. Many members were added to the church. During his stay there, he was called to the Third Temple Church of Christ Holiness U.S.A., Jackson, Mississippi. There, Elder Burley and his loyal wife accomplished great achievements in the improvement of the interior decoration of the church. He is now pastoring the following churches: Christ Temple at Cleveland, Miss. Rose Hill at Pinola, Miss. Christ Temple at Port Gibson, Miss. and Christ Temple at Canton, Miss.

Elder Burley came to us from the Baptist Church 18 years ago. He left the Baptist Church, in love and full fellowship and on his own accord. He has worked cooperatively with the Church of Christ Holiness and has followed the "directives" sent from the National Convention.

291

Rev. Robert J. Davis

Rev. Robert J. Davis of Tulsa, Oklahoma, was converted and started in this work in July 1899.

He worked in the Sunday School, H.Y.P.U. and gave support to Foreign Mission.

He gave more than 60 years of his life in the service of the Lord. He recently retired from the active pastorate.

Rev. L. M. Relf

Rev. L. M. Relf became a member of the Church of Christ (Holiness) U.S.A., when he was 15 years of age in Gordonville, Alabama.

Following his "call" to the ministry, he served as "supply pastor" for several years at churches in Montgomery, Birmingham and Selma, Alabama. He worked in every department of the home church at Montgomery, Alabama, later serving as Financial Secretary to the National Convention for approximately 10 years.

After being ordained, he was sent to pastor the church in Indianapolis, Indiana, where he served for two years. Other churches, in which he pastored are:

First Church, Chicago, Illinois
Christ Temple, Kansas City, Kansas
Christ Temple, Omaha, Nebraska
Christ Temple, Chicago Heights, Illinois
Christ Temple, Jackson, Tenn. and Brownsville, Tenn.
Bethel Temple, St. Louis, Missouri
Christ Temple, Gary, Indiana

Rev. Willie Kendrick

Rev. Willie Kendrick is the son of one of the "Pioneers", Deacon Charley Kendrick of Terry, Miss. He spent several years as a student and farm manager at C.M. and I. College.

He married Miss Rebecca Gates, also a former C.M. and I. College Student from Yazoo County, Miss.

Rev. Kendrick was Vice-President of the Jackson and Terry Ministers and Deacons Institute. He was President of the Jackson and Terry District Assembly of the South Central Diocese.

He pastored Cynthia and Second Temple Churches at Jackson, Mississippi; Little Zion Church at Carpenter, Mississippi; and Christ Temple Church at Tougaloo, Mississippi.

Elder & Sister J. B. Burley

Rev. Robert J. Davis

Rev. Willie Kendrick

293

Rev. A. J. Perkins

Rev. A. J. Perkins was President of the H.Y.P.U. and Superintendent of the Sunday School of the Church at Hollandale, Mississippi.

He was ordained in 1936. He pastored the churches at Kansas City, Kansas; Arlington, Virginia; the First Church of Christ, Washington, D.C., and Zion Chapel Church at Detroit, Michigan.

He is President of the Indiana-Michigan District of the Northern Diocese, and Corresponding Secretary of the National Convention.

He is a graduate of C.M. and I. College at Jackson, Mississippi; attended the American Bible College and the Moody Bible Institute of Chicago, Illinois. He is an instructor in the Minister's Seminar.

Rev. Will D. Roberts

Rev. Will D. Roberts was born November 23, 1888. He was ordained by Bishop O. B. Cobbins.

He pastored the churches at Indianola and Shaw, Mississippi. He was President of the Greenville District Assembly of the South Central Diocese.

Rev. Willie Bingham

Rev. Willie Bingham, Jackson, Mississippi, was the pastor of Sweet Home Church, Brookhaven, Miss.; Moral Grove Church, Byram, Miss.; White Oak Church, Utica, Miss.; and Sweet Home Church, Pelahatchie, Miss. He passed away September 1965.

Rev. L. P. Camper

Rev. L. P. Camper of Jackson, Mississippi, is one of the growing young ministers of the church. His wife, Mrs. Rosie Lee Vance Camper, is the daughter of the late Rev. John Vance.

Rev. Camper is a member of the faculty of C.M. and I. College, pastor of the Second Temple Church of Jackson, Mississippi, and Recording Secretary of the National Convention.

Rev. C. L. Carhee

Rev. C. L. Carhee is son of Elder and Sister C. C. Carhee. He was converted in early life and acknowledged his call to the ministry.

He was president of the National Sunday School and HYPU

Rev. A. J. Perkins   Rev. Will D. Roberts

Rev. Willie Bingham   Rev. L. P. Camper

Congress. He was Recording Secretary of the National Convention from 1947-1949, again 1956-1960. He was assistant and Acting Pastor of Christ Temple Church, Los Angeles, Calif. He pastored the First Church of Christ, Washington, D.C., and Christ Temple Church at Memphis, Tennessee, and presently is pastoring Christ Temple Church, Seattle, Washington.

Rev. John Hill

Rev. John Hill of Hazlehurst, Mississippi, is president of the Jackson District of South Central Diocese. He is pastoring the Sweet Home, Sweet Rest, and Mount Bethel churches. The latter two churches have been rebuilt under his administration.

Rev. Joseph E. Holland

Rev. Joseph E. Holland joined the Bright Star Missionary Baptist Church of Merigold, Mississippi, at the age 12, under the ministry of Rev. Adam Newsome. He was the only child of Mr. Robert and Mary Holland.

The family moved from Merigold, Mississippi, to Holly Grove, Arkansas, and lived there for five years.

Rev. Holland came to Indianapolis in 1924 at the age of 21. Later he attended night school for a few weeks where he met Rev. David Caldwell who was then Assistant Pastor to Rev. F. E. Williams.

In June 1930 he united with the Church of Christ (Holiness) U.S.A. under the pastorate of Rev. F. E. Williams, Indianapolis.

He was elected President of the H.Y.P.U. appointed teacher of the Adult Sunday School class, became a member of the Senior Choir, and was placed on trial for deacon until he was ordained in 1931.

He was placed on the trustee board in 1933, and made Sunday School Superintendent and choir director in 1943, and later became chairman of the deacon board.

In 1953 he acknowledged the call to the ministry. He became acting Pastor of the church in 1960, following the resignation of Rev. J. E. Bearden.

Rev. Marcus Irons

Rev. Marcus Irons, a pioneer in the work of the churches of Christ (Holiness) U.S.A. has built three churches in and around Chicago Heights, Illinois.

Rev. John Hill

Rev. C. L. Carhee

Rev. Marcus Irons

Rev. Willie Jenkins   Rev. Joseph E. Holland

He is the district president of the Illinois-Indiana District of the Northern Diocese. He has held this position for thirteen years.

At present he is the pastor of Christ Temple No. 2, East Chicago Heights, Ill., which was built and remodeled by him.

Rev. Willie Jenkins

Rev. Willie Jenkins of Pearson, Mississippi, is a product of the Sweet Rest Church. Among the many churches that he has pastored are Mt. Zion, White Oak, Wolf Lake, Caney Creek, Fairview, New Lake and Canton, Mississippi. He has been a strong supporter of the work throughout his ministry.

Rev. W. L. Jerome

Rev. W. L. Jerome was an active officer in the First Church in Washington, D.C. He founded the Zion Chapel Church where he pastored for several years. He is Secretary of the Eastern Diocese and is now pastoring the First Church of Christ Holiness, U.S.A. in New York City.

Rev. Charles Price Jones, Jr.

Rev. Charles Price Jones, Jr., the oldest son of the late Charles Price Jones, Sr., became the Acting Pastor of the Christ Temple Church, Los Angeles, California, following the death of Bishop Albert Hamilton. He is now the pastor of the First Church, Washington, D.C.

Rev. Samuel Kendrick

With a very small membership, Rev. Samuel Kendrick has built a most unique church, in Inkster, Mich., an area that has possibilities for growth.

Rev. W. S. Kilgore

Rev. W. S. Kilgore is pastor of the church in Atlanta, Georgia. He has been with the work since the church was started in Atlanta.

Rev. L. J. May

Rev. L. J. May was formerly a deacon of Christ Temple, Los Angeles, Calif. He pastored the churches at Fresno and Long Beach, California, and was superintendent of the Southern District of California.

Rev. L. J. May

Rev. W. L. Jerome

Rev. W. S. Kilgore

Rev. Samuel Kendrick

Rev. Charles Price Jones, Jr.

Rev. James Stuart, Sr.

The name of Rev. James Stuart, Sr., of St. Louis, Mo., appears in the records of the establishing of the two churches in St. Louis. The church which he is now pastoring has been pastored by him before.

He has been steadfast throughout the years.

Rev. James Stuart, Jr.

Rev. James Stuart, Jr., formerly of St. Louis, Mo., is now the pastor of the church at Memphis, Tennessee. Aside from pastoring, he is active in the Youth Program of the church. He formerly pastored the church at Kansas City, Kansas.

Elder George A. Thomas

Elder George A. Thomas was born May 15, 1882, in Neshoba County, Northeast Mississippi, to George and Dorcas Thomas. In 1891, his father moved to Forest, Miss. He died in 1892 leaving seven boys and five girls. George Thomas finished high school in Jackson, Mississippi, and Professor Lanier was one of his teachers.

In 1900 Rev. C. P. Jones was conducting a revival meeting at Mt. Helm Baptist Church with Rev. L. W. Welch, the revivalist. In this meeting, he joined the Church of Christ Holiness, U.S.A.

He married Miss Maggie Crawford. His second wife was Miss Annie Matt Murdock and his third marriage was to Mrs. Lottie Lyons.

He served as deacon, trustee, clerk, superintendent of the Sunday School for twenty-three years, director of the choir, succeeding Brother E. W. Crane, and organized the first H.Y.P.U. in Monroe, La. in 1906.

He was called to the ministry and was ordained in 1926. He pastored at Tougaloo, Mt. Bethel, Second and Third Temple of Jackson, Miss., and Callis Hill in Terry, Miss.

The Third Temple Church was bought for $10,000 from another denomination. The present building at Terry was built in 1919 and the Tylertown Church in 1920. The present church in Prentiss, known as Thomas Chapel was built in 1945.

Rev. Thomas is now pastoring at Damascus Church, Hazelhurst, Miss., and has been there for 33 years, also at Collis Hill, Terry, Miss., and Thomas Chapel Prentiss, Miss

Rev. James Stuart, Jr.

Rev. James Stuart, Sr.

Elder George A. Thomas

Mrs. Maggie Crawford—Thomas

Rev. L. D. Webb

Rev. L. D. Webb, of Hazlehurst, Mississippi, was ordained in 1940. He had been Sunday School Superintendent, deacon, and trustee at the Damascus Church. He pastored the Wilderness of Judea Church, at Hazlehurst, the Berean Church at Lexington, and the Mount Olive Church at Jackson, Mississippi.

ORDAINED ELDERS

Rev. J. S. Allen, B.S.D.D.

Rev. J. S. Allen is an evangelist for the Christ who came to us in Chicago, Ill., and taught us the way. He is a crusader who loves to carry the message to a sinful world.

Rev. Albert Banks

Rev. Albert Banks has been the stabilizing force of Beulah Church of Christ, Holiness, Atlanta, Ga., for about 40 years, as trustee, a deacon, and as a minister. He has been a good and faithful steward having steered the Beulah Church through its troublesome times. During the most dismal hour he was called to the ministry, licensed, and in time was ordained. Thus he was clothed ecclesiastically to serve a greater need of the church.

He has worked in the local church, the district, diocese, and the National Conventions.

Brother Roscoe C. Cook
Licensed Lay Teacher

Brother Roscoe C. Cook of Jackson, Mississippi, in early life became deeply impressed with the doctrine of Holiness as taught by the late Bishop Charles P. Jones. Following his college days Brother Cook pursued the teaching profession but soon followed the business trend, successfully establishing Cook Funeral Homes

302

Rev. L. D. Webb

Mrs. L. L. Worthie—Thomas

Brother Roscoe C. Cook

Rev. Albert Banks

and Enterprise Burial and Undertaking Company with branches in the major cities of Mississippi and East Louisiana.

Brother Cook gave extensive support to Bishop Jones in his general ministry but most especially in the publication of the song books "His Fullness" and "Jesus Only" several editions of which he personally financed. He is a supporter of the ministry in general and is at present a member of the Mother Church at Jackson, Miss.

Rev. D. L. Dyson

The Reverend Douglas Lawrence Dyson was born March 12, 1903, a member of Calton Hill Church of Christ (Holiness), U.S.A.

"I was baptized at Calton Hill Church of Christ, (Holiness), U.S.A. in Jackson, Miss. In 1919 I changed my membership from Calton Hill Church of Christ, (Holiness) U.S.A. to Third Temple Church of Christ, (Holiness). I began preaching at Third Temple Church of Christ, (Holiness) in 1942.

"In the early days, I was a pastor and a missionary. I am still holding the position of a missionary this day."

Rev. J. C. Smith

Rev. J. C. Smith, financial secretary of the National Convention and Chairman of the Foreign Mission Board also pastor at St. Timothy Church, Newport News, Virginia.

Joseph C. Smith was born on September 5, 1909, to W. B. and Lucy Smith at Pine Bluff, Arkansas. He received his elementary education from Professor Clark at Pine Bluff and at Capitol Hill School in Little Rock, Arkansas. After moving to Los Angeles in 1920 he attended Nevin Avenue School and later graduated from Jefferson High School. He did undergraduate studies at Biola Bible College and also Los Angeles Business School.

Joseph Smith was baptized by Bishop J. A. Jeter at Little Rock, Arkansas. Later in 1920 when the Smith family moved to Los Angeles he became a member of Christ Temple Church with Bishop C. P. Jones, pastor. Here Joseph remained a faithful member until the age of 18 at which time he decided to "try the world."

After eight sinful years he found it rough going and returned to the church. At the age of 29, Joseph was ordained to the deaconship by Bishop C. P. Jones. In 1951 with Rev. C. L. Carhee

as pastor of Christ Temple, Joseph Smith acknowledged the call
to the ministry. The young Rev. Smith became the first pastor of
Calvary Mission of Fontana, California, and was ordained Thanks-
giving day of 1953 by Bishop A. M. White then presiding Bishop
of the Western Diocese.

Upon the death of Bishop White in September 1955, Rev.
Smith was appointed temporary pastor of Christ Temple, Los
Angeles, by Senior Bishop Conic until the National Convention
of 1956. In this convention Rev. Smith was elected Financial
Secretary of the National Convention and the Chairman of the
Foreign Mission Board. The following November he assumed
his first pastorate which was to be a long and joyious one at St.
Timothy Church, Newport News, Virginia.

Rev. J. C. Smith has carried the Foreign Mission Board to
great heights and after eight great long years of struggles purchased 135 acres for a mission post in Baja California, Mexico,
under his fine leadership.

Rev. J. C. Smith

OTHER MINISTERS

Name	Address	Church	Services
Clarence Goodwin	Fontana, Calif.	Calvary	Pastor
Lester Hughes	Oakland, Calif. 839 13th St.	Emmanuel	Pastor: Emmanuel Former Pastor: Pilgrim Deacon: Pilgrim 1947-50 Chairman: Diocese Mission Board
V. Jackson	Washington, D.C. 2523 Capitol St. NW	Zion Chapel	Pastor
Bennie Lee	Marrero, La. 1220 Marshall St.	Plain View New Salem	Pastor President of Ministers & Deacon's Institute President Diocese Mission Board Vice President District 3
R. Luster	Seattle, Wash.	Christ Temple	Associate Minister
O. C. Miller	Baton Rouge, La.	Plain View	Pastor
A. J. Olive	Chicago, Ill.	Bethel	Pastor
A. J. Parrish	Arkadelphia, Ark.	New Testament	Pastor

OTHER MINISTERS

Name	Address	Church	Services
John Plummer, Jr.	Los Angeles, Calif.	New Testament	Founder and Pastor Secretary of Publications
W. H. Hollins	Lexington, Miss.	Mt. Perea	Pastor: Mt. Perea, RFD Lexington, Miss. Ruleville, Miss. Former District Pres. Hazlehurst and Brookhaven District
	Jayess, Miss.	New Home	
O. C. Burns	Chicago, Ill.	Retired	Founder of Bethel
J. E. Graham	Jackson, Miss.	Retired	
Luther Jenkins	Detroit, Mich. 2975 Webb St.	Zion Chapel	Associate Minister
J. H. Young	Los Angeles, Calif. 1832 E. 41st Place	First Church	Charter Member
E. N. Haggans	Starkville, Miss.	First Church	Pastor
Eddie Jones	Jackson, Miss. R4 Box 126	Wolf Lake Canay Creek Galilee	Pastor

CHAPTER VII

NATIONAL AUXILIARIES

THE CHRISTIAN WOMEN WILLING WORKERS

In August 1909 there was organized through the Movement what was called Sisters' Meetings, Bible Bands, or Prayer Bands. Women of the Church met at stated times and held meetings, singing and praying, testifying and teaching bible lessons, and ministering to the needy.

Sister Maria J. Williams of Pine Bluff, Ark., reported that the Lord gave to her the name "Willing Workers" for the Sisters' gatherings. It appears that she discussed the matter with Sister Fannie Jones, wife of the Founder, for at the Convention in 1909 Sister Jones met with a group of women, called a fast and organized the Christian Women Willing Workers auxiliary.

Among those present were Sisters Harriet Poole, local president, Maggie Patterson, Bible teacher, Maria J. Williams, Sally J. Adams, all of Pine Bluff, Ark.; Irene Dunn, Josephine Cann, National Missionary and Sister Ruffins, all of Monroe, La. Sister Jones was National President until she left this life in October 1916.

Through the efforts of Pastor J. A. Jeter this group was given a place in the state work at this convention. In 1910 the band was named an "Auxiliary". The brethren recognized and felt the need of the C.W.W.W. In the National Convention in 1912 the set-up became a National Auxiliary which set about to aid the cause of missions and to help promote Christian Education.

There were Senior and Junior C.W.W.W., the latter consisting of younger women who in time became independent of the former parent C.W.W.W. as a National group. In 1954 the National Convention voted the change in the name of this group to the Women's Auxiliary of the Church of Christ (Holiness) U.S.A. (W.A.C.C.) taking in women of any age not actively engaged in church work.

House to House Prayer Bands

The All-Prayer Band and Choir of Praise was a ministry of prayer for those willing to live the life for Jesus, meeting where as many as three in one place were of one mind and heart, walking as children of Light, to engage in prayer daily for one another, to go from strength to strength; for healing when sick or in any other strait; for the upbuilding of the cause of Christ, for a general outpouring of God's Spirit upon the Churches.

Mrs. Gladys Moore

Mrs. Gladys Moore was born in Pine Bluff, Arkansas. She was married to Sandy John McIntyre in 1921. Of this union, three children were born. She is a graduate of Arkansas State College, and taught for several years. She married Brother Walter Moore on December 26, 1965.

She became National President of the Christian Women Willing Workers in 1947—an office she held until 1964. She was instrumental in arousing interest and raising the bulk of finances which led to the erection of the Girls' Dormitory of C.M. and I. College in Jackson, Mississippi.

National Executive Board of the Christian Women Willing Workers.

National Executive Board of the Christian Women Willing Workers
Left to right: Sisters Matilda Bingham, C. R. Gatling, Lenoll Dunn, Anna Willis, Dollye Brown, Sarah Caver, Gladys Moore, Murla Bennett, Leola Ballard, Bessie Moore, E. Coffin, Cora Harvey, and Arville Keetch.

309

Mrs. Gladys Moore   Mrs. Tennessee Washington
Pres. of C.W.W.W. 1947-1964

National C.W.W.W. Officers—1961

Mrs. Gladys Moore, Chicago, Illinois—President
Mrs. Leola Ballard, Los Angeles, California—Vice President
Mrs. M. Bennett Little Rock, Arkansas—Second Vice President
Mrs. Bessie Moore, Compton, California—Recording Secretary
Mrs. Arveal Keetch, San Diego, Calif.—Assistant Recording Secy.
Mrs. Dolly Brown, St. Louis, Missouri—Corresponding Secretary
Mrs. Matilda Bingham, Jackson, Mississippi—Treasurer
Mrs. C. R. Gatling, Gary, Indiana—Senior Missionary
Mrs. Anita B. Jefferson, Jackson, Mississippi—Junior Missionary
Mrs. Esterlena Coffin, Los Angeles, California—Board Member
Mrs. Cora Harvey, Ruleville, Mississippi—Board Member
Mrs. Lenell Dunn, Norfolk, Virginia—Board Member
Mrs. Margie Crain, Seattle, Washington—Board Member
Mrs. Anna Willis, Memphis, Tennessee—Board Member
Mrs. Sarah Caver, Detroit, Michigan—Board Member

Presidents
Sister Fannie Jones, Jackson, Miss.
Sister P. E. Frazier, Jackson, Miss. Cleveland, Ohio
Sister Loretia Dunn Pruitt, Los Angeles, Calif.
Sister Irene Dunn, Norfolk, Va.
Sister Tennessee Washington, Los Angeles, Calif.
Sister Gladys Moore, Chicago, Ill.
Sister Cora Harvey, Ruleville, Miss.

Mrs. Fannie Jones

Mrs. Fannie Jones was the first wife of Bishop C. P. Jones and lived through twenty-one years of his dynamic struggles in establishing the new church.

Sister Jones organized The Christian Women Willing Workers in 1909 and became the first president of this auxiliary.

During the stormy period of the church struggle, a shadow of gloom was cast over the family in the death of their only child.

Sister Jones died in Jackson, Mississippi, October 1916.

Sister P. E. Frazier

Mrs. P. E. Frazier was an active and ardent working member of the church. She was a tireless, energetic and faithful worker.

311

dent of The National Christian Women Willing Workers, serving from 1917 until about 1936. She passed in Cleveland, Ohio.

Mrs. Loretia Dunn Pruitt

Sister Loretia Dunn Pruitt was one of the most beloved women of the church. She was a tireless energetic and faithful worker. She often said, "I want to wear out in the service of my Lord." No task was too humble for this Godly woman if she was convinced that it was for the good of humanity, for the word spoken by her Lord, Matthew 25:40, was ever in her mind: "In as much as ye have done it unto one of the least of these my brethren, ye have done it unto me." With this in mind, she conscientiously went about her work, comforting the sorrowing, encouraging and strengthening the weak and offering charity and sympathy to the needy. It can be truthfully said of her "she has done what she could."

She was a loving, devoted and courageous mother, who in spite of widowhood educated her six children—thus preparing them to be useful citizens.

Her love for her church was unbounded. Day and night she would plan for its success. She took an active part, not only as a member, but as an auxiliary worker. She was interested in every department of the organization. She was a great leader: president of the local C.W.W.W., vice president of the Western Diocese C.W.W.W., president of the National C.W.W.W. Also, in other capacities she gave the full measure of her strength and ability to help foster the cause of Christ in the world. She died April, 1939.

In the home, in the school room, and in the church, she was a bright and shining light.

> Servant of Christ, well done,
> Rest from thy loved employ.
> The battle fought, the victory won,
> Enter thy Master's joy.
> —Bishop William A. Washington

Mrs. Irene Dunn

The late Mrs. Irene Dunn, the widow of the late Bishop W. H. Dunn, was president of the Mississippi C.W.W.W. before moving to Norfolk, Virginia.

Mrs. Loretia Dunn Pruitt

313

She succeeded Sister L. D. Pruitt as president of the National
C.W.W.W.

Mrs. Eva M. Holt

Sister Cecelia Roberta Gatling

Sister Cecelia Roberta Gatling, a veteran church worker of
long standing, is known throughout the church.

She is a member of the executive board of the National Christian Women Willing Workers, and National Missionary.

A resident of Gary, Indiana, she is active in the local church
serving as president of the C.W.W.W. group I, directress, and
pianist of the Fellowship Chorus.

Mrs. Eva M. Holt

Mrs. Eva Bingham Holt of Los Angeles, California, was born
in Terry, Mississippi. She was reared of Christian parents. She
accepted Christ at an early age and began her missionary work
at the age of seventeen (17).

She served as local missionary from 1923 to 1945, and served
as diocesan missionary from 1945 to 1950.

After serving as national missionary from 1951 to 1960, she
became active on the National Foreign Mission Board.

Miss C. B. Kimbrough, Missionary

Miss Claracy Kimbrough was a private secretary to Elder C. P. Jones in Jackson, Mississippi and Los Angeles, California. She was one of the founders of the Jungle Sunday School in Jackson, Mississippi which later became a church. Another Sunday School was set up in South Jackson next to the Martin Public School. She was founder and first National President of the Standard Bearers and Sunbeam Bands.

The missionary and charitable work of Miss Kimbrough was very outstanding in Cleveland, Ohio. The following excerpts are found in a Cleveland newspaper article entitled "She Finds Blessing in Giving to Others" by Henry Gordon. "She took in the sick and homeless, old and young, helpless and unfortunate, sheltered and fed them with her means, asking nothing in return. Often she could be seen with a tray of food hurrying to the home of the sick.

"For 17 years to my personal knowledge, Miss Claracy Kimbrough has given herself in service to others" writes a minister. "She has housed the helpless, fed the needy and destitute, cared for the sick and unfortunate with her own hands and means."

Long active in the Church of Christ (Holiness) U.S.A., Miss Kimbrough for years helped to operate a free church nursery

315

school. Until she spent most of her resources on others Miss Kimbrough maintained a modest haven, gratis, for elderly folks who couldn't fend for themselves. You ask Claracy Kimbrough why she has given so much to others and left so little for herself. "I can't help it," she replies timidly. "I guess I was just born a missionary. In giving, you are blessed."

THE NATIONAL SUNDAY SCHOOL
AND
H.Y.P.U. CONGRESS

Its Organization:

Professor Charles F. Jones, (no relation to Charles P. Jones) later editor of Young People's Department in *Truth* informs us in the issue of April 13, 1910, that the Holiness Young People's Union was organized that year as their work might be more effective. Then he asks for reports on their work, telling what they have done, how their work is carried on, what causes they are helping, what definite plans they have on foot.

The plan for the latest youth section in the *Truth* was born out of a discussion among Misses Mollie Hughes, Rudd and Marie Gordon during a National Sunday School & H.Y.P.U. Congress of the need of a specified section for expression from young people. Dr. Howard, then editor of the *Truth Messenger,* a periodical serving as official church organ during a temporary discontinuance of *Truth,* was favorably impressed with the idea and asked Miss Gordon to lead out in the endeavor. Accordingly, Miss Marie Gordon of Chicago became first and most efficient editor of the latest youth section. She was spirit taught as well as intellectually fitted for that work.

Presidents of the National Sunday School & H.Y.P.U. Congress: O. B. Cobbins, 1940-1944; M. R. Conic, 1944-1948; C. L. Carhee, 1948-1956; F. A. Moore, 1956-1964; and Maurice Bingham 1964-.

Presidents prior to 1940, when it was known as National S.S. & H.Y.P.U. Convention: C. F. Jones, W. J. Johnson and N. S. Cann.

Current Departmental Leaders of the Congress: Adult—Mrs. Anna Willis; Daily Vacation Bible School—Mrs. Opsy Lee Jenkins; H.Y.P.U. Group Leaders—Leonard Moore; Junior and Intermediate Teachers—Mrs. Elaine Williams; Ministers—Rev.

ANNUAL SESSION
NATIONAL S.S. & H.Y.P.U. CONGRESS
Norfolk, Virginia
August 16-20, 1961

O. B. Cobbins; Ministers' Wives—Mrs. Hattie C. Burley; Music —Ralph Moore; Primary—Mrs. Rosa Lee Camper; Secretaries and Treasurers—Miss Susie B. Jones; S.S. Superintendents and H.Y.P.U. Presidents—Myrtis Amecker; Young Adults and Senior Teachers—Mrs. Eugenia Magee.

Professor Frank A. Moore
President, National S.S. & H.Y.P.U. Congress, 1956-1964; Principal, C.M. and I., 1957; Secretary, South Central Diocese.

THE WOMEN'S AUXILIARY
CHURCH OF CHRIST (HOLINESS), U.S.A.

The Women's Auxiliary of the Church of Christ (Holiness) was officially organized in 1954 under the administration of Bishop M. R. Conic with Sister Alice Hamilton, as president.

The organization received the blessings of the presiding official in its plans for raising funds to erect a much needed home for the aged and orphans over the various dioceses. To date, the auxiliary has raised in the area of $25,000 for this effort, while at the same time carrying its share financially for the National Body with respect.

In addition to the Home for Aged project, the auxiliary is instrumental in encouraging the youth of the Churches of Christ (Holiness) who have chosen a musical career, by presenting each year, at the National Convention, one student in formal recital, vocal or instrumental. The deserving young person is given a cash scholarship award of $100.00 in addition to the H. L. Caver Award in memory of the late Bishop H. L. Caver, a lover of music.

Succeeding Sister Hamilton as president beginning the year 1965 is Sister Maude Conic of the Western Diocese.

Professor Frank A. Moore

Sister Alice Hamilton

Mrs. Hattie C. Burley   Mrs. Julia A. Miller

Sister Hattie C. Burley

Sister Hattie C. Burley is a member of Christ Temple Church, Jackson, Miss., where she worked as an outstanding group captain, and Sunday School teacher for many years.

She is W.A.C.C. president of the South Central Diocese. She has organized five Bands in this work. She is a loyal worker and a helper with her husband, Rev. J. B. Burley, in his pastorate. She also taught in her church school for 17 years. She is now operating a private Nursery and Kindergarten, with four workers and enrollment of 70 children.

She also is serving as Supply Teacher, in the City Public School System. She is Second Vice President in the National Convention of the Women's Auxiliary. She has also been National leader for the Minister's Wives, of the National Sunday School Departtment for many years.

Mrs. Julia A. Miller

Mrs. Julia A. Miller serves as Recording Secretary of the Women's Auxiliary under the administration of Sister Alice Hamilton and Sister Maude Conic. She is the wife of Pastor Miller of Louisiana. Mrs. Miller is known as a sincere faithful Church Worker.

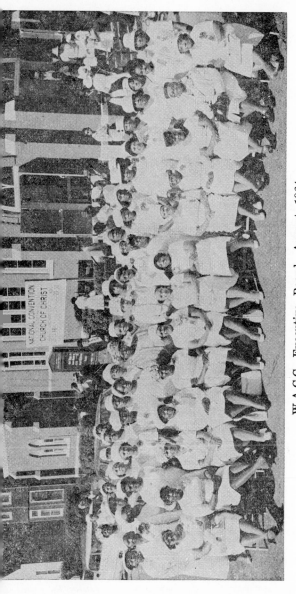

W.A.C.C. Executive Board, August 1964

Seated front row: beginning 3rd from left, Sisters Maude Conic, Board Member and succeeding President Nadie White, Board Member; Susie B. Jones, 1st Vice President; (2nd Vice President, Sister Hattie Burley, not shown) Alice Hamilton, National President 12 years; Julia Akines Miller, Secretary; Virginia Jerome, Treasurer; Perlena Ross, Board Member; Lydia Relf, Board Member and Musician C. B. Kimbrough, Esther Roebuck, Missionaries (not shown) Ada L. Wilson, Assistant Secretary not shown.

CHAPTER VIII

THE CHURCH ENTERPRISES

C.M. AND I. COLLEGE

The formal educational program of the church did not emerge in a formal way, but rather was the results of changing circumstances, and conditions. The places of schooling that were once normal became intolerable. The new church became a target of intolerance. The children of parents of the new religion were looked upon with scorn in some of the public schools. This became distasteful to the children.

The leaders began to plan a way out of this dilemma for these children.

The first reaction from the convention took place in July, 1901.

The Convention Action

The Committee on Education made the following report to the Christ Sunday School Convention of Mississippi at the White Oak Church of Christ, Carpenter, Miss. July 14, 1901.

Heretofore, it has been the custom of this convention to send its educational money to Jackson and Natchez Colleges.

We recommend that hereafter the money be held in the treasury and then be given to the support of some student in a Christian training school until the Lord shall direct us what to do with the educational money.

Your Committee: W. S. Keys, S. A. Gainer, Miss L. A. Pleasant, John Smith, Ned Wormack, and E. M. Gibson.

The report was adopted.

The above action was taken after the body withdrew from the Baptist Convention and had organized a new convention under the newly established church.

The next year, 1902, the group in Jackson, Mississippi, was put out of Mt. Helm Baptist Church. But before they were put out a parochial school had been set up and maintained in the Mt. Helm Baptist Church. This fact is verified by the following narrative: by Sister Sarah J. Thomas-Land.

Christ's Holiness School was born in Mt. Helm Baptist Church in 1897. Sister Alice Brown, one of the first women of the church to believe and accept the whole truth, came to the pastor with the message of the school master, stating that the Lord had told her that He wanted among us a school where the pupils could be taught the Bible as well as the regular text books.

At first he gave it little thought, but her continual coming moved him to ask the Lord about it. He then came with the confirmation that the Lord did want such a school started, but that the Lord did not want him to bother with the school, for the Lord had called him to preach the Gospel and not to build schools; so he sent her to the brethren.

She succeeded in getting some of the brethren interested in starting the school. She also claimed the Lord had shown her who should be the first teacher and she made this known to them. They were willing and elected trustees and the teacher; but the teacher didn't want the job and strove hard through tears, fasting and praying to keep out of it. But Sister Brown said, "If you will begin and teach the first year you may leave, if you wish." Just why the Lord wanted that particular person to begin that school has never been known. However, after much prayer the school was opened in due time with that one teacher and 45 pupils.

Sarah J. Thomas-Land was afraid not to accept the position if the Lord wanted her to teach. It was a very successful year. The school was continued in Mt. Helm by other teachers until the group was put out of the church and parsonage.

The first Christ Temple Church was a frame building located on the corner of Grayson and Monument Streets. In the basement, a chapel, a classroom and other conveniences were prepared. At the same location on the church yard the printing office was built. This building had a second floor with several rooms thereon. Unfortunately all this was destroyed by fire set by a mob.

The printing office was staffed by J. H. Green, a Mr. Filler, Eddie Crane, and Mrs. Sarah J. Thomas-Land. Professor L. W. Lee, a former public school teacher of Lexington, Mississippi, was the first principal of the school and its first president. But Mrs. Alice Brown was a great advocate of the starting of the school. The city public school principal whipped the daughter of Elder W. S. Pleasant because of her testimony of holy life. This apparently had something to do with the eagerness of the founding fathers to establish a school.

According to the cornerstone from the frame building which was destroyed by fire, the building was erected in 1902. Unfortunate, a picture of the first building is not available for this work.

After the frame church was destroyed by fire a brick church was constructed in 1906. This larger building provided more space and better accommodations for the school. A large two-story frame building, across East Monument Street to the north of the church, was bought and used as a dormitory for boarding girls.

Following the death of Prof. L. W. Lee, Prof. J. S. Land of Tchula, Miss., became the second Principal of the School. (He was the husband of Mrs. Sarah J. Thomas-Land).

Prof. Land was an earnest Christian gentleman, an ardent church worker, a devoted husband and father, a good neighbor and quiet citizen and an exceptionally good man.

Our School
by C. P. Jones

Our attitude toward our school is the same as it ever was. God did not send me to build schools, but to preach the Gospel. When God can find a man on whose heart He can put the school as his life's work, a man who will expect great things from God, the school will prosper.

It is Heaven's decree that *the just shall live by faith*—faith not in a convention, or a set of men, or a budget, as a business plan, but faith in God, then will a great work be done there, and not until then. God is a jealous God. He wishes to be known and to be trusted; to be given a chance to do exploits. He must be personally trusted. *God wants a man.*

Brethren, let us pray for *a man of faith* to take our school. No matter how gifted a man, he must walk by faith to please God. Without such man the school is only a stumbling block to the holy faith which we are sent to propagate. "Who hath believed our report, and to whom is the arm of the Lord revealed?" Isaiah is said to have been torn assunder by unbelievers, but it is still true that *the just live by faith* and that God is jealous. Men of faith, please humble yourselves and seek the Lord with me. This work must not fail. It is the Lord's. Come to the help of the

Lord against the mighty, lest the curse of Meroz fall upon us. (Judges 5:23)

I see no hope for our young people today with all sorts of vain notions being taught daily in our magazines and newspapers, I see, I say, absolutely no hope, but in the Holy Ghost and religious education. It is the one thing needed today. Let us pray for more laborers; laborers capable and God-fearing, who have a vision of their appointed task and who will follow that vision to the goal; men like Ezra and Nehemiah and John the Baptist and Paul. And why should we not have them? They were of like passions with us. Grace made them what they were. Is God less loving and merciful? Is He at last impoverished? Has He lost power? Has He said I change not? (Mal. 3:6) His grace is sufficient.

Picture of the Faculty During the Transition Period

Back Row: Mrs. Luella Russel, Mrs. Margaret Murdock Dunlap, Principal J. S. Land, Mrs. Elizabeth Bennett and Mrs. Annabell Polk Pleasant.

Front Row: Mrs. Amy Horn, Mrs. Luticia Jones Ferguson, Mrs. Mary Stewart Johnson and Mrs. Anna M. Thomas.

NEW NAME FOR SCHOOL
Christ's Missionary and Industrial College
In 1907, the trustees agreed that the school needed more and

325

larger physical and personal facilities to broaden and increase the scope of its Christian and educational influence.

They bought for the school, a 142 acre farm from Mr. Woodruff, three miles north of Jackson, Mississippi, on the Livingston Road, which was quite unique for the New Christ's Missionary and Industrial College Campus.

There were several buildings already there. The large frame building provided the home for the principal's family, the lady teachers, and boarding girls. Another building was repaired for men teachers and boys. A large barn and a large shop building were also available.

The four new buildings that were erected were chapel with classrooms, dining hall, laundry, and boys' dormitory.

The transfer from the city location to the new campus was probably consummated during the summer of 1909, according to information given in the school catalogue, the title page of which is given below.

College Status

The Christ Missionary and Industrial College was incorporated in the state of Mississippi on the collegiate basis as a college, but never functioned on the accredited college level.

As a new movement, its educational program had to be formulated according to the needs of its heterogeneous adherents.

The type of training pursued during the first decades was in keeping with the intent of the name: missionary, industrial and academic, but was carried forward on the secondary school level.

CATALOGUE

of

Officers and Students

of the

College, Biblical, Academy, English, Musical and Industrial Departments

of

CHRIST'S

Missionary & Industrial College

Jackson, Hinds Co., Mississippi

(R.F.D. No. 3)

Session 1909-1910
Under the auspices of God's people led by the
Holy Spirit according to His will.
Truth Publishing Company
Jackson, Mississippi
First Trustee Board of C.M. and I. College
based on the most reliable available record
1908-1909
Term of Three Years
Elder T. Sanders, Jackson, Miss.; Elder C. P. Jones, Jackson,
Miss.; Mr. Thomas Grant, Jackson, Miss.; Mr. Hyram Wright,
Jackson, Miss.;
Elder N. Sanders, New Orleans, La.; Elder L. J. Brunson,
Fernwood, Miss.; Elder J. L. I. Conic, Cynthia, Miss.; Mr. H.
Moore, Jackson, Miss.;
Term of One Year
Brother Charles Kendrick, Terry, Miss.; Elder G. H. Funches,
Raymond, Miss.; Elder J. A. Jeter, Little Rock, Ark.; Elder W.
S. Pleasant, Hazlehurst, Miss.;
Officers of the Board
Elder T. Sanders, Jackson, Miss., Chairman; Elder J. L. I.
Conic, Cynthia, Miss., Secretary; Mr. H. Wright, Jackson, Miss.,
Treasurer.
NOTE: Every member of that original 12 member trustee board
is now dead. Elder G. H. Funches was the last member to die.
He was said to have been 96 years old when he died.
C.M. and I. College, Jackson, Mississippi
Following the death of Prof. J. S. Land, it became necessary
for Elder C.P. Jones to become president of the school. He ap-
pointed Prof. George Moseley as Principal to live on the campus
and conduct the academic aspect of the school. Later, Prof. Mose-
ley accepted the position of farm Superintendent at Tougaloo
College, and resigned the C.M. and I. College Principalship.
Elder J. L. I. Conic became the next president. He soon be-
came involved in responsibilities in other areas of the church and
found it necessary to resign.
Prof. C. F. Jones, head of the English department at Alcorn
A. & M. College, Alcorn, Miss., was selected to succeed Elder
J. L. I. Conic. Because of his commitments at Alcorn A. & M.
College, his services as president could not be much more than
titular and were brief. Following this the trustee board saw fit to

lease the school to one Mr. L. W. Williams who was a specialist in canning vegetables and fruits. This contract was short-lived. In the meantime, a Mr. A. Brown of Tougaloo College, followed by Mr. Holmes of Utica Institute acted as academic principals.

When this administration was cleared, the trustee board elected Prof. O. W. Jones president of the school. This became a spectacular administration and showed signs of real progress. The faculty was strengthened by the inclusion of the scholarly J. M. Edwards and securing the service of Rev. Henry L. Caver (later, Bishop Henry L. Caver of the North Central Diocese) a graduate of and a member of the faculty of Philander Smith College. His wife was with him to make her worthy contribution.

The curriculum was improved and the student body increased to maximum capacity. It seemed new heights were being approached.

Without warning, the end came. Most of the buildings went up in flames from an uncontrolled fire.

The educational hopes and aspirations that the aspirants of the new faith had cherished for nearly a quarter of a century were daunted and seemed to have fled like a dove. Thus the school closed.

Suspension of School Operation

It goes without saying, that the trustee board and those who were supporters of the school were stunned by the colossal fire losses so early in the history of the school and the church, which was limited both in numerical strength as well as in financial resources. Like Israel of old, they could only hope in God.

Boydton Institute, Virginia, Gift

Some solace was found in the conditional gift of Boydton Institute in Virginia by the Christian Missionary Alliance. The gift was conditioned on the school being successfully operated for a certain number of years. The attempt was made by the brotherhood, but they were not fully able to live up to the stipulated requirement.

The C.M. and I. College had become too endeared to its supporters and the church constituency to be lured away by the Boydton offer, even though attractive it was. Rev. Henry L. Caver was sent to head the project. This project was discontinued in 1929.

Faculty and Dormitory Girls (1890?)
C.M. and I. College, Jackson, Mississippi

This picture was probably taken fifty-six years ago on the front porch of the girls' dormitory at 915 North Lamar Street (then Grayson Street), Jackson, Mississippi. By the next year all of the school had been transferred to the new one hundred forty-two (142) acre school site three miles northwest of Jackson, Mississippi on the Livingston Road.

Only a few of the persons shown here can be identified by name. President C. S. Land of Tchula, Mississippi, seated first to the left. Seated last to the right is Matron, Mrs. Luella Russell-Robinson of Selma, Alabama. Seated to her right is a student, Mrs. Manerva Bingham-Walker of Terry, Mississippi. Standing directly behind Matron Robinson is Mrs. Rosa L. Jones-Vance of Pine Bluff, Arkansas. On the back row to the left standing is Mrs. Luticia Jones-Ferguson of Hermanville, Mississippi. To the right of the back row is Mrs. Annie Murdock-Thomas of Starkville, Mississippi. Directly in front of Mrs. Thomas is student, Mrs. Elizabeth Cobbins-Hines of Lexington, Mississippi. To the left of Mrs. Hines is Professor Y. A. Lenoir of Jayess, Mississippi, shop teacher and Principal George G. Mosely.

329

The Faculty at the New C.M. and I. College Campus
(1910-1911)
Seated left to right: (11) Mrs. Luella Russell Robinson Bogan;
(10) Miss Malinda Imes; (1) President C. P. Jones; (9) Mrs.
Margaret A. Washington; (8) Mrs. Luticia Jones-Ferguson.
Standing left to right: (3) Miss Della Viola Brown; (4) Mrs. M.
E. Jackson Mosely; (5) Mrs. Mary Wright Owens; (2) Professor
George G. Mosely; (6) Mrs. Annie Murdock Thomas; (7) Mrs.
Rosa L. Jones Vance.

Principal Moseley and Some Dormitory Boys (1910-1911)
Left: Principal George G. Moseley. *Back row, left to right*: Joseph
Horton, Samuel T. Cobbins, Leonidas F. Dunn, (unknown),
(unknown). *Front row, left to righht*: Roy Thomas, Homer
Dyson, David Huey, Fletcher Dyson. *Single*: (unknown).

The Move to Rebuild and Reopen C.M. and I. College

In 1927, moves were made to borrow money to build a dormitory for girls which would include mess-hall, classrooms and other accommodations, and also to build a chapel with additional classrooms.

These two buildings formed the nucleus for the re-building of the C. M. and I. College.

It was after the school was rebuilt and he had been there for two years as a teacher 1929-31 that Rev. M. R. Conic returned as president, 1932-36. He was acquainted with the previous operation of the school, and realized the difficulties to be encountered in the attempt to reestablish the school.

He and Bishop W. E. Holman worked together sponsoring a quartette to raise much needed money for the school.

In August 1936, Prof. O. B. Cobbins, Supervisor of Jackson Public Schools for Negroes, was elected president of the school by

Girls' Dormitory

New Building Erected
This is a picture of the girls' dormitory built in the year of 1928. The picture was taken eighteen years after the building was erected and was in need of much repairs.

The chapel was the second of the two new buildings erected in the new building program.

These two buildings made possible the reopening of the school on a limited basis, and tended to abate the clouds of disheartenment and to lift a touch of light to illuminate the pathway to future progress.

CHAPEL

the convention. In September Bishop W. E. Holman returned from the field with the members of the quartette. A trustee board meeting was called. At this meeting Prof. O. B. Cobbins was asked to resign as president in favor of Bishop Holman and to serve as executive Vice President, to allow Bishop Holman to travel as President and collect money for the school.

Prof. Y. A. Lenoir, who was a blacksmith shop teacher during the early history of the school, returned in 1937 as president, and served for two years 1937-39. He was quite versatile, ambitious and attracted students to the school.

The third building that was erected in the new building program was a small house to accommodate a limited number of out-of-town boys whose parents were still interested in sending them to this school because of the quality and nature of its teaching.

The credit for this building went to Prof. Y. A. Lenoir who was president of the school at the time, 1937-39. Though small, this building was an approach to a real felt need.

Prof. M. W. Wilson succeeded Prof. Y. A. Lenoir, 1940-43. Rev. O. B. Cobbins served as President, 1943-47.

A part of the 1944-45 faculty is here pictured. (page 334)

Lack of Modern Facilities

For nearly 40 years, from the beginning of the school to the year 1944, the school had operated without modern conveniences. Wood and coal were used for fuel for cooking and heating with space heaters. Kerosene lamps were used for lighting buildings. Water was supplied from a cistern. The old outdoor pit toilets were used.

After some years gas was installed, providing the much needed heating system and supplanting the old coal heaters.

Getting electric service proved a major problem for the school. War conditions, restrictions and shortage of essential materials made it necessary for the electric project to be cleared and approved by the War Production Board in Washington, D.C.

The approval was forthcoming in the early spring of 1945. Immediately, the contract was let to a reputable electrical company in Jackson, Miss. The company began and expedited the work.

Boys' Cottage

Picture of Faculty

Reading from left to right: Prof. D. C. Lee, Miss Viola Jones, Miss Willie Mae Hayden, Mrs. C. L. Johnson, Mrs. Elva Cobbins, Miss Elnora Ellis. Prof. D. C. Lee was principal, he was followed in 1945-46 by Prof. Cara Hamilton.

334

Picture of Student Body

The students who attended the school were well behaved and very studious. Most of them seemed to have been from well regulated homes. A group of the students is shown.

Again due credit was given to the general church constituency for the instant response to the appeal for money to pay in full for the project at the designated time.

The installing of water from the city and sanitary sewerage system involved major problems. The nearest sewer line was nearly one half mile away. The special city water line was more than 2,000 feet away. The 2,000 feet of galvanized pipe needed could not be secured in the state; but the problems had to be solved.

First, the services of one of the largest plumbing companies in the state were secured. At some distant point, more than 2,000 feet of copper pipe were located and purchased. Two large septic tanks were selected. Other plumbing equipment, fixtures and fittings were made available with difficulty.

With those problems solved, the installation of the sanitary sewerage and city water became a reality for the first time on the school campus.

The improvement program was concluded in 1946 with general repairing of the three buildings.

The school enrollment for 1945-46 was 232.

335

Summary—School Plant Improvement
June 1, 1944—November 1, 1946

Electrical installations	$ 975.00
Installation of natural gas and fixtures	1,450.00
Installing City water, sewerage and fixtures	4,250.00
Repairs on the three buildings	8,500.00
Total	$15,175.00

Faculty 1946-1947

Prof. Jerome Nelson, B.S., Principal and Vocational Agriculture
Mrs. Mary Whittington, B.S., Matron and Home Economics
Mrs. Elva Cobbins, 1st and 2nd grades
Mrs. Hattie Bonds, 3rd and 4th grades
Miss Lela Mae Aust, 5th and 6th grades
Miss Agnes Bingham, A.B. English and Social Science
Prof. J. M. Edwards, A.B. Science and Mathematics
Rev. W. H. Lewis, A.B. Director of Religious Leadership training
Bishop O. B. Cobbins, A.B., A.M,, D.D., President

In 1944, the name of the board was changed from "Trustee Board of C.M. and I. College to National Education-Trustee Board," and the number of members increased from 12 to 29 members.

The circumstances under which the board was enlarged from 12 to 29 members in 1944 was probably expedient at the time when the board was set up on the stagger basis, 10-10-9, instead of 4-4-4 as was the original.

From 1908-1944 the board which governed C.M. and I. College officially and legally was properly known as the Trustee Board of C.M. and I. College.

This was a self-constituted and self perpetuating board acting under a Mississippi Charter of Incorporation, issued by the state of Mississippi through the office of the Secretary of State.

As the church or the convention began to assume responsibility for the financial obligations of the school, it also began to move into the realm of management and control of the school.

Later, there was the establishment of a national board of education by the national convention of the church. The line of demarcation between the two boards were never sufficiently defined. Some conflict of thinking began to appear. First in 1942 the national convention voted (1) to remove the incumbent president

336

of the trustee board, (2) elect a new president of the trustee board, and (3) elect other members for the trustee board, thus ignoring the legal stipulations of the charter of Incorporation, which provided that the trustees and the officers of the trustee board be elected by the trustee board itself.

Second, without a resolve by the trustee board itself, in 1944, the National Convention voted to merge the national board of education and the trustee board of C.M. and I. College and elect a chairman or president of the new board formed by combining the other two boards. The purpose back of the action was a harmony move, but officially the legal status of the trustee board still remained as provided in the charter.

Since then, three measures have been instituted with the view of amending the charter.

List of Members of the Board 1908-1965

Rev. W. S. Pleasant, Hazlehurst, Miss.; Rev. Thomas Sanders, Jackson, Miss.; Bishop Willie A. Thurmond, Lexington, Miss.; Mr. R. C. Cook, Bogalusa, La.; Bishop O. B. Cobbins, Jackson, Miss.; Mr. Fletcher E. Dyson, Franklinton, La.; Rev. George A. Thomas, Jackson, Miss.; Bishop Clifton Goodloe, Canton, Miss.; Bishop A. J. Torry, Canton, Miss.; Rev. John Sanders, Jackson, Miss.; Mr. William Castella, Jackson, Miss.; Prof. W. H. Howard, Los Angeles, Calif.; Mr. Wilbert Robinson, Canton, Miss.; Mr. Ernest White; Bishop O. W. McInnis, Chicago, Ill.; Rev. J. T. Hill, Hazlehurst, Miss.; Rev. A. J. Parrish, Little Rock, Ark,.; Rev. W. D. Roberts, Shaw, Miss.; Rev. Ezekiel Moore, Cleveland, Ohio; Rev. Maurice Bingham, McComb, Miss.;

Rev. W. L. Jerome, New York, N.Y.; Rev. L. M. Relf, Gary, Ind.; Prof. Frank A. Moore, Jackson, Miss.; Mr. Willis J. Burris, Pine Bluff, Ark.; Mr. William Callion, Sr., Chicago, Ill.; Mr. Walter Moore, Chicago, Ill.; Mr. Adolphus Dixon, Jackson, Miss.; Mr. Willie Davis, Jackson, Miss.; Mr. W. L. Sutton, Silver Creek, Miss.; Mrs. Cora Harvey, Ruleville, Miss.; Miss Susie B. Jones, Chicago, Ill.; Mrs. Carrie Johnson, Los Angeles, Calif.; Mrs. Mentha Richards, Ruleville, Miss.; Rev. H. R. McInnis, Utica, Miss.; Rev. D. S. Michael, Jackson, Miss.; Mr. Elmore Fizer, Jackson, Miss.; Mrs. Gussie Brinkley, Jackson, Miss.; Mr. S. M. Brinkley, Jackson, Miss.; Rev. L. J. Jackson, Jackson, Miss.; Rev. G. H. Funches, Raymond, Miss.; Bishop W. E. Holman, Los Angeles, Calif.; Mrs. Rosa A. Lee, Lexington, Miss.; Bishop

William A. Washington, Los Angeles, Calif.; Rev. W. D. Roberts, Shaw, Miss.; Miss Pearl Clark, Washington, D.C.; Rev. Alonzo Beasley, Indianapolis, Ind.; Rev. James Stuart, Jr., Memphis, Tenn.; Rev. Zed Crawley, Yakima, Wash.; Mr. Eddie Anderson, Jackson, Miss.;

Rev. F. A. Boyd, Leland, Miss.; Rev. O. D. Henry, Newport News, Va., Mr. E. L. Hall, Silver Creek, Miss.; Mr. Jesse Bell, St. Louis, Mo.; Bishop J. M. Haywood, Chicago, Ill.; Rev. J. E. Bearden, Jackson, Miss.; Mrs. Ruth Mixon, Jackson, Miss.; Mrs. C. B. Spruille, Ruleville, Miss.; Mr. Albert Hamilton, Sr., Pocahontas, Miss.; Prof. Myrtis Amacker, Franklinton, La.; Mrs. T. M. Washington, Los Angeles, Calif.; Mr. Q. M. Green, Ruleville, Miss.; Bishop William Mitchell, St. Louis, Mo.; Rev. S. B. Thomas, Jackson, Miss.; Rev. J. R. Perkins, Jackson, Miss.; L. F. Dunn, Chicago, Ill.; L. D. Webb, Hazlehurst, Miss.; Eliza J. Gibson, Jackson, Miss. and Annie E. Butler, Jackson, Miss.

Members of the first newly-combined National Education-Trustee Board, as of August 1944—Term expires August 1945:

Mr. Jesse Bell*, St. Louis, Mo.; Mr. J. E. Conic*, Jackson, Miss.; Mr. F. E. Dyson*, Franklinton, La.; Mr. Q. M. Green*, Ruleville, Miss.; Rev. L. M. Relf, Gary, Ind.; Mrs. R. C. Lee, Lexington, Miss.; Mrs. T. M. Washington*, Los Angeles, Calif.; Rev. H. R. McInnis*, Utica, Miss.; Bishop J. M. Haywood, Chicago, Ill.; and Mr. H. E. Guy, Bogalusa, La.

Term expires August 1946:

Bishop E. W. Butler*, Little Rock, Ark.; Bishop O. B. Cobbins, Chicago, Ill.; Mr. R. C. Cook, Jackson, Miss.; Mr. E. L. Fizer*, Jackson, Miss.; Mr. Albert A. Hamilton*, Los Angeles, Calif.; Rev. L. J. Jackson*, Jackson, Miss.; Rev. D. S. Michael*, Jackson, Miss.; Mrs. C. B. Spruille*, Ruleville, Miss.; Bishop W. A. Thurmond*, Jackson, Miss.; and Rev. J. R. Perkins*, Jackson, Miss.

Term expires August 1947:

Miss Pearl Clark, Washington, D.C.; Rev. O. D. Henry*, Newport News, Va.; Mr. S. M. Brinkley*, Jackson, Miss.; Mr. E. L. Hall*, Silver Creek, Miss.; Bishop W. E. Holman, Los Angeles, Calif.; Prof. W. H. Howard, Los Angeles, Calif.; Rev. S. B. Thomas*, Jackson, Miss.; Bishop William A. Washington*, Los Angeles, Calif.; Bishop William Mitchell*, St. Louis, Mo.; and Rev. G. A. Thomas, Jackson, Miss.

Only three members are still on the board. Only seven members are still living. *Twenty members of this board are dead as of October, 1964.

There were 30 members of this first combined board instead of the authorized 29 members. The two boards had 12 members each making a total of 24 members. The plan provided for the addition of all of the bishops. Six bishops were elected, with the understanding that at the following election the office of one member whose term of office expires that place on the board would not be filled. Then the board would have the proper number 29 members.

The record shows that Bishop W. A. Thurmond died during the year. The terms of office of both Bishop E. W. Butler and Bishop W. A. Thurmond expired the next. Bishop E. W. Butler was elected to fill the unexpired term of Bishop W. A. Thurmond.

National Education-Trustee Board
Membership as of 1964-65:

Bishop A. J. Torry, President, Jackson, Miss.; Rev. John Sanders, Executive Sec., Jackson, Miss.; Mr. Wilbert Robinson, Rec. Sec., Canton, Miss.; Rev. George A. Thomas, Treasurer, Jackson, Miss.; Dr. W. H. Howard, President C.M. and I., Los Angeles, Calif.; Mr. Ernest White, Ass't Rec. Sec.; Bishop M. R. Conic, Los Angeles, Calif.; Bishop O. W. McInnis, Chicago, Ill.; Bishop Clifton Goodloe, Canton, Miss.; Rev. Maurice Bingham, McComb, Miss.; Rev. Willis J. Burris; Mr. William Callion, Sr., Chicago, Ill.; Mr. W. Castilla, Jackson, Miss.; Mr. R. C. Cook, Jackson, Miss.; Mr. Willie Davis; Mr. A. Dixon, Jackson, Miss.; Mrs. Cara Harvey, Ruleville, Miss.

Mrs. Carrie Johnson, Los Angeles, Calif.; Miss Susie B. Jones, Chicago, Ill.; Rev. Ezekiel Moore, Los Angeles, Calif.; Mr. Walter Moore, Chicago, Ill.; Prof. Frank A. Moore, Jackson, Miss.; Rev. A. J. Parrish, Little Rock, Ark.; Rev. W. D. Roberts, Shaw, Miss.; Rev. L. M. Relf, Gary, Ind.; Mr. W. L. Sutton, Silver Creek, Miss.; Mrs. Mentha Richards, Ruleville, Miss.; Rev. J. T. Hill, Hazlehurst, Miss. and Rev. W. L. Jerome, New York, N.Y.

Ground Breaking Ceremony for Howard Hall

The ground breaking ceremony for the new administration building on C.M. and I. College was the beginning of a new era for the educational program of the Church of Christ (Holiness) U.S.A. The building was named for Dr. Willard H. Howard who was elected president of C.M. and I. by the National Convention of the Church of Christ (Holiness) U.S.A. Under the direction of Dr. Howard the following persons served as principals: Professor Jerome Nelson, Professor Cary Hamilton who was principal at the time of the ground breaking ceremony, and Professor Frank A. Moore who was principal when the building was completed in 1959.

Rev. George Thomas, with spade in hands, indicated that he was happy about the whole event and was ready for any new eventuality.

Howard Hall was built under the administration of Dr. Howard at a cost of approximately $200,000.

Howard Hall

Chapel, Howard Hall. Seating Capacity 350

Dr. Willard H. Howard

Dr. Howard served as president of the Christ Missionary and Industrial College from 1947 to 1962. Thereafter he served as president emeritus.

Presidents of the C.M. and I. College Trustee Board 1908-1965: Rec. Thomas Sanders, Rev. W. S. Pleasant, Bishop J. L. I. Conic, Bishop Willie A. Thurmond, Mr. R. C. Cook, Bishop O. B. Cobbins, Mr. Fletcher Dyson, Rev. George A. Thomas, Bishop Clifton Goodloe and Bishop A. J. Torry.

Executive Secretaries 1946-1965,
Trustee Board of C.M. and I. College

At the National Convention in 1946, on recommendation of the N.E.-T.B., the office of executive secretary of the board was created and Bishop O. B. Cobbins was elected the first executive secretary.

Bishop O. B. Cobbins, Bishop M. R. Conic, Rev. John Sanders, Mr. W. Castella and Rev. John Sanders (returned).

Past Principals: George Mosley, N. S. Cann, Jr., A. D. Otis, D. C. Lee, Cara Hamilton and Jerome Nelson.

The title president and principal at time have been used synonymously. The title principal has been used chiefly when the presi-

341

dent was non-resident as in the cases of C. P. Jones, C. F. Jones, O. B. Cobbins, W. H. Howard, and as the case of A. J. Torrey in 1964-65. The principals involved have been George Mosley, A. D. Otis, N. S. Cann, Jr., D. C. Lee, Cara Hamilton, Jerome Nelson.

Past Presidents of C.M. and I. College: L. W. Lee, C. S. Land, C. P. Jones, J. L. I. Conic, C. F. Jones, A. Brown, Holmes, O. W. Jones, M. R. Conic, J. M. Edwards, W. E. Holman, Y. A. Lenoir, M. W. Wilson, O. B. Cobbins and W. H. Howard.

The school has had fifteen administrations in less than sitxty years. The lack of administrative continuity may have hampered constructive administrative policies.

Past Matrons: Mrs. Bettie Trammel, Mrs. Luella Russel Robinson Bogan, Mrs. Mary J. Jones, Mrs. L. W. Williams, Mrs. Luticia Jones-Ferguson, Mrs. Willa Ella Lofton, Miss Bertha Matthews, Miss Elnora Ellis, Mrs. Ruth Conic Brumfield and Miss Katie Mae Robinson.

Faculty: C.M. and I. College 1956-57

Seated from left to right: Dr. W. H. Howard, President; Bishop O. W. McInnis, Seminar Director. *Standing from left to right*: Professor Cara Hamilton, Principal; Miss Katie Mae Robinson; Mrs. Annie Murdock Thomas; Mrs. Annie E. Butler; Mrs. Eliza Gibson; Mrs. Hattie Burley.

While the above Faculty was serving, the new administration building was under construction.

Faculty: C.M. and I. College

Seated from left to right: Rev. J. Morgan Hodes, Mrs. Gladys Davis, President W. H. Howard, Mrs. Mary Lyles, Principal Frank Moore, Mrs. Pauline Singleton, Mr. G. Hayes and Mrs. Hattie Burley.
Standing: Mrs. Eliza Gibson, Rev. L. P. Camper, Mrs. S. B. Thomas.

Brother Willenham Castella

Brother Willenham Castella of Jackson, Mississippi, is a High School graduate of C.M. and I. College. He was Sunday School Superintendent and Chairman of the Deacon Board of New Lake Church. He has served as executive secretary of the National Education-Trustee Board for three years. He is a graduate from Jackson College and is now employed in government Postal Service.

343

C.M. and I. College Investment Building
The first investment building for the school was purchased in Chicago, Illinois, in 1960 under the direction of Bishop M. R. Conic, at a cost of more than $100,000.00.

Ground Breaking at C.M. and I. College (1965)
Twenty years ago, the C.W.W.W. began raising money to build a new dormitory for the girls at the school. Little by little, year by year, they have kept adding to this building fund until now the first physical step is being taken toward the erection of the proposed structure.

No names are given of the persons at this ground breaking ceremony. With hands on the shovel in the act of digging seem to be the new president of the National C.W.W.W., Sister Cora Harvey of Ruleville, Mississippi, and Bishop A. J. Torrey, the acting president of the school. Principal Frank A. Moore, executive secretary, Rev. John Sanders, and the treasurer, Rev. George A. Thomas are shown in the background.

Mrs. Gussie Gertrude Grayson Brinkley
Mrs. Gussie Gertrude Grayson Brinkley of Jackson, Mississippi, spent all of her adult life in the services of the church. She was consistent in her support of the church and all its departments. She was among the first members of the Christ Temple Church Choir; one of the first members of Truth Club; and later, chair-

344

C.M. and I. College Investment Building

Miss Pearl Clark

Mrs. Gussie Gertrude Grayson Brinkley

men of the Truth Club; a life time teacher of the Young Women's Sunday School Class. She was a member of the Junior C.W.W.W.; she was a member of the C.M. and I. College Trustee Board.

As a vocation, she was a teacher in the Jackson, Mississippi, Public Schools for more than a decade.

She was never too busy to take time out to attend the various conventions of the church.

Miss Pearl Clark

Miss Pearl Clark is a member and trustee of the First Church of Christ (Holiness), U.S.A., Washington, D.C. She was President of the Eastern Diocese C.W.W.W. and a member of the National Education-Trustee Board.

She was formerly secretary in the Office of Bishop Jones at the National headquarters at Jackson, Mississippi.

Honor Students

L. F. Dunn, Manervia Bingham, David Huey

L. F. Dunn, Manervia Bingham and David Huey were three of the outstanding musical personalities on the campus of C.M. and I. College. They were examples of the high quality of students that graced the school campus.

All three of them have passed within the last five years but their memory lives on.

A roster of some of the former students of C.M. and I. College selected at random and without reference to year of attendance. In this random selection, no attempt is made to alphabetize the roster. When known, the present location and married name are given. In many cases, names of persons known to be dead are also listed, as a matter of record. In some cases the trade, occupation or profession may be given. Titles may or may not be used. No definite policy has been adhered to. In some cases where "Mrs." is used the maiden name is not known.

Partial Roster of Graduates, Former Students of Christ's
Missionary and Industrial College

Name	Vocation	Location
Mrs. Elizabeth Bennet	Teacher	Jackson, Miss.
Rev. George A. Thomas	Minister	Jackson, Miss.
Rev. Robert J. Davis	Clergy	Los Angeles, Calif.
Bishop M. R. Conic	Churchman	Deceased
Mrs. Nellie McField Green	Teacher	Jackson, Miss.
Fletcher Dyson	Insurance agent	Jackson, Miss.
Adolphins Dixon	Dairyman	Deceased
Eddie Anderson	Farmer	Deceased
Rev. L. F. Dunn	U.S. Mail Service	Chicago, Ill.
S. B. Thomas	U.S. Mail Service	Jackson, Miss.
Bishop O. B. Cobbins	Educator	Jackson, Miss.
Willenham Castilla	U.S. Postal Service	Chicago, Ill.
Cara Hamilton	Teacher	Deceased
Mrs. Elizabeth Cobbins Hines	Housewife	Deceased
Rev. S. T. Cobbins	Minister	St. Louis, Mo.
David M. Huey	Teacher	Chicago, Ill.
George Avery	Florist	Chicago, Ill.
Mrs. Mabel Baker	Insurance agent	Deceased

348

Pastoral Roster of Graduates, Former Students of Christ's
Missionary and Industrial College

Name	Vocation	Location
Mrs. Elva Stevenson Cobbins	Housewife	Chicago, Ill.
Mrs. Frances Mitchel Dunn	Teacher	Deceased
Mrs. Sarah Sanders Huey	Housewife	Chicago, Ill.
Zebedee Jones	Churchman	Jackson, Miss.
Mrs. Rebecca Gates Kendrick	Housewife	Inkster, Mich.
Rev. Samuel Kendrick	Minister	Gary, Ind.
J. E. Lucas	Railroad Service	Deceased
Rev. C. E. Owens	Minister	Jackson, Miss.
Rev. Willie Kendrick	Minister	Detroit, Mich.
Rev. A. J. Perkins	Minister	Chicago, Ill.
Mrs. Eliza Neal	Housewife	Jackson, Miss.
Daisy Shackelford	Public School Teacher	Jackson, Miss.
D. J. Speech	Farmer	Hattiesburg, Miss.
Mrs. Rhoda Crawford Tademy	Teacher	Deceased
Lillian Miller	Printing office service	Deceased
Mrs. Idella Patrick		Deceased
Alice Pleasant		
Mrs. Demeris Farley Sanders		

NATIONAL PUBLISHING BOARD BUILDING
CORNER 69th and YALE AVENUE
CHICAGO, ILLINOIS

TRUTH

THE ORIGIN OF THE "TRUTH CLUBS"

Truth Club was founded by Sister Cora Lani Flood, associate Editor of *Truth* in 1949. The idea grew out of a need for support for the *Truth* paper. It is reported that the idea came to Sister Flood, April, 1949 in Los Angeles, California. Sister Flood sent her ideas to the Editor of the *Truth,* Brother L. Dunn. The Pastors began organizing Truth Clubs in their local churches to aid in publishing the *Truth* paper.

350

Sister Cora Lani Flood

Sister Cora L. Flood resided in Los Angeles, California. She was a member of Christ Temple Church, Los Angeles, California; served as Associate Editor of the *Truth* in 1949; and founder of the *Truth* Clubs. She has served as Private Secretary to the late Senior Bishop C. P. Jones, Sr. and Relations and Publicity Officer of Christ Temple.

Mother Luella Bush

CHAPTER IX

BIOGRAPHIES

Rev. Benjamin Akins

Rev. Benjamin Akins united with the Church of Christ (Holiness) U.S.A. at Jackson, Miss., in 1929; recognized his call to the ministry in 1930; and was ordained a few years later under Bishop E. W. Butler. Without an assigned field in which to work, he chose Crystal Springs, Miss., a small town 25 miles south of Jackson, Miss.; gathered some people and organized the First Church of Christ (Holiness) U. S. A. in that town. Their Testimonies of his help to them through his sacrificial ministry were rewarding to him for his suffering for them.

He helped to organize the Church Extension Board. His ministry reached many in Jackson through a radio program which he sponsored. He also pastored Wolfe Lake Church of Christ (Holiness) U.S.A. at Yazoo City, Miss.

During the 8 years, 1948-56, he pastored New Home Church of Christ (Holiness) U.S.A. at Jayess, Miss., he raised $5,000.00 to build a new edifice. Regretfully, his illness prevented him from completing his plans. He died February 12, 1957.

Mr. Henry G. Anderson

Mr. H. G. Anderson was born in Copiah County, Miss., in 1874 and died in Chicago, Ill., in 1961. Mrs. Amelia Anderson was born at Hermanville, Miss., in 1876 and died in Chicago, Ill., in 1959. They were charter members of the Wilderness of Judea Church near Hazlehurst, Miss.

In 1919, they moved to Omaha, Nebr., where they were instrumental in establishing a church with the assistance of Elder A. T. Rucker. They were charter members of the church and Brother Anderson became the first deacon.

Sister Anderson used her musical talent in writing songs for the church. She wrote the words to the songs "Shine On My Soul", number 103, and "Jesus My Lord", number 135 in the Jesus Only

352

Mr. Henry G. Anderson

Rev. Benjamin Akins

Sister Sidney L. Austin   Mrs. Armelia Gaynor Anderson

Standard Hymnal, the Hymnal of the general church. She wrote many other songs.

The words of the song "Glorify His Name" were written by Sister Armelia Gaynor Anderson, with music by C. P. Jones. The full text of the song with the music is presented on page 408.

Sister Sidney L. Austin

Sister Sidney L. Austin, born October 2, 1873 of 1342 West Pearl Street, Jackson, Miss., is the oldest living member of Third Temple Church of Christ (Holiness) having celebrated her 91st birthday on October 2, 1964. She is truly a pioneer in the Holiness movement having been with the group that left Mt. Helm Baptist Church with Bishop C. P. Jones the night they left to form a new church. She is one of the organizers and charter members of the Third Temple Church of Christ (Holiness) on Morehouse Street. With a small band of saints prayer meetings were held from house to house. Then the sisters got together and obtained a used tent and together they patched for days on the tent. Finally it was finished and the brothers put it up and the saints worshipped here until they built a church on Dalton and Barrett Streets. Rev. H. R. McInnis was their first pastor. This was at least 50 years ago. She has always been quiet and faithful, serving in many capacities in the church. Although physically feeble, her mind is still alert and she attends church regularly. At 90 years old she attended the National Convention which was held in Chicago in 1963. She lives with her only daughter, Mrs. Wyllie Austin Singleton.

Deacon Israel Ball

Deacon Israel Ball, born June 22, 1885 in Pickensville, Ala., the son of Sam and Alice Ball. He attended school in Mississippi and Alabama, and evening school in St. Louis.

He accepted Christ under the ministry of Rev. Caesar Waddell and Rev. J. K. L. Clark and became deacon of the church in Columbus, Miss.

In November 1905, he was married to Miss Irene Brownrigg. To this union 13 children were born. He moved to St. Louis, Mo. in 1917 and joined the church there and was placed on the deacon board. In 1935 he moved and became a member of the Church in Detroit, Michigan, under the pastorate of Rev. Louis Randall, and served as chairman of the deacon board and treasurer. He died January 7, 1960 in Detroit, Michigan.

Rev. Albert Banks

Rev. Albert Banks of Atlanta, Ga., has been the stabilizing force of the Beulah Church of Christ (Holiness) U.S.A. on Harwell Street, for about forty years. As trustee, as deacon and as minister, he has been the good and faithful steward that has steered the Beulah church during the troublesome times through which the church has traveled. During the most dismal hour, he was called to the ministry, was licensed, and was soon ordained. Thus he was clothed ecclesiastically to serve a greater need in the church. He has worked in the local church, the District, the Diocese and National Conventions.

Brother Jesse Bell, deceased, formerly of 4305 Cook Avenue, St. Louis, Mo. Brother Bell was a charter member of the church at Starkville, Miss. He was a member of the trustee board of C. M. & I. College and a member of the deacon board of Christ Temple Church, 4301 Page Blvd. St. Louis, Mo.

Mr. John Askerneese and Mrs. Dora Askerneese

Mr. John and Mrs. Dora Askerneese were members of the Damascus Church of Hazlehurst, Miss.

In 1902 Brother John Askerneese was ordained as a deacon by

Rev. W. S. Pleasant, and served as deacon in the church at Fernwood, Miss., under Pastor Wm. Webb.

After living in Hazlehurst for a while, they moved to Glendora, Miss., and started a Sunday School and prayer band in their home in 1914. From the Sunday School the Glendora Pilgrim Rest Church was organized, since there was no Holiness church there. Brother John Askerneese was the deacon; Sister Dora Askerneese, his wife, was the missionary. Rev. H. R. Hicks became the pastor. The man who owned the land built a church for them. Soon afterward a church was organized at Sumner, called Second Pilgrim Rest.

In 1919 they moved to Lambert where again they found no holiness church. They had set the pattern. So they began their missionary work and soon began Pilgrim Rest No. 3 with Rev. A G. Belton of Hollandale as pastor.

In 1922 they moved to Chicago and joined the Christ Temple Church and Brother Askerneese became a deacon and worked until he was called from labor to reward. In 1941 Sister Askerneese went to live with her son, Pastor O. A. Askerneese in Omaha, Nebr.

Brother Matthew Chase

Brother Matthew Chase was a charter member, and deacon of White Rock Church, just west of Jackson Miss. He was secretary of a special North Jackson district of which Rev. Judge Hayes was the president. He is survived his two daughters; Mrs. Fannie Gant and Mrs. Mary Sims.

356

Rev. Samuel T. Cobbins

Rev. Samuel T. Cobbins was one of four children born near Lexington, Miss. There were two sisters, Elizabeth Cobbins Hines, now living in Chicago, Illinois and Hallie who died in her young womanhood and one brother, O. B. Cobbins.

During their youth, they were reared by their grandfather, for the four children were orphaned while they were very young.

The grandfather was a Baptist minister. The last church he pastored was the big Community Baptist near his home, which he pastored for 20 years until he retired to his quiet country farm life. His father was recognized as a prophet by his community peers. The grandfather had three sons, all of whom were ministers; one Lee Porter Cobbins was among the early ministers of the Church of Christ (Holiness) U.S.A., pastored Mt. Perea, his home church in Carroll County, the churches at Tchula and Goodmiss, Miss., until his death in 1913.

Rev. S. T. Cobbins founded the church at Hattiesburg, Miss: pastored the Lord's Tabernacle Church at Lucas, Miss.; and was called to pastor the Christ Temple Church at St. Louis, Mo. The church sent him money for moving expenses. Rushing back home from the Lucas church from which he was resigining, he was caught in the Big Black Flood river, his car was washed off the road bed, and he with his son Lemuel was drowned in December 1926. The church at St. Louis kept the chairs in the pulpit draped for him for 30 days, and refused to accept the return of the moving expense money from his widow, Mrs. Rosa Walker Cobbins.

The widow with the four remaining children, Lillie Mae Cobbins-

Anderson, Sammie Christine Cobbins-Phillips, Alberta Cobbins-Bunton, all of Chicago; and the son Charles Cobbins in New York City.

Rev. Samuel Cobbins was with the first group of students who moved with the C. M. &. I. College when it was moved to the new 43 acre campus three miles north west of Jackson, Miss. While a student, at intervals, he traveled and gathered provision and money for the school. On one occassion—during an emergency, he raised nearly $1,000 for the school.

When he left the school he went immediately to Hattiesburg, Miss. where he established Mt. Olive Church of Christ (Holiness), now pastored by Rev. Willie Bingham, Sr. He never missed the sessions of the National Conventions.

At his death, he was secretary of the Publishing Board, and Financial and Statistical Secretary of the National Convention. For 100 years the gospel has been cared by the ministers in the direct lineage of the Cobbins family.

Brother Oscar Davis

1. *What is thy talent?*   2. *Use what thou hast.*

No one questioned what was Oscar Davis' talent, nor whether he could use it to the glory of the Lord, nor if he would use it to the glory of the Lord. He was naturally musical. He had a tenor musical voice of exceptional good quality. He usually sang with a quartette, often made up of J. E. Conic, G. A. Thomas, Eddie Crane, Sims or R. Lowe, all members of the Christ Temple Church, pastored by the late C. P. Jones. His musical voice was enjoyed by thousands during his active lifetime; and especially in the rendering of these two numbers:—"One Sweetly Solemn Thought". "O Soul Beset With Sorrows Deep".

Mother Rachel Dees

Mother Rachel Dees is the oldest living member of Caney Creek Church. She was a member of Caney Creek at its early stage and is still active and a faithful servant of the Lord.

Sister Bettie A. Dorsey

Sister Bettie A. Dorsey was born April 30, 1870 in Jackson, Miss. She was a member of Mt. Helm Baptist Church, and was with Elder Jones and the group when they were put out of Mt. Helm Baptist Church. She continued with the Holiness movement

Brother Oscar Davis   Mother Rachel Dees

Sister Bettie A. Dorsey

until her death October 2, 1953 in St. Louis, Mo., under the pastorate of Rev. M. F. Brown. She organized the Sunbeams, was a Sunday School teacher, member of the Senior Choir, and was president of the C. W. W. W.

A Summary of My Life and Work in the Church and Vocation
Mrs. Luticia Ferguson

My mother, born in slavery was given to her young mistress when a girl, and when the mistress married, she took her little slave with her and reared her as there were no children born to her and her husband. The child was Darcas Ball. She became almost as a member of the family.

Finally her young master got in debt and mortgaged his slaves, and ran them off south and sold them. It grieved the mistress and she asked her slave to let her get her a home in St. Louis. Mother said, "I don't like the city." Not aware of the hardships of slaves down south, she said no. She was put on the block here in St. Louis, sold and taken to Mississippi. After eight years in slavery married Lexous Thomas; ten children were born to them. In Clairbourne County, Mississippi, while I was quite young, my widowed mother Mrs. Darcas Thomas, the mother of seven children, let me live with an older sister, Mrs. Paulina King, who was married and had one little girl younger than myself. As they had to work on the farm I was a companion to her child, now Mrs. Clara Anderson of Omaha, Nebraska.

My teachers saw my desire to learn and encouraged me to go to college. My sister did her best to help me until I was 14 years of age and at the age of 15 for the next two years they sent me to Summer Normal held in Port Gibson, Mississippi. At 17 years of age I went to school at Jackson Missionary Baptist College.

In 1896 I finished at Jackson College, I then went down to take an examination which I passed, and received my first grade license. I had my license transferred to Capiah County in which I taught 4 years. In 1897 my niece Miss Clara King and I attended the first National "Holiness" Convention held at Mt. Helm Church. Rev. C. P. Jones was the Pastor. My niece and I were saved in December 1896 and still kept by His power. Try Him, He is able. I continued teaching and in 1899 I was married to the late Mr. Robert Jones and began housekeeping. I gave up teaching for a while and moved to Jackson, Mississippi, bought a home and settled down.

In 1905 my husband died, in Sept., 1905 I went to Christ Temple and began to review my subjects. In a short time I was elected and put on the teachers staff in 1906. Prof. P. Lee was the principal. I worked there until 1907 until mid year, when the trustees bought a tract of land with the mansions, and added more room to it, and opened up the high school department. Being in need of a matron and teachers I was sent out as a teacher and matron. It has been 55 years since I went, served out that term and was sent back to town and made principal of that department at the Temple and served until 1914, when my health became poor for a while.

In 1920 I came to St Louis, Missouri, worked out in service, went to night school and took vocational English and general

360

mathematics and vocal music at our church. In 1925 I went to Jackson, Mississippi, to the convention where I met Rev. A. B. Ferguson of Luray, Tennessee. Rev. Ferguson was pastoring a church in Huntington, Kentucky. He finally gave that church up and worked at the home church in Luray teaching the Bible in the community.

Sister Pauline King

In 1944 I got a letter from Professor O. B. Cobbins to come to Christ Missionary & Industrial College to serve as matron. I accepted the challenge. But during the session I was called back to St. Louis twice in two weeks time. This caused me to ask Prof. Cobbins for a leave of absence. Before school opened the next session I had received the leave and returned to St. Louis, in 1946 to work in the Sunday School and church. I served as a Sunday School teacher, and President of the C.W.W.W. for eight years and I also sang in the choir. At all times I endeavored to continue in the doctrine of Holiness. And in all things I did by best, thank God. I am still sowing the seed of righteousness. I am now 87 years old and by the power of God I am kept saved and happy in the Lord.

William Funches

Brother William Funches came up with the old line guards of the church. He hailed from Copiah County, Mississippi, where he was born in 1892. He traveled around through the Mississippi Delta, the Greenville District in particular, and aided the administration of Rev. N. Sanders.

He is acquainted with the church, knows of its actions, has talked with many of its leaders and has apprehended their religious thinking.

He was particularly interested in the educational work of the church. He helped to raise funds for the support of the school and spent some time working there at the school.

Mrs. Mary Graves

Mrs. Mary Graves has allowed the Lord to use her time and her talents in the service of the church.

She is teacher in the Sunday School, secretary of the Usher Board, Bible teacher for the Woman's Auxiliary and has three "Child Evangelism Classes" which meet on different days in three different neighborhoods. She also likes to attend the conventions. Mrs. Graves is a member of the Golden Gate Church of Christ Holiness) in San Francisco, California, where she resides.

Sister Annie R. Hines

Mrs. Annie R. Hines was born in 1880 and became a member of the Lord's Tabernacle Church of Christ, (Holiness) U.S.A. at the age of 25, during the ministry of the late Bishop Wm. A. Washington, and she has been a member for the past sixty years. She is the only living charter member of the church at Selma, Alabama.

Sister Hines has faithfully served the church in various capacities as indicated below: Sunday School teacher, H.Y.P.U. leader, choir member, president at C.W.W.W., member church trustee board and church treasurer. Hers was a life well spent in the sevvice of the Lord. Her home was the minister's home.

Brother Jesse Bell

Brother Jesse Bell was a charter member of the church at Starkville, Miss. He was a member of the Trustee Board of C. M. &. I. College, and a member of the deacon board of Christ Temple Church, St. Louis, Mo.

Rev. Leonidas Francis Dunn

Rev. Leonidas Francis Dunn, the sixth son and the youngest of the ten children of Richmond and Elizabeth Dunn, was born December 24, 1890 in Monroe, La., Cadwell Parish. Rev. Dunn was reared in a Christian home. He received educational training at C. M. &. I. College in Jackson, Mississippi, and Arkansas Bap-

362

Mrs. Mary Graves

Sister Annie R. Hines

Rev. Leonidas Francis Dunn

tist College, Little Rock, Arkansas. He taught school in Monroe, La.

On December 11, 1917, he married Miss Frances Mitchell. They moved to Chicago, Illinois, in 1919 where they united with Christ Temple Church under the Pastorate of Rev. C. E. Owens.

He served as Editor of *Truth* and manager of the Printing Office. He has served as Sunday School Teacher, Superintendent, and Choir Director. His work with the Truth Clubs was progressively pronounced. He was President of the local club and director of the clubs nationally. He answered the call and entered the ministry in 1957. He died April 6, 1964, in Chicago, Illinois.

Mrs. Frances Mitchell-Dunn

Mrs. Frances Mitchell-Dunn is the daughter of Missionary Louise A. Mitchell of Monroe, La.

She is a former student of C. M. &. I. College and was a member of the school's noted choral group.

She was married to Mr. Leonidas F. Dunn and they moved to Chicago in 1919, where they joined the Christ Temple Church. She became an active worker in the church. She was organist, member of Truth Club and President of Sunday School Class Number Three Club.

During the lifetime of her husband, he accumulated a large collection of religious books. When her husband died, she contributed the books to the Christ Temple Church, Chicago, library in memory of her husband.

Mr. E. L. Fizer

Mr. E. L. Fizer was a charter member of Mt. Olive Church, located about seven miles southwest of Jackson, Mississippi, on Raymond Road. He was a Sunday School and lifetime Deacon of the Church. He was also a member of C. M. & I. College Trustee Board until his death.

Mrs. Florence Johnson

Mrs. Florence Johnson was the president of the Illinois-Indiana District C.W.W.W. of the Northern Diocese.

She was the chairman of the Deaconess Board of Christ Temple Church, Chicago, Illinois.

Mrs. Omega Askerneese

Mrs. Omega Snipes-Askerneese, the daughter of Mr. and Mrs. Jordan Snipes, was born in Searcy, Ark., April 28, 1913.

She joined the church at Searcy Arkansas.

On November 2, 1946 she was married to Rev. O. A. Askerneese, and worked faithfully to help him in his church ministry.

Mrs. Florence Johnson   Mrs. Omega Askerneese

Mrs. Ruth Conic-Brumfield   Sister Sarah Caver

She died May 27, 1957 at Memphis, Tenn.

Rev. Maurice Bingham

Rev. Maurice Bingham, A. B., of Jackson, Miss., is a graduate of Moody Bible Institute of Chicago, Illinois. His religious activities have included summer Bible camp work, boys club work, Christian service brigade, radio ministry, general evangelistic work, H.Y.P. U. leader, and Sunday School teacher.

He was pastor, Mt. Olive, Hattiesburg, Miss., and Pastor, Christ Temple Church, McComb, Miss.

Mrs. Ruth Conic-Brumfield

Mrs. Ruth Conic-Brumfield was a former student of Southern Christian Institute of Edward, Mississippi.

She became matron of girls at the same institute, and, later, became matron of girls at C. M. & I. College. She was married to the late Bishop J. L. I. Conic, and was the step-mother of Bishop M. R. Conic.

Sister Annie E. Butler

Sister Annie E. Butler is the widow of the late Bishop E. M. Butler of Jackson, Mississippi. Sister Butler comes from a family of intellectuals. She received her educational preparation in institutions of higher learning in Louisiana and Texas, and Jackson, Mississippi, at Jackson College.

She taught in the Jackson, Mississippi, Public Schools and C. M. & I. College. Sister Butler manifested a keen interest in the work of the Church and became the president of the South Central Diocese C.W.W.W. She was gifted in writing poetry.

Sister Maude L. Conic

Sister Maude L. Conic was born in Indiana, Miss. She was reared in a Christian home. When she was quite young, her family moved to Little Rock, Arkansas. She was married to Reverend M. R. Conic, in December, 1933. Her husband has since become Senior Bishop of the Churches of Christ (Holiness) U.S.A.

While rearing the family of four children she continued her activities in the church. She worked faithfully with, and in, every church pastored by her husband. In the Woman's Auxiliary, of the Church of Christ (Holiness) organization, she undertook the leadership in a project known as "The Home for the Aged" and sponsored a recital program annually in the National Session of the W.A.C.C. The latter effort has as its aim, the encouraging of youthful talent to continue education and specialized interest in line of personal improvement and development.

In 1964 she was elected to the position of National President of the W.A.C.C. She is director of the Young Mother's Service Unit, a missionary and social welfare effort. Sister Conic is a gifted vocalist and has served in different choirs under the pastorates of her husband.

Elder C. C. Carhee

Elder C. C. Carhee, a former student of C. M. & I. College has been actively engaged in the work of the church.

He has seen the Church grow from its inception to its present status. He is acquainted with all departments of the church.

He has traveled and preached in all the dioceses during his missionary career.

Rev. O. B. Cobbins, The Sunday School Missionary

Rev. O. B. Cobbins, a former student of C. M. & I. College, served as Sunday School Missionary for three years in thirteen counties in Southeast Alabama., under the auspices of the American Sunday School Union of Philadelphia, Penna.

The slogan was: "Reaching the otherwise unreached."

The city dwellers can hardly conceive of the many vast rural areas with no existing church offerings; with schools exhibiting nothing to justify the name; and with many human beings, but no society.

Thus the befitting saying, "Ignorance is bliss."

Dangers had to be faced in taking the messages and serving the needs of these people.

On one occasion as the Missionary was walking up a pathway to a cross-road, less than a half block away where four men were standing, suddenly a shot was fired from a pistol. The bullet passed close to the right of the Missionary's head. Presently a second shot was fired with the bullet passing within a few inches of the left of the Missionary's head. Finally, the third shot was fired. The bullet passed directly over the Missionary's head but did not strike his hat. Naturally by this time, the Missionary was doing some thinking.

But he reasoned that he had been commissioned to do a certain task. He was within the realm of his domain. He felt that he was within the will of God and God would surely preserve his life.

Shortly the Missionary was with the people who had conveyance to take him into the rural for the purpose of starting a Sunday School.

On the journey out, they told the Missionary that a Negro was lynched the month before in the town and his body was tied to the rear of an automobile and dragged around the court house. They then loosed the Negro's body for his people to get and bury. That was the end of the episode. . .

The second incident they reported to the Missionary was the community meeting the week before which was broken up by some shooting into the little meeting place. So it was doubtful if any would dare meet again.

However, the Missionary went alone to the meeting place and went in. Surely enough there were signs of shooting. The Missionary took his pocket knife and picked a few of the pellets out of the wall of the little pulpit, prayed and then left.

Sister Elva Cobbins

Sister Elva Cobbins was born July 16, 1896. She was a faithful minister's wife, the companion of the editor, Rev. O. B. Cobbins. A faithful church worker, she also taught in the Jackson, Mississippi, Public School system.

On November 7, 1964 the Master called her home.

Sister Leanna Moore

Mrs. Leanna Shaw-Moore (1891-1945), the deceased wife of Brother Walter Moore, Chicago, Illinois, was a former member

368

Sister Elva Cobbins

Sister Leanna Moore

of the Christ Temple Church, Jackson, Mississippi.

After moving to Chicago, she became interested in the C.W.W.
W. work. Across the years, she served as President of the local
C.W.W.W., the District C.W.W.W., the Northern Diocese C.W.
W.W. and at her death she was the Vice-President of the National
C.W.W.W.

Rev. T. C. (Neal) Dyson

Mr. Q. M. Green

Rev. T. C. (Neal) Dyson

Rev. T. C. (Neal) Dyson was one of the Veteran Ministers
of Franklinton, La. He was a zealous worker during the early
period of the movement.

Rev. Jesse Edward Graham

Rev. Jesse Edward Graham was born April 13, 1875 at Edwards, Mississippi. At age 23, he was united in holy wedlock with
Miss Mary M. Hatch. He moved to Jackson, Mississippi, in 1943.
During a serious illness in the hospital, Bishop M. R. Conic visited
and consoled him. And talked to him of God's goodness. He was
constrained to unite with the Holiness Movement. He was sent to
the Cynthia Church to rebuild the church. He also rebuilt the
Church at Little Zion. He was faithful to the end. He passed away
in July, 1965.

Mr. Q. M. Green

Mr. Q. M. Green of Ruleville, Mississippi, was a typical family
man. He had a large family with a devoted Christian wife. He sent
his children to College and taught them to love and support the
church.

He was a staunch member of the C. M. & I. College Trustee Board.

Sister Cora Harvey

Sister Cora Harvey of Ruleville, Mississippi, is a substantial supporter of C. M. & I. College and a member of the Trustee Board.

In 1964, she was elected President of the National C.W.W.W., the organization sponsoring the erection of the new Dormitory for girls at C. M. & I. College.

Sister Martha Jackson

Sister Martha Jackson of Jackson, Mississippi, was a charter member of the Holy Mt. Zion Church at Hermanville, Mississippi.

She died in May, 1964, in Jackson where she held membership in the Christ Temple Church.

Sister Viola Jones

Sister Viola Jones is one of the workers in the Sweet Home Church of Christ Holiness, U.S.A. in Rankins County, East of Jackson, Mississippi. The Church is pastored by Rev. John Hill. The church was started in her house.

Sister Viola Jones

Sister Frances M. Dunn

371

Rev. J. D. King

Rev. J. D. King of Hazlehurst, Mississippi, was a Bible scholar; an expert in quoting scriptures, giving book, chapter and verse from memory throughout his sermons.

The Bethel Church at Franklinton, La., was built under his pastorate. He was the supply minister at Christ Temple, the Mother church, Jackson, Mississippi. He also pastored the Washington addition church (now Third Temple) Jackson, Mississippi, and he also pastored the New Lake Church near Jackson for 28 years.

Mrs. Fannie Burrell-Jones

Mrs. Fannie Burrell-Jones of Jackson, Miss., was born March 29, 1876, the daughter of the late Joseph and Susie A. Burrell.

At the age of 12, she accepted Christ and united with the Mt. Helm Baptist Church in 1888. She was 19 years old when Bishop C. P. Jones became pastor of the Mt. Helm Baptist Church. She became one of the first charter members of Christ Temple founded by Bishop C. P. Jones, Jackson, Miss.

She was the mother of Horace L. Floyd and Bernard C. Jones; Mrs. Hattie Jones-Hutchins and Mrs. Mary Jones-Younkins, Jackson, Miss.

She died Feb. 18, 1962 at Jackson, Miss., at the age of 86.

Miss Susie Bell Jones

Miss Susie Bell Jones, Chicago, Illinois joined Leland, Miss., Church of Christ, Holiness in 1933 under the pastorate of Rev. J. W. Coleman.

She moved to Chicago in 1943 where she became a member of Christ Temple Church. Her church activities have included: Secretary of Truth Club, member of the Gospel Choir, Sponsor of the Junior Usher Board and president of the Woman's Auxiliary of the Northern Diocese.

Professor John A. Lee

The Rev. Prof. John Anthony Lee, second child of six children in the family of Anthony and Kitty Lee, was born in Holmes County, Miss., Aug. 30, 1875. He was converted at the age of 12 years and served faithfully in many offices in the church. In 1902, he united with the Church of Christ (Holiness). He was Bible instructor in various organizations in the state of Mississippi and was licensed as a minister by Pastor C. P. Jones, founder of the

Mrs. Fannie Burrell-Jones

Rev. J. D. King

Miss Susie Bell Jones

Professor John A. Lee

Church of Christ (Holiness),U.S.A. and Pastor J. A. Jeter. He acted as pastor of the Berean Church for several years. He was an honest, intelligent, law abiding citizen. Prof. Lee was the first "exempted" public school teacher to be appointed in Holmes County. He entered Civil Service and was R.F.D. Mail Carrier from 1907 till he retired in 1938. He was census clerk in Washington, D.C., for 2 years. He was active in all civic and religious work. He was the life-time deacon on the Berean Church. His generous donations meant much in the practice of the motto, "Lifting As We Climb."

In young manhood, Prof. Lee was married to Miss Rosa C. Calcote. He was an honor roll member of the Prayer Room Club, sharing the pleasure of helping his most devoted wife to sponsor the building of the Prayer Room. This long life of service closed August 31, 1957 in Memphis, Tenn. where they had moved 16 months before from Lexington, Miss. His last repeated song was "Jesus Christ is made to me all I need, all I need." Now he rests.

Prof. J. S. Land

Prof. J. S. Land of Tchula, Mississippi, was the second President of C. M. & I. College. He was a devoted husband and father. He was a quiet loyal citizen, a congenial and exceptional good man, an earnest Christian gentleman and an ardent church worker.

It was during the time of his administration that the school was established on its present site.

Rev. York A. Lenoir

Rev. York A. Lenoir, a graduate of Alcorn A. and M. College in Mississippi, was born in 1877.

He was a veteran educator; one of the first industrial teachers at C. M. & I. College and later became President of the same institution.

He was Pastor of the Bethel Church in St. Louis, Missouri, where he died, December 12, 1960, at the age of 83.

Mrs. Sally Lowry

Mrs. Sally Lowry was born in 1872 in Terry, Miss. She was the mother of twelve children. She was charter member of the church at Ruleville, Miss., where she was a Sunday School Teacher for many years. She was a member of the Christ Temple Church at Jackson, Miss., 1947-1953.

374

Mrs. Sally Lowry

Rev. Sandy J. McIntyre

She moved to Christ Temple Church in Chicago, Illinois, in 953, and died Feb. 7, 1955.

William T. McDonald

Deacon William T. McDonald, Norfolk, Va., and his sister, Mrs. Emma Jackson of New York, N. Y., were the only surviving harter members of the Church of Christ (Holiness) in the Tide-vater area.

Elder Parker Williams of Langley, S. C., came to Norfolk in 895 and held street meetings. Preaching "without holiness no nan shall see the Lord in Peace." His converts to sanctification vere Brother William T. McDonald and his sister, Mrs. Emma ackson.

They rented meeting space, and finally built a small building nd organized the Grant St. Holy Church. It was the first Holiness hurch in Virginia or anywhere nearby. Rev. Samuel was the first pastor. The first deacons were Deacons William T. McDonald, Edward Cox, and Riddick.

Deacon William T. McDonald was born November 7, 1869.

Rev. Sandy J. McIntyre

Rev. Sandy J. McIntyre was born in Louisiana. He attended Normal College in Pine Bluff, Ark., and Wiley College in Marshall, Texas.

He was married to Miss Gladys Means and moved to Pine Bluff, Ark., where he became a member of the Church of Christ, Holiness.

375

He was soon called to the ministry, ordained and pastored th
church at Texarkana, Texas; Madisonville, Ky.; Omaha, Nebrask
and had been pastoring the church at Cleveland, Ohio for nin
years before he died.

He was courageous in his belief for the truth that he preache(

He had two daughters: Mrs. Eloise Lesane of Cleveland, Ohi
and Mrs. Dymple McIntyre Robinson of Chicago, and one so
Sandy John, II.

Brother Henry McGee

Brother Henry McGee joined the Holiness church early in life.

Soon after he moved to Canton, Miss., he became a membe
of the deacon board of the Pleasant Green Church of Christ, Hol
ness, U.S.A. He remained deacon until he died April 15, 1936.

After Deacon Henry McGee died, his wife, Mrs. Hattie McGe(
born 1890, moved to Chicago where she became a faithful membe
of the Christ Temple Church.

She became a deaconess and worked with C.W.W.W. until he
health failed. She died January 23, 1964, age 74.

Her two daughters Mrs. Nadie White and Mrs. Lena Bake
both live in Chicago.

Deacon Alex Matthews,

Deacon Alex Matthews served as a deacon of the church a
Cleveland, Miss., for 25 years.

He was a member of the Trustee Board of C. M. & I. Colleg
and a substantial supporter of the school, During the early days
the establishment of the school, he gave $1,000 at one time.

He was always concerned about the welfare and the best intere
of the church.

His widow, Sister Bettie Matthews, is still a faithful worker
the church.

Deacon Henry Moore

Deacon Henry Moore was born about 1857. He was one of th
six, including Elder Jones, to make selection of the new churc
site with plans. The six met at the same corner near the same tim
He gave the first $100 to purchase the site on the corner of Ea
Monument and Lamar Streets, Jackson, Miss. This was done th
Sunday after they were put out of Mt. Helm Baptist Church
1902.

376

Brother Henry McGee   Sister Hattie McGee

Deacon Alex Matthews, Deceased   Sister Bettie Matthews

Deacon Henry Moore

He served for almost 50 years as deacon of the mother church. He was chairman of the trustee board. Deacon Moore was one one of the oldest deacons of the movement.

When Elder Jones was a victim of smallpox during the smallpox epidemic in 1900, Elder Jones stayed in the home of Deacon Moore. Deacon Moore was one of the first charter members of the Christ Temple Church.

He died in 1945 at the age of 88.

Deacon Larkin K. Neal

Larkin K. Neal was a charter member of the church at Cleveland, Miss.

He served his church as a member of the Senior Choir. Superintendent of the Sunday School, and Church Treasurer.

He was active in the church services until a few weeks before his death in 1964.

Sister Agnes Bingham-Nelson

Sister Agnes Bingham-Nelson, a graduate of Jackson State College for Teachers, Jackson, Mississippi, is a teacher in the Jackson Public Schools.

Mrs. Nelson was a former teacher at C. M. & I. College, and a worker in the Women's Auxiliary program.

Rev. Johnnie James Peterson

Johnnie James Peterson was born in Columbus, Mississippi, on March 9th, 1894. He was the only child of Joshua and Dinah Peterson. He grew up in Columbus and attended Baldwyn and Union Academy Schools. At an early age he accepted Christ and joined the Ten Mile Holiness Church, under the pastorate of Elder Noah Smith. He was joined in Holy Matrimony to Juanita Alexander, February 1, 1915. To this union three children were born. He moved to Chicago Heights, Ill., in 1916. He helped to organize and was a leader of the Church. This church later affiliated with the National Convention of the Churches of Christ, Holiness, U.S.A. became known as Christ Temple Holiness Church.

In 1920, he began his ministry and was inspired to build a comfortable church for his people to worship God. This church is located at 1610 Shields Ave. Chicago, Ill. In 1931 he became Assistant Pastor at Christ Temple Cathedral, Chicago, under Elder William Webb.

In March of 1932 he was assigned by Bishop J. L. I. Conic to build a church in Gary, Indiana. In addition to building this edifice he was also responsible for building the Christ Temple Rest Home located at 2369 Taney Street, Gary. The house next door north was also purchased and added to the church property.

Elder Peterson realized a need for expanding the church, and started this project in the fall of 1961.

Acording to God's will Elder Peterson did not live to see this remodeling completed. He was called home by our Savior from his labor to reward at 9:50 A.M. Friday, June 15, 1962, Methodist Hospital, Gary, at the age of 68. This was the expiration of our Lord's good and faithful servant and our loyal and devoted leader.

Elder Peterson served at this church for 30 years, 2 months and 15 days. He was a man of sincere prayer, eternal faith and bold courage. He had a deep belief in divine healing and prayed for many people with visual results. Rev. Peterson loved and was loved by old and young people. We considered him an asset to this comunity. Christ Temple Church suffered a great loss but we realize it is heaven's gain.

Brother Moses Phillips and Sister Nettie Phillips

Mrs. Nettie Phillips

Sept. 15, 1878 — July 27, 1964

Mrs. Nettie Harness Phillips was born in Clarksburg, Mississippi.

When she was fourteen years old, she sought the Lord and was converted and joined the Baptist Church.

She was a young lady when her family moved to Jackson, Miss. It was at Lane Chapel Methodist Church in Jackson where she heard the late Bishop C. P. Jones preach.

381

In Sept. of 1902, she met Moses Phillips, and was married March 4th 1903.

After she was married, she still felt the need of a deeper consecration and wanted to tbe filled with the Holy Ghost. One day her mother said to her: "Nettie, I heard you are going to join that Sanctified Church. You are plenty good enough;" but she knew within herself that she was not filled.

In 1906 she joined the Carlton Hill Church of Christ, (Holiness) out from Jackson, under the pastorate of the late Rev. H. R. McInnis. She still felt that she needed to grow deeper in the faith and one morning in 1910, as she was scrubbing the floor, it was so white and clean that she asked the Lord to cleanse her heart and make it as pure and white as the floor. On this day she was truly filled with the Holy Ghost. Her husband, mother and other members of her family joined the Holiness Church. At last she knew it was real.

A couple of years later a few sisters in Washington's Addition in Jackson began a prayer meeting in Sister Phillips' home and asked for a Church there. She wanted a Church close by where her children could attend Sunday School and church services. After much fasting and prayer, the Lord sent the Rev. McInnis there who organized a church and was the first pastor. It was now called the Third Temple in Jackson, Washington Addition.

On May 19, 1917, Sister Phillips moved to Chicago. At the time she had five children. She was reluctant about leaving the south for she feared that there would be no church of her faith in Chicago. She prayed earnestly and a voice spoke to her and said, "The Lord will provide."

After her arrival she and the children had prayer every day and the Lord blessed and provided her with everything He had promised. The church of her choice was organized. All of this happened in 1918. She testified the Sunday of the organization and said, "I was glad when they said unto me, let us go into the house of the Lord."

The sisters met in her home and prayed for a work for themselves. Out of this prayer meeting, the Christian Women Willing Workers was organized, and she suggested that they meet on Tuesday night, and this has been their regular meeting night for forty-seven years.

Several years ago she suggested to the sisters that they start a Calendar Birthday celebration which has been a great help financially and socially.

In 1945 she was appointed a deaconess and served faithfully in that capacity until her passing.

Sister Phillips was a member of the Third Temple at Jackson, Miss., and also a charter member of Christ Temple of Chicago.

Brother Moses Phillips
Jan. 26, 1873 — Sept. 27, 1957

Brother Moses Phillips was born in Jackson, Miss. In March, 1903, he was married to Miss Nettie Harness. As a result of his wife being a devout Christian and being filled with the Holy Ghost, he sought the Lord and wanted to be filled also. In 1910 he joined the Carlton Hill Church of Christ (Holiness) then pastored by the late Rev. H. R. McInnis.

In 1912 Brother Phillips and his wife felt the need of a church closer to their home. They prayed earnestly and continued to trust God. Their prayers were answered when Rev. H. R. McInnis organized and pastored the church in Washington Addition. He served as a deacon of the church. This church was built with only a few members.

Brother Phillips' home served as haven for the pastor of the church who lived out of town. Other visiting ministers were always welcome at his home.

In 1917 he moved his family to Chicago. Immediately after arriving here he began to seek the church of his choice. Prayer was again answered when Christ Temple Church of Christ, (Holiness) was organized. Rev. C. E. Owens was called to pastor. Brother Phillips was oppointed a deacon under his pastorate. He served faithfully in this office under five different pastors. He was known to visit the members in his district more than any other deacon on the board. He was a very devout servant of God and the church.

Elder Louis Randall

Elder Louis Randall was born on the 3rd day of March 1880 to slave parents, Willis and Nancy Randall, just 12 miles from Lexington, Mississippi. As a young man Louis was an industrious farmer working his share of his father's 350 acre spread until he noticed the over 100 acres of virgin timber and set out to harvest this natural resource. Louis was the first Negro in Holmes County to set up and run a steam gin saw mill which was later blown up by the white folks as his prosperity grew. In the summer

Elder Louis Randall

of 1898 Louis attended revival meetings near his home which were conducted by a fiery young minister by the name of Elder C. P. Jones. Elder Jones preached a fire and brimstone gospel that found the hearts of men "when holiness first broke out". That gospel found Louis and placed him among the holiness saints. January 15, 1903, Louis was wed by Elder Blackman to Almeda Spurlin, daughter of Owen and Amenda Spurlin also slave parents, all of whom he brought to holiness from the Methodist Church. Louis' young family's life was made miserable by the whites because he could not be satisfied with nothing and no future for his family but rather wanted to grow and expand. He had to begin his migration to the north with his wife and 7 children; first to Jonestown, Mississippi, then to Poplar Bluff, Missouri, and finally to Cleveland, Ohio. By 1925 Louis was doing well in Cleveland as the largest Negro contractor there, building large tracts of new homes; until this time he managed to keep his preaching in the background but the Lord's call was too great to ignore. He was appointed pastor of the church in Cleveland by Bishop J. L. I. Conic in 1920. The great depression came and separated Louis from all his earthly possessions in 1931 but being the great man of faith that he was he moved with his 11 children to Detroit, Michigan; and soon afterward Elder W. Webb resigned and Elder Randall was appointed pastor of Zion Chapel of Detroit in 1932. By 1938 Elder Randall had harvested the small group of less than 25 to over 125 and trained young Elder Gilbert to carry forth.

In November 1938 Elder Randall accepted pastorate with a small group at Indianapolis, Indiana, and the fruits of his labors were to be reaped here. A man of faith and vision set out to do a task for the Lord. As he undertook a building program during the war he knew that God was with him. He ordered steel when there was no steel and God delivered steel. He ordered bricks and lumber and nails and God delivered everything; so the man of faith and his flock who believed completed their church in 1947. In 1950 Elder Randall was elected president of the Illinois-Indiana District Convention. He was the gospel father of Bishop A. M. White, Bishop David McPherson, Elder Ezekiel Moore, Elder Alonzo Beasley, Elder M. D. McGee, Elder Joseph Holland, and Elder Allen Myers. Elder Randall slipped away to his reward on January 12, 1956, at the age of 75. "He fought a good fight, he kept the faith, he finished the course".

Deacon Jeff Robinson

Deacon Jeff Robinson

Deacon Jeff Robinson came to the Mt. Helm Baptist Church in 1897 from the Pleasant Baptist Church at Clinton, Miss.

He was counted with the number put out of Mt Helm in 1902. He was one of the first deacons at Christ Temple Church and continued until his death Oct. 13, 1916.

Sister Eliza Ricks

Sister Eliza Ricks is another one of the dependable church workers of Norfolk, Virginia. The Church could not achieve without the services of such faithful willing workers.

The consecrated, devout women of the church have helped to perpetuate the influence of the church in the community.

Elder Thomas Sanders

Elder Thomas Sanders of Jackson, Mississippi, was one of the first to lead the way in establishing the new church.

He with Elder W. S. Pleasant were two first trustees of C. M. & I. College and they were the first two chairmen of the Trustee Board.

He stood for the high principles of the church until his death.

Sister Fannie Washington Seaton

Mrs. Fannie Washington Seaton, the daughter of the late Dicey Jordan and Wade Washington of Brandon, Miss., was born in 1877. She was reared in Madison County.

Her early education was received from the Mary Holmes School, the Smith-Robertson School and Tougaloo College.

On May 31, 1901, she was married to Mr. Aaron Seaton. Of the nine children born, the six now living are Miss Fannie Mae Seaton of Detroit, Michigan; Mrs. Hester Curry of Chicago, Illinois; and Mrs. Mildred Turner, Mrs. Julia Seaton May, Mr. Aaron Seaton, and Mr. William Seaton.

She was a loving and thoughtful mother who tried to give her children the right start in life while they were easily impressed.

Mrs. Seaton was converted during her youthful life. She soon became a member of the Christ Temple Church pastored by Elder C. P. Jones, Jackson, Mississippi.

Pictured with Mrs. Seaton is her daughter, Mrs. Mattie Seaton-Bailey who preceded her mother in death, September, 1961. She was a devout member of Christ Temple Church. She had served as

Elder Thomas Sanders

Sister Eliza Ricks

Mrs. Fannie W. Seaton
and daughter
Mrs. Mattie Seaton Baily

387

an efficient ecretary of the Sunday School, a member of the choir, and an usher. She joined the church under the pastorate of Bishop E. W. Butler.

Mrs. Mildred Seaton Turner, the daughter of Mrs. Fannie W. Seaton, is also a member of Christ Temple Church.

Sister Maude Simon

Sister Maude Simon was born 1882. She was a charter member of the Christ Temple Church and had grown up with the choir through the years. Age did not wear away her smiles, nor the mellowness of her spirit. She had a depth of understanding of human of human cares.

It was her pleasing and lovable disposition that made it possible for her to build up such a massive insurance debit in her business. For many years, she was president of the Christ Temple Church's Senior Choir and the members never sought a change of President.

Sister Hattie Potter Simms

Sister Hattie Potter Simms was born in Copiah County, Miss. in 1883. She was married to one Mr. Simms who became a successful business man.

They had four children: G. E., Percy, Julius, and Mrs. Mable Simms Lewis. Being an educator herself, she educated all of her children, and they were taught in the way of righteousness.

She was one of the charter members of the church where Rev. S. T. Cobbins was the pastor in Hattiesburg, Miss.

Sister Carrie Bell Spruille

Sister Carrie Bell Spruille was born Nov.17, 1885 in Smithville, Mississippi. She was converted in 1910 and became a member of the Ruleville, Mississippi, Church.

She served as member of the Senior Choir, deaconess, President of the local C.W.W.W., President of the Greenville District C.W. W.W. and a member of the Trustee Board of C. M. & I. College. She was a devoted wife and a loving mother. She died Feb. 24, 1951, in Robins, Illinois.

Mrs. Mildred Seaton Turner

Sister Maude Simon

Sister Hattie Potter Simms

Sister Carrie Bell Spruille

Rev. Walter Smith

Rev. Walter Smith is a member of the First Church of Christ Holiness U.S.A., 1935 Madison Ave., New York City, N.Y. He was the assistant pastor under Rev. Wm. Acty. He has made several trips abroad.

Mrs. Armanda Spurlins

Mrs. Armanda Spurlins was born a slave, and was one of the first in her community to accept teachings of the new church through the preaching of Elder C. P. Jones and Elder C. H. Mason. She and her family lived in Acona in Holmes County, eight miles north of Lexington, Miss.

She was a charter member of the Pine Grove Church. At one time Rev. Hick of Selma, Ala., was her pastor.

Mrs. Minnie Stevenson

Mrs. Minnie Stevenson, 87, was born in 1878, at Hazlehurst, Copiah County, Mississippi.

Her husband, Gus Stevenson, died in August, 1945.

She was the mother of six children: Mrs. Elva Stevenson-Cobbins (deceased, 1964), the wife of Rev. O. B. Cobbins of Chicago, Mr. Joseph Stevenson of Birmingham, Ala., Mrs. Bettie Pearl Martin of Chicago, Illinois, Mrs. Leora Stevenson-Lewis, the wife of Deacon Lewis of Hattiesburg, Miss., Mrs. Emma Lee Stevenson-Hill, the wife of Rev. John T. Hill of Hazlehurst, Miss., Miss Ambrosia Stevenson of Seatle, Washington, an adopted son, Mr. Roosevelt Stevenson of Detroit, Michigan.

She is one of the oldest of the very few living charter members of the "Wilderness of Judea Church" in Copiah County. She is now a member of the Damascus Church at Hazlehurst, Miss., pastored by Elder Geo. A. Thomas.

The Late Rev. J. S. Williams

Prominent among the staunch supporters of the cause of the General Church was Rev. J. S. Williams of Shreveport, La. A life-long friend and advisor to the late Bishop E. W. Butler, he served as layman and pastor. He was a member of the National Publishing Board and for many years treasurer of the National Convention, serving on the original Episcopal Committee.

His success in the business world is attested to by the high esteem held of him by the citizens of both Shreveport and the State of

Rev. Walter Smith

Mrs. Armanda Spurlins

Mrs. Minnie Stevenson

The Late Rev. J. S. Williams

Louisiana. A monument to his memory is the J. S. Williams Funeral Home in Shreveport, dedicated April 11, 1965. He was one of the founders of the National Funeral Directors Association. The National Negro Business League and the National Negro Insurance Association. He passed December 22, 1938.

Sister Bettie Thomas-Trammel

Sister Bettie Thomas-Trammel, a consecrated Christian woman, was born in Hermanville, Mississippi. She was a devoted matron of the girls at C. M. & I. College and a consistent worker in the church at St. Louis, Missouri.

The Late Sister Charlotte Washington

Sister Charlotte Washington, a Mississippi-born slave, lived to a ripe old age to tell men and women that Jesus still doth indeed save from sin and make men free. (John 8:32-36)

Sister Washington was a leader among church women and a devout saint. She was a charter member of the Mt. Perea Church of Christ, (Holiness), U.S.A. in Carroll County, Mississippi.

She was the mother of seven sons who entered the ministry. Three of the seven sons became ministers in the Church of Christ, (Holiness) They are Rev. Daniel J. Washington, Bishop William

A. Washington and Rev. G. B. Washington, who succeeded Bishop Washington as pastor of Bethel Church of Christ (Holiness), Los Angeles, California.

Rev. William Ward

The Rev. William Ward was born October 5, 1863, during the Civil War period. He made his home in St. Louis, Missouri, and was active in the work of the church. He was chairman of the trustee board and was assistant pastor under Elder Henry L. Caver. He died August 17, 1943.

Sister Rebecca V. Means

Sister Rebecca V. Means was a strong and staunch supporter of the Church in Pine Bluff, Arkansas. She was always ready and willing to do what she could to help God's work along. She went to be with the Lord on April 16, 1965.

Deacon Stephen Lewis

Deacon Stephen Lewis became a member of the Church of
Christ (Holiness) in Jackson, Miss. in 1899. He moved to Indianapolis, Ind. in 1918 and was one of the founders and pillars of
the First Church of Christ (Holiness) there. His faithful service
was, for years, a great mainstay of righteousness in the life of
the Indianapolis church until he moved to Detroit, Mich. in 1953.
Presently, September 1964, at the age of 87 years, he is an
honorary deacon at Zion Chapel Church of Christ (Holiness)
Detroit, Mich.

*　　*　　*

The following charts give brief information about persons who
have played an active role in the history of the Church. It is re-
gretted that no write-ups are available about them, however, their
work is known by the Editor.

Name	Address	Church	Function
Rev. Wm. Acty	Montgomery, N.Y.	Christ Temple	Sec. Nat. S.S. Convention
Brother A. W. Adams	St. Louis, Mo.		Deacon
Israel Ball 1885-1960	Detroit, Mich.	Zion Chapel	
Rev. F. A. Boyd	Deceased		Pastor Little Rock, Ark., St. Louis, Mo., Shreveport, La., Leland and Hollandale, Miss.
Brother Felix Ball	Detroit, Mich.	Zion Chapel	Musician
Rev. G. L. Bogan			Pastor Mt. Perea
Brother Harry Brown	Los Angeles, Calif.	Christ Temple	Deacon
Mrs. Matilda Bingham	Jackson, Miss.	Third Temple	Secretary
Mr. W. J. Burris	Franklinton, La.		Pres. S.S. & H.Y.P.U. district
Mrs. Emma Beasley	Jackson, Miss.	Christ Temple	Pianist 30 years.
Rev. J. Boatner	New Orleans, La.		Pastor
Rev. James Brewer	Searcy, Ark.		
Brother. Wm. Burton	Franklinton, La.	Bethel	First Deacon
Rev. L. W. Capshaw	Jackson, Miss.	Christ Temple	First S.S. Supt.
Brother E. W. Crane		Charter Member	Choir director
Sister C. Dixon	Lexington, Miss.	Mt. Perea	Charter member Deaconess
Brother J. S. Farley	Ruleville, Miss.	Christ Temple	Deacon
		Charter Member	
		Galilee-Hazlehurst	
Prof. J. T. Franklin	Memphis, Tenn.	Christ Temple	
Brother Geo. Freeman	Tchula, Miss.		Deacon

395

Name	Address	Church	Function
Brother Wm. Goodloe	Maghee, Mich.	Toledo Church	Deacon
Rev. Richard Hines	Hattiesburg, Miss.	Mt. Perea	Pastor
Mother Ellen Hobbs	Lexington R.F.D. Miss.		Deaconess
			Charter member
Sister Martha Cobbins	Lexington R.F.D. Miss.	Mt. Perea	Pastor's wife
			Charter member
Brother L. M. Lanton	Montgomery, Ala.	Sutter Street	Chair. Dea. Board
			Charter member
Sister Martha Jackson	Jackson, Miss.	Christ Temple	
Brother D. W. Lee	Chicago, Ill.	Christ Temple	Church Clerk
Rev. Felix Lewis	Hazlehurst, Miss.		
Brother Joe Lewis	Leesville, La.	Christ Temple	Dea. and Trustee
Mr. Pleas McCadney	Utica, Miss.	Christ Temple	Dea. and Trustee
Brother C. C. Phillips	Indianola, Miss.	Christ Temple	Chair. Deac. Bd.
		Charter member	
Brother Elijah L. Relf	Montgomery, Ala.	Suter Street	Deacon
Mrs. Georgia Renegar	Chicago, Ill.	Christ Temple	Organist
Sister Pearlena Ross	Chicago, Ill.	Christ Temple	S.S. Teacher
Rev. A. T. Rucker			Pastor, Omaha, Neb.
Sister Slaughter	Tougaloo, Miss.	Christ Temple	C.W.W.W. Worker
Brother Butha Smith	Jayess, Miss.	New Home	Chair. Dea. Bd.
Brother Pat Smith	Tougaloo, Miss.	Christ Temple	Deacon
Brother Tom H. Smith	Los Angeles, Calif	Christ Temple	Deacon
		Charter member	
Mrs. Norah Thompson	Franklinton, La.	Sweet Home	Pres. First C.W.W.W.
Brother Geo. Townsend	Lexington R.F.D. Miss.	Mt. Perea	Deacon
Brother L. Townsend	Detroit, Mich.	Zion Chapel	Deacon
		Charter member	
		Mt. Perea	
		R.F.D. Lexington	

Name	Location	Church	Notes
Brother Ezekiel Virgil	Hazlehurst, Miss.	Galilee	Deacon
Rev. Comic M. Wallace	Chicago, Ill.	Charter member Christ Temple	Founded mission North side
Rev. Dan Washington	Los Angeles, Calif		Former pastor Treas. Nat. Convention
Rev. J. S. Williams	Shreveport, La.		
Brother E. H. Younger	Pocahontas, Miss.	Cynthia	Deacon
Mrs. Sarah L. Williams	Chicago, Ill.	Christ Temple	Teacher S.S. Class No. 3, Pres. Truth Club, Mem. Sr. Choir
Mrs. Dora Roman Widow of the Late Rev. Eugene Roman.	Hermanville, Miss.	Little Zion	
Mrs. Ruby E. Luster 1706½ 24th Ave.	Seattle, Wash.	Old member (108)	
Deacon Hugh N. May 1909-1964	Chicago, Illinois	Christ Temple	Deacon, S.S. Supt. 27 yrs., Mem. Bd. of Chr. Ed., Mem. Sr. Choir, Pres. S.S. Conv. Church pianist, Directress Gospel Choir Pres. Dist. C.W.W.W. Chair. Dea. Bd.
Mrs. Lydia Relf			
Mrs. Florence Johnson	Chicago, Illinois	Christ Temple	Charter member Christ Temple Church-Jackson Pioneer: Greenville Dist., Miss.
Mrs. M. Kimbrough Born 11-17-1885 died 2-24-1951			
Elder N. Sanders			
Rev. J. E. Burris		Little Zion	Carpenter, Miss.
Mrs. Luella O'Quinn			

Name	Address	Church	Function
Mrs. M. Wright-Owens Charter member		Christ Temple Chicago	Teacher C.M. and I. College
Christ Temple-Jackson			
Rev. R. L. Bradley	2033 No. Corlet Los Angeles	Founder of Church	Church consolidated with Pilgrim Church of Christ, Los Angeles Pastor
Rev. Jesse L. Burris	Pine Bluff, Ark.		
Rev. Emanuel L. Campbell	903 So. 7th St. Yakima, Wash.	Morning Star Church	S.S. Supt., H.Y.P.U. Pres., Adult S.S. Teacher, Church Treas., Choir Director
Rev. Rogie Doles	5 Downes Portsmouth, Va.		Pastor Pastor
Rev. Robert Durr	R2 Box 180 Prentiss, Miss.	Mt. Perea Church Rock Hill Church	Pastor Pastor

CHAPTER X

THE MINISTRY OF SONG

The "Ministry of Song" was one of the moving stimuli during the emergence of the church movement.

A befitting introduction to the ministry of song was penned by the Late Bishop Wm. A. Washington, D.D., as follows:

"Oh Sing unto the Lord a New Song," David, the sweet singer of Israel exclaimed; his songs inspired by the spirit of the living God were not only melodious but prophetical; and even though the strings of his harp are broken and the fingers that moved them to tones of ecstasy have crumbled into dust, the Psalms of David still cheer the weary pilgrim along the highway of life.

There are two kinds of poets: the natural and the spiritual. The natural poet may sing to the intellect and sweeten the memory of the human mind with the achievements of mortal success, but the inspired poet sings to the soul and pours into it both inspiration and conviction—for inspired songs are born of God.

The songs written by Bishop Chas. P. Jones, D.D., LL.D., are truly inspired—they are not the mere product of the human mind, but the breathing in of the Spirit of God, giving to the earth the melody of heaven, the gospel of Jesus in poetical strains.

The songs in "Jesus Only" and "His Fulness" carry the message of the movement (The Church of Christ Holiness). Without these songs there is a lack of completeness in the service where the message of this movement is being proclaimed. These songs are in the truest sense Gospel Songs. For in them the fundamental doctrines of salvation are definitely set forth.

As you read the history of these songs written by the author, your soul will be inspired; your faith will be strengthened and your zeal for righteousness will be fanned into a holy flame. You can't read the history of these songs and sing them without acknowledging that the author was only a messenger of the Eternal Spirit.

399

The Exponent of the Ministry of Song
Bishop Charles Price Jones, D.D.LL.D.

The History of the Ministry of Song

Bishop C. P. Jones, the writer of the songs, tells the history of the "ministry of songs" in his own words. The songs presented in this narrative are found in the "Jesus Only Standard Hymnal," Edited by Bishop C. P. Jones. The numbers listed denote the pages on which the songs may be found in the hymnal.

The History of My Songs
by C. P. Jones

Perhaps the history of the songs themselves would not be understood unless there was something known of the history of the writer. Therefore I shall tell something of the experiences of life that led up to the writing of these songs.

And what mercy, what grace, that I, less than the least of all saints (Eph. 3:8) should be called upon, after I am seventy years of age, to give the history of my songs! I, who in childhood had a spell of sickness nearly every year, and who was so afflicted as not to hope to reach my thirtieth year.

Happy with Jesus Alone

The Lord gifted me to sing from a child. Among the many drawbacks of my life has been my bashfulness, a natural timidity that has caused me to hide the light of my very faith, let alone the light of any talent I might have.

The first song I wrote and sang was "JESUS HAS MADE IT ALL RIGHT." Some kind brother heard me sing it at the parsonage when I had finished writing it. During the service there was a lull. "Sing your song," said the brother. I was bashful about it, but his urging encouraged me, and I sang it. The ice once broken, it was not hard after that to put my song messages over. Praise the Lord!

(2)

Then I wrote HAPPY WITH JESUS ALONE. This I sang several years before the music was printed. For it was written in 1897 and the music was brought out in 1900.

It celebrated my soul's determination to stick to Jesus and to the word as it was written and revealed by the Holy Ghost. Severe trials had beset me. My meetings had been shot into at Lexington. C. H. Mason had started his meeting, but that night the meeting had been turned into my hands and I had preached. Five people were shot—none seriously hurt. When the meeting got hot and the foe fierce I had been telegraphed for. This was just following our first holiness convention at Jackson, in 1897. I had been scorned by my brethren and the women of our denominational gatherings; tho I found some staunch supporters among them, such as Elders Richard Morris, Philip Capshaw, W. S. Pleasant, F. S. Sheriff, George Robinson, Dr. R. J. Temple, the father of Doctor Ruth Temple; R. H. Thompson and many others.

I was looked on as a fanatic by some; by others as weak of brain; by yet others as a sharper trying to distinguish myself by being different; by nearly all as a heretic. The leaders set themselves against me and those who did not were intimidated by the others.

(43)

At McComb City a white bootlegger shot at me five or six times as I was calling people up for prayer. I had preached from Isaiah 32:1-3. Of course his action broke up the meeting that night.

This man had two companions with him, so I was reliably informed. One of these killed him the next night. Then this other went to New Orleans and, in a few weeks, killed himself, so I learned. Anyway, the man shot at me Friday night, and when I (having gone home to preach) got back Monday night to resume my meetings, he was dead and buried. And not a white minister

Jesus Has Made it All Right.

Rom. 5: 10.

C. P. J.

Revival.

CHAS. P. JONES.

1. I once was a self-ban-ished soul from the Lord, And wan-dered to death in my flight, Till Je-sus o'er-took me, all sin-sick and sore, And vent-ured to make it all right.

2. It cost Him a life of a-base-ment so sad, And ma-ny a pray'r-la-den night; It cost Him a death of great an-guish and pain: But now He has made it all right.

3. He rose from the grave all tri-umph-ant o'er sin, As-cend-ing to heav-en in might; There at the right hand of the Fa-ther to plead. Come, sin-ner, He'll make it all right.

4. Say not, "I am too mean a sin-ner to come," And give up the strug-gle to-night: A-rise, for the Sav-ior is call-ing for thee; Come, Je-sus will make it all right.

CHORUS.

All right, all right; Je-sus has made it all right; The Fa-ther ac-cepts me, Sal-va-tion is sure; For Je-sus has made it all right.

899, by Chas. P. Jones.

402

I'm Happy With Jesus Alone.

C. P. J.   CHAS. P. JONES.

Moderato.

1. There's noth-ing so precious as Je-sus to me; Let earth with its
2. When sin ful and doom'd to a life of des-pair, No light on my
3. When noth-ing but death for my ransom could pay, And make me ac-
4. 'Twas Je-sus who call'd me and show'd me the way To peace up-on
5. Should fa-ther and moth-er for-sake me be-low, My bed up-on

treas-ures be gone; I'm rich as can be when my Sav-ior I see;
path-way to shine,'Twas Je-sus who found me and made me an-heir
cept-ed with God, 'Twas Je-sus who free-ly Him-self made a prey
earth and in heav'n;'Tis Je-sus who teach-es me dai-ly to pray
earth be a stone, I'll cling to my Sav-ior, He loves me I know,

CHORUS.

I'm hap-py with Je-sus a-lone.
To man-sions of glo-ry di-vine.
And ransom'd my soul with His blood. I'm hap-py with Je-sus a-
And walk in the light He has giv'n.
I'm hap-py with Je-sus a-lone.

lone, I'm hap-py with Je-sus a-lone; Tho' poor and de-

sert-ed,thank God, I can say I'm hap-py with Je-sus a-lone.

1900, by C. P. Jones.

403

in the city would bury him. They said he "interfered with that colored man's meetings, and had no business to do it." ....

Mr. R. L. Cotton, a noble white man who attended my meetings, told me about it.

(242)

Here at McComb, I stayed with Professor (now Doctor) A. J. Scarborough, one of the finest men God ever made and redeemed. It was at his home that I wrote HAPPY WITH JESUS ALONE, which was born out of these experience and others. (Ps. 73) My wife, herself a good, well-reared woman, misunderstood me and had little sympathy with my high spiritual aspirations. This is a song for the determined, the misunderstood, the persecuted, the forsaken witness. (Rev. 2:10; Ps. 46.) Who can really sing it?

My next popular song was "Deeper, Deeper"; it grew out of my dissatisfaction with my limited ability to do good. The Savior had said, "He that believeth on me the works that I do shall he do also, and greater works than these shall he do because I go to my Father." Not understanding thoroughly the oneness of the Christ body as revealed in I Corinthians 12, and Ephesians 4, I did not see how anyone could do greater works than the Savior had done. I felt that nevertheless I was coming short of my highest privileges of service in Christ. I wonder if I was not right. Nevertheless I prayed in that song for deeper grace, deeper wisdom, more perfect conformity to and willingness to do God's will. I think, too, that the simplicity and the happy lift of the melody had something to do with its popularity. If ever there was an inspired song I feel that 'Deeper, Deeper' was inspired. Anyway, so I felt when it was written. But I do not say this in spiritual exaltedness or pride. The Spirit gave me a song with which to express the need of my soul. And, Oh, how many need to sing it with me! DEEPER! DEEPER!

(72)

Next to DEEPER, DEEPER came I WOULD NOT BE DENIED. Many have been sanctified under this song—ministers and laymen, and of all races. This song grew out of a distressing soul experience. I was walking in the fervor of constant spiritual comfort. But I was told on an occasion not to give communion. The church was not in a good condition of spiritual unity; God, the Spirit knew this. But, as King Saul obeyed the people (I Sam. 15), I obeyed the deacons rather than the Spirit. My joy departed, my comfort fled, I knew not what to do. I fasted and prayed, yet

404

fears distressed me and the consolations of the Spirit were denied me, or seemed to be. It was all, however, a besetment of Satan. I know now.

(7)

Having been rebuked, I refused to be comforted. But oh, how I prayed in every closet, behind every door; wherever I could hide I went to my knees begging for mercy. But no comfort came. You who have been tried in spirit can understand this. Satan tempted me to despair.

I seemed, like King Saul, forsaken of the Lord who under the new covenant said, "I will never leave thee nor forsake thee." (Hebrews 13)

I began to fear the losing of my mind. Satan said I had sinned against the Holy Ghost and the Lord would never hear me again. I said, "I won't take that. God will have to tell me that from the throne." I prayed on.

Then one night I was given a "song in the night." The room seemed filled with angels, who sang a song I had heard when a child:

> "Brother dear, never fear, for the Savior is near,
> With His hand He will lead you along
> And the way that is dark Christ will graciously clear
> And your mourning shall turn into song."

And so it happened. Praise the Lord, it came to pass. My mourning became a song. When all the trial was over, thinking of it all one day while alone communing with God and thanking Him for His mercy to me, my soul felt that it must express itself in song; and so was born "I WOULD NOT BE DENIED." Out of the depths I had come. (Ps. 130) Grace had triumphed. My soul sang unto the Lord a new song.

Jesus Only

Perhaps few songs I have been given the grace to write are sung more among our people than number one in "Jesus Only." Perhaps none has a more glorious history. But it is a long story.

Between the Holiness convention of 1897 and 1898 I began to be impressed with the inconsistencies of our Baptist churches, being myself almost a fanatical Baptist. Our slogan was that we were the only scriptural people; the only people who preached the whole Bible without adding to or taking from—without changing the word of God to add the traditions of men. (Mark 7:6-13;

405

JESUS ONLY.

Jesus Only.

"And Jesus came and touched them and said, Arise, and be not afraid. And when they had lifted up their eyes, they saw no man, save Jesus only."—Matt. 17: 7, 8.

C. P. J.
Slowly and with much feeling.

CHAS. P. JONES.

1. Je-sus on-ly is my mot-to, Je-sus on-ly is my song,
2. Je-sus on-ly shall com-mand me, Je-sus on-ly guide my way;
3. Je-sus on-ly is my Cap-tain, He shall lead me forth to fight;
4. Then a-way with ev-'ry i-dol, Let my Lord be all to me;

Je-sus on-ly is my heart-tho't, Je-sus on-ly all day long.
On-ly He to choose my chang-es, None but Je-sus ev-'ry day.
Je-sus on-ly is mine ar-mor, Je-sus on-ly is my might.
Je-sus on-ly is my Mas-ter, Je-sus on-ly let me see.

CHORUS.

None but Je-sus, Sav-ior, Cap-tain, None but Je-sus help me sing;

Fill me ev-er with Thy pres-ence, Je-sus, Je-sus, Lord and King.

406

Prov. 30:5,6; Rev. 22:18,19) We boasted of our scripturalness. If it was, "Thus saith the Lord," it was Baptistic; if not, it was the mere tradition of men and unworthy of authority. This was our claim as Baptists.

But I was taken to account before God. "You Baptists are liars," said the Spirit. "You profess to love me, but you do not. You love yourselves, but you do not love MY NAME. You praise yourselves, but you do not praise ME. You glory in yourselves, but you do not GLORY IN MY NAME." (Ps. 105:3)

"It was the NAME OF JESUS for which the apostles suffered shame. (Acts 5:41) It was for my name's sake I said you should be hated of all men. You are hated merely for your sect name.

"It was in the NAME OF JESUS that miracles were wrought. You have neglected His name and you work no miracles. (Acts 3:6-16) It is the Name of Jesus alone that has salvation in it. You expect salvation because you are Baptists." (Acts 4:12) (The same could be said of Methodists, Presbyterians, Campbellites, Holiness, or any cult that has degenerated into a self-exalting "ism".) Christ must be all. Holiness belongs to God. Christ is the life. All else is failure. The Spirit came to show us Christ and the things of Christ. He can glory in or exalt no one else. (John 15:12-15)

"You rob Jesus of His glory. You call the church, which is His bride, after His best man, John, (the Friend of the Bridegroom), rather than after the Bridegroom Himself. Any bridegroom would feel dishonored, insulted, robbed, by such treatment. John said "He must increase, I must decrease." (John 3:22-36) Jesus gets nothing out of all His sufferings and ministry but a name, and you rob Him of that and go not in His name but in your own name and the name of your crowd. (Phil. 2:1-13; Isa. 63:12-14; Ps. 71:16; Deut. 28:10)

"The name of God alone is holy. Jesus is not only the Prince of Life but THE HOLY ONE of Israel. How can you be holy when you glory in every name but His? The Name of the Lord is a strong tower; the righteous runneth into it and is safe. How can you be a saved people when you run into the name of a sect, a crowd, a lodge, a party and not into the name of the Lord?" (Prov. 18:10; Psalms 118)

But I said, "Lord, our denominational name is only a convenience of operation. We stand on principle; on the word; on

Glorify His Name.

AMELIA GAYNOR ANDERSON.   "Do all to the glory of God."—1 Cor. 10:31.   C. P. JONES.

1. Praise Him, praise Him all ye na-tions, All His wondrous love proclaim,
2. Let us do the things He bids us, Let the world de-ride or blame,
3. Tho' at times He seems not near us, And the world would us beshame,
4. When our Sav-ior in His glo-ry, Comes His blessed ones to claim,

Sing with rap-ture of His blessings, Sing and glo-ri-fy His name!
We shall con-quer if we ev-er Live to glo-ri-fy His name.
Yet, O saints, thro' all the darkness, Live to glo-ri-fy His name.
We shall meet Him and be with Him, There to glo-ri-fy His name.

D. S.—All ye ransomed children, ev-er Glo-ri-fy the Savior's name.

CHORUS.

Sing to glo - - ri-fy His name, . . , . .
Sing to glo-ri-fy His name, Sing to glo-ri-fy His name,

Sing to glo - - ri-fy His name;
Sing to glo-ri-fy His name, Sing to glo-ri-fy His name.

408

scripture. We must gather in one name to distinguish us, as we stand for scriptural principles." Thus I spake because I was a decided Baptist; not that the NAME Baptist was essential. Our history taught us better than that. "Baptist" was merely an epithet applied first in derision to those who practiced immersion to comply with the meaning of the Greek term "baptidzo".

(173)

But as I contended, He said, "My people hate my name and so they hate Me. Try them and see." (Jer. 6:27-30) Take the attitude of Paul. Know nothing among them but Christ and Him crucified. (I Cor. 2) and you will be hated of all men; even Methodists and sinners will hate you. They have all set up their idols in the plains and have the fiery furnace ready for those who know nothing but Jesus. Each wants to set himself above his fellow, but none glory in me. My "all-in-allness" they know not. They do not bless Him who comes in the name of the Lord. Matt. 23:39, etc. How can they see Me?

It was this attitude that brought the severest persecution upon me. I was carried to law. Baptists and Methodists held a congress and counsels against me. They reported six hundred preachers present. But I know according to our denominational principles I was a better Baptist than any of them, I held on and was determined to know nothing but Jesus. (I Cor. 2; Phil. 3:1-12)

I admit that in view of the fact that Christ loves all men, and that Paul became all things to all men, it seemed foolish to be so contentious about a name. But this name had salvation in it. It was the only name to which everything bowed. His people had become creed worshippers; they hated their Lord and the authority of His Name. At a bank, it is the name signed on a check that gives it value or worthlessness. The devil knew that was what Christ died for—a name. Therefore they denied His Power by neglecting and even denying His name. I had to prove this to them, to myself, to the world. He did not love His people less. Yet said He, "If I be a Father where is mine honor? If I be a Master where is my fear?" (Mal. 1:6) "Glory ye in his holy name." (Ps. 105:3; Phil. 2:1-11; Isa. 63:8-14; Rev. 3:8-10)

I had chosen to be hated of all men for His name's sake. I was not carried to law for stealing or murder or rape or slander, but because I would know nothing but Jesus. No name but His. No master but Him. No law but His word. No creed but Jesus. I had to be "Happy with Jesus alone." All else was trash to me.

409

This sounds foolish; but once in a while someone must be a fool for Christ's sake. Does He not take the foolish things to confound the wise? (I Cor. 1:22-31) Did God speak in vain: "He that glorieth let him glory in the Lord"? (See Jer. 9:23) Thine is the kingdom, the power and the glory. (Matt. 6) Men have no right to rob Jesus of His glory; that is all He gets out of all He suffered. Vain peacocks standing glorifying themselves and belittling their Redeemer! What could Satan ask for more?

I shall now proceed to tell the story of "Jesus Only," reserving for it the next chapter. This story embraces tragedy. But out of death comes life.

All this time I was a young man in my early thirties. But in the eternal verities I was old, for with and in me teaching me was the "Ancient of Days."

Jesus Only

There was a preacher, a member of Mt. Helm Church, named George Wright, who had a brother named William. There was a school teacher in Lexington, Mississippi, named Sam Brown. Geo. Wright was a brown-skinned man of medium size. Professor Brown was a large, burly gentleman of decided Ethiopian features and complexion—the type you loved to see. He was intellectual, energetic, brave, ambitious and therefore religiously "a bull in a china shop."

One mistake he made: in his spiritual ignorance, he undertook to be a champion against the Lord. Both Solomon and Paul declared in the Spirit that there is no wisdom nor counsel nor might against the Lord. There may seem to be for a while, but God lives forever. He inhabits eternity. He waits to be gracious. He can also afford to wait to take vengeance. He is patient, but sure. (Judges 5:23)

There was a Sunday School convention held at Mt. Olive Baptist Church near Jackson in 1899. At this convention I was to be killed. Rev. Mr. Wright himself told the story. He got Professor Brown to come from Lexington—more than 70 miles— to help him. They carried pistols, it was reported, for the express purpose of sending me on to be with my Master while I was young. There was to be a row raised—something the blessed Baptists of that day seemed to regard as the spice of the program. That was a part of their enjoyment. They took it as a part of their liberty in Christ, but they seldom hurt anyone. However, this time murder was planned. One man, a school teacher, too, a

Professor Bracy, drew back to strike me, but I answered him so meekly, and, I dare say, looked so astonished and frightened that he thought better of it. You see, it was that they desired to get me to fight. That would break the power of my message and later the tone of my ministry. No more holiness thunder to disturb flustered consciences! O they would have been delighted to have me fight. They got Elder G. W. D. Gaines with that in Arkansas, and spiked his guns. And he had wonderful power before. After that he followed on, but could never be courageously with us in full. He lost his wonderful power to heal and to convince of the need of holiness.

But always someone fought for me. I had armed myself with the mind to suffer, thru the mercy of the Most High; and heaven stood by me. (I Peter 4; II Tim. 4:16-18)

Directly came dinner time. Now I seldom ate at such times, lest a full stomach should bring an empty mind and a sluggish spirit. (Luke 21:34-36) I generally deferred eating till after the night service.

But a lady whose name I regretfully disremember came and asked me to go home with her to dinner. To my astonishment the Spirit said, "Go." You see I had to be Spirit led. Times were too dangerous for such as I to be left to his own inadequate mind, to his own devices.

I went with the lady. She took an astonishingly long time to prepare a rather poor meal. Had I not feared hurting her feelings, I would have gone back without it. She must have known what she was doing. Just before I got back to the meeting house the row occurred. When I got opposite the church house my friends were all in the road and the pastor, the Reverend Love, of Crystal Springs, saw standing in the door calling everybody back. Brown and Wright, I suppose, were in the house. I do not remember seeing them at that time. I learned the lady's name was Mrs. Fizer.

"Come on, Brother Jones," said my friends; "they drove us out and we are going down to Carleton Hill and organize another convention." So I kept right on up the road and beat everyone to Carleton Hill. I sat down before the deacons' table and wrote and tuned "Jesus Only is My Motto." From this song my first two song books were named.

Rev. S. F. Sheriff, an exceptionally fine man and a Bible Christian, was pastor at Carleton Hill. With him came J. H. Green, my superintendent and printer and leader of the young people, and Professor N. M. Jones, the secretary of the convention and a number of others, among them A. B. Essex, my friend.

The new convention was organized in the name of Jesus and continued under the leadership of Fathers W. S. Pleasant and Thomas Sanders till the reorganizations of our work in 1906.

Elder George Wright died of smallpox in 1900.

Shortly after this meeting Professor Sam Brown was elected to a professorship in Alcorn College thru the influence of a white friend in Holmes county. When he was on his way down he must needs change cars in Jackson. I was on my way somewhere to preach and came into the station. Professor Brown greeted me with a pitiful cordiality. "O here is Brother Jones. Brother Jones, I want to buy some of your books." (I wrote, printed and sold books in those days, for I had a limited printing plant). I sent the professor some of the books I had. Then said he, "Pray for me, Brother Jones, I am not well." He went on to Alcorn and possibly in less than three months was dead. I may be mistaken as to the exact length of time. I think of him with a tender heart. He was so full of life and vigor, it seemed a pity that he was cut off. But there is a sin unto death. (I John 5:14-17) Who has read about the mill stone? (Matt. 18:6; 21:43,44)

"Why should I live, O Lord, if not for Thee?
Why shouldst thou health afford daily to me?
Why should I daily live hopeful and free
If I that life withhold, dear Lord, from Thee?"
—Page 65, "His Fulness."

Whenever I hear "None but Jesus" I think of Professor Sam Brown and Rev. George Wright who set themselves against the Lord—dead now more than thirty-five years. What is their reward? (Isa. 30.) They were not wilful sinners. They were God's children destroyed for lack of knowledge. (Ho. 4; Isa. 9:16)

Men do these things thru ignorance and are destroyed for lack of knowledge. Yet often they think they are doing God service. Trouble yourself to read Luke 19 and I Corinthians 2 and you will find that Jerusalem, who thought herself especially wise and highly favored, was destroyed for lack of knowledge. O Jerusalem!

Fathers Pleasant and Sanders are dead. Father Sheriff is very old. But their works abide. They were all devout men, the salt of the earth. And they lived long as well as holily. Indeed they live yet, for all live unto Him, and "being dead they yet speak."

412

Other Songs
(4 & 5)

"WHERE SHALL I BE" was once greatly used, to warn and win souls. A white brother from Texas wrote me about 1905, "Brother Jones, I think you ought to know this. Last night a young lady sang your song, 'Where Shall I Be,' and people began to get blessed and filled and converted and kept it up so that the preacher was unable to preach." This was an old Alabama plantation melody to which I put music and words.

(254-155)

"LIST TO THE SOUND OF THE TRUMPET" has blessed thousands. A missionary from Jerusalem told me that he had seen two thousand people at once saved, blessed, sanctified and filled under the power of that song. I have seen it apparently shake a place of assembly with power. It celebrates the Lord's reign on earth. Lo, He comes. It is the hope of the earth.

"PERFECTED IN THEE" was born out of a desire that all God's people be one, as Jesus prayed. We are becoming tolerant, but are still saying, I am of Paul; I am of Apollos and I am of Cephas; and do not know real oneness—oneness on Calvary, oneness in the upper room, oneness in God, oneness in heaven and earth, oneness in Glory. (John 17) Have you ever noticed where they dwell together in Unity? There is power, there is life there. Heaven is there. We join with him in prayer in this matter. (Ps. 133) We all know the psychological power of oneness in a large congregation and among a determined people. If a threefold cord is not easily broken, how invincible must God's people be when at last they see eye to eye. Then will "God bring again Zion."

(248)

"IT IS ALL ON JESUS" was written one day when He gave me the grace to pray myself from under a distressing fever.

(151)

So was "I WILL MAKE THE DARKNESS LIGHT." I was in Louisiana preaching every night for Pastor L. J. Brunson, now of Bogalusa, Louisiana. I was in the home of Deacon Burton. I had distressing fevers every day and sleep was taken from me at night. I would go and preach, for the Spirit of truth teaches me to walk by faith rather than by feeling. One day I said, "Well, Lord, I guess that the end has come." That was about twenty-eight years ago. I walked down the road praying and contemplating the end. When I got back into my room and knelt, as I usually was com-

Where Shall I Be?

"For the Lord Himself shall descend from heaven with a shout, with the voice of the archangel, and with the trump of God."—I Thess. 4:16.

C. P. J.
Moderato.

CHAS. P. JONES.

1. When judg-ment day is draw-ing nigh, Where shall I be?
2. When wick-ed men His wrath shall see, Where shall I be?
3. When heav'n and earth as some great scroll, Where shall I be?
4. All troub-le done, all con-flict past, Where shall I be?

When God the works of men shall try, Where shall I be?
And to the rocks and moun-tains flee, Where shall I be?
Shall from God's an-gry pres-ence roll, Where shall I be?
And old A-pol-yon bound at last, Where shall I be?

When east and west the fire shall roll, Where shall I be?
When hills and moun-tains flee a-way, Where shall I be?
When all the saints redeemed shall stand, Where shall I be?
When Christ shall reign from shore to shore, Where shall I be?

How will it be with my poor soul; Where shall I be?
When all the works of men de-cay, Where shall I be?
For-ev-er blest at God's right hand, Where shall I be?
And peace a-bide for ev-er-more, Where shall I be?

General arrangement, words and music, by C. P. Jones, 1899.

Where Shall I Be?

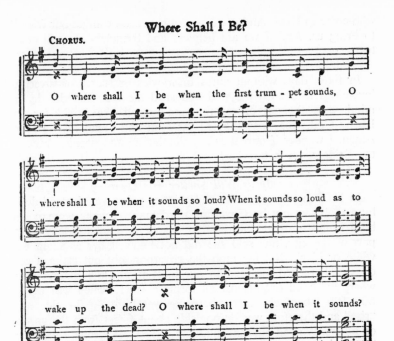

O where shall I be when the first trum - pet sounds, O where shall I be when it sounds so loud? When it sounds so loud as to wake up the dead? O where shall I be when it sounds?

pelled by the Spirit to do. He said, "Write a song." And there upon my knees I wrote the words, then went to the organ and set them to music. And God has fulfilled every word of it to me. O how many have been helped and blessed by it!

(203)

"THERE'S A HAPPY TIME COMING" was written like "List to the Sound of the Trumpet" as I longed and prayed and looked for the coming of the Lord. Who loves His appearing? Is not His coming the hope of His people and the joy of the world?

(3)

"COME UNTO ME" was written in Selma, Alabama, as I was waiting for a lady, whose name I have unfortunately forgotten, to prepare dinner. Some have called that my best song. I do not know, but it always sings well. It ALWAYS sings well and easily. It is a Savior's invitation of love. I've never known a congregation to fail in the attempt to sing it. For always He gives rest to those

415

who come to HIM. And if we cannot come, we can get our friends to bring us. And if we are helpless and friendless He will come to us.

(262-263)

In those days without autos or movies or scores of diverting inventions to deaden the soul and steal the time and delude the mind, men thought of eternity and longed like David for the Living God. Yea, they thirsted for Him and found rest in Him. Amen. I wonder if now they are slumbering and sleeping because the Bridegroom is tarrying?

Jesus Will Shelter His Own

In 1905 my church house and printing office were burned down by a mob sent out by Governor Vardaman. A white woman had been found mistreated in a white man's yard in a strictly white part of the city. She said she did not know if her assailant was white or black. But the mob the governor sent out claimed that dogs had tracked the man to our meeting house (the one place where we cried out against all forms of sin), which was then a 60 x 100 tabernacle. Our tabernacle was built on the side of a "rise" and therefore was on one side about 6 feet from the ground on pillars. We had built this building in 1903. A strong, substantial building that held twelve hundred people safely; fourteen hundred had been counted going in the doors.

The mob got coal oil and set the meeting house on fire; they said the culprit was under it, which, of course, nobody believed at all. It was a piece of malicious vandalism. (Ecc. 5:8)

Our printing office with two thousand new *Jesus Onlies I and II* just shipped to me from the Baptist Publishing house at Nashville, and a new book of my own not quite finished, and a new issue of Truth, a paper I published more than 20 years, were all burned up, with thousands of dollars of office material, type and presses, etc. The mob would not allow the fire put out.

But next day friends white and black began to give me money to rebuild—not large sums, for the poor have mostly cared for God's work. I knew, however, that had I been gifted with the power to approach the wealthy as my friend Dr. J. A. Jeter was, they no doubt would have rebuilt my work for me. For the better whites felt ashamed of this vandalism. For only that class who could say, and did say, "The idea of a Nigger printing books!" could do or endorse such a thing. Mr. Vardaman, otherwise a

416

great man, kept that class stirred up against us. Others helped me rebuild. He would not, tho' I went personally to him.

God helped me to rebuild the house—all of brick and capable of holding 800 more people than the one so debasedly and undeservedly burned down. God is like that. He gives our souls great and sore troubles, then increases our greatness and comforts us on every side. (Psalms 71)

That house yet stands and I saw it filled with people last year and years and years before that. Mr. Vardaman and most of his mob met God years ago—a merciful God, I am happy to say. Still I am rejoicing in the exceeding riches of His grace. For after all, "A man's life consisteth not in the abundance of the things which he possesseth." Luke 12:15. God bless them all. What a debt we owe the souls of men! The Savior bids us to bless those who curse us and do good to those who hate us and pray for those who despitefully use us and persecute us. (Matt. 5:38-43) So this is all on the program. How could we obey that unless we were used despitefully? It is written: "The Lord trieth the righteous." It is sometimes His way. He loves ALL MEN. All souls are His. He died for all. What if one soul must suffer with Him to save another? In the end it will be glory, glory eternal. And that glory is not far off for such as I. For who has suffered with and for Him as much as He deserves that we should? Surely I have not. Praised be He.

Two weeks before this trial a song was given me as I stayed in the home of Deacon Charley Kendrick of the Terry Church.

I was reading Ecclesiastes and this prophecy formed itself into words and became a song:

"He that observeth the winds shall not sow,
Let them blow; let them blow;
He that's discouraged success cannot know,
Let the bleak winds blow.
                    Chorus:
Jesus will shelter His own,
Guide them till life's work is done.
Be not discouraged, the Lord is thy stay,
Jesus will shelter His own."

There were other stanzas, but unfortunately this song which came out in the "Sweet Selections" song book and was much sung at one time does not appear in my latest book; and "Sweet Selections" is out of print.

In 1906 I became dissatisfied with my spiritual condition. I was making a hard fight for righteousness, but needed the renewing of the Holy Ghost to rob my spirit of that hardness that makes a man a "pulpit scold" rather than a shepherd who gives his life for the sheep in tender love.

The Lord sent along at this time a man (with his wife) from Chicago named Brother Norton. He heard me preach and perceived that I needed another anointing and a fuller view of the atonement, the all-sufficiency of Christ and His blood and His finished work and HIS COMPLETE SALVATION. He perceived that I had become a scolder. Thru his visits I was set seeking a renewing of the Holy Ghost (Titus 3:5.) I gave myself to three or four days fasting for this. At last I got a new vision of Jesus and His all-in-allness; the power of His atonement, the all-sufficiency of HIS Holy merits; a new view of the cross and what it meant. Oh the rest and victory of faith! For the Holy Ghost does not speak of Himself but takes the things of Christ and shows them to us. After law, the gospel. The mind of Christ. Bread instead of stones. Christ the One Life given us in resurrection glory.

Out of this glorious renewing was born the songs: "JESUS CHRIST IS MADE TO ME ALL I NEED" and "O HIDE ME" and several other songs that were much used by the Holy Spirit to save and comfort souls. Amen.

(257, 25)

I have written more than a thousand songs, most of them born out of significant experiences—experiences of trial or of victory or both. Of this class is "I WILL NOT YIELD," which was written in New Haven, Conn., in 1906. This song was greatly used by J. T. Brown, the evangelist, formerly of Nashville, Tenn., now of San Diego, California.

(6-7)

Also "I'll Go All the Way With My Savior," written in Americus, Georgia, in the home of Professor A. S. Staley. "HAPPY DAY AT HAND" was written in the home of Deacon Geo. O. Freeman, one of the truly great business men who was with us. I was on my way to Lexington, Mississippi, to a convention. I was in my room at prayer, for in those days of strenuous seeking after God and souls we literally "gave ourselves to the word of God and prayer." And what a wonderful occupation for the young! It bears rich fruit and gives sweet memories in after years.

As I knelt and wrote the vision unfolded to my soul. And when

418

I got to Lexington, the song took the convention. At Jackson an amusing thing was said. They had a way of mocking me about praising the Lord. Men at work would mock me as I went along the street, calling the attention of one another to my nearness by saying, "Praise the Lord." This never hurt me or aroused resentment in me, I knew they were spiritually ignorant. So I would say to myself "Thank God, I've got you praising Him somehow," as Paul said to the Philippians, *"So Christ is preached."* (Phil. 1) When I sang this "Happy Day at Hand" in Jackson, they said, "You can't do anything with Brother Jones now; he's got him a song, 'Praise the Lord.' " And so grace conquered.

"O HOW SAD TO HAVE LIVED" or "THE HARVEST IS PAST," so greatly used in the ministry of Bishop Jeter, was written in the home of a merchant in Okolona, Mississippi. His name was Mr. McIntosh. His was my first home in that city.

(82-83)

One song greatly used in my ministry is *"The Strong Man Bound."* This was the result of a revelation of the truth that Christ had already conquered for us and that we are more than conquerors by our experiences, "thru Him that loved us and gave Himself for us." (Ro. 8:26-39) Truly Jesus is mighty to save.

(121)

Two other songs "THERE'S COMING A TIME," so greatly used by Geo. H. Thomas, and "PRECIOUS SAVIOR" have a great history of service. Souls break down under them. But they were simply born out of deep conviction and intense longing after God and the salvation of men.

(253, 26)

All of my greatest songs were written before I was fifty years of age, most of them before I was forty.

Truly it is good for a man to bear the yoke in his youth. (Lamentations 3) David's and Solomon's and Paul's greatest work was done when they were young men. So were Isaiah's, Jeremiah's and Ezekiel's. And M. Spurgeon's. Do not wait for old age to serve God. Remember tny Creator in the days of thy youth. Give unto the Lord glory and strength. (Ps. 28; Ps. 96 and 94) The king hath desired thy beauty—the beauty of youth.

Sing unto the Lord, sing praises. Sing unto the Lord, sing praises. He is the best friend youth or age ever had. Amen.

The Jesus Only Standard Hymnal has become the hymnal for the general church. The following are titles of nine songs from

419

The Harvest is Past.

Jer. 8: 20. Gal. 6: 9.

C. P. J.
Con espressione.

C. P. JONES.

1. O how sad to have lived as did Is-rael of old, In a land where
2. Brother, what shall we say when the Lord shall withdraw, And seek us
3. When at last we shall see that the Bi-ble is true, And we have
4. O how sad to look back on the deeds we have done; On the words of

Je-ho-vah is known, With His good word to guide us to glo-ries
in mer-cy no more? When His good Spirit, griev'd that we love not
re-ject-ed its light, Oh, tell me, dear brother, what then shall
un-kindness we've said, On the vows yet unkept, and the priv-i-

un-told, And make us bright heirs to a throne, And still to neg-lect
His law, Shall no long-er knock at the door? Oh, what shall we plead?
we do, When Judgment is roll-ing in sight? When Nin-e-veh stands
lege gone, Be-fore us e-ter-ni-ty dread! How sad then to meet

His way to pur-sue, And drive His good Spir-it a-way;
oh, how shall we do When Mer-cy and Truth shall de-part?
with So-dom of old, Con-demn-ing the men of this day,
the Sav-ior we scorn In or-der to walk with the world!

, 1899, C. P. Jones.

420

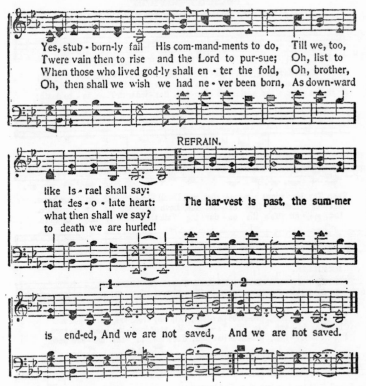

The Harvest is Past.

Yes, stub-born-ly fail His com-mand-ments to do, Till we, too,
'Twere vain then to rise and the Lord to pur-sue; Oh, list to
When those who lived god-ly shall en-ter the fold, Oh, brother,
Oh, then shall we wish we had ne-ver been born, As down-ward

REFRAIN.

like Is-rael shall say:
that des-o-late heart:
what then shall we say?
to death we are hurled!

The har-vest is past, the sum-mer

is end-ed, And we are not saved, And we are not saved.

this book which make up a small part of the compositions for the "Ministry of Songs" commision given to the late C. P. Jones, the servant of God: "Be of Good Cheer," "I Will Trust and Never Fear," "I Care Not for Riches," "I Have Surrendered to Jesus," "Calling Us Deeper," "O Jerusalem," "O Soul Beset," "None But Christ," and "I Am Waiting, O Lord, For the Power." He was told, "You shall write the hymns for your people. "The songs bear testimony of his travails and the manifestation of his faith and trust in God. Several songs from the *Jesus Only Standard Hymnal** can be found in the following section.

Through the leading of the spirit, he wrote more than a thousand songs, many of which have been sung around the world by

* Jesus Only Standard Hymnal can be ordered from James Hart, 717 East 74th Street, Los Angeles 1, California.

421

Precious Saviour.

"That ye might be filled with all the fulness of God."—Eph. 3: 19.

C. P J   Chas. Price Jones.

1. Pre-cious Sav-iour, I im-plore Thee, All Thy full-ness now im-part;
2. Let not sin a-gain de-file me, Keep me ho-ly, faith-ful, pure;
3. Hide me from the world's al-lur-ing, Bur-ied with Thee in-to death;

Keep Thy love-wings hov-ered o'er me, Dwell Thy-self with-in my heart.
Nev-er from Thy face ex-ile me, Love me, keep me ev-er-more.
Let me, all life's ills en-dur-ing, Walk the ho-ly way of faith.

REFRAIN.

Pre-cious Sav-iour, pre-cious Sav-iour, All my treas-ure, Lord, Thou art.
In Thy fa-vor, in Thy fa-vor, My poor long-ing heart as-sure.
Pre-cious Sav-iour, pre-cious Sav-iour, Keep me in the nar-row path.

Chas. P. Jones, owner, Jackson, Miss. Used by per.

people who knew him not. There has been an untold spiritualizing effect of these songs within the church.

During his middle-life, two of the song books he published were: "His Fullness" and "Sweet Selections." These were jewels and were precious in the spiritual life of the church. They were published after his Jesus Only, Numbers One and Two.

The Jones Foundation

The Jones Foundation was organized to carry on the publications started by Bishop C. P. Jones.

Under the chairmanship of Mother Luella Bush, Los Angeles, California, the church has been provided with the *Jesus Only* Standard Hymnal. The Foundation has done well under the adverse circumstances which it has faced.

There's Coming a Time.

C. P. J.

"And these shall go away into everlasting punishment; but the righteous into
life eternal."—Matt. 25: 46.

C. P. JONE

1. There's com-ing a time, when all who have jour-neyed Pa - tient-ly
2. There's com-ing a time of judg-ment e - ter - nal, Day when the
3. There's com-ing a time when sin - ners shall hear Him, Say-ing in
4. This won - der-ful time is swift - ly ap-proach-ing,—Will you not

in the heav - en-ly way, Will hear the dear Mas - ter
works of men shall be tried; When on - ly the pure, the
an - ger, "From me de - part!" And driv - en to doom, shall
now to meet it pre - pare? Re-pent and be-lieve, be

ten - der-ly say - ing, "En - ter my rest, O child of the day.
god - ly, the ho - ly, Hap - py with Christ in heav'n shall a - bide.
wail that they nev-er Gave to the Lord the love of their heart.
filled with the Spir-it; Hur - ry! the time of judg-ment is near.

Fine.

D. S.—On His right hand, . O will you be one?

CHORUS.

Will you be one? O will you be one? Will you be there, your

D. S. al Fine.

life's work all done? As the re-deemed shall hear the glad wel-come,

Perfect. Perfect.

"Be ye therefore perfect, even as your Father which is in heaven is perfect."—Matt. 5: 4b.

NATHANIEL STUART.   CHAS. P. JONES.

1. O God, we pray to be like Thee, Pure, true and ho-ly night and day,
2. O purge each heart from ev'ry sin And take it for Thy throne to be
3. Let truth's light shine upon our way, As thro' this e-vil world we go,

All filled with love and pur-i-ty, And walking in the perfect way.
And let Thy Spir-it reign within And ev - er keep us true to Thee.
Fill us with love each passing day, And in Thy fa-vor let us grow.

CHORUS.

Per-fect, per - - - fect, Lord as Thou! . . . .
Per - fect, Lord, as Thou,   Per-fect, Lord, as Thou,

Cleansed from   all sin!   Hal - le-
Cleans'd from all sin,   from all sin!

lu - jah! Christ doth now   Make His throne with - in.
Hal - le - lu - jah!

Grace to Die.

C. P. J. Matt. 16: 24-26. CHAS. P. JONES.

1. O my gen-tle, lov-ing Sav-ior, Who so free-ly died for me,
2. Oh, my ho-ly, ho-ly Sav-ior, Let me fill my min-is-try,
3. When allured by strong temptations, Still, my Sav-ior, 'tis my plea,

In these hours of sin and per-il, Give me grace to die for Thee.
Spite of hell's in-tim-i-da-tion, Give me grace to die for Thee.
To all self-ish-ness and e-vil, Give me grace to die for Thee.

See the hosts of hell are rag-ing! Fain would they force me to flee!
On the land or on the o-cean, Let my heart from fear be free;
Morn and ev-'ning watch my footsteps, Let me ne'er from danger flee,

But I want to be a sol-dier; Give me grace to die for Thee.
Yea, when dangers thick be-set me, Give me grace to die for Thee.
When my standing will ex-alt Thee—Give me grace to die for Thee.

Rit.

But I want to be a sol-dier; Give me grace to die for Thee.
Yea, when dangers thick be-set me, Give me grace to die for Thee.
When my standing will ex-alt Thee—Give me grace to die for Thee.

CHAPTER XI

THE EXPANDING PERIMETER

What had its beginning seventy years ago, with realignment with the basic tenets within the framework of the already established church, has resulted in the establishment of several different religious organizations with many thousands of local units and possibly a half million communicants; and possessing many millions of dollars worth of property.

Even though organized into separate religious groups, in the main, they have all held to their original fundamental tenets.

The dispersion has created a greater sphere and a more favorable climate in which the tenets may evolve.

There is now less antagonism among the separate groups; all advocating more or less portions of the same tenets.

Persons have for various reasons left the original movement.

Some of these were honorable characters and have remained useful and proved themselves fruitful in their fields of service.

In 1906 there arose a contention among the leading brethren relative to what constituted the baptism of the Holy Ghost. All had taught that after repentance and forgiveness of sins of the past, the new convert should receive the Holy Ghost as keeping power from committing known sins henceforth, and that the fruits of the daily life are the evidence of either having thus received Him or having not so received Him, according to Matthew 7:20 and Galatians 5:22-23, and corroborating scripture passages.

Now came the teaching that everyone must speak in an unknown tongue as evidence of the baptism of the Holy Ghost. This teaching came through some of the brethren who imbibed the doctrine on their visit in Los Angeles, California. Those supporting this view or belief banded together. After fruitless conferences among the brethren, supporters of the "New Tongues" doctrine banded together, and organized under the charter of the "Church of God in Christ," with headquarters in Memphis, Tennessee, and began the publication of their organ, the "Whole Truth."

426

Until this time the original movement was generally referred to as the "Holiness Church" or "Church of God," and had existed without a charter from its beginning in 1897. It was later incorporated under the name "Church of Christ (Holiness) U.S.A.," with headquarters at Jackson, Mississippi, 329 East Monument Street.

EVENTS WHICH LED TO THE FOUNDING
OF THE CHURCH OF GOD
IN CHRIST
From Fifty Years Achievement, Church of God in Christ
By Charles H. Pleas

CHAPTER I

The closing years of the last century and the early years of the present century heralded, what was then thought to be, an insignificant religious upheaval. That period, it can be truthfully said, extended from 1894 to 1906. A part of what occurred pertaining to that movement is taken from the Manual of the Church of Christ (Holiness) U.S.A. written by Bishop C. P. Jones, to wit:

"In the year 1894, I was pastor of the Tabernacle Baptist Church, Selma, Alabama, and my ministry with that church and with Alabama Baptist Ministry at large seemed to be accepted and much loved. But as I read my Bible and observed conditions, I felt that we were not, as a brother once said to me, 'toting fair with Jesus'. I began then to seek Him with all my heart for that power that would make my life wholly His, so that I might realize both the blessedness and usefulness of real Bible religion.

"I was not satisfied with a faith that brought no fruit, or else fruit of so poor a quality, spiritually, and a religion that none of the signs spoken of in the Scriptures followed. (Mk. 16:14-18; Heb. 2:1-11) I wanted to be one of wisdom's true sons and, like Abraham, 'a friend of God'. As we sought God, the Spirit promised that if we would fast three days and nights, He would sanctify us: which we did and were filled with light, with joy and with the Holy Ghost. O, the splendid glory of that exalted state. Do not be satisfied with the attitude that holiness is right. Get the experience, get saved, get a knowledge of it. Have the mind of Christ. You will really know something then that you never knew before. Try it out. (Jn. 14:12-23)

"From then on, with more or less zeal, we sought renewings of power and pushed the claims of Christ on the churches, could

I not help it, for then I knew Him that He was in the Father, and I in Him and He in me. (John 14:15-18) I beg, again, get the real experience of the fullness of the Spirit. Amen.

"In 1895, I accepted a unanimous call to the Mount Helm Baptist Church, Jackson, Mississippi. Here I began my deeper spiritual labors among the people. I worked in the Association; at Byrum, Big Creek, Mt. Olive, and Charlton of which latter, Elder F. S. Sheriff was then pastor. From the first I found Elder Sheriff an industrious, farming minister, who bore an excellent reputation among black and white. (Ecc. 7)

"In 1895 we preached at the General Baptist Association in Vicksburg, Mississippi, and there Elder A. J. Bradley was much affected by the message but he proved later unable to go all the way; yet for a time he seemed a friend to our dear Master. Also a Brother H. C. Tate of Tougaloo, Mississippi, who afterward became an Adventist. God bless him.

"But in 1896 the General Association of the Baptist Church was held at Mt. Helm Church, Jackson. At that time we came to better know Elder Kelly Bucks, A. Reed, R. J. Temple, W. S. Pleasant, and others who regarded our zeal with more or less apparent favor. At this Association we sold our first booklet, a treatise on the 12th chapter of First Corinthians, under the title, "The Work of the Holy Spirit in the Churches". We also began about this time to publish the *Truth*.

"Sometime after this Association, the Holy Spirit bade me call a Holiness Convention. Said I, "When, Lord?" "The sixth of June", said He. "What day will that be, Lord?" I asked. "Sunday," said He. Later when the almanac for 1897 came out, I found it was Sunday. Then I, young as I was in the way, 'knew it was the Lord'.

"In due time we made the call. We had, already in 1896 as I said, begun to publish *Truth*. So it became a special organ of the call. But special invitations, I think, were sent out to those men who seemed interested in their own souls and the souls of the people. We began the meeting, Sunday, June 6, and continued two weeks, studying the Bible and praying night and day.

*   *   *   *

"But we were persecuted by the churches, eventually; and Associations and all sects combined against us. But this persecution compelled us to build another sect, which was not our aim nor desire. We contended that Christ is all. But we were extreme in our fight. The time demanded it. But we, from the first, only wanted to exalt Jesus and put down man-made tradition. (Mk. 7:1-7) "During our second convention, the fight began against us hard and we had much persecution to endure to God's glory. But I have not time to tell you all. It would take a very long history. This move on the part of the Mt. Helm Church gave the enemies of the Holy Ghost a chance and they put us in court, and though we won our liberty in the lower court, the Supreme Court put us out, not on general law, but on a technicality involved in the Mt. Helm holdings, but we were out and that for the Name's sake of the Lord. (John 16) But God was with us and year after year we have held on and come up to the help of the Lord, like Israel of old. (Judges 5:23)"

CHAPTER II

Along with the events stated by Bishop C. P. Jones, revivals continued, unabated, and persecutions continued also. Along with C. P. Jones were others of the same belief including Elders C. H. Mason; W. S. Pleasant, Hazlehurst, Miss.; J. E. Jeter, Little Rock, Ark. They preached relentlessly that which they saw in the Scriptures: "Follow peace with all men and holiness, without which no man shall see the Lord". They contended that all who had that conviction and patterned their lives accordingly were doing as God would have them do.

CHAPTER III

During those years, Elder C. H. Mason was doing the work of an evangelist. Also during those years, the Baptists were operating a college for females at Natchez, Miss. In the mid-winter of the school year 1985-96, the dormitory of the school was destroyed by fire. Immediately plans were put in operation to rebuild it. As a result each young woman attending the school was appointed a financial missionary for the purpose of raising funds for rebuilding. A Miss Margaret Ann Lee was one of these. During the activities for the raising of funds, she made a request of the pastor, Rev. H. L. Young of the Asia Baptist Church and congregation to allow her to invite Rev. C. P. Jones to assist her. This request was granted and Rev. Jones was invited. He responded and conducted a revival for one week. As a result quite a number of persons were sanctified. These included the principal of the school, Professor L. W. Lee. This brought on a fight and the pastor lost his pastorate. As a result Rev. Jones was asked to return and modify or correct that which he had preached. However, he was not able to respond. In his stead Rev. H. C. Mason was substituted. Rev. Mason conducted a week's revival and gained one convert, Charles Pleas, Jr. This was in 1896.

CHAPTER IV

Rev. Mason returned the following year, 1897. But the doors of all churches were closed against him and all others who believed and supported the doctrine of sanctification. Therefore, he was forced to deliver his first message from the south entrance of the courthouse. At this time, a Brother John Lee granted Elder Mason the privilege of holding the meeting in the front room of his home. However, it proved to be far too small for even the first night. Because of that, one Mr. Watson gave consent for the meeting to be conducted in an old abandoned gin-house which he owned. He was also assisted in this meeting by Rev. C. P. Jones and W. S. Pleasant. This service proved to be a miraculous success. In that particular meeting one Jennie Watson was healed of an affliction which the doctors had pronounced as hopeless. She lived for twenty years afterwards. On the same night there were five pistol shots and two shots from a double barrelled shotgun. Some persons were wounded but none of the wounds were fatal.

CHAPTER V

At the close of this meeting it was found necessary to organize for the purpose of a continuation in the faith. Upon the advice of Elders Mason, Jones, and Pleasant a meeting was called and votes were allowed in order to give the people an opportunity to express themselves as to what they wanted. In response to that privilege, sixty stood as charter members.

CHAPTER VI

It was readily seen that this organization could not survive without a leader. As a consequence, Rev. C. H. Mason was the unaminous choice. He performed his first baptismal service on the first Sunday in March 1897. Those who were baptized in that service were Addie Golden, Lulu McCullough, Charles, Jr., and an elderly man named Mac McMillan. We would have associated with the Mt. Leaventon Baptist Association but they scoffed at this idea before any application was made for membership. They ruled against all who claimed sanctification. The first church added to the number professing sanctification was located in Carroll County sixteen miles north of Lexington, Mississippi, Pastored by Rev. Lee Porter Cobbins.

CHAPTER VII

During the time of the events aforesaid, Elder Mason learned from a minister's message delivered in Memphis, Tennessee, that there is a difference between the baptism of the Holy Spirit and being filled with the Holy Spirit. The illustration went in this wise: "There is a difference in a jug being filled with water and a jug being buried or baptized in water." Elder Mason then acknowledged that he saw the difference and would continue to seek for the baptism of the Holy Spirit.

Having been rejected by the Baptists, Elder Mason sought God prayfully for the correct name of the church. While walking along a certain street in Little Rock, Arkansas, the Lord revealed this name, "Church of God in Christ", with the following scriptures to support it: (I Thess. 2:14) "For ye brethren became followers of the churches of God which in Judea are in Christ Jesus: for ye have suffered like things of your own countrymen even as they have the Jews." His strong and forceful message concerning the same so influenced the other of the brethren that it was agreed to accept it as the name of the church. However, this caused much trouble with the Clergy Bureau. It was then further revealed to Elder Mason in view of the scriptures, to name it The Church of God in Christ. This was readily accepted and there was no more trouble with the Clergy Bureau.

After this, the church was further organized. As a result Elder C. P. Jones was chosen as General Overseer. Elder C. H. Mason was appointed as Overseer of Tennessee and Elder J. A. Jeter was appointed as Overseer of Arkansas.

CHAPTER VIII

During the year 1906, the news reached Elder Mason that the Baptism of the Holy Spirit was being received by some believers in Los Angeles, Calif. He was made aware that they tarried for it just as Jesus commanded the disciples in Luke 24:49. "And behold I send the promise of my Father upon you: but tarry ye in the city of Jerusalem until ye be endured with power from on high." Being convinced by these momentous happenings in Los Angeles, Elder Mason was determined to go there. In company with Elders D. J. Young and J. A. Jeter, who were also anxious to know about this new experience, the trip was made. A few days after their arrival in Los Angeles they received the baptism of the Holy Ghost according to Acts 2:4.

Upon their return home with that experience, the hearts of many

431

were open to receive the same. Therefore, it spread rapidly among them. Unfortunately, at that time, Elder Jeter claimed that the experience was a delusion and that he had been deceived by it. As a consequence of that deflection much harm was done and evil work of every description was generated among the brethren. The then General Overseer also took a stand against it and fought it from every angle. That attitude created such an influence among the body of ministers (which had been greatly increased by that time) that it was decided to sever relationship with all who claimed the baptism of the Holy Ghost according to Acts 2:4. Elder Mason was included in that number.

An acount of the events that transpired after Elder Mason's return is taken from the pages of the "Manual of the Church of God in Christ", to wit: "This union lasted until the year 1906, when a great revival in Los Angeles, California, under the auspices of Elder W. J. Seymour. Elder C. H. Mason, among many others, attended this revival and received the baptism of the Holy Ghost with signs of speaking with other tongues according to Acts 2:4, "and they were all filled with the Holy Ghost and began to speak with other tongues as the Spirit gave them utterance." Elder Mason came back preaching this as a New Testament Doctrine to which many of the brethren were adverse.

CHAPTER IX

In August, 1907, the General Assembly convened at Jackson, Mississippi, with Elder C. P. Jones presiding as General Overseer, who was also averse to the new doctrine promulgated by Elder C. H. Mason and others. After a lengthy discussion, the Assembly withdrew from Elder C. H. Mason and all who promulgated the doctrine of speaking with tongues, the right hand of fellowship.

Later in the same year, Elder Mason called a meeting in Memphis, Tennessee, of all the ministers who believed in receiving the baptism of the Holy Ghost according to Scriptures, Acts 2:4. Among the group of Elders who responded to this call were: E. R. Driver, J. Bowe, R. R. Booker, W. M. Roberts, R. E. Hart, W. Welch, A. A. Blackwell, E M. Page, R. H. I. Clark, D. J. Young, James Brewer, Daniel Spearman, J. H. Boone. These pioneer ministers were responsible for the early strides in the Church's growth. They spoke with authority the things concerning the Kingdom of God.

They realized that the practice and development of Christian religion, in this hectic age, was just as necessary and paramount as in the days of the early Church when the inhabitants of the earth in many regions had not seen nor even heard of Christ.

If there was ever any group of sanctified persons capable, (and who went a long way), in erecting a monument to the righteousness of God, it was this assembly of early preachers of the faith of holiness. Records of the activities of some of them will be found on these pages. These brethren formed the first assembly of the Church of God in Christ, whose faith was founded upon the doctrine of the Apostles as received on the day of Pentecost."

CHAPTER X

As a result of that action, law suits followed for the control of church property in Memphis, Tenn., Lexington, Miss., and elsewhere. The brethren who were excluded were advised by Dr. R. E. Hart not to reorganize until all law suits were ended. Elder J. Bowe of Arkansas refused to accept that advice and proceeded to reorganize the first convocation in the State of Arkansas in 1908. By doing so all church property in the State of Arkansas at that time was lost. However, those in Memphis, Tennessee, and Lexington, Mississippi, who accepted Dr. Hart's advice, were successful in the courts in their claims of church property. In 1909 law suits were ended and advice was given by Dr. Hart to reorganize.

CHAPTER XI
Dr. Hart

It is necessary, at this point, to pay tribute to Dr. Hart. He was a prominent minister of the A.M.E. Church in the state of Tennessee and also a lawyer. He was among those who had been excluded who had accepted the doctrine of the baptism of the Holy Ghost according to Acts 2:4. He was one of the pioneers in the new organization and his services proved to be invaluable.

CHAPTER XII

Up to this time there had been no national meeting of the new organization. It followed, then, that the brethren were called together by Elder Mason for a national convention which should last for twenty days, extending from November 25 to December 14 annually. The reason for calling the meeting at this time of the year was the fact that practically all of the communicants of the faith at that time lived in the farming districts of Mississippi, Tennessee, and Arkansas. By that time their crops were all harvested and enough finance and other provisions were available which would enable them to attend and support a national meeting.

Editor's Notes

In the matter of Tongues referred to in Chapter IX above in the article by Elder Charles H. Pleas, Elder C. P. Jones, Senior, took the following position:

1. That no one gift is the specific sign or evidence of the Holy Spirit's presence, but faith (Heb. 11) and Love (I Cor. 13; 35) are the evidences; not even power alone is the evidence for that may be of Satan.

2. That these gifts, though they may be of use to edification, may be counterfeited and are not to be trusted as evidence. (Thes. 2:7-12; II Tim. 3:8).

3. That there are three essential evidences of true religion. They are Faith, Hope, and Love, (I Cor. 13:13).

4. That the Bible endorses speaking in tongues, or a gift of tongues, but that no one really speaks in tongues unless he speaks a language understood by men, as in Acts 2:4, 8.

5. That though one speak witth tongues, it is no evidence of the Holy Ghost at all, but merely a sign.

Bishop K. H. Burruss

Bishop K. H. Burruss of Atlanta, Georgia, was the host Pastor to the 1920 Annual Session of the National Convention of the Churches of Christ (Holiness) U.S.A. He had erected a spacious

434

sanctuary and had built up quite a large following.

However. this was the last session the Pastor and Church affiliated with the National Convention.

Rev. Burruss founded a group which has its strength in the Eastern Section of the Country, operating under the name "Church of God Holiness" with headquarters in Atlanta, Georgia.

The Tennessee Brethren, Et Al.
by C. P. Jones, Sr.

On both sides, there seemed to have been made tentative efforts to unite with these Brethren. I believe, with a hope, that it will yet come, but I do not think, judging from the failures of earnest efforts on both sides, that the time is yet ripe.

Circumstances would not allow me to attend the meetings on the matter nor did I feel sent of God. We need them! They are the Lord's people! They need us! . . .

(The Tennessee Brethren referred to were once among us but now operate under the name of "The Church of God Sanctified," with headquarters in Nashville, Tenn. Bishop T. D. McGee, Leader.)

So with Dr. Fisher of Durham, North Carolina, and his people in Christ, and Brother Collette and His followers. (Dr. Fisher is believed to be the founder of the United Holy Church of America, with headquarters in Goldsboro, North Carolina.)

At Chicago in 1924, the Nazarene Brethren sent a delegation to invite us to join them as a colored contingent. They are earnest, industrious, persevering, prosperous and on the whole, sanely Evangelical.

I prayed God to direct the affair, for the matter was hard to decide. The Lord seemed to decide it for us by causing the Brethren to cease their efforts. We need and want Jesus, Jesus, Jesus. Amen.

The Church of Christ (Holiness) Incorporated
By the Editor

The Church of Christ (Holiness), Incorporated, in reality was organized in 1915 in California by the late William Washington.

For several years he had been working separately from the original movement founded by the late Charles Price Jones in Jackson, Mississippi.

William Washington invited Charles Price Jones to come to Los

435

Angeles, California, to conduct a series of services.

This led first to Charles Price Jones' asking William Washington to rejoin him in the convention in Jackson, Mississippi. This was done.

Next, Charles Price Jones went back to Los Angeles, California, and worked out an understanding with William A. Washington with reference to organizing CHRIST TEMPLE CHURCH OF CHRIST, (HOLINESS) U.S.A. in Los Angeles, California.

The BETHEL CHURCH OF CHRIST HOLINESS, Incorporated, pastored by William A. Washington, had already been established, and incorporated under the laws of the state of California. This incorporation remained, but the two prelates entered into an agreement to work together.

The general constituency of the church was never made fully aware of this agreeable understanding between the two clergymen.

This agreement continued for thirty years until the convention year of 1946-1947. The manipulating of some adminstrative problems in the upper circles of the church, finally resulted in an organizational eruption. The 1945 convention yearbook shows Bishop Charles Price Jones, President Emeritus, and Bishop William A. Washington, President. As a result of the eruption, Bishop William A. Washington was no longer in the Church of Christ, (Holiness) U.S.A. He was still legally entitled to continue under under his continued incorporation—Church of Christ, Holiness, Incorporated, dated 1915. The end result was two organizational administrative units, but one in doctrine and practice.

Bethel Church of Christ (Holiness)

Bethel Church of Christ (Holiness) was organized May 19, 1915, by Bishop William A. Washington at the home of Mother Rebecca Williams, 945 Naomi St., Los Angeles, California, with sixteen persons present who constituted the church.

The first public service was held in a mission on East First St., in Boyle Heights, which was loaned by Sister Marshall who conducted a Nazarene Mission. On May 25th of the same year a special meeting was called for the purpose of planning for a place of worship. A place was leased on East 14th Street, for a short while, then moved to a place on Hooper Avenue near 14th Street. A few months later a contract was given for a more comfortable place on Paloma Avenue. But while still looking for a more convenient location and giving much time to prayer and meditation, the property on which the present edifice stands was offered to the Pastor. With the council and cooperation of the Pastor and Officers, the property was purchased. A small building was placed on the rear of the lot, and used until the congregation out-grew their facilities.

Finally, this building was replaced with a larger building which was remodeled and enlarged to meet the needs of the congregation.

The present edifice represents thirty years of earnest planning, patient striving, many sacrifices and prayers to meet the housing requirement of a congregation which grew from 16 members to over 1200 members under the administration of one Pastor, Bishop William A. Washington. This great man of the Church was respected and honored in the community, the city, the state and the nation.

Bethel Church of Christ (Holiness) has to her credit many endeavors and achievements:

1. A massed church property and facilities valued at over $100,000.00.
2. Developed a membership over 1200.
3. Nine men inspired to enter the ministry.
4. Sponsored the establishing of nine missions and churches.
5. Financed Missionary efforts in the Foreign Mission Field.
6. Loan space for the first tangible efforts to establish a creditable Publishing House on the West Coast by the National Publishing Board.
7. Host two sessions of the National Conventions of the Churches of Christ (Holiness) U.S.A., (1930 and 1938, and facilities used for the National Convention in 1959).
8. Three of the church's most honored Bishops were consecrated at her altars.

The first charter members of the organization were Brothers Wm. A. Washington, L. Lewis, T. H. Smith, J. A. Witherspoon, Wesley Baker, T. J. Lomack, Edward Clements, Sisters T. M. Washington, Emma Lewis, Rebecca Williams, Alberta Baker, Ella Clements, Pennie Smith, Sallie Baker, Sallie Garner and Bettie Dunton.

The first officers were: Rev. Wm. A. Washington, Pastor; Deacons: T. J. Lomack, Wesley Baker; L. Lewis; Treasurer, Sister Pennie D. Smith. Secretary Pro-Tem. Brother T. J. Lomack.

Bethel Church, under the pastorate of Elder G. B. Washington, operates independently, sharing a responsible role in the religious life of Los Angeles.

The August, 1955 Session of the National Convention of the Church of Christ, Holiness, Incorporated, held with the Washington Memorial Church of Christ, Holiness, Incorporated on McKinley Avenue, and 43rd Place in Los Angeles, California.

Deacon Albert Young
Deacon Albert Young was a consistent, devoted worker of the First Tabernacle Church of Christ Holiness, Alabama Avenue, Washington, D.C. He was the reliable vanguard of the church, from the layman's point of view, for more than twenty years.

Mrs. Savanah Young
Mrs. Savanah Young, the wife of Brother Albert Young, has been a faithful worker among the women of the First Tabernacle Church of Christ, Holiness for two decades.

Rev. and Mrs. J. E. Young
Rev. and Mrs. J. E. Young are credited with establishing the First Tabernacle Church of Christ, Holiness, 2451 Ainger Place, S. E. Washington, D.C.

They owned the property where the church services were held throughout the years until the membership had grown enough numerically and financially to purchase a lot on Alabama Avenue near Ainger Place. On this lot a $75,000 edifice was erected under

438

Deacon Albert Young   Mrs. Savanah Young

Rev. and Mrs. J. E. Young

the Pastorate of Dr. J. E. Young, who remained Pastor until he retired at the age of 90.

He remained steadfast and unwavering in his contentions for the teaching of holiness.

He and his wife have both passed.

Rev. John Turner Woodson

Rev. John Turner Woodson was born in Carroll County near Blackhawk, Mississippi.

In 1923 he moved to Jackson, Mississippi, where he joined the Christ Temple Church pastored by Rev. E. W. Butler.

In 1924 he was married to Miss Hattie Spencer of Wesson, Missisippi. To this union one daughter, Dora, was born.

In 1925 he proclaimed his call to the ministry, and was soon ordained, and called to pastor the Mt. Olive church near Jackson.

He pastored the following churches: Mt. Perea, Carroll County, Miss., Berean, Lexington, Miss., Colis Hill, Terry, Miss., Mt. Bethel, So. Galliton Street, Jackson, Miss., Christ Temple, Utica, Miss., and Christ Temple, Hazlehurst, Miss.

Rev. John Turner Woodson died July 21, 1958.

Chapter XII

THE FAMILY
The CORE of the CHURCH

"Be not unequally yoked together with unbelievers"
"Train up a child in the way he should go"
Proverbs 22:6

Family life is an important aspect of any developing church. The Family was ordained of God that Children might be trained up for Himself.

The Family was before the Church, and the First Form of the Church on earth.

THE M. F. BROWN Family

The members of the M. F. BROWN Family, Deborah, Rev. M. F. Brown, Mrs. Malinda.

"Happy is the Family where the government
of the parents is the reign of affection, and
obedience of the children, the submission of
love."

The M. F. Brown Family worked together in home, church and community. There a common interest existed.

M. F. Brown united with the Christ Temple Church, Wolfe Lake, out of Yazoo City, Mississippi, at eight years of age and was baptized by Bishop J. L. I. Conic. M. F. Brown was married to

441

Malinda Basset on September 4, 1931, at Yazoo City, Mississippi. He left Wolfe Lake with his wife and went to Memphis, Tennessee, where they united with the Church of Christ Holiness, 907 South Lauderdale Street. Bishop J. L. I. Conic was pastor there when they united with the church. He was licensed to preach by Bishop Conic. He was ordained in the diocesan Convention in Cleveland, Ohio, by a Presbytery of ministers—S. J. McTyre, G. W. Hemphill, D. J. Washington, and J. W. Johnson, presiding Bishop Conic, Clerk M. R. Conic. In 1940 he was made pastor of the Christ Temple Church, Jackson, Tennessee. From Jackson he went to Memphis to take charge of the church there. He remodeled the church there and took many new members into the church. He served under Bishop W. M. Mitchell until Bishop Mitchell died in 1951. Then Reverend Brown was chosen to be overseer of the N. C. Diocese for eight years, and pastor of the Christ Temple Church, St. Louis, Mo. The church purchased a parsonage on Fountain Court. He resigned the church in 1957 and was sent to Chicago Heights to pastor where he had served for seven years. His stand-bys have been his wife, Malinda, and his daughter, Deborah.

Mr. George B. Hines—deceased, and his widow
Mrs. Elizabeth Hines, and their first two
children: S. B. and Helen

Brother Geo. B. Hines and Mrs. Elizabeth Cobbins-Hines were charter members of the Mt. Olive Church of Christ Holiness, U.S.A. Hattiesburg, Miss. Later they were charter members in organizing the Christ Temple Church, Chicago, Illinois.

Brother Geo. B. Hines was one of the first deacons in the Hattiesburg, Mississippi, and when they moved to Chicago, he became one of the first deacons of the Christ Temple Church, Chicago, Illinois.

THE O. B. COBBINS FAMILY
All were former members CHRIST TEMPLE CHURCH
Jackson, Mississippi

Left to right; Charles Price Cobbins, youngest child. I.B.M. Data Processing, Chicago, Illinois. Rev. O. B. Cobbins, father. Joseph Samuel Cobbins, A. B., Tougaloo College, I.B.M. Data Processing, Chicago. Mrs. Ruth Cobbins-Jones, oldest child, A. B., Tougaloo College, Chicago, Ill. Mrs. Elva Cobbins—Mother—Deceased November 7, 1964. Teacher, Special Education, Chicago Public Schools. John Cephus Cobbins, Junior College Graduate, Southern Christian Institute. Career: U.S. Postal Clerk, Chicago. Mrs. Esther Cobbins-Hawkins, 2nd oldest child. A. B. Tougaloo College, Physical Education Major, Howard University, Washington, D.C.; Teacher, Special Education, Inglewood Public Schools. Inglewood, California.

The JOHN A. JETER, Sr., Family
(His son John not shown)

Elder John A. Jeter was married in October 1885 to Miss Lena Elizabeth Evans in Little Rock, Arkansas.

This Christian home of three, John, Jr., included, was marked by its mutual love, companionship and cooperation. A prince among men, Pastor Jeter everywhere and always showed distinct respect to "Sister Jeter," as he affectionately called her.

He died September 15, 1945 at the age of 91. Sister Jeter died in May, 1958, also at the age of 91.

THE POSTUM DESCENDANTS
THE FOUR GENERATIONS

444

Mrs. Maria Postum, the mother
Mrs. Anna Hines-Dexter, the daughter
Mrs. Christine Hines-Jackson, the granodaughter
Mrs. Ruth Hines-Jones, the other granddaughter
Mrs. Flora Mae Jackson-Gilliam, the great granddaughter
These generations spread from those final historic days at the Mt. Helm Baptist Church to the present time. Only the great-granddaughter still lives. All were former members of the Christ Temple Church of Christ, Holiness, U.S.A., 329 E. Monument Street, Jackson, Mississippi.

Victor and Juanita
Smith
and introducing
Vania Phyllis

Mr. Victor Smith, the son of Rev. J. C. Smith, a minister of Newport News, Virginia, is the manager of the National Publishing House, 234 W. 69th Street, Chicago, Illinois.

He is making good his printing and publishing career.

He is a former member of the Christ Temple Church in Los Angeles, California. He is now a member of Christ Temple Church in Chicago, and is a Sunday School Teacher, Choir member, and Junior Deacon. His wife, Juanita, was reared in the Christ Temple Church, Chicago. She has participated in the various activities of the Church.

Vania Phyllis has a worthwhile inheritance to which to aspire in her parents and grandparents.

445

THE FAMILY

OF THE LATE SENIOR BISHOP CHARLES PRICE JONES

BISHOP CHARLES PRICE JONES SR.

MRS. PEARL E. JONES
CHARLES PRICE JR.
PEARL JOSIE
CHARLES III
VANCE R. JONES
SAMUEL S. JONES

446